PCI DSS

An Integrated Data Security Standard Guide

Jim Seaman

Apress®

PCI DSS: *An Integrated Data Security Standard Guide*

Jim Seaman
Castleford, West Yorkshire, UK

ISBN-13 (pbk): 978-1-4842-5807-1 ISBN-13 (electronic): 978-1-4842-5808-8
https://doi.org/10.1007/978-1-4842-5808-8

Managing Director, Apress Media LLC: Welmoed Spahr
Acquisitions Editor: Susan McDermott
Development Editor: Laura Berendson
Coordinating Editor: Jessica Vakili

Distributed to the book trade worldwide by Springer Science+Business Media New York, 233 Spring Street, 6th Floor, New York, NY 10013. Phone 1-800-SPRINGER, fax (201) 348-4505, e-mail orders-ny@springer-sbm.com, or visit www.springeronline.com. Apress Media, LLC is a California LLC and the sole member (owner) is Springer Science + Business Media Finance Inc (SSBM Finance Inc). SSBM Finance Inc is a **Delaware** corporation.

For information on translations, please e-mail rights@apress.com, or visit http://www.apress.com/rights-permissions.

Apress titles may be purchased in bulk for academic, corporate, or promotional use. eBook versions and licenses are also available for most titles. For more information, reference our Print and eBook Bulk Sales web page at http://www.apress.com/bulk-sales.

Any source code or other supplementary material referenced by the author in this book is available to readers on GitHub via the book's product page, located at www.apress.com/978-1-4842-5807-1. For more detailed information, please visit http://www.apress.com/source-code.

Printed on acid-free paper

Table of Contents

About the Author xv

About the Technical Reviewer xvii

Introduction xix

A Tribute To xxv

Chapter 1: An Evolving Regulatory Perspective 1

Introduction 2

Revolution or Evolution? 6

    Europe 8

    Canada 8

    United States 9

    Australia 10

    China 10

    Japan 10

    Argentina 10

    Malaysia 10

    Brazil 11

    India 11

    Financial Services 11

Data Privacy Hierarchy 13

    PCI DSS Validation Requirements 14

Recommendations 16

    Behaviors 19

    Leadership 24

    Consent or Legitimate Use 25

Conclusion 26

Key Takeaways.. 27

Risks 27

Chapter 2: The Evolution of PCI DSS **29**

Associated Costs (Non-compliance/Data Breach).. 35

Introduction.. 36

PCI DSS Controls Framework Architecture 36

    Primary (Core) Ring 37

    Secondary Ring 38

    Tertiary Ring 38

    Quaternary Ring 38

    Quinary Ring 38

    Senary (Outer) Ring 38

Historic References... 40

    Build and Maintain a Secure Network 40

    Protect Cardholder Data 45

    Maintain a Vulnerability Management Program 46

Implement Strong Access Control Measures 49

Regularly Monitor and Test Networks 54

Maintain an Information Security Policy 57

Reality Bites 58

Recommendations 58

Conclusion 58

Key Takeaways.. 59

Risks 60

Chapter 3: Data Life Support System... **61**

Introduction.. 61

Concept... 62

Lessons Learned 63

Layered Defenses 63

24/7 Monitoring 65

Physical Security 66

Incident Response 67

Blood Life-Cycle Management 68

Recommendations 69

Conclusion 71

Key Takeaways 71

Risks 72

Chapter 4: An Integrated Cyber/InfoSec Strategy **73**

Introduction 74

Components of an Effective Strategy 77

Data Privacy 79

Cyber Security 83

Information Security 98

Physical Security 105

Resilience 108

Recommendations 109

Conclusion 109

Key Takeaways 110

Risks 110

Chapter 5: The Importance of Risk Management **113**

Introduction 120

What Is a Risk Assessment? 120

Background 121

Scenario Development 124

Think Like an Attacker 124

Risk Scenarios 127

Risk Assessment Process 139

Reality Bites 141

Recommendations 143

Conclusion 144

Key Takeaways.. 144

Risks 145

Chapter 6: Risk Management vs. Compliance – The Differentiator 147

Introduction.. 152

PCI DSS Is Not a Legal Requirement. 154

   ...But Should Be a Business Requirement?.. 154

Concept... 156

   How Is This Achieved?... 159

   Qualitative vs. Quantitative Risk Assessment.. 161

   Quantitative Risk Assessments 162

   Risk Appetite/Tolerance 162

Case Studies 162

   Case Study 1: Telephone-Based Payments Risk Balance Case 164

   Case Study 2: Enhanced PCI DSS Program Through Integration into
   Enterprise Risk Management (ERM).. 178

Reality Bites 189

Recommendations 191

Conclusion 192

Key Takeaways.. 192

Risks 193

Chapter 7: PCI DSS Applicability 195

PCI DSS Overview 195

Introduction.. 198

The Precious Cargo 198

   Structure of a Payment Card 199

   Precious Cargo Categories 199

Accessing Applicability 206

The Future 208

Key Takeaways 210

Risks 210

Chapter 8: De-scoping the Scoping Risk 213

Introduction 216

Lessons Learned from History 217

Thinking Like the Enemy 218

The Way Forward 219

Reality Bites 220

Recommendations 224

    High-Level Overview 225

    Detailed-Level Overview 225

Conclusion 228

Key Takeaways 228

Risks 229

Chapter 9: An Introduction to the PCI DSS Controls Framework 231

Brief History of PCI DSS 231

My Life Before PCI DSS 234

My Life Living with PCI DSS 237

PCI DSS Structure 240

PCI DSS: 6 Goals, 12 Requirements 241

Goals 242

6.3 Ps: People, Policies, and Processes *(Maintain a Policy That Addresses*
Information Security for All Personnel) 243

    Documentation, Documentation, Documentation 243

    Reality Bites 244

Secure Architecture (Build and Maintain a Secure Network) 245

    Layered Defenses 246

    Identify and Manage IT Assets 247

Traffic Control 248

Reality Bites.. 249

Secure by Design/Secured by Default 249

Reality Bites.. 250

Secure Data at Rest and in Transit (Protect Cardholder Data) 252

Reality Bites.. 253

Secure Maintenance (Maintain a Vulnerability Management Program) 254

Reality Bites.. 255

Gate Keeping *(Implement Strong Access Control Measures)*.............................. 257

Reality Bites.. 258

Routine Assurance (Regularly Monitor and Test Networks) 258

Reality Bites.. 260

PCI DSS 12 Requirements 263

Introduction 263

Requirement 12: 3 Ps (People, Policies, and Processes) 265

Requirement 1: Layering the Network... 266

Requirement 2: Secure by Design/Default.. 270

Requirement 3: The Vault... 271

Requirement 4: Secure in Motion 273

Requirement 5: Entry Search.. 275

Requirement 6: Build and Maintain 276

Requirement 7: Role-Based Restrictions... 276

Requirement 8: Logical Entry Control 277

Requirement 9: Physical Entry Control 278

Requirement 10: Monitor and Detect.. 279

Requirement 11: Assurance Testing 280

Conclusion 283

Risks 284

Chapter 10: Payment Channel Attack Vectors **285**

Introduction.. 286

    Card Not Present 291

    Card Present.. 292

Card Not Present (CNP) Attack Vectors 295

    "Payload" Delivery Attacks... 297

    CNP Perimeter Attacks 302

    Perimeter Network Attacks.. 302

    Perimeter Web Attacks... 305

Card Present (CP) Attack Vectors 306

    ATM Attacks... 308

    POI/PTS/POS/PDQ Device Attacks 310

Third-Party Attack Vectors 313

Recommendations 314

    Stage 1 316

    Stage 2 316

    Reality Bites... 317

Conclusion.. 319

Key Takeaways.. 320

Risks 321

Chapter 11: Compliance – A Team Effort **323**

Introduction.. 328

It's All in the Game 331

Team Structure.. 332

Rugby League Game Play 334

Team Player Development 335

    Sounds Unrealistic?.. 337

Applying "Team Tactics" to Win the PCI DSS Compliance Game.. 340

    1LOD 341

    2LOD 342

    3LOD 342

Reality Bites 345

Military Lessons Applied 347

Recommendations 356

Conclusion 357

Key Takeaways.. 357

Risks 358

Chapter 12: PIE FARM – A Project Managed Approach to PCI DSS...................... 359

Introduction.. 359

Integrated Project Management 360

    Benefits 364

Background.. 367

PIE FARM Methodology 368

    How to Bake Your PIE? 368

Conclusion 382

Key Takeaways.. 382

Risks 383

Chapter 13: Proactive Defense 385

Maturing the Five Pillars of Defense 385

Introduction.. 385

    Asset Management.. 386

    Vulnerability and Patch Management... 393

    Privileged Access Management (PAM) 399

    Security Information and Event Management (SIEM)... 400

    Incident Management.. 403

    Reality Bites.. 406

Coincidence? 408

    Recommendation 409

    Conclusion 410

Key Takeaways 411

Risks 411

Chapter 14: People, People, People... **413**

Introduction.. 417

Documentation... 420

    Policies Development *(Establishing the Laws)* 422

    Procedures 426

    Supporting Documents 429

Continual Security Awareness/Education 433

    Maintaining Specialist Knowledge/Skillsets.................................... 435

Building an Effective Security Culture.. 437

Managing Change 438

Reality Bites 439

Key Takeaways 441

Risks 442

Chapter 15: The Ripple Effect **445**

Introduction.. 448

PCI DSS: Appropriate Technical and Organizational Measures 451

    Requirement 1: Install and Maintain a Firewall Configuration to Protect Sensitive Data 454

    Requirement 2: Do Not Use Vendor-supplied Defaults for System Passwords and Other Security Parameters 456

    Requirement 3: Protect Stored Sensitive Data 457

    Requirement 4: Encrypt Transmission of Sensitive Data Across Open, Public Networks 458

    Requirement 5: Protect All Systems Against Malware and Regularly Update Anti-virus Software or Programs 459

    Requirement 6: Develop and Maintain Secure Systems and Applications 459

    Requirement 7: Restrict Access to Sensitive Data by Business Need to Know 460

Requirement 8: Identify and Authenticate Access to System Components 460

Requirement 9: Restrict Physical Access to Sensitive Data 461

Requirement 10: Track and Monitor All Access to Network Resources and
Sensitive Data... 462

Requirement 11: Regularly Test Security Systems and Processes.................................... 462

Requirement 12: Maintain a Policy that Addresses Information Security for
All Personnel.. 463

Conclusion 463

Key Takeaways.. 464

Risks 464

Chapter 16: Cometh the Year, Month, Day, Hour **467**

Introduction.. 470

Background 471

Formal Assessment Expectations 473

Principles... 473

Offering.. 476

Execution 477

Closure 478

Annual PCI DSS Assessment.. 478

Planning and Preparation 479

Assessment Process 483

Reality Bites 485

Recommendations 486

Conclusion 487

Key Takeaways.. 488

Risks 489

Chapter 17: Quick Fire Round – Five Commonly Asked Questions 491

Five Commonly Asked Questions 494

Where can I enhance my or my team's knowledge on securing
the business's payment card security? 494

What are the biggest inhibitors to a successful PCI DSS strategy for
the protection of my customer cardholder data? 494

I have outsourced all payment card operations to a third-party supplier, so as neither
my business systems nor personnel interact with *any* cardholder data, surely, I do
not need to validate my compliance? 495

I am not a Merchant or a Service Provider, so does PCI DSS apply to me and how
am I meant to validate my annual compliance? 496

I have undergone multiple onsite assessments and there appears to be a wide range
of inconsistencies in the way that different QSAs interpret the PCI DSS controls. 497

Bibliography 515

Goal 1: Build and Maintain a Secure Network and Systems 515

Goal 2: Protect Cardholder Data 516

Goal 3: Maintain a Vulnerability Management Program 516

Goal 4: Implement Strong Access Control Measures 518

Goal 5: Regularly Monitor and Test Networks 519

Goal 6: Maintain an Information Security Policy 520

Index 523

About the Author

Jim Seaman has been dedicated to the pursuit of security for his entire adult life. He served 22 years in the RAF Police, covering a number of specialist areas including physical security, aviation security, information security management, IT security management, cyber security management, security investigations, intelligence operations, and incident response and disaster recovery. He has successfully transitioned his skills to the corporate environment and now works in areas such as financial services, banking, retail, manufacturing, e-commerce, and marketing. He helps businesses enhance their cyber security and InfoSec defensive measures and work with various industry security standards.

About the Technical Reviewer

Michael Gioia is an information security leader with 17 years of experience delivering security solutions across several industries. He was an officer in the United States Air Force and has worked in higher education, the Department of Defense, retail food services, and security consulting. He has performed most of his information security work in higher education as an Information Security Officer at Eastern Illinois University, Rose-Hulman Institute of Technology, and Bentley University. Michael holds various professional certifications that include a Certified Information Security Manager (CISM) from ISACA, Certified Information System Security Professional (CISSP) from ISC2, GIAC Security Leadership Certification (GSLC) from SANS, and Payment Card Industry Professional (PCIP) from the PCI Security Standards Council.

Introduction

Figure 1. *Image Designed by Laura Scopel*[1]

For any business involved with taking payments from their customers for their goods and services using credit cards, there needs to be a secure chain of trust *(this chain of trust extends out to all your third-party suppliers, who support your payment card operations)*. Your customers are entrusting their payment card data to you and, in return, expect that their payment card data is used in a business justified and legal manner and protected from harm.

All the while, opportunist attackers are seeking to identify potential weak links in this chain, which they are able to exploit and profit from.

Long before I started helping businesses to successfully align with the Payment Card Industry Data Security Standard (PCI DSS), I was fortunate enough to have been responsible for the protection of sensitive data assets, whose impact is described in Figures 2–4.

The compromise of this **HIGHLY SENSITIVE** information or material would be likely to:

- *threaten directly the internal stability of the UK or friendly countries;*
- *lead directly to widespread loss of life;*
- *cause exceptionally grave damage to the effectiveness or security of UK or allied forces or to the continuing effectiveness of extremely valuable security or intelligence operations;*
- *cause exceptionally grave damage to relations with friendly governments;*
- *cause severe long-term damage to the UK economy.*

Levels of Protection
Information and other assets should be held, processed, transmitted or transported and destroyed under conditions which ensure that only those who can be trusted with them and have been authorized gain access to them, that actual or attempted compromises will be detected, and those responsible will be identified.

Figure 2. *Highly Sensitive Category*

The compromise of this **SENSITIVE** information or material would be likely to:

- *raise international tension;*
- *damage seriously relations with friendly governments;*
- *threaten life directly, or seriously prejudice public order, or individual security or liberty;*
- *cause serious damage to the operational effectiveness or security of UK or allied forces or the continuing effectiveness of highly valuable security or intelligence operations;*
- *cause substantial material damage to national finances or economic and commercial interests.*

Levels of Protection
Information and other assets should be held, processed, transmitted or transported and destroyed under conditions which make it highly unlikely that anyone without authorized access will, by chance or design, gain access to them, that compromise will go undetected or that those responsible will remain unidentified.

Figure 3. *Sensitive Category*

The compromise of this **PROTECTED** information or material would be likely to:

- *materially damage diplomatic relations (i.e. cause formal protest or other sanction);*
- *prejudice individual security or liberty;*
- *cause damage to the operational effectiveness or security of UK or allied forces or the effectiveness of valuable security or intelligence operations;*
- *work substantially against national finances or economic and commercial interests; substantially to undermine the financial viability of major organizations;*
- *impede the investigation or facilitate the commission of serious crime; to impede seriously the development or operation of major government policies;*
- *shut down or otherwise substantially disrupt significant national operations.*

Levels of Protection

Information and other assets should be held, processed, transmitted or transported and destroyed under conditions which inhibit casual or willful access by unauthorized people, and which are likely to assist in the identification of compromises.

Figure 4. *Protected Category*

Consequently, the value of ensuring that these assets were adequately protected was fully understood by the organization, and comprehensive defenses were applied using the Defence Manual of Security (Joint Service Publication (JSP) 440).

Each asset was categorized against the category descriptions (Figures 2–4) and afforded the appropriate levels of protection. The need for suitable protection was fully appreciated, and as a result, the concept of applying the minimum standard was never a consideration, with the protective measures being aligned with their perceived levels of risk.

Thus, during my 10 years working on Counter Intelligence duties, even through security risk assessments, I never heard the term "compliant."[2] Some of these principles and lessons learned have been incorporated into the development of this book.

---

[2]www.lexico.com/definition/compliant

INTRODUCTION

The PCI DSS framework can be seen as being extremely complex, expensive, and difficult to achieve and maintain. However, the reality is that it provides a comprehensive suite of baseline of mitigation security controls to help businesses fortify their payment card operations and to help reduce the opportunist attackers to exploit bad practices. The cost of not, at least, establishing a baseline and allowing your payment card operations to be compromised or your customers' payment card data to be stolen would far exceed time, resources, and costs associated with aligning with PCI DSS.

There are many good books on the market that have been developed to help explain the content of the PCI DSS framework:

- *PCI DSS Quick Reference Guide*[3]

- *PCI DSS 3.2: A Comprehensive Understanding to Effectively Achieve PCI DSS Compliance*[4]

- *PCI DSS: A Pocket Guide, 6th Edition*[5]

However, I wanted to design and develop a book that went a little bit further so as to expand on the intent of the PCI DSS framework, the objective being not to be a direct regurgitation of the underlying controls but to provide both Cyber/Information Security professionals and the company's key stakeholders with a comprehensive guide on the benefits of aligning your business's payment card operations with the PCI DSS framework and how this might be applicable to different business types.

Consequently, the readers do not need to have a detailed understanding of the specifics of the PCI DSS framework *(as the latest version and additional supplementary support information is made freely available in the PCI council's Document Library[6])* to gain an improved appreciation for the framework and how it might be applicable to your organization.

---

[3]www.pcisecuritystandards.org/documents/PCIDSS_QRGv3_1.pdf
[4]www.goodreads.com/book/show/40169207-pci-dss-3-2---a-comprehensive-understanding-to-effectively-achieve-pci-d
[5]www.oreilly.com/library/view/pci-dss-a/9781787781641/
[6]www.pcisecuritystandards.org/document_library

Additionally, this guide provides examples of real-life events and incidents, where the attackers have pounced on vulnerabilities which would have been addressed through the implementation of the PCI DSS mitigating controls.

The readers of this book will gain an improved understanding of the principles and objectives of the 6 goals and 12 requirements of PCI DSS and how this can be used in support of building an effective data privacy and security strategy.

Having read this book, the readers will better appreciate how alignment with the PCI DSS framework should be seen as an important business investment, helping to defend the company from opportunist attackers and to reduce the risks associated with a compromise or data breach.

A Tribute To

I would like to dedicate this book to the memory of my late father, who died because of cancer. Unfortunately, this cancer robbed him of his plans to enjoy early retirement *(from the age of 60)*, as he died in hospital just 6 days after his 60th birthday.

Maurice J Seaman
Sept 1942 – Sept 2002

My father had been an extremely intelligent and determined individual, who dedicated his life to building a successful business and supporting his family.

Despite losing his father, when he was just 17 years of age, he showed outstanding determination and resilience to balance supporting his mother and younger brother and sister while successfully becoming a chartered account and going on to found his own company.

Throughout the time that I had known my dad, he had been plagued by illness, having undergone multiple surgeries to treat Crohn's disease. However, despite all of this, he remained extremely supportive of me throughout my childhood and early military career.

In fact, I remember him driving me and a friend to and from the lake district (an approximately 2-hour drive) for our very first solo holiday (10 days hiking and camping) and being extremely supportive following my return to the United Kingdom, after sustaining serious injuries while deployed to the Falkland Islands, on my very first overseas deployment.

During my deployment to the Falkland Islands, I had been involved in a serious road traffic accident, where the Land Rover I had been travelling had left the road at speed and rolled over several times, during which I suffered a fractured skull, fractured neck *(although not discovered until around 3 years later)*, lacerations to the side of my head, a severed ear, and 42 stitches. On my return to the United Kingdom, my father drove the 7-hour return journey to pick me up from RAF Brize Norton, so that I was able to continue my recovery at home. This included him driving me to the nearest RAF medical facility to have my stitches removed and finding me a suitable lawyer to sue the Ministry of Defense (MOD) for the poor treatment I had received post accident.

Basically, I was immediately airlifted from RAF Mount Pleasant to Stanley hospital and then left completely alone (as a 23-year-old, on my first ever overseas deployment), under the care of the hospital for approximately 3 weeks. During this time, I underwent surgery to stitch the ear back together and to skin graft it, a repair to the side of my head, following which I was flown back to the United Kingdom and left to convalesce at home and with very little support or contact from the MOD. My father was outraged at the way his son had been treated and wanted to ensure that their failure to provide adequate "Duty of Care" did not go unpunished.

I appreciate that times have changed and that the aftercare that service personnel receive is completely different from what I received back then, where the only consideration was for the repair of the physical injuries that were visible and without any consideration for any potential mental health or brain injuries that may have been caused as a consequence.

For example, as part of the legal case, 3 years after the accident, a fracture to the C5 joint in my neck had been found *(undetected by the RAF Medical Services)*. Even 23 years after this accident, an MRI scan *(as part of an investigation into prolonged migraines)* identified evidence of a brain injury sustained during the accident *(another thing left undetected by the RAF Medical Services)*, and I suffer consistent pain in my upper spine and neck, caused by early onset (wear and tear) arthritis.

On my frequent visits to see my father, we would sit and discuss the latest world issues, and he would ask me what was happening with me and be genuinely intrigued by my life in the RAF Police.

Unfortunately, he died before he was able to see some of my greatest successes. Consequently, the purpose of this book is to deliver a "double-edged sword." The first is to pass on some of my knowledge and experiences to help the reader to better appreciate the importance of the PCI DSS integrated controls framework. Second, this also provides me with an opportunity to recount some of my tales and successes from my career that occurred after the loss of my father.

You see, my father died just as I was commencing my career into the field of Information Security and Cyber Security. In the few months leading up to the commencement of my 10-week residential counter intelligence (CI) course, my father had succumbed to another bout of illness. However, this was to be his very last fight, and approximately 4 weeks after I had started the course, he would lose his life, on the very same day that he was diagnosed with colon cancer (following the discovery of two tumors).

During his life, my dad was dedicated to delivering the best services to his clients and strived to be utmost professional, and this is something that I have always aspired to embrace in my chosen career.

I hope that you enjoy reading this book and, if my dad is out there somewhere, that he is proud of what I have achieved so far.

CHAPTER 1

An Evolving Regulatory Perspective

Much like the evolution of the motor vehicle, the digitalized business is going through its own revolution, where any increasing reliance on the technology becomes an integral part of a successful business.

As modern successful businesses are seen to embrace technological advances and have established an increasing reliance on personal data, the danger to these technologies and data assets increases. Such assets have far-ranging uses, helping businesses to be more efficient, and can be a game changer for organizations involved in the provision of goods or services to customers.

Technological advances help businesses to track the habits of their customers and thus help them to deliver an improved service or tailored products to their customers.

However, such technological advances have not gone unnoticed by the modern criminals, and they are increasingly looking at opportunities to exploit poorly configured/operated systems or bad practices. Additionally, some organizations may choose to act unscrupulously, and rather than respecting the trust provided to them by their customers, they seek to gain additional profit from their customers' personal data, such as in the event of an immoral activity (e.g., Cambridge Analytica) by an organization that impacts the consumer's rights and calls into question the value of the data made available to consumers or criminal actions that compromise the confidentiality, integrity, or availability of personal data records entrusted to a business, which has the potential to directly impact the associated consumer.

Consequently, regulators and governments across the globe have started to recognize the need for updated data privacy laws, to help protect the consumer and to encourage companies to respect the need to safeguard such data across defined life cycles, and to use it for the purpose to which it had been originally provided.

© Jim Seaman 2020
J. Seaman, *PCI DSS*, https://doi.org/10.1007/978-1-4842-5808-8_1

If you are a business that handles *any* personal data, the value of that data should be identified and appropriate measures applied to help appropriately protect the data to which they have been entrusted. Payment card data is one such high-value personal data asset which criminals are seeking to illegally obtain, so as to make a considerable profit from through payment card fraud.[1]

Imagine the attraction of being able to use the credit of complete strangers to purchase goods for resale on the black market. One platinum credit card with $10,000 credit availability can provide a considerable return on investment.

Unfortunately, personal data has been very much taken for granted for far too many years, with the ease at which it can be reproduced and locally stored, making data security as complicated as "herding cats." This makes for very easy pickings for today's opportunist criminals.

However, now the enhancement of the data privacy regulations increases the need to ensure that such data is processed, stored, and transmitted safely. Fifteen years ago the payment card industry recognized the importance of secure payment card operations and introduced the global data security standards. This is referred to as the Payment Card Industry Data Security Standard, or PCI DSS, and is applicable to *any* organization with the handling of payment card data.

Although the current version does not cover all the data privacy requirements, it does provide businesses with a baseline of controls that cover three quarters of the legal and regulatory requirements.

Introduction

To remain competitive in the payment card industry, it is essential that you balance having customer-friendly, polished payment card operations with the perceived risk. Increasingly, your customers are from the technology generation and are attracted to well-designed, ergonomic, quick, efficient, and convenient payment options. However, your dynamic solutions need to be balanced against the inherent risks and also your customer base is likely to span many generations.

---

[1]www.financederivative.com/inside-payment-card-fraud/

Much like age statistics of the victims of identity theft,[2] users of social media,[3] the age population demographics,[4] and the Internet and Home Broadband are all very similar spreads to that of the motor vehicle accident rates[5] by age (see Figures 1-1 through 1-5).

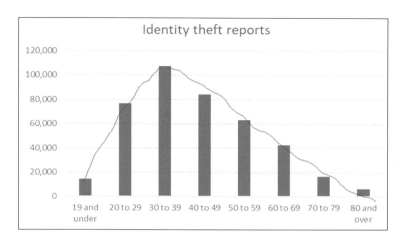

Figure 1-1. *ID Theft*

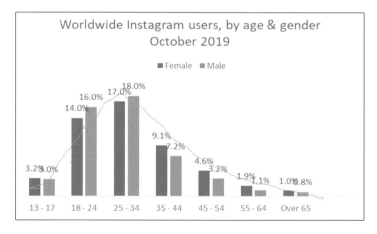

Figure 1-2. *Instagram Users*

---

[2]www.fool.com/the-ascent/research/identity-theft-credit-card-fraud-statistics/
[3]www.statista.com/statistics/248769/age-distribution-of-worldwide-instagram-users/
[4]www.worldometers.info/demographics/world-demographics/
[5]www.iii.org/fact-statistic/facts-statistics-highway-safety

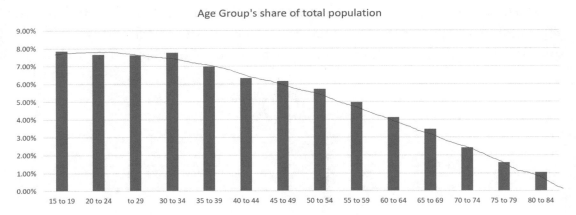

Figure 1-3. *Age Demographics*

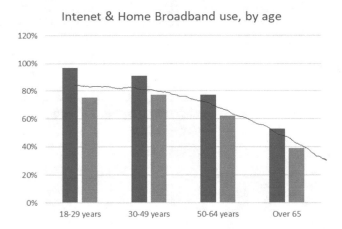

Figure 1-4. *Internet and Home Broadband Use*

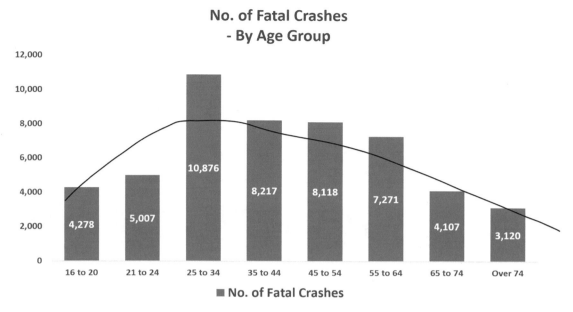

Figure 1-5. *Fatal Vehicle Crashes*

Much like the motor industry changed the supporting legislations and safety requirements to mitigate the increased risks presented by the increased volumes of drivers and the increased speeds of the vehicles on the road, the past few years have seen significant legal and regulatory enhancements (see Figure 1-6).

UK Motor Safety Timeline[6]

---

[6]https://blog.motoringassist.com/history-of-automobile-safety/

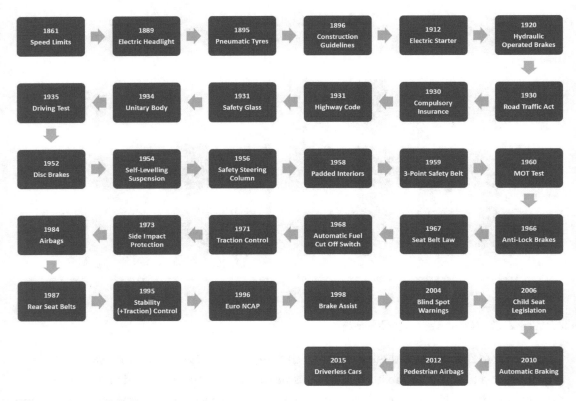

Figure 1-6. *UK Motoring Timeline*

Consequently, as the trend for the digital sharing of personal data has increased, the number of companies suffering data breaches has increased and, as a result, the number of consumers being impacted has significantly grown. Understandably, given the rate of technological advancements, this was unsustainable and the laws and regulations needed to be enhanced to ensure that any businesses receiving personal data did so in a safe and secure manner and in respect of the rights of the individual. Failure to do so would result in regulatory fines and compensation of the affected persons.

Revolution or Evolution?

Often regarded as the revolution of data privacy laws, in May 2018 the European Union (EU) introduced 99 Principles of data privacy that applied to ALL organizations provisioning goods or services to EU members or monitoring the behavior of EU members.[7]

---

[7]https://gdpr-info.eu/art-3-gdpr/

This was the EU General Data Protection Regulation (GDPR),[8] which had a global reach and had considerably larger administrative fines:[9]

- **Tier 1**

  Up to **€10 Million** or, in the case of an undertaking, up to **2%** of the total worldwide annual turnover of the preceding financial year, whichever is higher

- **Tier 2**

  Up to **€20 Million** or, in the case of an undertaking, up to **4%** of the total worldwide annual turnover of the preceding financial year, whichever is higher

This includes the requirement to maintain secure data processing:

- The basic principles for processing, including conditions for consent, pursuant to Articles 5, 6, 7, and 9

  - *Processed in a manner that ensures appropriate security of the personal data, including protection against unauthorized or unlawful processing and against accidental loss, destruction or damage, using appropriate technical or organizational measures ("integrity and confidentiality")*

Previously, under the earlier legislation, the administrative fines had been limited to a maximum of **€1 Million**. Suddenly, businesses were starting to recognize the need to embed security into their Business-As-Usual (BAU) processes – something that was introduced into PCI DSS, in November 2013, with the release of version 3.0.

The enhancement to the EU Data Privacy laws included the requirement for Data Controllers and Data Processors to notify both the Regulators and the affected Data Subjects within 72 hours of a data breach that is suspected to impact the Data Subjects. This particular requirement is a game changer for data privacy, as it supports timely mitigation against data theft, allowing the monitoring to detect and deny potential malicious use.

The introduction of the EU GDPR created a ripple effect across the globe,[10] with other countries enhancing or implementing additional data privacy laws being introduced.

---

[8]https://gdpr.eu/

[9]https://gdpr-info.eu/issues/fines-penalties/

[10]www.dlapiperdataprotection.com/

Europe

- UK Data Privacy Act 2018

  - Aligned with EU GDPR

- EU Directive on Security of Network and Information Systems ("NIS Directive")[11]

  - **Scope**

    - "Operators of Essential Services" (OES)

    - "Relevant Digital Service Providers" (RDSPs)

  - **Penalties**

    - **€20 million** or **4%** of annual global turnover – whichever is higher

- EU Privacy and Electronic Communications Regulations (PECR)[12]

  - **Scope**

    - Organizations that provide a public electronic communications network or service

    - Organizations that market by phone, email, text, or fax; use cookies or a similar technology on your web site; or compile a telephone directory (or a similar public directory)

  - **Penalties**

    - Up to £500,000

Canada

- Personal Information Protection and Electronic Documents Act (PIPEDA)[13]

---

[11]https://ec.europa.eu/commission/presscorner/detail/en/MEMO_16_2422

[12]https://ico.org.uk/for-organisations/guide-to-pecr/

[13]www.priv.gc.ca/en/privacy-topics/privacy-laws-in-canada/the-personal-information-protection-and-electronic-documents-act-pipeda/

United States

- US Federal Trade Commission (FTC)

    - Has jurisdiction over a wide range of commercial entities under its authority to prevent and protect consumers against unfair or deceptive trade practices, including materially unfair privacy and data security practices

- California Consumer Privacy Act of 2018 (CCPA)

    - Effective January 1, 2020

- Massachusetts MA 201 CMR 1[14]

    - The objectives of 201 CMR 17.00 are to ensure the security and confidentiality of customer information in a manner fully consistent with industry standards, protect against anticipated threats or hazards to the security or integrity of such information, and protect against unauthorized access to or use of such information that may result in substantial harm or inconvenience to any consumer.

- Illinois 815 ILCS 530 – Personal Information Protection Act (PIPA)[15]

- New York[16]

    - SHIELD Act[17]

    - Identity Theft Protection and Mitigation Services Act[18]

---

[14]www.mass.gov/doc/201-cmr-17-standards-for-the-protection-of-personal-information-of-residents-of-the/download

[15]www.ilga.gov/legislation/ilcs/ilcs3.asp?ActID=2702&ChapterID=67

[16]www.ropesgray.com/en/newsroom/alerts/2019/08/New-York-Updates-Privacy-Laws?utm_source=Mondaq&utm_medium=syndication&utm_campaign=View-Original

[17]https://legislation.nysenate.gov/pdf/bills/2019/S133

[18]https://legislation.nysenate.gov/pdf/bills/2019/A2374

Australia

- Information Privacy Act 2014 (Australian Capital Territory)

- Information Act 2002 (Northern Territory)

- Privacy and Personal Information Protection Act 1998 (New South Wales)

- Information Privacy Act 2009 (Queensland)

- Personal Information Protection Act 2004 (Tasmania)

- Privacy and Data Protection Act 2014 (Victoria)

China

- People's Republic of China (PRC) Cyber security Law

Japan

- The Act on the Protection of Personal Information ("APPI")

Argentina

- Personal Data Protection Law (PDPL)

  - Law 25 § 326

    - Includes the basic personal data rules. It follows international standards and has been considered as granting adequate protection by the European Commission.

Malaysia

- Personal Data Protection Act 2010 (PDPA)

Brazil

- Brazilian General Data Protection Law (LGPD)[19]

India

- Personal Data Protection Bill 2018[20]

Financial Services

Despite being heavily regulated, the Financial Services industry is not exempt from their applicable data privacy rules. However, if they are involved in the processing of any branded payment cards (Mastercard, Visa, American Express, JCB, Discover), they are expected to align to the PCI DSS and, under the recent changes to the Mastercard Rules (Chapter 2, para 2.2.7),[21] have a formal Information Security program.

The strength of the PCI DSS controls framework has been recognized by the Regulators (e.g., Information Commissioner's Office (ICO),[22] Federal Trade Commission (FTC),[23] etc.), with it being noted that in the event of a personal data breach, the effectiveness of an organization's PCI DSS compliance program will be taken into account.

Note   It is important to remember that the PCI DSS does not incorporate ALL of the data privacy requirements and only provides a baseline against the Cyber Security, Information Security, and Physical Security domains and omits the Rights of the Individual and the need for Resilience. The focus of the PCI DSS is to ensure that the Confidentiality and Integrity of the payment card data and supporting Information Systems are protected.

---

[19]www.dlapiperdataprotection.com/index.html?t=law&c=BR

[20]www.dlapiperdataprotection.com/index.html?t=law&c=IN

[21]www.mastercard.us/content/dam/mccom/global/documents/mastercard-rules.pdf

[22]https://ico.org.uk/for-organisations/guide-to-data-protection/guide-to-the-general-data-protection-regulation-gdpr/security/

[23]www.venable.com/insights/publications/2019/02/ftc-2019-insights-and-priorities-for-the-payments

In the event that a financial services company were to be compromised and personal data is stolen, they could be liable to be penalized from a variety of regulators and, in some countries, private litigation.

This has been highlighted through numerous penalties levied against Financial Services companies:

- **2016**:[24] Financial Conduct Authority (FCA) fines Tesco Personal Finance plc (Tesco Bank) **£16.4 Million** for failing to exercise due skill, care, and diligence in protecting its personal current account holders against a cyber-attack.

  - 136,000 current accounts frozen, following "online criminal activity," resulting in the theft of funds from at least 20,000 customers

- **2017**:[25] Federal Trade Commission (FTC) fines Equifax up to **$700 Million**, as part of a settlement with federal authorities over a data breach in 2017.

  - 209,000 credit card details

- **2018**:[26] Ireland's central bank fines the Bank of Montreal, Toronto, **€1.25 million** for breaching license conditions.

  - 90,000 clients of the Canadian banks Simplii and Bank of Montreal (BMO).

  - Simplii and BMO are now facing a class action lawsuit, with those involved arguing that the banks failed to properly protect sensitive information.

- **2019**:[27] FTC investigating the Capital One breach.

  - **106 Million** credit card customers and credit card applicants in the United States and Canada

---

[24]www.fca.org.uk/news/press-releases/fca-fines-tesco-bank-failures-2016-cyber-attack
[25]https://techcrunch.com/2019/07/22/equifax-fine-ftc/
[26]www.ctvnews.ca/business/bmo-fined-1-25m-euros-by-ireland-s-central-bank-for-breaching-licence-conditions-1.4399691
[27]www.consumer.ftc.gov/blog/2019/07/capital-one-data-breach-time-check-your-credit-report

Data Privacy Hierarchy

Whether you are a small Merchant or a large Global Bank, if you are a business that relies on payment card data, you have an obligation to align with the PCI DSS for both legal and regulatory obligations. Consequently, a natural hierarchy has developed where your compliance obligations are aligned to the potential risks associated with particular business types (see Figure 1-7).

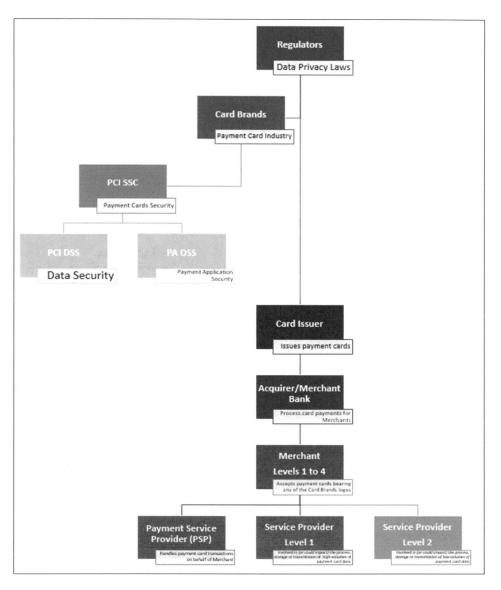

Figure 1-7. *PCI DSS Hierarchy*

The manner in which you validate your PCI DSS compliance varies based upon the perceived risks for a heavily regulated industry or the volume of payment card data involved within your business operations.

PCI DSS Validation Requirements

As previously mentioned, it is extremely important to keep track of your PCI DSS compliance status, all year around, to ensure that you have the evidence to support any breach investigations and not for a "Once-A-Year" compliance obligation, as per Table 1-1.

Banking Industry

- **Card Issuer/Acquirer**

  - Self-regulation

  - Incorporated into a formal Information Security program

  - Compliance status called upon as evidence, in the event of a data breach

Table 1-1. *Mastercard Compliance Criteria – Merchants*[28]

Level	Criteria	Validation
1	• Any merchant that has suffered a hack or an attack that resulted in an Account Data Compromise (ADC) Event • Any merchant having **greater than 6 Million** total combined Mastercard and Maestro transactions annually • *Any merchant meeting the Level 1 criteria of Visa* • Any merchant that Mastercard, in its sole discretion, determines should meet the Level 1 merchant requirements to minimize risk to the system.	• **Annual Onsite Assessment**[29] • **Quarterly Network Scan conducted by an Approved Scanning Vendor (ASV)**[30]

(*continued*)

---

[28]www.mastercard.us/en-us/merchants/safety-security/security-recommendations/merchants-need-to-know.html

[29]Level 1 merchants that choose to conduct an annual onsite assessment using an internal auditor must ensure that primary internal auditor staff engaged in validating PCI DSS compliance attend PCI SSC ISA Training and pass the associated accreditation program annually in order to continue to use internal auditors.

[30]www.pcisecuritystandards.org/assessors_and_solutions/approved_scanning_vendors

Table 1-1. (*continued*)

Level	Criteria	Validation
2	• Any merchant with more than **1 to 6 Million** total combined Mastercard and Maestro transactions annually • Any merchant meeting the Level 2 criteria of Visa	• **Annual Self-Assessment** *(Self-Assessment Questionnaire (SAQ))*[31] • **Onsite Assessment at Merchant Discretion**[32]
3	• Any merchant with **greater than 20,000** combined Mastercard and Maestro e-commerce transactions **annually but less than or equal to 1 Million** total combined Mastercard and Maestro e-commerce transactions annually • Any merchant meeting the Level 3 criteria of Visa	• **Annual Self-Assessment** • **Onsite Assessment at Merchant Discretion**[33] • **Quarterly Network Scan conducted by an ASV**
4	• All other merchants[34]	• **Annual Self-Assessment** • **Onsite Assessment at Merchant Discretion** • **Quarterly Network Scan conducted by an ASV**

---

[31] www.pcisecuritystandards.org/documents/SAQ-InstrGuidelines-v3_2_1.pdf?agreement=true&time=1575476486348

[32] Level 2 merchants that choose to complete an annual self-assessment questionnaire must ensure that staff engaged in the self-assessment attend PCI SSC ISA Training and pass the associated accreditation program annually in order to continue the option of self-assessment for compliance validation. Alternatively, Level 2 merchants may, at their own discretion, complete an annual onsite assessment conducted by a PCI SSC-approved Qualified Security Assessor (QSA) rather than complete an annual self-assessment questionnaire.

[33] Level 3 and Level 4 merchants may alternatively, at their own discretion, engage a PCI SSC-approved QSA for an onsite assessment instead of performing a self-assessment.

[34] Level 4 merchants are required to comply with the PCI DSS. Level 4 merchants should consult their acquirer to determine if compliance validation is also required.

Table 1-2. *Mastercard Compliance Criteria – Service Providers*[35]

Level 1	• All Third-Party Processors (TPPs) • All Staged Digital Wallet Operators (SDWOs) • All Digital Activity Service Providers (DASPs) • All Token Service Providers (TSPs) • All 3-D Secure Service Providers (3-DSSPs) • All Data Storage Entities (DSEs) and Payment Facilitators (PFs) with **greater than 300,000** total combined Mastercard and Maestro transactions annually	• **Annual Onsite Assessment conducted by an appropriate PCI SSC-approved QSA** • **Quarterly Network Scan conducted by an ASV**
Level 2	• All Data Storage Entities (DSEs) and Payment Facilitators (PFs) with **300,000 or less** total combined Mastercard and Maestro transactions annually • All Terminal Servicers (TSs)	• **Annual Self-Assessment** • **Quarterly Network Scan conducted by an ASV**

Recommendations

It is abundantly clear that the world has moved on both in regard to the increasing use of technology and data and relation to data privacy regulations.

Consequently, it is highly recommended that you embed the data privacy principles and PCI DSS controls into your business operations, so that it becomes a seamless part of your organization. To achieve this, it is extremely important to ensure that your PCI DSS validation efforts are incorporated into your business-as-usual activities and not treated as a "standalone" compliance effort.

Data privacy and data security go "Hand in Glove" and should be treated as complementary to one another. Therefore, the components for data privacy, data security, and PCI DSS compliance should be incorporated into a single data privacy and security program (see Figure 1-8).

---

[35]www.mastercard.us/en-us/merchants/safety-security/security-recommendations/service-providers-need-to-know.html

Figure 1-8. *Data Privacy and Security Cycles*

Embed data privacy and information security into your risk programs to ensure that senior management is fully apprised of the risks associated with your various data processes, be that payment card (PCI DSS) or personal data (e.g., GDPR), and that formal information security programs provide regular updates on the status, baselined against the most appropriate security controls frameworks.

The objectives of your data privacy program should be supported by defined roles (e.g., Risk Director, Information Security Manager, Data Privacy Officer, Privacy and Security Steering Committee, Privacy Manager, Risk Management Committee, Data

Controller, Data Processor, and various representative Business Unit Managers), which would form your cohesive process enablement to help deliver the following:

- Evaluation, direction, and monitoring

- Alignment, planning, and organization

- Secure development, procurement, and implementation

- Quality delivery, service, and support

- Monitoring, evaluation, and assessment

Additionally, the objective of this committee is to discuss any perceived risk and to provide guidance on the best practices to their representative teams. The processing, storage, or transmission of personal data has become an integral part of running a successful business. Consequently, this is an essential element of any successful privacy and information security program, as employee interaction with personal data and personal data processing IT systems is regarded as the greatest risk.

Establishing enterprise-wide security cultures, ethics, and behaviors is embedded throughout PCI DSS, seen at the conclusion controls of every requirement and in its entirety at requirement 12. It is important to remember that the foundations of effective security cultures, ethics, and behaviors must be endorsed and supported from the very top of the corporate hill and should not be seen as a once-a-year compliance "tick box" requirement.

Think of your data privacy program as you would regard a road safety program. Every road user needs to understand the "rules of the road" and to appreciate the risks associated with careless driving or breaking the rules. In order to be licensed to navigate the roads, each road user must achieve a minimum standard (pass their driving test) and then maintain these driving standards. Failure to do so results in re-education (e.g., warning, caution, speed awareness training, etc.) or disciplinary action (e.g., fine, driving ban, etc.).

A similar approach should be applied to the development of an effective data privacy program.

Behaviors

At the organizational level, behaviors are determined by the values of your business (e.g., PCI DSS Charter) and at an individual level, where the behaviors are defined by personal values:

- **Data privacy is as natural as breathing *(practiced in daily operations)*.**

- Data protection becomes an integral part of business. Rarely do employees wish to do badly by their employers or consumers, but do so out of complacency, neglect, or poor understanding.

  - At the corporate level, behavior indicates that data protection is accepted as a business imperative in business goals setting.

  - At the individual level, the employee recognizes the importance of applying data protection principles into their daily routines for the safeguarding of the consumers and the reputation of the business.

- **People respect the data protection policies and principles.**

Think of this like your "Rules of the Road," where the employees do not need to be fully conversant with all the content of the data privacy legislations, only those controls that apply to their business functions. For example, if you take the example of the Highway Code,[36] this is deemed to be essential reading for anyone intending to use the UK road (e.g., pedestrians, equestrians, cyclists, motorcycle riders, car drivers, bus drivers, truck drivers, etc.) and with the sole purpose of reducing the associated risks.

When you are entrusted driving a vehicle on the highways, there are a number of legal requirements that you need to comply with, as detailed in the Highway Code *(e.g., safe driving, maintaining an operational vehicle, having insurance, etc.)*. Any drivers or businesses failing to comply with the guidance from the Highway Code understand that there are consequences, as detailed in Table 1-3.

---

[36]www.gov.uk/guidance/the-highway-code/introduction

Table 1-3. *Driving Penalties*

Offence	Imprisonment	Fine	Disqualification	Penalty Points
Causing deaths or grievous bodily injury by dangerous driving	14 years	Unlimited	Obligatory – two years minimum	3 to 11 (if exceptionally not disqualified)
Dangerous driving	Five years	Unlimited	Obligatory	3 to 11 (if exceptionally not disqualified)
Causing death or grievous bodily injury by careless driving under the influence of drink or drugs	14 years	Unlimited	Obligatory – two years minimum	3 to 11 (if exceptionally not disqualified)
Aggravated vehicle taking causing death or grievous bodily injury	14 years	Unlimited	Obligatory	3 to 11
Careless and inconsiderate driving	None	£5,000	Discretionary	3 to 9
Driving while unfit through drink or drugs or with excess alcohol, or failing to provide a specimen for analysis	Six months	£5,000	Obligatory	3 to 11 (if exceptionally not disqualified)
Failing to stop after an accident (collision) or failing to report an accident (collision)	Six months	£5,000	Discretionary	5 to 10
Driving when disqualified	Two years	Unlimited	Discretionary	6
Causing death or grievous bodily injury by careless or inconsiderate driving	Five years	Unlimited	Obligatory	3 to 11
Driving without insurance	Six months	£5,000	Discretionary	6 to 8

(*continued*)

Table 1-3. (*continued*)

Offence	Imprisonment	Fine	Disqualification	Penalty Points
Causing death or grievous bodily injury by driving unlicensed, uninsured, or while disqualified	Two years	Unlimited	Obligatory	3 to 11
Failure to have proper control of vehicle or full view of the road and traffic ahead or using a handheld mobile phone while driving	None	£1,000 (£2,500 for PCV or goods vehicle)	Discretionary	3
Speeding	None	£1,000 (£2,500 for motorway offences)	Discretionary	3 to 6 or 3 (fixed penalty)
Traffic light offences	None	£1,000	Discretionary	3
No MOT certificate	None	£1,000		
Seat belt offences	None	£500		3
Dangerous cycling	None	£2,500		
Careless cycling	None	£1,000		
Failing to identify driver of a vehicle	None	£1,000	Discretionary	6

Similarities between the legal requirements for driving a motor vehicle can be correlated against the expectations for being a data controller or processor.

- **At the corporate level**

  - Data protection policies and principles are endorsed and supported by senior management and communicated to all. Individuals are encouraged to provide constructive feedback.

  - All systems supporting the personal data processing operations are well maintained.

- Individuals receive periodic refresher training, so as to keep their knowledge of the data Protection policies and principles fresh in their minds.

  - *This should be delivered through a variety of mediums (e.g., face to face (department security champions), emails, posters, newsletters, quizzes, etc.).*

  - *Consider the potential Return on Investment (ROI) of outsourcing the production and delivery through a third-party service (e.g., KnowBe4[37]).*

- Adherence to policies and procedures is policed.

- **At an individual level**

  - Employees/contractors have read, understood, and adhere to the data protection policies and principles *(actively encouraged to provide feedback on the content/applicability to their role).*

  - Personnel adhere to their intent *(raising a formal approval requests for temporary deviations, when required).* Individuals receive periodic refresher training, so as to keep their knowledge of the data Protection policies and principles fresh in their minds.

- **Individuals are given sufficient guidance and are encouraged to provide constructive feedback.**

  Employees/contractors are provided sufficient instruction and are encouraged to challenge the data protection practices to ensure that they remain effective.

  - A two-way communicative process is established.

  - The culture supports the questioning of data protection practices, identifying potential issues/problems and providing comments, when requested.

---

[37]https://info.knowbe4.com/one-on-one-demo-partners?partnerid=0010c000022xCHUAA2

- **Everyone is deemed responsible for data protection.**

  - Discipline and sanctions are implemented for non-adherence of policy, with stakeholders confirming enforcement.

  - Individuals understand their data protection policies and principles that apply to their specific roles/duties.

- **Stakeholders identify and respond to threats to the organization.**

  - Threat intelligence is embedded into your company to enhance your ability to identify and respond to such breaches.

  - Personnel receive refresher training that includes relevant data breaches and how they should respond and report to such events.

- **Data Protection challenges are embedded into business projects and innovations.**

  - Research and development has an embedded security culture to ensure that data protection considerations are considered.

  - Individual data protection culture is included when stakeholders introduce new ideas.

- **Cross-functional collaboration supports the efficiency and effectiveness of the data protection programs.**

  - An integrated approach to data protection strategies is embedded into your organization.

  - Individual participation is encouraged for the identification of data protection risks, providing a synergy for the establishment of new data protection mitigations.

- **Executive management understands the business value of data protection.**

  - Data protection is recognized as a means to improve business value (e.g., revenue, expense, reputation, competitive advantage, etc.), maintain trust, and enhance brand value. Failure to be transparent, in the event of an incident/breach, can significantly undermine consumer confidence.

  - Individuals are seen to generate creative ideas that improve the value of any data protection efforts.

Leadership

Never has the "Tone at the Top" been more important than in support of an effective data protection program, and this example needs to cascade down with the same message communicated through the departmental leads. Executive management are not expected to know the "ins and outs" of the data protection program; however, their actions should not undermine such a program.

The value of good leadership was a valuable lesson that I learned during my 22 years in the RAF Police and was often seen as being the deciding factor between success and failure. Organizations with weak or ineffectual leadership are doomed to fail, whereas organizations that have clear-sighted and courageous leadership are able to overcome virtually any problem.

The task of leadership is not to put greatness into humanity, but to elicit it, for the greatness is already there!

—John Buchan, Lord Tweedsmuir of Elsfield

Some of the traits of a good leader include

- Creating a sense of belonging
- Developing a sense of duty and service
- Supporting good morale
- Courage
- Communication
- Leading by example
- Knowing your people
- Showing vision and decisiveness
- Creating an air of trust
- Providing command

All of these traits help to influence behavior across your business. Failure to embrace and support your data protection program can lead to incidents like these:

- I recall a visit to a client where their reception staff had made the visitor process redundant so that no visitor was being booked into the visitor log. Why had this happened? A board member had deemed this to be an inconvenience for them and had set a precedent for everyone else. As a consequence, they had no record of the comings and goings of strangers.

- On another occasion, I was carrying out a PCI DSS gap assessment for a UK football club. During the review of the logical access control practices, the IT Manager reassured me that the Active Directory Group policy had been configured to comply with the PCI DSS requirements (e.g., seven characters, strong complexity, etc.). However, when reviewing the Mail Order Telephone Ordering practices, carried out in a warehouse, it was revealed that the user was using a six-character password. When asked of the complexity used, I was informed that they were only using a six-character simple password. As a result, it would only take 500 milliseconds to crack the password[38] and be able to gain unauthorized access to the corporate network.

"How could this have happened?", I hear you shout. During a lunchtime period, when the IT help desk was being manned by a junior member of the IT team, a member of the Board demanded that the password complexity be changed, so as to make it easier for them.

Consent or Legitimate Use

Just requesting and collecting personal data from an individual are not acceptable practices. The consumer can reasonably expect that their data will explicitly be used in

---

[38]https://howsecureismypassword.net/

a manner that they have approved or with which you are able to demonstrate a legal or legitimate business reason for doing so, for example:

- A consumer provides their personal and payment card data for the purchase of annual car insurance. It is reasonable for that consumer to believe that the payment card data shall not be retained once the payment has been processed. Therefore, without the explicit permission of the consumer, it is not acceptable to retain that personal data so that the insurance company can auto-enroll that consumer onto subsequent renewals.

  - Any deviation from this must be through transparent consent from the consumer.

Conclusion

Changes to data privacy laws have made the need to ensure that all systems and personnel involved in the processing of personal data (including payment card data) are securely managed a high priority for business. However, the changing legislation should be less influential than the ROI the business will achieve from safeguarding and using the entrusted data correctly.

Failure to prioritize the data protection program, so that it becomes integral to the organization, may lead to complacency which would increase the risk of a compromise of your personal data processing operations. Such a compromise can lead to significant regulatory fines and reputational damage.

An effective data protection policy needs to be set through the "Tone at the Top" and embraced throughout the company, with leadership and management responsibilities being delegated to departmental business unit managers but managed through a Data Protection Committee.

As a business, you are expected to maintain safe processes throughout the year, with the status being formally validated (for PCI DSS) on an annual basis.

"Many hands make light work" – applying a team approach helps embed good security practices across the organization, which will be observed by your customers and employees to increase their trust levels and, thus, make them more comfortable with your brand. Such a ROI is priceless!

Key Takeaways

When consumers provide their personal data, in exchange for goods or services, to your data processing operations, it is like they are entrusting their children (or other most valued items) to a taxi, courier, or bus service.

Consequently, they quite rightly expect that the drivers will be licensed and safe and the vehicles are well maintained and subject to an annual safety check.

The same applies to your personal data processing operations.

Maintaining fleet safety requires leadership, support, and teamwork!

Do you set the "Tone at the Top"?

Do you understand your personal data processing operations?

Do all personnel understand what "Safe Driving" looks like?

Do you have a well-maintained fleet?

In the case of an event/incident, do you have sufficient fleet maintenance records?

Is Data Protection embedded into your business culture?

Do you apply a team effort?

Do all personnel receive initial and periodic refresher training?

Are your fleet drivers policed?

Are your personnel encouraged to report any potential incidents of "Dangerous Driving"?

In the event of an accident (incident), do your staff know what to do?

Risks

Criminals are constantly looking at opportunities to collect any loose pieces of the "personal data" jigsaw puzzle.

Consumers provide you with their personal data for a specific reason, and this does not automatically give you the rights to use this data as you feel fit.

Failure to securely retain and appropriately use all of the pieces of the jigsaw is seen as a lack of respect for the consumers and can lead to considerable reputational damage, as well as potential regulatory and legislative fines.

Ask yourself:

- *Do I have an integrated Data Protection program which spans further than members from the IT teams?*

- *Do I have a Data Protection team program?*

- *Do I share regular updates with a Data Protection Committee?*

- *Do I have sufficient representation across the organization?*

- *Do I have an embedded security culture?*

- *Is the "Tone at the Top" established?*

- *Does everyone understand what is (and what is not) acceptable practice?*

- *In the event of a data breach, do I have sufficient evidence of an effective Data Protection program?*

- *Am I solely reliant on my annual compliance validation (a great deal of data processing activity occurs in the 12 months between validation dates)?*

- *Am I confident in my staffs' levels of skill, knowledge, and experience needed for to ensure that they know how to "Drive Safely"?*

CHAPTER 2

The Evolution of PCI DSS

Many believe that the Payment Card Industry Data Security Standard (PCI DSS) began in December 2004. However, much like Darwin's theory of evolution, the evolution of the PCI DSS controls framework has a much longer history.

To truly appreciate the evolution of the PCI DSS integrated framework, it is important to take a look at its roots to ascertain the lessons learned from history, previous associated controls frameworks, and the evolutionary changes that inspired the need for the development of an effective defensive controls framework for the protection of payment card data.

Over the centuries (yes, centuries), we have seen significant changes in the way customers purchase goods and services using payment cards:

1. Starting with the clay tablets[1] used by the ancient Mesopotamians in around 3300 BC which were used as means of credit for the purchase of goods.

Figure 2-1. *Clay Tablet*

---

[1]www.metmuseum.org/toah/works-of-art/1988.433.3/

© Jim Seaman 2020
J. Seaman, *PCI DSS*, https://doi.org/10.1007/978-1-4842-5808-8_2

2.   Next came, in the 1800s, the United States' use of charge plates[2] as the precursor to the modern-day payment card.

Figure 2-2. *Charge Plate*

3.   In the 1880s, the Provident Clothing Group (United Kingdom) introduced a credit voucher[3] – often regarded as one of the precursors to the modern-day payment card.

4.   The 1950s saw the introduction of the Diners' Club card.[4]

Figure 2-3. *Diners' Club Card*

5.   In 1958, American Express introduced the first embossed plastic cards.[5]

---

[2]www.digibarn.com/collections/small-items/charga-plate/index.html
[3]www.theukcardsassociation.org.uk/history_of_cards/index.asp
[4]www.timetoast.com/timelines/credit-card-in-1950
[5]www.relativelyinteresting.com/evolution-credit-card-paper-plastic-virtual/

Figure 2-4. *AMEX Payment Card*

6. In the 1970s, a joint pilot project by American Express,[6] American Airlines, and IBM took place at Chicago's O'Hare Airport. American Express issued hundreds of new cards to frequent travelers in the Chicago area and allowed for electronic payment for tickets and other services using these new cards.

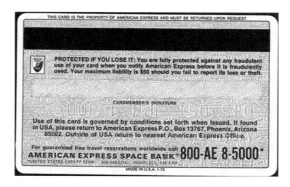

Figure 2-5. *AMEX Mag Stripe Payment Card*

7. The 1990s saw the introduction of the first form of digital wallet.[7] However, the early versions were extremely unreliable, and these did not become popular until Apple debuted their version in October 2014.

---

[6]https://postalmuseum.si.edu/americasmailingindustry/American-Express.html
[7]https://due.com/blog/digital-wallet-revolution/

Figure 2-6. *Mobile Payments*

It is very clear that over the centuries advancements in technologies have increased the convenience of making instant payments through the use of payment cards. Hence, the consumers are increasingly choosing payment cards as their preferred choice for making payments.[8]

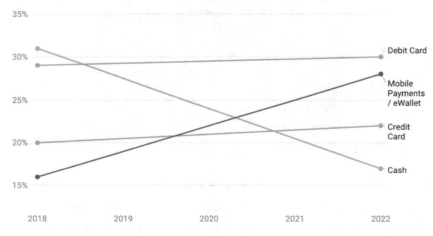

Figure 2-7. *Global Share of Point-of-Sale (PoS) Payment Methods*

---

[8]https://worldpay.globalpaymentsreport.com/#/

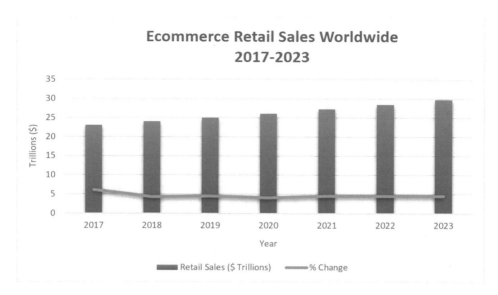

Figure 2-8. *Global E-commerce Trends[9]*

This progressive move toward more convenient technical based payments[10] has made this increasingly attractive to opportunist criminals, with the volume of data breaches[11] and cases of identity theft continuing to grow, with business being the greatest victim of criminal activity.

---

[9]www.emarketer.com/content/global-ecommerce-2019
[10]www.ukfinance.org.uk/sites/default/files/uploads/pdf/UK-Finance-UK-Payment-
  Markets-Report-2019-SUMMARY.pdf
[11]https://safeatlast.co/blog/data-breach-statistics/#gref

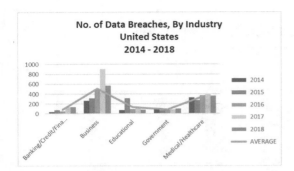

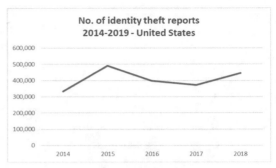

Source: Statistica[12]

Source: FTC Consumer Sentinel Network Databook 2018[13]

As a consequence, the Card Brands (Mastercard, Visa, American Express, JCB, and Discover) started to develop their own suites of defensive control sets:

- *Visa's Cardholder Information Security Program*

- *Mastercard's Site Data Protection*

- *American Express's Data Security Operating Policy*

- *Discover's Information Security and Compliance*

- *JCB's Data Security Program*

In 2004, the Payment Card Industry Security Standards Council (PCI SSC) had been appointed to develop and manage a single integrated controls framework (Payment Cards Industry Data Security Standard (PCI DSS) v1.0). The intended purpose being to provide payment card processing businesses with a suite of security controls to help them harden the payment card defenses. Consequently, any business involved in the processing, storage, or transmission of payment card data must apply the applicable controls from the PCI DSS catalogue of controls.

---

[12]www.statista.com/statistics/273572/number-of-data-breaches-in-the-united-states-by-business/

[13]www.ftc.gov/system/files/documents/reports/consumer-sentinel-network-data-book-2018/consumer_sentinel_network_data_book_2018_0.pdf

Failure to demonstrate their annual compliance to these controls *(using the self-assessment questionnaire (SAQ) or report on compliance (RoC) formats (or self-attested for regulated Merchant/Acquirer/Issuer Bank))* would likely lead to a monthly non-compliance (miscellaneous) charge,[14] fine, or withdrawal of license to take payments through payment cards.[15]

Associated Costs (Non-compliance/Data Breach)

- **Card reissuance costs** (*for each card involved that must be reissued*)
  - **$2–$5** or more per card
    - *The average number of cards compromised per breach is typically in the thousands for small businesses and in the hundreds of thousands to millions for larger businesses.*
      - *For example, British Airways Breach of 380,000 payment card records = **$760k–$1.9 Million**.*
- *Non-compliance fines*
  - Passed from the Acquiring banks
    - ***$5000–$10,000*** *per month*
    - ***$60,000–$120,000*** *per annum*
- Additional fraud detection services costs (*enforced by the card brands such as costly financial and forensic audits*)
- Additional fraud monitoring programs and technologies (*as mandated by the card brands*)

Much like the evolution of the payment card processes, the PCI DSS controls framework continues to evolve in response to the changing technologies; the attackers Tactics, Techniques, and Protocols (TTPs); and any new or emerging payment channel specific threats. Consequently, the PCI DSS controls framework employs industry best practices. This chapter will investigate the potential origins, from history, that can be seen within the latest version of PCI DSS.

---

[14]www.worldpay.com/en-us/insights-hub/article/how-to-become-pci-compliant
[15]www.theukcardsassociation.org.uk/security/Non_compliance_PCIDSS.asp

Introduction

Frequently, businesses do not understand the PCI DSS controls framework and believe it to be a new standard that is purely technical and not applicable to them if they are not processing, storing, or transmitting payment card data electronically. However, these organizations have many opportunist attackers who will seek to steal payment cardholder data in any format, gaining unauthorized access through *any* means presented to them.

Payment card processing has evolved and changed significantly over many years, and payment card theft/fraud activities have adapted to meet these business changes. However, despite the evolution of the PCI DSS controls framework to help mitigate these risks, businesses have been slow to recognize the maturity of the PCI DSS controls framework and the effectiveness it has in reducing the associated risks to their payment card processing operations.

Understanding the heritage of the PCI DSS controls and framework should help businesses to better appreciate the structure and the benefits to your organization.

Aligning your business to the PCI DSS controls framework will help you to layer your defenses around your payment card data operations, improving your ability to maintain the Confidentiality and Integrity of your customers' payment card details *(entrusted to you in payment for goods or services)*. The unforeseen benefits being the safeguarding of your company's reputation.

PCI DSS Controls Framework Architecture

The PCI DSS controls architecture employs a layered defensive structure, whereby each layer provides an isolated barrier in order to slow or deter an attacker's ingress or egress. As a result, an attacker would need to peel back each layer of defense to move toward (or away from) the payment card data. Think of the architecture as being similar to the structure of an onion.

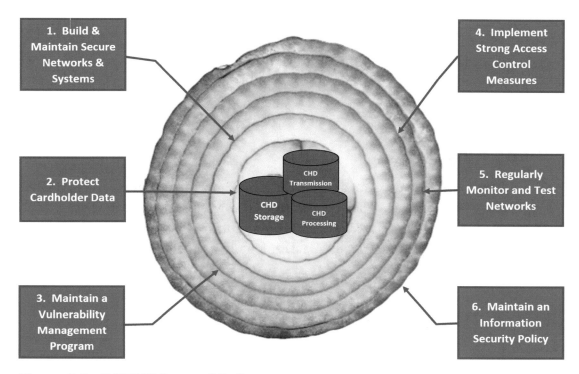

Figure 2-9. *PCI DSS Layered Defenses*

Primary (Core) Ring

At the core of the PCI DSS controls framework is the need to safeguard the payment card data (Storage, Transmission, and Processing) by ensuring that the aggregated risk associated with data retention is strictly limited based upon strict legal, regulatory, and/ or business requirements and with the most sensitive data (Sensitive Authentication Data (SAD) being prevented from being retained post authorization. Where the Primary Account Number (PAN) needs to be viewed, the risk is reduced to only the first six and last four digits. Having strictly controlled the retained payment card data, any unavoidable data stores need to be securely stored and, if encrypted, supported by robust key management processes to ensure that if the data vault becomes compromised, then the data appears to be worthless to the criminal. Additionally, all data in transit is also to be protected through the use of strong encryption.

Secondary Ring

The next ring requires the supporting network and systems to be robustly configured to ensure that the network traffic is filtered to only allow authorized traffic into the trusted zone and to ensure that the supporting IT systems are locked down, so as to prevent misuse.

Tertiary Ring

Having limited your data retention to a minimum and implemented robustly configured the supporting IT systems, you then need to strictly limit the access to only those with a legitimate need to know/need to access. The more personnel with authorized access, the greater the number of potential targets to be exploited by criminals and, thus, the greater the risk.

Quaternary Ring

IT systems and software applications are dynamic by their very nature and, as such, need to be well maintained to ensure that they are protected from malware and any higher risk emerging vulnerabilities, and all software development activities have security considerations embedded within them to ensure no known high-risk vulnerabilities are introduced into your secure environment.

Quinary Ring

This is the "checks and balance" ring, whereby the inner rings are monitored for ABNORMAL activities and are periodically tested to provide reassurance to confirm that no vulnerabilities exist. In the event that vulnerabilities are detected, they are remediated against in a timely manner *(based upon the perceived risks)*.

Senary (Outer) Ring

The final outer ring is the "People Management" to ensure that all personnel supporting the payment card business operations understand the rules, their responsibilities, and the standard operating procedures (SOPs) that relate to their roles.

Each of these rings has subsequent sub-rings and micro-rings that need to be applied to provide robust rings of defense.

For example, see the following data taken from v3.2.1.

Requirement 3: Protect Stored Cardholder Data

3.1   Data Retention

3.2   Sensitive Authentication Data (SAD)

- 3.2.1. Prohibit storage of full track data
- 3.2.2. Prohibit storage of card verification code or value
- 3.2.3. Prohibit storage of personal identification number (PIN) or the encrypted PIN block

3.3   Mask primary account number (PAN)

3.4   Render stored PAN unreadable

- 3.4.1. Disk encryption

3.5   Formal key management practices

- 3.5.1. Service Providers – Documented description of the cryptographic architecture
- 3.5.2. Restrict access to cryptographic Keys
- 3.5.3. Secret and private keys secure storage
- 3.5.4. Cryptographic keys storage

3.6   Formal key management processes and procedures

- 3.6.1. Strong cryptographic key generation
- 3.6.2. Secure cryptographic key distribution
- 3.6.3. Cryptographic key secure storage
- 3.6.4. Cryptographic key change management
- 3.6.5. Cryptographic key retirement/replacement
- 3.6.6. Manual clear text cryptographic practices
- 3.6.7. Prevention of unauthorized substitution of cryptographic keys
- 3.6.8. Cryptographic key custodians' acknowledgment of their responsibilities

3.7   Policies and Procedures for securing CHD

Based upon the structure of an onion, the outer skin layer is paper thin, while the inner layers get progressively thicker, and the closer you get to the center of the onion, you will be feeling increasing layers of discomfort *(eyes watering)*.

The same principles apply within PCI DSS, to provide five Ds of defensive methodology:

- **De**ter
- **De**tect

- **D**elay

- **D**eny

- **D**efend

The concept of layered defenses (a.k.a. Defense in Depth) were believed to have been applied to protect the City of Troy,[16] between 1174 BC and 1184 BC, to successfully repel a 10-year period of Greek army invasion attempts and finally succumbing to the attacker's Trojan horse delivery. The Roman Empire were,[17] in fourth century AD, to provide flexibility with efficient defenses for their rapidly expanding frontiers.

In 2001, the SANS Institute created a comprehensive paper[18] on the very same topic, which still remains a fundamental defensive concept to this day and which remains a resource provision in their Reading Room.

Historic References

The original version of the PCI DSS controls framework was first released in December 2004.[19] However, the source of some of the content are clearly evident before 2004.

Build and Maintain a Secure Network

Your network infrastructure should be configured so as to prevent the misuse of unused Ports, Services, Protocols, and unchanged vendor default settings and to filter the network traffic between the untrusted and untrusted zones.

Each layered network interface (e.g., Internet connection, De-militarized zone (DMZ), and the internal network zones) requires a securely configured Firewall/Router to act as a "Gatekeeper" to help control the data flows.

You need only look at the structure of any medieval castle or a Cold War (1947–1991) military weapons storage facility to see this concept successfully applied for the protection of valued, sensitive, or critical assets.

During my time as an RAF Police Dog handler (1989–1994), I patrolled numerous RAF bases that had exactly the same principles applied to produce a layered security architecture.

---

[16]www.nationalgeographic.org/thisday/apr24/fall-troy/
[17]www.romanarmy.net/Latearmy.shtml
[18]www.sans.org/reading-room/whitepapers/basics/defense-in-depth-525
[19]www.davidfroud.com/wp-content/uploads/2016/07/PCI-DSS-v1.0.pdf

For example, at one high-risk establishment, there were a number of access/egress points around the perimeter of the base. However, these were strictly controlled and locked down, with the only entrance/egress being allowed through a permanently manned, main controlled access point.

Only authorized personnel were granted access to the facility, but this access did not provide them with automatic authorized access to the Cold War Special Weapons storage facility. This was a separate secure silo facility located within the confines of the main RAF base and which had its own security defenses and access control measures.

RAF Base: Perimeter

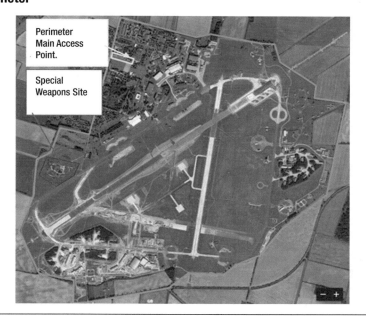

Perimeter Access Control

Cold War Special Weapons Site

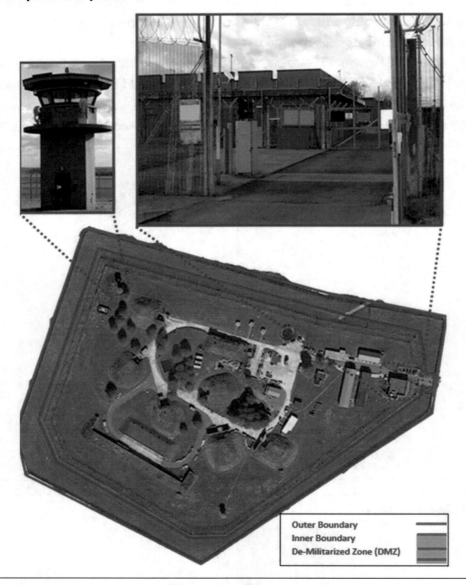

Outer Boundary	
Inner Boundary	
De-Militarized Zone (DMZ)	

Additionally, a great deal of the content from requirement 1 regarding Firewall configurations can be seen in the very first NIST SP800-41 (*Guidelines on Firewalls and Firewall Policy*),[20] which was published in January 2002 and superseded with version 1.0 in September 2009.

---

[20]https://nvlpubs.nist.gov/nistpubs/Legacy/SP/nistspecialpublication800-41.pdf

Table of Contents

Executive Summary ix

1. Introduction 1

    1.1. Document Purpose and Scope 1

    1.2. Audience and Assumptions 1

    1.3. Document Organization 2

2. Overview of Firewall Platforms 3

    2.1. General Introduction to Firewall Technology 3

    2.2. Packet Filter Firewalls 5

    2.3. Stateful Inspection Firewalls 10

    2.4. Application-Proxy Gateway Firewalls 12

    2.5. Dedicated Proxy Servers 14

    2.6. Hybrid Firewall Technologies 16

    2.7. Network Address Translation 16

    2.8. Host-Based Firewalls 18

    2.9. Personal Firewalls/Personal Firewall Appliances 19

3. Firewall Environments 21

    3.1. Guidelines for Building Firewall Environments 21

    3.2. DMZ Networks 22

    3.3. Virtual Private Networks 23

    3.4. Intranets 25

    3.5. Extranets 26

    3.6. Infrastructure Components: Hubs and Switches 26

    3.7. Intrusion Detection Systems 27

    3.8. Domain Name Service (DNS) 29

    3.9. Placement of Servers in Firewall Environments 30

4. Firewall Security Policy 33

    4.1. Firewall Policy 33

    4.2. Implementing a Firewall Ruleset 34

    4.3. Testing Firewall Policy 37

    4.4. Firewall Implementation Approach 37

    4.5. Firewall Maintenance & Management 38

    4.6. Physical Security Of The Firewall Environment 39

v

Figure 2-10. *NIST SP800-41*

5.5

Manage

This last phase of the firewall planning and implementation model is the longest lasting, because managing the solution involves maintaining firewall architecture, policies, software, and other components of the solution chosen to be deployed. One example of a typical maintenance action is testing and applying patches to firewall devices. Policy rules may need to be updated as new threats are identified and requirements change, such as when new applications or hosts are implemented within the network, and should also be reviewed periodically to ensure they remain in compliance with security policy. It is also important to monitor the performance of firewall components to ensure that potential resource issues are identified and addressed before components become overwhelmed. Logs and alerts should also be monitored continuously to identify threats—successful and unsuccessful—that are made to the system. Another important task is to perform periodic testing to verify that firewall rules are functioning as expected. Also, firewall policies and rulesets should be backed up regularly. Some firewalls can store this information in multiple formats, such as a binary format that is used to configure the firewall and a human-readable format that can be read by auditors. If multiple formats are available, backups should be kept in all of them. Changes to firewall rulesets or policies impact security and should be managed as part of a formal configuration management process. Many firewalls have auditing of changes as part of their administrative interfaces, but this does not necessarily track policy changes. At a minimum, a log should be kept of all policy decisions and ruleset changes—and this log should somehow be associated with the firewall. For example, the log can be attached to the device physically, or the log file can be kept in the same part of the organization's inventory management system as the firewall. Also, some firewalls permit comments to be maintained for each rule; wherever practical, rulesets should be documented with comments on each rule. Most firewalls allow restrictions on who can make changes to the ruleset; some even allow restrictions on the addresses from which administrators can make such changes. Such restrictions should be used when possible.

Be aware that firewall rulesets can become increasingly complicated with age. For example, a new firewall ruleset might contain entries to accommodate only outbound user traffic and inbound email traffic (along with allowing the return inbound connections required by TCP/IP)—but will likely contain far more rules by the time the firewall system reaches the end of its first year in production. While new user or business requirements typically drive these changes, they can also reflect other influences within an organization. It is important to review the firewall policy often. Such a review can uncover rules that are no longer needed as well as new policy requirements that need to be added to the firewall. It is best to review the firewall policy at regular intervals so that such reviews do not only happen during policy or security audits (or, worse, only during emergencies). Each review should include a detailed examination of all changes since the last regular review, particularly who made the changes and under what circumstances. It is also useful to occasionally perform overall ruleset audits by people who are not part of the normal policy review team to get an outside view of how the policy matches the organization's goals. Some firewalls have tools that can do automated reviews of policies, looking for such things as redundant rules or missing rules that are widely recommended. If such tools are available for an organization's firewall, they should be used periodically, probably as part of the regular policy review. Organizations may want to consider conducting penetration testing to assess the overall security of their network environment. This testing can be used to verify that a firewall ruleset is performing as intended by generating network traffic and monitoring how it is handled by the firewall in comparison with its expected response. Penetration testing should be employed in addition to, rather than instead of, a conventional audit program.

Figure 2-11. *NIST SP800-41, r1*

The elements of requirement 2 can be seen within the Carnegie Mellon Software Engineering Institute's "Securing Network Servers" report, published in April 2000.[21]

---

[21]ftp://ftp.sei.cmu.edu/pub/documents/00.reports/pdf/sim010.pdf.

4   *Offer only essential network services and operating system services on the server host machine.*

Ideally, each network service should be on a dedicated, single-purpose host. Many computers are configured by default to provide a wider set of services and applications than required to provide a particular network service, so you may need to configure the server to eliminate or disable them.

Why this is important	Offering only the essential network services on a particular host can enhance your network security in several ways:

- Other services cannot be used to attack the host and impair or remove desired network services. Each additional service added to a host increases the risk of compromise for all services on that host or for any computer trusting that host.
- Different services may be administered by different individuals. By isolating services so each host and service has a single administrator, you will minimize the possibility of conflicts between the administrators (also known as separation of duties).
- The host can be configured to better suit the requirements of the particular service. Different services might require different hardware and software configurations, which could lead to needless vulnerabilities or service restrictions.
- By reducing services, the number of logs and log entries is reduced, so detecting unexpected behavior becomes easier.

How to do it	We strongly recommend that you use the configuration principle "deny first, then allow." That is, turn off as many services and applications as possible and then selectively turn on only those that are absolutely essential. We recommend you install the most minimal operating system configuration image that meets your business requirements.

➤ *Determine the functions that you intend to support with your network server.*

The services you enable on a selected host depend on the functions you want the host to provide. Functions could support the selected network service, other services hosted on this computer, or development and maintenance of the operating system and applications. Providing multiple services or combining the role of workstation and server on the same machine results in a less secure configuration and makes security maintenance more difficult.

Determine the configuration of the host for

- file systems (e.g., whether any file services will be used by this host. NFS should be avoided as it has many known vulnerabilities.)
- system maintenance (e.g., with multiuser systems, whether all maintenance will be done only via the console or remotely)

Figure 2-12. *"Securing Network Servers" Extract*

Protect Cardholder Data

As detailed in the SANS's History of Encryption Paper,[22] from January 2002, encryption is one of the oldest forms of science that has been carried out by the human race, and from Egyptian times to modern times, it concerns the desire to disguise, masquerade, or protect certain sensitive information from inquisitive eyes.

---

[22]www.giac.org/paper/gsec/1555/history-encryption/102877

Consequently, being that the objective of PCI DSS is to safeguard customer cardholder data, if you are storing or transmitting over public networks, it makes sense to ensure that it remains under lock and key.

Figure 2-13. *Encrypted Storage and Transmission*

Maintain a Vulnerability Management Program

Malware software has been an ever-present risk since 1971 with the Creeper and Reaper viruses,[23] whereas the birth of the term Trojan horse spans back the successful use of a hidden payload in the first Trojan Horse during the siege of the City of Troy. NIST produced some comprehensive guidance, in November 2005, with the publication of their NIST Special Publication 800-83 (*Guide to Malware Incident Prevention and Handling*)[24] and which was superseded with r1 in July 2013.[25]

Since the late 1940s, the Royal Air Force Police have employed arms and explosives search (AES) dogs,[26] as well as manual entry searches to help identify suspicious payloads. In 1970 *(in response to an increase in the incidence of hijackings during the late 1960s and early 1970s)*, the United States' civilization aviation industry started using X-ray and metal detector machines[27] to augment their use of search dogs and manual searches.

---

[23]https://pandorafms.com/blog/creeper-and-reaper/

[24]https://nvlpubs.nist.gov/nistpubs/Legacy/SP/nistspecialpublication800-83.pdf

[25]https://nvlpubs.nist.gov/nistpubs/SpecialPublications/NIST.SP.800-83r1.pdf

[26]www.k9history.com/uk-royal-air-force-police-dog-history.htm

[27]www.nap.edu/read/5116/chapter/3

The need to apply regular updates can be seen in the NIST Special Publication 800-40 (*Procedures for Handling Security Patches*),[28] which was first published in August 2002 and which has been subsequently superseded with the latest revision (R3, *Guide to Enterprise Patch Management Technologies*[29]).

5.1

Patching Priorities

With the exception of small networks, it is a complex and difficult endeavor for network administrators to install all patches in a timely manner. This is attributed not only to time and resource constraints but also to the much greater complexity and heterogeneity of larger networks. Thus, setting priorities for which systems to patch in what order is essential for an effective patch process. The first step in this prioritization process requires an organization's systems to be inventoried (if such an inventory does not already exist). This inventory would include the following:

- **Hardware**—Type, manufacturer, and unique identifier (e.g. serial number or government property number)
- **Operating System**—Type, manufacturer, version number, and current patch level
- **Major Applications**—Type, manufacturer, version number, and current patch level.

Once a reasonably complete inventory is available, a risk assessment needs to be performed to determine the prioritization of the systems to be patched. Consult NIST Special Publication 800-30, Risk Management Guide for Information Technology Systems, for guidance on performing risk assessments. The general idea in performing a patch-focused risk assessment is to evaluate each of your systems for the following:

- **Threat**—An activity with the potential of causing harm to a computer system or network. Examples of systems that frequently face high threat levels are web servers, email servers, and other hosts traditionally accessible to external users and servers that contain high-value information such as financial databases, proprietary information, or other items of interest to internal and external entities. Threats can be determined through the analysis of the specific threat level historically faced by the organization and by general threat updates from external organizations (e.g., CERT/CC, NIPC).
- **Vulnerability**—A flaw, misconfiguration, or weakness that allows the security of the system to be violated. In some instances it may allow harm to occur to a computer system or network. Systems that often have significant vulnerabilities include web servers, systems installed by inexperienced personnel, and systems that allow unauthenticated access to resources. A quick search of vulnerability resources (e.g., ICAT) should assist in the identification of vulnerable hosts.
- **Criticality**—A measure of how important or valuable a system is to the organization's mission. Systems frequently considered mission-critical include mail servers, database servers, and network infrastructure nodes. Interviews with appropriate staff should help determine mission-critical systems.

Systems that face significant threats, are vulnerable, and are mission-critical should be patched before hosts that face few threats, are secure, and are not mission-critical.

Figure 2-14. *NIST SP800-40 Extract*

The Open Web Application Security Project (a.k.a. OWASP) was established in 2001[30] in response to an increasing number of data breaches being attributed to vulnerabilities created through insecure software development practices (e.g., SQL injection attacks

---

[28]https://nvlpubs.nist.gov/nistpubs/Legacy/SP/nistspecialpublication800-40.pdf
[29]https://csrc.nist.gov/publications/detail/sp/800-40/rev-3/final
[30]www.owasp.org/index.php/History_of_OWASP

in 1998[31]). As a result, OWASP began to develop top 10 lists of the most critical web application security risks[32] and supporting guidance/mitigation advice.

OWASP Top 10 Entries (Unordered)	Releases				
	2003	2004	2007	2010	2013
Unvalidated Input	A1	A1	X	X	X
Buffer Overflows	A5	A5	X	X	X
Denial of Service	X	A9	X	X	X
Injection	A6	A6	A2	A1	A1
Cross Site Scripting (XSS)	A4	A4	A1	A2	A3
Broken Authentication and Session Management	A3	A3	A7	A3	A2
Insecure Direct Object Reference	X	A2	A4	A4	A4
Cross Site Request Forgery (CSRF)	X	X	A5	A5	A8
Security Misconfiguration	A10	A10	X	A6	A5
Missing Functional Level Access Control	A2	A2	A10	A8	A7
Unvalidated Redirects and Forwards	X	X	X	A10	A10
Information Leakage and Improper Error Handling	A7	A7	A6	A6	X
Malicious File Execution	X	X	A3	A6	X
Sensitive Data Exposure	A8	A8	A8	A7	A6
Insecure Communications	X	A10	A9	A9	X
Remote Administration Flaws	A9	X	X	X	X
Using Known Vulnerable Components	X	X	X	X	A9

Figure 2-15. *Comparison of 2003, 2004, 2007, 2010, and 2013 Releases*

Mitigating the risks associated with poor software development practices continues to be the cause of a high volume of web site compromises and data breaches. Consequently, both the Payment Card Industry Security Standards Council (PCI SSC)[33] and NIST[34] have produced supporting guidance/standards.

---

[31]www.esecurityplanet.com/network-security/how-was-sql-injection-discovered.html

[32]www.owasp.org/images/7/72/OWASP_Top_10-2017_%28en%29.pdf.pdf

[33]www.pcisecuritystandards.org/documents/PCI-Secure-Software-Standard-v1_0.pdf?agreement=true&time=1576693614480

[34]https://csrc.nist.gov/CSRC/media/Publications/white-paper/2019/06/07/mitigating-risk-of-software-vulnerabilities-with-ssdf/draft/documents/ssdf-for-mitigating-risk-of-software-vulns-draft.pdf

Despite Injection[35] attacks remaining at the very top of the OWASP top 10 risks *(since 2010)*, the Magecart Hacking Group[36] continues to be extremely successful at leveraging this style of attack against e-Commerce businesses.

Implement Strong Access Control Measures

If something is deemed to be of value either to your business or to your customers, it is essential that these assets are secured behind a lock and key *(whether physical or logical)*. The requirements for convenient access control measures have been around for far longer than you might imagine. In fact, the very first keyless (combination and rotation) locks were used in the year **1206 AD**.[37] The higher the value of the asset, the greater the need for a robust access control system.

During my RAF Police Special Weapons protection duties, in the late 1980s, I was taught a very valuable phrase which remains current today:

Sir,

Please don't confuse your rank with my authority!

Despite the fact that an RAF officer may have been a higher rank to myself, my job provided me with the authority of the Provost Marshal of the Royal Air Force Police in order that I was able to restrict access based upon strict Need to Know/Need to Access criteria. Consequently, if their details were not on the approved access list, they would be denied access to the Special Weapons facility. In PCI DSS, the same principle applies, with access to the cardholder data environment (CDE) needing to be strictly limited to approved personnel only and those with the formal approval having their access appropriately managed. This applies to both physical and logical CDEs.

The "Need to Know" principle is not a new term, having been applied during World War II and is referenced in the original NIST SP800-12 (*An Introduction to Computer Security: the NIST Handbook*)[38] – first published in October 1995.

---

[35]www.owasp.org/index.php/Top_10-2017_A1-Injection

[36]https://threatpost.com/magecart-infestations-saturate-web/148911/

[37]https://prezi.com/oqwyu-nb9yym/the-history-of-combination-locks-and-rotations/

[38]https://nvlpubs.nist.gov/nistpubs/Legacy/SP/nistspecialpublication800-12.pdf

"The LAN server operating system's access controls provide extensive features for controlling access to files. These include group-oriented controls that allow teams of users to be assigned to named groups by the System Administrator. Group members are then allowed access to sensitive files not accessible to nonmembers. Each user can be assigned to several groups according to **need to know**."

Having a secure network and systems is significantly undermined by poor access control facilities or poor access practices. Consequently, it is essential that the access control measures are appropriate to the sensitivity of the payment CDEs. For example, in a data center the systems risk has an aggravated value, and Privileged user accounts and user accounts that have authorized access into the CDE are a high priority target for criminals. Consequently, these accounts need to employ robust access controls applied to ensure that the Need to Know/Need to Access principles are applied.

Think of your access control measures as being like you lending your expensive car to your son/daughter and discovering that while you had loaned your car to them, the car had been stolen. The theft had occurred, as the result of your son/daughter been careless with the keys and had left the keys in the ignition of your car while they went into the Petrol/Gas station to pay for fuel, after having refueled the car. Your son/daughter had not regarded this as being a high-risk act and it had been more convenient to them. However, being convenient to them also made it extremely convenient to the opportunist criminal, who happened to be walking by at the time.

The act of bypassing access controls is nothing new, with the term "*husbryce*" (House Breach)[39] being used in Anglo-Saxon England. Consequently, it is a requirement that all authorized users be given individual access credentials, so that should an investigation be needed, you are able to identify the time, location, and person accessing the CDE.

In terms of physical access controls, the physical environment should be robust enough so as to ensure that access can only be gained through the official, recorded, access points. Remember that the integrity of a physical space is interdependent on each other.

---

[39]https://englishlegalhistory.wordpress.com/2013/05/30/history-of-burglary/

Figure 2-16. *Physical Security Perspectives*

When reviewing the effectiveness of your physical security measures, it is important to look at it from multiple dimensions. The attacker may not always look for opportunities via the main access/egress points and may look to exploit weaknesses in the ceiling or underfloor spaces or seek to exploit vulnerabilities in the fitting of the door/window frames, hinges, or locking mechanisms. More importantly, the integrity of your physical security measures is undermined by the "Human Firewall":

- Propping open doors/windows

- Sharing access cards

- Tailgating

- The ability to clone telemetry access cards[40]

If you are a business that has valuables or sensitive data assets that need to be physically protected, it is essential that the physical barriers to unauthorized access remain effective and that, in the event of an incident, you are able to identify who accessed the facility at the specified time. This can be achieved through an electronic automated access control system (EAACS), with personal identification number (PIN) to identify and validate the access to a particular person and/or the use of a manual lock

---

[40]https://totalsecuritysummit.co.uk/industry-spotlight-secure-your-rfid-access-controls-against-card-cloning/

(or EAACS without PIN) and an appropriately sited closed circuit television (CCTV). The CCTV needs to meet the operational requirements[41] needed to be able to identify the individual using the manual or EAACS to gain authorized access to the CDE.

Note of caution

When using CCTV, be careful that you are not capturing images of your customers' cardholder data (CHD) and especially Sensitive Authentication Data (SAD).

For example, in retail environments where CCTV is installed for crime reduction that overlooks the physical card reading device, can the CHD be identified/recovered from the CCTV recording? If so, this may bring you into conflict with PCI DSS and also extend the "In-Scope" environment to include the CCTV monitoring and image storage.

However, it is worth remembering that this is the core of your onion (in-scope) and should be further enhanced by the application of additional outer rings of defense. This will help prevent an opportunist malicious actor from gaining unauthorized access through gaining entry to the facility in which the CDE resides.

Clearly, having created your secure citadels and strictly restricted the numbers of personnel that are granted access, you are going to have occasions where temporary visitor access needs to be allowed. PCI DSS does not prohibit temporary access, as long as their visits are easily identifiable, logged, and escorted at all times.

Technological advancements have not decreased the threat from physical security breaches and have, in fact, increased the threat. Where you have hardened your logical perimeter, preventing unauthorized access, attackers will pounce on any opportunity to circumvent your defenses through gaining physical access to your network and systems.

For instance, for not a great deal of money the attackers may build rogue devices to place on your network or may even purchase commercial products[42] to help them bypass your defensive efforts. Additionally, the increased use of mobile technologies makes them increasingly valuable to opportunist thieves, where they are not looking at the data value but the resale value of the technology.

---

[41]https://assets.publishing.service.gov.uk/government/uploads/system/uploads/attachment_data/file/378443/28_09_CCTV_OR_Manual2835.pdf

[42]https://shop.hak5.org/collections/hak5-field-kits

Finally, in this onion ring, physical security measures need to be applied for the protection of media and pin transaction security (PTS) and point-of-sale (POS) devices.

Versions of the PCI DSS physical security and media protection controls can be seen through many different guidance documents, spanning many generations, to provide barriers and monitoring capabilities for malicious inbound and outbound movements.

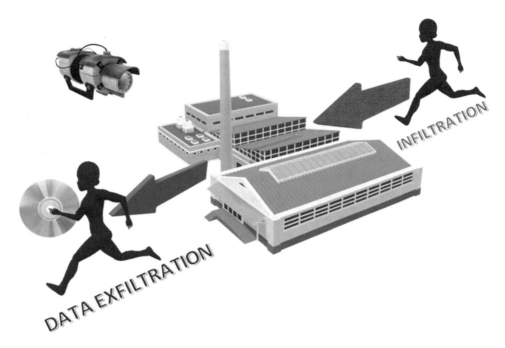

Figure 2-17. *Physical Security*

- **January 2001 – United States: Physical Security (FM 3-19.30)**[43]

  - *"IDENTIFICATION SYSTEM*

    An ID system is established at each installation or facility to provide a method of identifying personnel. The system provides for personal recognition and the use of security ID cards or badges to aid in the control and movement of personnel activities."

---

[43]www.wbdg.org/FFC/ARMYCOE/FIELDMAN/fm31930.pdf

- **October 1995 – NIST SP800-12 (*An Introduction to Computer Security: The NIST Handbook*).**

  - **"14.5 Media Controls**

    Media controls include a variety of measures to provide physical and environmental protection and accountability for tapes, diskettes, printouts, and other media. From a security perspective, media controls should be designed to prevent the loss of confidentiality, integrity, or availability of information, including data or software, when stored outside the system. This can include storage of information before it is input to the system and after it is output.

    The extent of media control depends upon many factors, including the type of data, the quantity of media, and the nature of the user environment. Physical and environmental protection is used to prevent unauthorized individuals from accessing the media. It also protects against such factors as heat, cold, or harmful magnetic fields. When necessary, logging the use of individual media (e.g., a tape cartridge) provides detailed accountability - to hold authorized people responsible for their actions."

Regularly Monitor and Test Networks

Having established secure systems and network operations, it is essential that this be monitored for ABNORMAL and potentially malicious activities (both inbound and outbound) across your various layers of your physical and logical onion rings. The objective being to rapidly identify potential malicious or dangerous activities occurring within your environment.

In December 2003, the SANS Institute produced a paper, entitled "The Importance of Logging and Traffic Monitoring for Information Security."[44] The content of this can be seen within this section of the PCI DSS controls framework, for example:

---

[44]www.sans.org/reading-room/whitepapers/logging/importance-logging-traffic-monitoring-information-security-1379

It is important for every security or network administrator to review the content of log files for suspicious entries indicating that a potential attack has occurred, or in the process of occurring in daily basis. Doing that will help him to enhance and maintain the security process.

With regard to the security testing controls, the NIST SP800-42 (*Guideline on Network Security Testing*),[45] as published in October 2003, shows a strong alignment to the content of this section, for example:

Penetration testing is important for determining how vulnerable an organization's network is and the level of damage that can occur if the network is compromised. Because of the high cost and potential impact, annual penetration testing may be sufficient. The results of penetration testing should be taken very seriously and discovered vulnerabilities should be mitigated. As soon as they are available, the results should be presented to the organization's managers.

---

[45]https://nvlpubs.nist.gov/nistpubs/Legacy/SP/nistspecialpublication800-42.pdf

Test Type	Frequency	Benefit
Network Scanning	Continuously to Quarterly	• Enumerates the network structure and determines the set of active hosts, and associated software • Identifies unauthorized hosts connected to a network • Identifies open ports • Identifies unauthorized services
Vulnerability Scanning	Quarterly or bimonthly (more often for certain high-risk systems), when the vulnerability database is updated	• Enumerates the network structure and determines the set of active hosts, and associated software • Identifies a target set of computers to focus vulnerability analysis • Identifies potential vulnerabilities on the target set • Validates that operating systems and major applications are up to date with security patches and software versions
Penetration Testing	Annually	• Determines how vulnerable an organization's network is to penetration and the level of damage that can be incurred • Tests IT staff's response to perceived security incidents and their knowledge of and implementation of the organization's security policy and system's security requirements
Password Cracking	Continuously to same frequency as expiration policy	• Verifies that the policy is effective in producing passwords that are more or less difficult to break • Verifies that users select passwords that are compliant with the organization's security policy
Log Reviews	Daily for critical systems, e.g., firewalls	• Validates that the system is operating according to policies
Integrity Checkers	Monthly and in case of suspected incident	• Detects unauthorized file modifications
Virus Detectors	Weekly or as required	• Detects and deletes viruses before successful installation on the system

Figure 2-18. NIST SP800-42 Extract

Maintain an Information Security Policy

Integral to the success or failure of any security controls framework is the establishment of formally defined rules and consistent policies. This was clearly an essential component for any organization wishing to successfully implement BS 7799[46] *(the precursor to the ISO/IEC 27001:2005 Information Security Management System[47])*, for example:

"Step 3:

Define the Security Policy

Security policy is the demonstration of management's intent and commitment for the information security in the organization. This should be based on facts about the criticality of information for business as identified during step 1. Security policy statement should strongly reflect the management's belief that if information is not secure, the business will suffer. The policy should clearly address issues like:

- *Why information is strategically important for the organization?*

- *What are business and legal requirements for information security for the organization?*

- *What are the organizations' contractual obligation towards security of the information pertaining to business processes, information collected from clients, employees, etc.?*

- *What steps the organization will take to ensure information security?*

A clear security policy will provide direction to the information security efforts of the organization as well as create confidence in the minds of various stakeholders.

The Chief Executive of the organization should issue the security policy statement to build the momentum towards information security and set clear security goals and objectives."

---

[46]https://cyber-defense.sans.org/resources/papers/gsec/implementation-methodology-information-security-management-system-to-comply-bs-7799-requi-104600

[47]www.iso.org/standard/42103.html

Reality Bites

In 1250 BC, the Greeks laid siege on the City of Troy.[48] For over a decade, the city's defenses had managed to thwart all the previous attacks. The Trojan defenses were undermined when they took receipt of an unexpected gift (a large wooden horse), which had contained an undetected clandestine payload (Greek Warriors).

The Trojans failed to effectively search and detect the presence of this malicious payload and, as a result, freely wheeled the wooden horse through the various layers of defense, nearer the core of the city.

The same tactics, techniques, and protocols (TTPs) can still be seen used in modern-day cyber-attacks, with Trojan Horse-style malware attacks still being recorded as the most common type of attack[49] *(along with phishing/spear-phishing, rootkit, and SQL injection)* in 2019.

Recommendations

Understanding the strong heritage of the PCI DSS is extremely useful in helping you understand how the integrated framework could assist you in appreciating the value of applying these controls to enhance your defensive efforts. Consequently, I would highly recommend that you become familiarized with the intent of the specific controls and apply them against historic events. This will ensure that you gain an improved appreciation of the benefits of these controls to your business.

Conclusion

I frequently hear references to the birth of the PCI DSS controls framework being with the release of PCI DSS v1.0.[50] However, as you will have read, the heritage of the PCI DSS goes back a great deal further than its launch date – December 2004.

The PCI DSS controls framework has a strong heritage to help you implement a robust baseline of defensive onion rings based upon your business processes.

---

[48]www.britannica.com/event/Siege-of-Troy-1250-BCE

[49]www.varonis.com/blog/cybersecurity-statistics/

[50]www.tasgroup.eu/solutions/cashless-world/certifications/tas-pci-dss-white-paper-2017

Consequently, understanding the origins of the PCI DSS controls framework, prior to this launch date, helps you understand the strength of its heritages to aid you in bolstering your defenses against the ever-growing criminal threat.

It is important that the payment card industry stretches back further than the digitally based or even the manual "knuckle scraper"-based payment card processes, and while the payment cards are regarded as valuable and attractive items to opportunist criminals, the threat will still need to be mitigated against.

Figure 2-19. *Manual Imprint Machine*

Looking through the historic development of security countermeasures can greatly help you appreciate the intent of the controls, so that you are then able to design, develop, implement, and manage the PCI DSS controls for your specific business environments.

This better understanding of the intent of the specific controls should also help you during the procurement of new security defenses to ensure that you are not sucked into the "Sales Pitch" for that security solution that is everything that you need. As you can see, the PCI DSS controls framework is an integrated catalogue of controls that need to be managed with suitable and usable tools that complement each other to provide an integrated view of your defenses.

Key Takeaways

PCI DSS compliance does not require special weapons grade countermeasures but provides a minimum baseline to help organizations defend their business against their attackers.

Today's criminals increasingly regard the electronic payment card business operations as an extremely viable target for identity theft and credit card fraud.

Consumers prefer to pay for goods and services through the convenience of instant payments, using payment card-enabled technologies. However, this ever-growing trend toward payment cards increases the potential opportunities for criminals to exploit poor practices.

PCI DSS continues to evolve based upon mature and well-established industry best practices. Consequently, to repay the consumer trust and to reduce the attractiveness to criminals, it is essential that businesses understand the heritage of the PCI DSS controls to better enable them to develop robust defenses.

Ever since the "Dawn of time" criminals have profited from stealing the valuable and attractive items belonging to others. Payment card data constitutes both personal information and payment data which make these data types a high-priority target for today's criminals.

Do you understand the threats to your business's payment card operations?

Are your defensive efforts providing you with a reasonable degree of reassurances?

Risks

Reported cases of identity theft and payment card fraud continue to grow, year on year. However, the reported rates of PCI DSS compliance are seen to be on the decrease, with just **37%** of businesses maintaining their PCI DSS compliance obligations *(Source: Verizon 2019 Payment Security Report).*

Without the baselining against the applicable PCI DSS controls, businesses will have an increased risk of running their business with unremedied vulnerabilities that are exploitable by malicious individuals or groups, seeking to profit from the exfiltration of the consumers' sensitive payment data.

Consequently, the number of data breaches continues to reach record levels.

Remember, your enemies only need to find a single exploitable infiltration opportunity to make a profit.

You need to identify and manage the exploitable infiltration opportunities to avoid reputational damage and a loss of profits.

Ask yourself:

Do I understand the advantages of applying the strong heritage PCI DSS controls to my organization?

Do I understand the implications for not applying lessons learned from history?

CHAPTER 3

Data Life Support System

Introduction

Much like the circulatory system within the human body, data has become the lifeblood of modern business feeding the vital organs of organizations (see Figure 3-1). These vital organs need to be continually fed with good quality data and be physically protected from harm:

- Skull

- Rib cage

- Pelvis

Similar to the circulatory system, the importance of this infrastructure is often not appreciated and remains unseen. That is until it goes wrong and the blood becomes infected or the system gets compromised and starts to lose its integrity and the vital organs do not get access at the time of need (availability). Unfortunately, in most cases businesses have not evolved their data life support systems to ensure that they provide effective support to their data circulatory system.

© Jim Seaman 2020
J. Seaman, *PCI DSS*, https://doi.org/10.1007/978-1-4842-5808-8_3

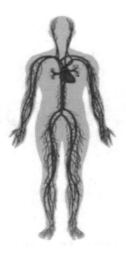

Figure 3-1. *Circulatory System*

Concept

Your major organs[1] can be harmed through direct actions or through indirect actions against the circulatory system. The same applies for today's corporate networks, where the perpetrator does not always need to directly attack the business's major organs (databases, file stores, business applications, etc.) but is able to target the supporting circulatory system to have an equivalent impact.

There are many similarities between the human body and a corporate network and many lessons that can be applied from human biology. Take, for example, the body's early warning system (nervous system), which sends rapid signals to its central monitoring system (brain) in the case of an event or incident. In the event of a major trauma (e.g., severed limb), the aggregated alerts from the nervous system allow the brain to instantly respond by segmenting the circulatory system to isolate the vital organs, cutting the flow of blood to the most critical organs within the body.

---

[1]www.education.vic.gov.au/school/teachers/teachingresources/discipline/science/ continuum/Pages/internalbody.aspx

For example, much like the military employs the "Golden Hour[2]" to improve the chances of saving the life of someone that has suffered major trauma, an effective security incident response capability refers to the use of the term "Golden Hour.[3]"

The faster that you can identify and respond to the presence of the abnormal, the better the chances you have of protecting your vital and critical organs before irreparable damage is done and recover becomes impossible.

Lessons Learned

The human body has one of the most sophisticated communications, storage, and transmission systems on the planet. Yet, in business, we still fail to recognize the benefits and apply similar concepts to our environments.

Layered Defenses

The very construction of the human body consists of various layers, with embedded alerting, which get denser the further into the body you go. Just take a look at the outer perimeter[4] (see Figure 3-2).

---

[2]www.reuters.com/article/us-health-trauma-transport/u-s-military-golden-hour-rule-saved-lives-idUSKCN0RU31F20150930

[3]www.cm-alliance.com/cybersecurity-blog/capital-one-data-breach-and-incident-response

[4]http://courses.lumenlearning.com/boundless-ap/chapter/the-skin/

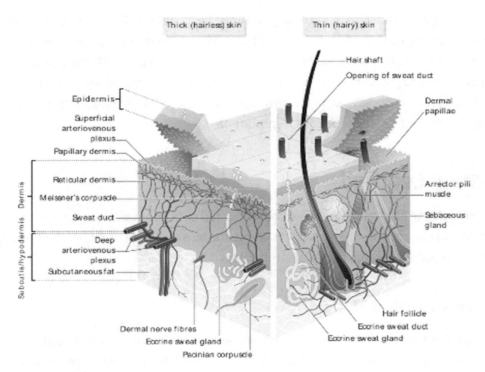

Figure 3-2. *Skin Layers*

Much as the human body's complex nervous system is able to alert the brain (sensing pain) as to the extent of trauma suffered (enabling the body to apply defensive measures), a corporate data privacy and security strategy should enable your organization to detect and respond to abnormal activity, and the alerting should become aggregated as the danger gets closer to the business's vital/critical organs (e.g., Critical systems, Processes and Sensitive data stores, etc.). This involves having adequate alerting and security defenses throughout your corporate network, for example:

- Perimeter intruder detection system (PIDS)
- Securely configured external firewall (restricted traffic from external sources)
- Internal detection system (IDS) at the boundary of the trusted zone
- Systems and device logs
- Change detection on data systems

24/7 Monitoring

The human body has an integral monitoring system (e.g., Nervous system) which sends alerts to the brain. This is then able to aggregate and analyze these alerts from many different resources across the entire body. Instantly, the brain is able to normalize, aggregate, and apply analytics to the alerts to discover trends, detect threats, and enable further investigation (seeing your doctor).

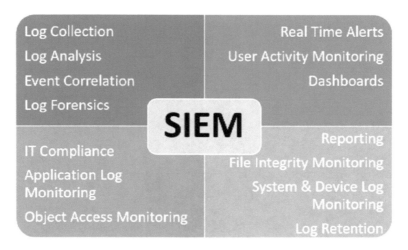

Figure 3-3. *SIEM*

Within your data privacy and security strategy, you should be seeking to imitate the activities of the human body's interaction between the nervous system and the brain. This is established through the use of a centralized monitoring, using a security information and event management security (SIEM) security tool (see Figure 3-3).

A SIEM solution provides real-time analysis of security alerts generated by applications and network hardware, sent to a centralized location, to show potential malicious activity (moving toward or away from the critical/vital organs).

Are your security system tools integrated, so as to provide you with an accurate picture of the activity occurring within your corporate architecture?

Physical Security

In addition to the multiple layers of defense, where the value of the organ is aggregated or deemed to be most critical, the human body's skeletal system provides additional protection to further enhance the protection of the vital organs and to support the overall integrity of the body.

Much like the skeletal system[5] of the human body, it is essential that a critical data path is supported by a physical and robust infrastructure (see Figure 3-4).

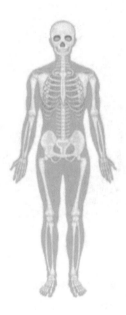

Figure 3-4. *Skeletal System*

For example, much like the human body provides additional protective measures around its most critical/vital assets (e.g., brain and skull), your data privacy and security strategy should ensure that any aggregated data stores or critical systems have additional protective measures to ensure their integrity.

---

[5]https://images.app.goo.gl/NvAECFsVuxgoVXbW8

Incident Response[6]

In the event of an incident, the human body has an extremely effective incident response capability.

For example, in the event of a cut, the body will immediately try to stem the loss of blood through clotting and in the event of a broken bone or dislocated joint will attempt to immobilize the affected area through elevating the sensation of pain. First Aid training simulates scenarios that could affect the human body and provides tried and tested responses that will provide assistance to the process (see Figure 3-5).

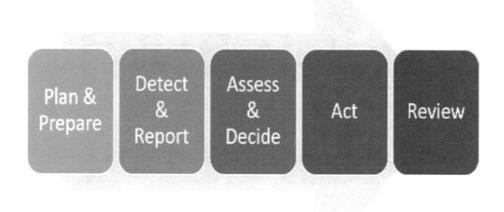

Figure 3-5. *Incident Response Process*

In your data privacy and security strategy, can you identify the activities of a malicious individual seeking to move laterally through your corporate network (after breaching your perimeter), before they get unauthorized access to your critical systems or sensitive data stores, or having compromised your sensitive data stores/critical systems, can you detect them navigating an egress route?

---

[6]www.cisecurity.org/controls/incident-response-and-management/

Remember, the attackers will not be supporting routine business functions and will, therefore, be carrying out activities that are not normal to your business. Therefore, it is essential that your monitoring teams are able to distinguish the NORMAL from the ABNORMAL.

Blood Life-Cycle Management[7]

The human body recognizes that blood has a specific lifespan and that it is extremely important to filter and cycle its blood flow, so that only good blood is pumped to the organs (see Figure 3-6).

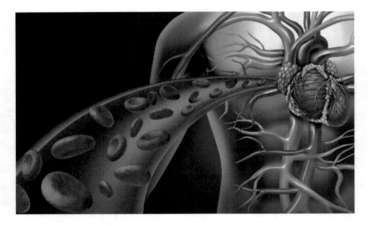

Figure 3-6. *Blood Flows*

Poor quality blood will impact the productivity of its organs and can lead to further complications, while excessive storage of old blood can lead to swelling and poor circulation.

Within the arterial and venous system, there are a number of filters/gateways that control the flow of blood and ensure that only authorized (good) blood is allowed to enter.

---

[7]http://newatlas.com/nanogenerator-blood-flow-electricity/51280/

Recommendations

Much like the structures of the human body, as shown in Figure 3-7, I would recommend that you start to look at your corporate infrastructure and connected business systems in the same way as a doctor may look at diagnosing the human body. Integral to any diagnosis is checking the quality of the blood flow (blood pressure), checking the blood quality (blood tests), and checking for early sign and symptoms.

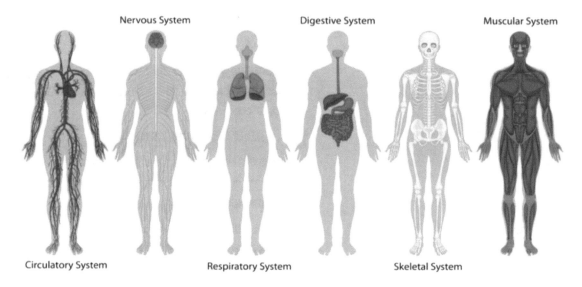

Figure 3-7. *Human Body Systems*

For example, see Table 3-1.

Table 3-1. *Human vs. Data Security*

Human Body	Data Privacy and Security Strategy
Understand and appreciate which are your vital and major organs and which are the connected organs that could have an impact.	Understand your circulatory system and how the data flows through your business.
• **Do you understand which are your major arteries?** • **Do you know which arteries service which major organs?**	• **Network Diagrams?** • **Data Flow Diagrams?**
Keep your blood flow healthy.	Ensure that you are cycling your data so that only good quality and the correct quantity of data are in your business.
• **Blood tests**	• **(Data Life-Cycle Management)**
Monitor your health.	Monitor your business for any changes (signs and symptoms) and ensure that your business remains healthy.
• **Medicals, Visits to the Doctor, etc.**	• **Periodic assurance review.** • **Independent physical and logical penetration tests** • **Independent web application testing**
Ensure that you can detect the early signs and symptoms and that you have an established and well-trained First Aid Team and that your employees understand what is (and what is not) acceptable, like teaching a child the dangers of boiling water, before they get scolded.	Ensure that you have an effective security incident monitoring and incident response team that are able to effectively detect and respond to signs of abnormal activity from known normal activities. This should be a cohesive approach, and to ensure the effectiveness, review the capabilities against plausible scenarios.

Conclusion

Likened to keeping the human body healthy, businesses need to protect the data circulatory system, and remember that the threats can be external (e.g., a punctured lung) or internal (e.g., food poisoning, disease, etc.). Therefore, understanding the intricate anatomy of your business architecture and how the data flows through this architecture and what vulnerabilities might be associated with specific architectures is essential to the maintenance of a healthy business.

Keeping your business healthy should be a commonsense investment of time, effort, resources, and costs rather than something that you are obliged to do because of compliance to a regulatory or legal requirement.

Yes, ensuring that your business data is secure may sound too expensive, time-consuming, and complex, but it is far less complex than the human body, and early intervention and response can be far less than missing the early signs and having your vital/major business organs suffer a traumatic failure.

Key Takeaways

Data has never been more important to business operations. In order to enable consumers to pay for goods and services, they entrust their payment card data to you. Therefore, in respect of this trust, it is essential that you safeguard the data and protect it from leakage, infection, or contamination and that the major organs of your business are sufficiently protected from harm.

Keeping your "Data Life Support System" healthy, ensuring that the data remains healthy through regular monitoring.

Do you understand your circulatory system?

When was the last time you checked the quality of your data?

Is your data healthy or are you storing old pools of data?

What about your major organs? Are they well protected?

Can you identify early signs of ill-health – the ABNORMAL from the Normal?

Risks

Much like the circulatory system within the human body, business needs to maintain good and healthy data (blood) flows to help maintain the critical processes (major organs).

Ask yourself:

- *Do I understand the threats to my circulatory system?*
- *How healthy is my business?*
- *When did I last have a checkup and was this done by someone who understands my business?*
- *Does everyone involved with my circulatory system understand the need to maintain its healthy functions?*
- *What measures do I employ to maintain my health?*
- *Do I have sufficiently trained "First Aiders"?*

"Diabetes can be successfully prevented and managed by a healthy lifestyle. When not managed, it can lead to severe organ damage and death"

Source: Tedros Adhanom
Director-General of the World Health Organization

Figure 3-8. Health Quote

CHAPTER 4

An Integrated Cyber/ InfoSec Strategy

The past few years have cemented my view that businesses are struggling to balance their juggle between keeping their payment card operations secure, aligning with new data privacy regulations, and ensuring that their business systems remain resilient.

Since the introduction of the European Union's new General Data Protection Regulation (GDPR), I have seen large FTSE 100 listed companies[1] make the mistake of treating the protection of personal data as a separate concern to their cyber/information security management operations and have cited the GDPR as their reason for making their Group Information Security Manager redundant.

Crazy idea, I know!

Especially when you consider that both Marriott[2] and British Airways[3] were issued statements of intent for considerable regulator fines based upon poor Cyber Security practices.

Consequently, it is important that you can understand and appreciate the differing components of an effective data privacy and security strategy for both fortifying your compliance operations and your sensitive data operations. This chapter will aim to provide you with the differing elements and to show how they should complement each other rather than act in isolation or in conflict with one another.

---

[1] https://merchantmachine.co.uk/profit-per-employee/

[2] https://ico.org.uk/about-the-ico/news-and-events/news-and-blogs/2019/07/statement-intention-to-fine-marriott-international-inc-more-than-99-million-under-gdpr-for-data-breach/

[3] https://ico.org.uk/about-the-ico/news-and-events/news-and-blogs/2019/07/ico-announces-intention-to-fine-british-airways/

© Jim Seaman 2020
J. Seaman, *PCI DSS*, https://doi.org/10.1007/978-1-4842-5808-8_4

Introduction

When looking at an integrated Cyber/InfoSec strategy, it is important to understand the four domains that are needed to achieve an effective program. Each domain is important to each other, but it is extremely important to remember that they are complementary to each other, with a considerable amount of overlap.

In essence, an effective strategy will divide your enterprise so that you are able to clearly understand the extent to which your "In-Scope" environment is protected by each domain.

The concept described in this chapter incorporates the core elements of ISACA's Business Model for Information Security (BMIS),[4] which has become an integral part of COBIT 2019.[5]

The problem with developing a suitable strategy is that organizations often regard it as being unachievable or expensive. However, in truth, we have an obligation to ensure that our customers' payment, financial, and personal data is adequately protected from misuse or loss. Your data processing operations are consistently at risk from opportunist attackers. This can be in the form of hackers, thieves, organized crime, or even that "trusted" employee.

Consequently, your strategy needs to be broad enough to mitigate the risks to an appropriate level while not be so aggressive as to appear to be "Boiling the Ocean."

It's all about balancing the risk!

By gaining an improved understanding of the four domains and their inter-relationships, you will be better able to understand the associated risks and to prioritize your efforts and to significantly reduce your potential for suffering a data breach.

---

[4]http://m.isaca.org/Knowledge-Center/BMIS/Documents/IntrotoBMIS.pdf
[5]www.isaca.org/COBIT/Pages/COBIT-2019-Publications-Resources.aspx

Remember, whether you are mitigating the external or internal attackers, they have some commonalities in the elements that drive them:

1. **Inquisitiveness**

   You've put up some defenses, so they want to know what is behind your defenses ("They want a peek inside") to see if there is anything that they can profit from.

   - They don't know whether your business is a viable target until they are able to take a look at what data lies behind your doors and windows.

2. **Challenge**

   A fact of modern life is that the attackers seek to develop work-arounds to circumvent your defenses. Often these will be the exploitation of your "Human Firewall," poor practices, or just looking at your web interfaces or networks through a different lens.

   - Think about an e-Commerce shopping basket, where the web developer has made the interface look appealing and easy to use for the consumer. In testing, the developer confirmed that all the required functionality works as expected, with consumers being able to add the number of goods they wish to order and the advertised price – the price is automatically calculated.

     - Can that consumer change the number of goods ordered to a minus figure?

       - List price $100 × **–100** items = Payment card is refunded to the tune of **£10,000**.

       Or

     - has your developer confirmed that the list price cannot be manually changed?

       - List price $100, changed to **$1** × 100 items = Your business sells $10,000 of goods for just £100 – **1%** of the list price.

Note   Neither of these examples are applicable to PCI DSS, as they do not impact the Confidentiality, Integrity, or Availability of the payment card data. However, they will impact your business!

3. **Reward**

   For your attackers, the term "Reward" comes in two forms:

   - **Financial**

     The modern criminal is looking to monetarize any stolen data, either by using the stolen data to commit identity theft, payment card fraud, to purchase "Black Market" goods or to resell the stolen data to other criminals.

   - **Kudos**

     Having cleverly created work-arounds, your amateur hacker may only wish to brag to their peer groups at how clever they have been. To do this, they need to retrieve evidence of their deeds so will steal your data to prove what they have done. Frequently, this data remains available on the "Dark/Deep" Web for many months, until it becomes useful for a criminal.

     - In 2013, Target was the victim of a piece of malware that was written by a 17-year-old Russian teenager.[6] Yet, just two weeks later, a Mexican couple[7] were caught crossing the US-Mexican border in possession of a large number of cloned payment cards related to the Target breach.

     - In 2015, TalkTalk (a UK Internet Service Provider (ISP)) was hacked, resulting in **157,000** customer records being stolen. Four years later, **4500** of the customer details were discovered to be still available online.[8]

---

[6]https://edition.cnn.com/2014/01/20/us/money-target-breach/index.html

[7]www.theguardian.com/world/2014/jan/21/texas-police-arrest-pair-linked-target-credit-card-breach-us-mexico-border

[8]www.silicon.co.uk/workspace/talktalk-breach-data-found-online-256555

All these drivers are driven by the attackers being presented with opportunities. Consequently, the belief that your business is not a credible target for an attacker is no longer a sensible approach, and if you are processing any personal data (especially payment card data), you are likely to become a victim without an effective defensive strategy.

Components of an Effective Strategy

At the heart of any effective strategy is maintaining secure technologies and having mature supporting processes, as the BMIS triangle.

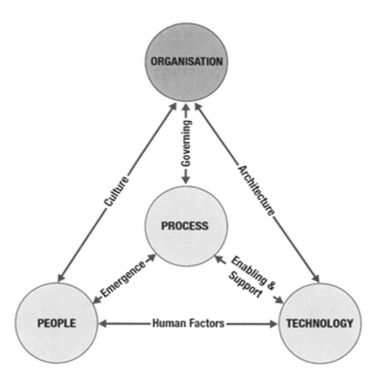

Figure 4-1. *BMIS*

Of course, this model needs to be prioritized against your particular business and the type of data that you are seeking to safeguard. To achieve this, your efforts need to be prioritized based upon your perceived attack vectors and aligned to the following domain areas.

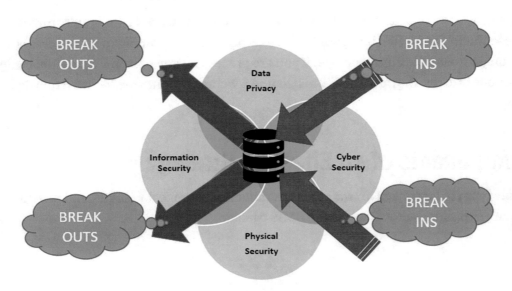

Figure 4-2. *Developing Data Security Strategy*

Consequently, an effective cyber security should reflect all of these components, aligned to your data processing operations/payment channels and prioritized based upon their potential impact to your business and with resilience being engrained throughout.

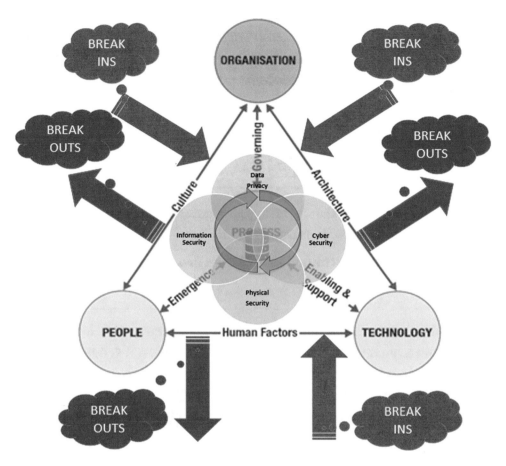

Figure 4-3. *An Integrated Data Security Strategy*

Data Privacy

Changing personal data regulations requires organizations to ensure that personal data is handled responsibly and in a manner that the data subject would approve and to ensure that their personal data is securely retained, processed, and transmitted in a manner that will ensure that it is adequately protected across its data life cycle.

Varonis[9] defines Data Privacy as

---

[9]www.varonis.com/blog/data-privacy/

Data privacy or information privacy is a branch of data security concerned with the proper handling of data – consent, notice, and regulatory obligations. More specifically, practical data privacy concerns often revolve around:

Whether or how data is shared with third parties.

How data is legally collected or stored.

Regulatory restrictions such as GDPR, HIPAA, GLBA, or CCPA.

Numerous updates to global data privacy laws now legislate that payment card data is deemed to be personal data, for example:

- **Article 4: European Union General Data Protection Regulation (EU GDPR)**

"Personal data" means any information relating to an identified or identifiable natural person ("data subject"); an identifiable natural person is one who can be identified, directly or indirectly, in particular by reference to an identifier such as a name, an identification number, location data, an online identifier, or to one or more factors specific to the physical, physiological, genetic, mental, economic, cultural, or social identity of that natural person.

- A payment card uses the PAN as an Identification number and contains the Initials and Surname of the cardholder.
- **Personal Information Protection and Electronic Documents Act (PIPEDA)**

"Information about an identifiable **individual**," essentially any **data** obtained in the course of a commercial activity.

- Payment card data is used in the course of commercial activities.
- **California Consumer Privacy Act (CCPA)**

Information that identifies, relates to, describes, is reasonably capable of being associated with, or could reasonably be linked, directly or indirectly, with a particular consumer or household; such as a real name, alias, postal address, unique personal identifier, online identifier Internet Protocol address, email address, account name, social security number, driver's license number, passport number, or other similar identifiers.

- Payment cards absolutely relate to a specific consumer.

Consequently, any business handling payment card data needs to ensure that it is handled in accordance with their appropriate Data Privacy regulations/laws, and the easiest way to achieve this is to apply and align with a suite of Privacy Principles and incorporate PCI DSS into these principles. To better aid your business's data privacy program in meeting the requirements of the various privacy regulations, ISACA recommends the use of their 14 privacy principles:[10]

1. Choice and Consent

2. Legitimate purpose specification

    - PCI DSS

        - *Requirement 3*

3. Personal information and sensitive information life cycle

    - PCI DSS

        - *Requirement 3*

4. Accuracy and Quality

5. Openness, Transparency, and Notice

6. Individual Participation

---

[10]https://next.isaca.org/bookstore/cobit-5/ipp

7. Accountability

    - PCI DSS

        - *Requirement 12*

8. Security Safeguards

    - PCI DSS

        - *Requirement 1*

        - *Requirement 2*

        - *Requirement 3*

        - *Requirement 4*

        - *Requirement 5*

        - *Requirement 6*

        - *Requirement 9*

9. Monitoring, Measuring, and Reporting

    - PCI DSS

        - *Requirement 10*

        - *Requirement 11*

        - *Requirement 12*

10. Preventing Harm

    - PCI DSS

        - *Requirement 12*

11. Third-party/Vendor Management

    - PCI DSS

        - *Requirement 12*

12. Breach Management

    - PCI DSS

        - *Requirement 12*

13. Security and Privacy By Design

- PCI DSS

  - *Requirement 1*

  - *Requirement 2*

14. Free flow of Information and Legitimate Restriction

    - PCI DSS

      - *Requirement 7*

      - *Requirement 8*

      - *Requirement 9*

As you can see, approximately **71%** of the data privacy regulatory requirements can be covered through the application of solely the PCI DSS controls framework. However, if you were to bolster this through using the ISACA privacy principles, you will be able to considerably reduce your data privacy and security risks. If all personal data is processed through PCI DSS compliant (or an equivalent standard) business operations, the remaining data privacy obligations are limited to maintaining the "Rights" of the Data Subject.

The identified **71%** will be further divided and explored in the following sections (Cyber Security, Information Security, Physical Security and Resilience) of this chapter.

Cyber Security

The term "Cyber" is believed to have become popular in the early 1990s but is thought to have had a loose association with the term "Cybernetics" which was first coined in the 1940s. However, in today's popularity of Internet-connected infrastructures, the term "Cyber Security" relates to the protection of any Internet/public-facing systems.

There are numerous differing definitions of the term "Cyber Security," for example, in Cambridge Dictionary:

Things that are done to protect a person, organization, or country and their computer information against crime or attacks carried out using the internet:

Ineffective cyber security and attacks on our informational infrastructure put our nation at risk.

A company's response to cyber security threats.

However, the most pertinent is the definition provided by TechTarget:[11]

Cyber security *is the protection of internet-connected systems, including hardware, software and data, from cyberattacks. In a computing context, security comprises cyber security and physical security -- both are used by enterprises to protect against unauthorized access to data centers and other computerized systems. The goal of cyber security is to limit risk and protect IT assets from attackers with malicious intent.*

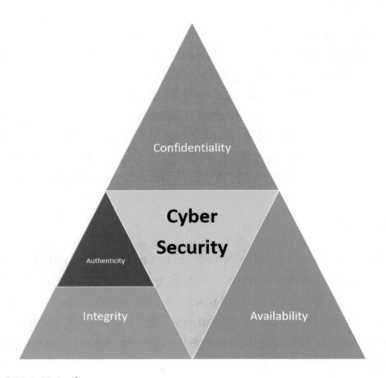

Figure 4-4. *CIAA Triad*

---

[11]https://searchsecurity.techtarget.com/definition/cybersecurity

External Attack Surface Reconnaissance

Hackers will look to surveil your external facing attack surfaces, looking to identify any possible opportunities to infiltrate the web application and Internet-facing technologies. Consequently, it is essential that you do the same and start to trace your consumer journeys to identify the external facing technologies that support the Points of Interaction through to the entry into your corporate network. It is important to note that the traditional hack through the network infrastructure are not the only Tactics, Techniques, and Protocols employed by hackers today, for example:

- **Avast**[12]

  Compromised employee's VPN credentials (no additional multi-factor authentication (MFA)), gaining access to their account.

- **Equifax**[13]

  The credit agency failed to update an external facing web server, which provided the attackers with unauthorized access, enabling them to move laterally across the corporate network.

- **Multiple Examples**

  - **2019 Application Security Risk Report**[14]

    1. There has been a reduction in the number of reported new High-severity vulnerabilities.

    2. Open source: A clear and present danger.

    3. Nearly all web apps have bugs in their security features.

    4. Mobile apps have shown a sharp increase in some vulnerability types.

    5. The adoption of DevOps approaches is increasing.

    6. Bug bounty programs have delivered a limited impact.

---

[12]www.zdnet.com/article/avast-says-hackers-breached-internal-network-through-compromised-vpn-profile/

[13]www.warren.senate.gov/imo/media/doc/2018.09.06%20GAO%20Equifax%20report.pdf

[14]https://content.microfocus.com/application-security-risk-tb/app-security-risk-takeaways?lx=qatCOj?utm_source=techbeacon&utm_medium=techbeacon&utm_campaign=00134846

Information Gathering

How well do you understand your business's digital footprint and what type of data is available to the opportunist attacker?

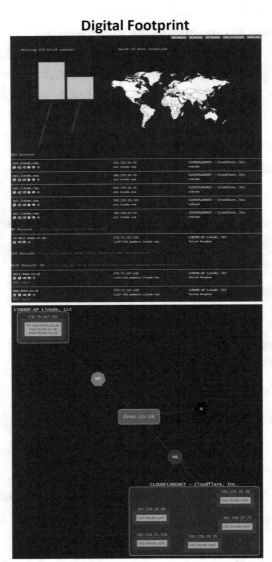

Figure 4-5. *DNS Dumpster[15]*

---

[15]https://dnsdumpster.com/

Geolocation

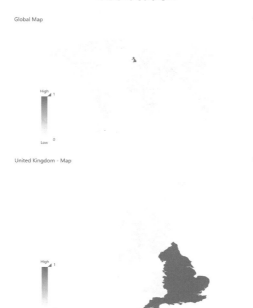

Figure 4-6. *Zoom Eye[16]*

Interconnections

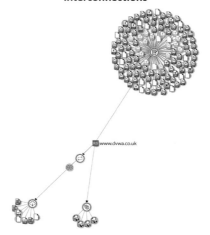

Figure 4-7. *VirusTotal[17]*

---

[16]www.zoomeye.org/

[17]www.virustotal.com/graph/

Figure 4-8. *Visual Site Mapper*[18]

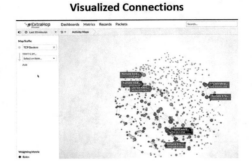

Figure 4-9. *ExtraHop*[19]

Figure 4-10. *Qualys*[20]

---

[18]http://visualsitemapper.com/

[19]www.extrahop.com/

[20]https://qualysguard.qualys.com/qwebhelp/fo_portal/maps/mapping_basics.htm

Asset Dashboard

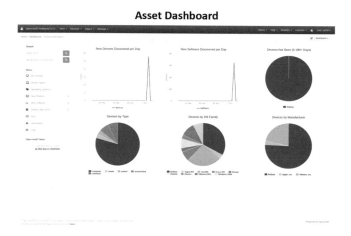

Figure 4-11. *Open-AudIT[21]*

Asset Mapping

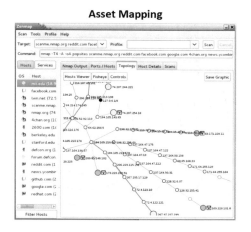

Figure 4-12. *NMAP[22]*

In order to effectively safeguard the interaction points, it is essential that the perimeter assets be differentiated from the internal technologies.

Within the PCI DSS controls framework, this is covered in the requirement to document your network assets and data flows, and you have a layered network.

---

[21]www.open-audit.org/

[22]https://nmap.org/

Consequently, to ensure that you understand the potential impact of your assets and you are able to prioritize your compliance activities, I recommend that you categorize your technologies, for example:

1. **Perimeter technologies**

   a. Web Servers

   b. Web Applications

   c. Perimeter Firewall

   d. Perimeter Intrusion Detection System (PIDS)

   e. External facing Server

   f. PIN Transaction Security (PTS) Devices

2. **Payment Card Data processing technologies**

   a. Databases

   b. Payment Applications

   c. Internal Firewalls

   d. Laptops

   e. Mainframes

   f. Intrusion Detection Systems (IDS)

   g. Internal Servers

3. **Supporting internal technologies**

Such an approach will greatly assist you in your ongoing Business-As-Usual (BAU) compliance efforts while aiding the vulnerability and risk management, more importantly helping to piece together the technology chains, so that any monitoring will improve the ability to readily detect malicious activities moving along the various customer journeys – toward the "Crown Jewels."

Additionally, early detection will help you respond in a timely manner so that you have improved chances of intercepting and blocking the activities of an attacker.

Remember, you are looking to be able to detect and block malicious "Inbound" and "Outbound" network traffic and unauthorized actions.

Attackers will look to gain a persistent presence within your network and will not always, necessarily, attempt to brute force their way through the "Main Gate."

Thinking like an attacker, carrying out periodic reconnaissance results should be compared against categorized external assets.

PCI DSS Applicable Controls – External Technologies

It is essential that you understand what is needed to maintain a secure perimeter, so as to reduce the opportunities for your attackers to exploit. Consequently, I have collated together a suite of example external technology-related PCI DSS controls, as well as some suggested supporting resources.

These will provide you with some resources that could help you create a schedule of auditing, will enhance your defensive efforts, and help identify and defend against any potential infiltration opportunities.

- **Requirements 1.1 to 1.5 – External facing Network Topologies**
    - "Detailed" Network Diagrams
        - *Visual Paradigm*[23]
        - Open-AudIT[24]
        - NMAP[25]

---

[23]https://online.visual-paradigm.com/diagrams/solutions/
free-network-diagram-software/

[24]www.open-audit.org/

[25]https://nmap.org/

- Summary Network Diagrams

  - Showing the interconnections between numerous environments

    - "In-Scope" Payment Channels

    - "Out-of-Scope" BAU network components

  - It is extremely important that you are able to clearly identify the "Air Gaps" between the "In-Scope" and "Out-of-Scope" network topologies.

- Data Flow Diagrams

  - Gliffy[26]

  - DrawIO[27]

- Firewall Rulesets

  - *Titania Nipper Studio*[28]

- Network Traffic Analysis

  - *Dsniff*[29]

  - *NetWitness NextGen*[30]

  - *Argus*[31]

  - *P0f*[32]

- Wireless Analysis

  - Aircrack[33]

---

[26]www.gliffy.com/
[27]www.draw.io/
[28]www.titania.com/products/nipper/
[29]https://sectools.org/tool/dsniff/
[30]https://sectools.org/tool/netwitness/
[31]https://sectools.org/tool/argus/
[32]https://sectools.org/tool/p0f/
[33]https://sectools.org/tool/aircrack/

- Approved Services, Ports, and Protocols

    - *Command Prompt*

- Software Firewalls enabled on portable devices

    - *ZoneAlarm*[34]

- **Requirement 2 – Securely configured external facing IT Assets**

    - Categorized Asset Inventory

        - "In-Scope" assets (supporting customer journeys)

        - "Out-of-Scope" (adjoining assets with the potential to impact)

    - Securely configured wireless technologies

    - Secure Configuration Standards

        - *CIS Benchmarks*[35]

        - *Titania PAWS*[36]

- **Requirement 4.1 – Encryption over public-facing networks**

    - Secure transmission

        - Wireshark[37]

        - SSL Labs[38]

- **Requirement 5.1 – External technologies protected by effective Anti-Malware software**

    - Checks to confirm that the AV software is active and effective

        - *Wicar Test Virus*[39]

---

[34]www.zonealarm.com/software/free-firewall/?AID=11556579&PID=6361382&SID=
trd-5293610212650605605&network=cj

[35]www.cisecurity.org/cis-benchmarks/

[36]www.titania.com/products/paws/

[37]https://sectools.org/tool/wireshark/

[38]www.ssllabs.com/ssltest/

[39]www.wicar.org/test-malware.html

- **Requirements 6.1 to 6.6 – Manage Secure web sites and Applications**

  - Vulnerability Risk Management

    - Tenable.io[40]

    - Cequence.ai[41]

  - Inventory

    - "In-Scope" web sites (supporting payments)

    - "Out-of-Scope" web sites (potential to impact, e.g., Man-In-The-Middle (MITM), where the customer journey can be redirected)

  - All changes to external systems formally managed to ensure that impact and rollback decisions are applied

  - Secure Software Development Operations

    - *Open Web Application Security Project (OWASP)[42]*

    - *OWASP Top 10[43]*

    - *OWASP Appendix A Testing Tools[44]*

    - *Application Security Platform*

      - *Cequence Security[45]*

---

[40]www.tenable.com/products/tenable-io/web-application-scanning

[41]www.cequence.ai/

[42]www.owasp.org/index.php/Main_Page

[43]www.owasp.org/images/7/72/OWASP_Top_10-2017_%28en%29.pdf.pdf

[44]www.owasp.org/index.php/Appendix_A:_Testing_Tools

[45]www.cequence.ai/

- *Web Application Firewall (WAF)*

    - *AppTrana*[46]

    - *StackPath*[47]

    - *Sucuri*[48]

- **Requirement 8.1 – Identify and manage third-party remote/external access**

    - Manage the remote/external access of vendors

- **Requirement 9.9 – Inventory and Inspection of PTS Devices**

    - Also known as PDQ (Pretty Damn Quick) Devices, an inventory and periodic checks must be carried out.

- **Requirements 10 – Monitoring users and systems use**

    - Based upon the categorized IT systems and users, the monitoring should be able to detect the **ABNORMAL** from NORMAL activities.

    - Centralized monitoring of the various logs sources should be collated to show unauthorized activities, as an attacker carries out reconnaissance to move through your network from the trusted to the untrusted environments.

    - All critical external systems have correct and consistent clock readings, received from secure and industry-accepted external resources.

        - *This is essential in the event of an investigation or forensic examination to piece together an accurate chain of events.*

---

[46]https://apptrana.indusface.com/?utm_source=PPC&utm_medium=Referral&utm_
campaign=Comparitech-Product-Listing
[47]www.stackpath.com/products/waf/
[48]https://sucuri.net/website-firewall/

- Secure audit trails of all user and external systems activities.

  - *This is essential in the event of an incident to help trace the activities back to the potential "Root Cause."*

  - *Consider enhanced archiving, exceeding the 12 months between PCI DSS compliance assessments, as attackers are known for remaining dormant for a number of months or years, for example:*

    - *Three months instant, 36 months archive (rather than limiting to the minimum 12 months)*

- Example solutions/products

  - Elastic Stack SIEM[49]

  - LogRhythm[50]

  - OSSIM[51]

  - SIEMonster[52]

- **Requirement 10.5 – External logs**

  - Logs from external facing systems are written to secure storage systems.

- **Requirement 11.2 – External Vulnerability Scans**

  - Quarterly Approved Scanning Vendor (ASV)[53] scans

---

[49]www.elastic.co/products/siem

[50]https://logrhythm.com/products/nextgen-siem-platform/

[51]https://cybersecurity.att.com/products/ossim

[52]https://siemonster.com/

[53]www.pcisecuritystandards.org/assessors_and_solutions/approved_scanning_vendors

- **Requirement 11.3 – External Penetration Tests and Segmentation Tests**

  - Confirming the integrity and effectiveness of the external network layers and network segmentation

    - *CREST PTMA*[54]

- **Requirement 11.4 – Intrusion Detection/Prevention**

  - Alerting on all external systems

    - *OSSEC HIDS*[55]

    - *Suricata*[56]

    - *BRO*[57]

- **Requirement 11.5 – Change Detection**

  - Alerting to notify any potential unauthorized changes made to external systems

- **Requirement 12.4 – Roles and Responsibilities**

  - All personnel with roles and responsibilities for the external systems understand their duties and the potential impact these systems present for the payment card operations.

- **Requirement 12 – People Management**

  - Maintaining a security culture for all personnel responsible for the management of (or with access to) the internal systems and payment card data

---

[54]www.crest-approved.org/2018/07/20/penetration-testing-maturity-assessment-tools/index.html

[55]https://sectools.org/tool/ossec/

[56]https://suricata-ids.org/

[57]https://sourceforge.net/projects/bro-tools/

- **Requirement 12.10 – An effective Incident Response Process**

  - Having an effective incident response process to rapidly detect and respond to incidents or suspected compromise of external technologies

    - *Demisto*[58]

    - *CREST IRMA*[59]

    - *YUDU*[60]

Information Security

Having secured your Cyber Security environment, you still need to ensure that the internal networks are safeguarded from harm. The attackers could be from unauthorized aggressors, who have managed to circumvent your perimeter defenses, or from an authorized employee or trusted contractor. Consequently, it is essential that the internal technologies that support the card payment process are securely maintained.

TechTarget[61] defines Information Security as:

Information security (infosec) is a set of strategies for managing the processes, tools and policies necessary to prevent, detect, document and counter threats to digital and non-digital information. Infosec responsibilities include establishing a set of business processes that will protect information assets regardless of how the information is formatted or whether it is in transit, is being processed or is at rest in storage.

The purpose of your InfoSec program is to complement the Cyber Security environments, so as to slow the potential infiltration into the data stores/transmissions and exfiltration from your corporate network. Once an external attacker has breached

---

[58]www.demisto.com/

[59]www.crest-approved.org/cyber-security-incident-response-maturity-assessment/
index.html

[60]www.yudu.com/sentinel/emergency-notification

[61]https://searchsecurity.techtarget.com/definition/information-security-infosec

the perimeter defenses, they will seek to gain a clandestine persistent presence within your corporate network, while they figure out the best opportunities to steal your data.

At the same time, you need to effectively manage the "Insider Threat," whether that be from deliberate, malicious, or accidental activities of an authorized individual, contractor, or third party. Consequently, I have collated together a list of some of the complementary controls that relate to the Information Security environment.

- **Requirements 1.1 to 1.5 – Internal facing Network Topologies**

  - Can you identify the demarcation points between the trusted and untrusted environments?

  - Do you have a clearly defined "Buffer Zone" between trusted and untrusted environments?

    - During my deployment to Basrah, Iraq, my role was to use my 42-toothed furry Exocet (military patrol dog) to patrol and defend the "Buffer Zone" between the Badlands *(untrusted environment)* and the internal secure military operational areas. In essence, this involved covert patrolling of the perimeter track which ran parallel to the perimeter fence, so as to provide a proactive defense and first response to any potential incursion attempts *(Firewall/IDS alerting)*.

    - During other deployments into hostile environments, the delineation would be a considerable De-Militarized Zone (DMZ) to act as the "Buffer Zone." At Camp Bastion, this had consisted of approximately 1.5 km of rough road between the outer perimeter checkpoint and the inner checkpoint. I recall, on one occasion, the effectiveness of the DMZ during the response to an incident. At the internal checkpoint, the Ammunition and Explosives Detection (AED) detection dog had shown an interest on an incoming Non-Potable water tanker. The dog had indicated to the region around an open tool box (located beneath the water tank). Further

> investigation revealed that the water tanker had been repurposed from its former function as a fuel tanker and that the tool box had been closed when the driver had parked up on the previous evening. The uneven drive along the 1.5 km DMZ had shaken free an Improvised Explosive Device (IED) from the former fuel tanker.

- Do you filter your network traffic to ensure that only approved network traffic flows between the trusted and untrusted network environments?

- Internal Firewall/Router configurations.

- Internal Rulesets.

- Detailed Network Diagrams.

- Data Flow Diagrams.

  - During multiple appointments in the RAF Police, the primary defense involved creating secure environments within the confines of the military base (e.g., Hardened aircraft shelters (HAZ), Secure bunkers, Weapons storage facilities, etc.) which had specific access control lists to ensure that only approved vehicles and personnel were granted access.

- **Requirement 2 – Securely configured internal facing IT Assets**

  - Securely configured wireless technologies

  - Securely configured internal IT assets, supporting the data life cycles

  - Asset Inventory (including End-of-Life dates)

- **Requirement 3 – Secure Data Storage**

  - Data Discovery. You can't protect what you don't know.

    - *GroundLabs Card Recon*[62]

    - Spirion[63]

    - Memoryze[64]

  - Encryption Key Management

    - Wireshark[65]

- **Requirement 5 – Internal IT assets protected by active Anti-Malware software**

- **Requirements 6.1 to 6.5 – Manage Secure Internal Applications**

  - Manage vulnerabilities and updates based upon the identified vulnerabilities, risk assessed against local factors.

  - Secure Software Development on all internal applications that support your payment card processes.

  - All changes to internal systems are formally managed to ensure that impact and rollback decisions are applied.

- **Requirements 7 and 8 – Role-Based Access Control**

  - All access to internal systems is strictly restricted, based upon explicit need to know.

    - John the Ripper[66]

    - Ophcrack[67]

---

[62]www.groundlabs.com/card-recon/
[63]www.spirion.com/sensitive-data-discovery/
[64]www.fireeye.com/services/freeware/memoryze.html
[65]www.wireshark.org/
[66]https://sectools.org/tool/john/
[67]https://sectools.org/tool/ophcrack/

- Brutus[68]

- SolarWinds Permissions Analyzer[69]

- ManageEngine ADManager[70]

- MaxPowerSoft AD Reports Lite[71]

- All users that are granted access should be categorized based upon their potential ability to do damage. These categorized and prioritized users should then be monitored as part of requirement 10.

- **Requirements 10 – Monitoring users and systems use**

  - Based upon the categorized IT systems and users, the monitoring should be able to detect the **ABNORMAL** from NORMAL activities.

  - Centralized monitoring of the various logs source should be collated to show unauthorized activities, as an attacker carries out reconnaissance of your internal network.

  - All critical internal systems have correct and consistent clock readings, received from secure and industry-accepted external resources.

  - *Note:*

  - *This is essential in the event of an investigation or forensic examination to piece together an accurate chain of events.*

    - Elastic Stack

---

[68]https://sectools.org/tool/brutus/

[69]www.solarwinds.com/free-tools/permissions-analyzer-for-active-directory/registration?program=1323&campaign=70150000000OzCs&CMP=BIZ-TAD-ITT-SW_WW_X_PP_PPD_CQ_EN_HLTH_SW-PAFT-X_X_X_X-Q316

[70]www.manageengine.com/products/ad-manager/download.html?utm_source=ITT&utm_medium=ppc&utm_campaign=ADMP_download

[71]www.maxpowersoft.com/adreportslite.php

- Secure audit trails

    - *This is essential in the event of an incident to help trace the activities back to the potential "Root Cause."*

    - *Consider enhanced archiving, exceeding the 12 months between PCI DSS compliance assessments, as attackers are known for remaining dormant for a number of months or years, for example:*

        - *Three months instant, 36 months archive (as opposed to the minimum 12 months)*

- **Requirement 11.1 – Rogue Wireless Devices**

    - Conduct periodic checks for rogue wireless checks, which can be used to circumvent your network egress controls.

    - *Physical inspections of the internal IT assets*

    - Kismet[72]

    - NetStumbler[73]

    - inSSIDer[74]

- **Requirement 11.2 – External Vulnerability Scans**

    - Scanning of internal systems for vulnerabilities

        - Security Content Automation Protocol (SCAP) tools[75]

        - Nessus[76]

        - OpenVAS[77]

---

[72]https://sectools.org/tool/kismet/

[73]https://sectools.org/tool/netstumbler/

[74]https://sectools.org/tool/inssider/

[75]https://csrc.nist.gov/Projects/scap-validation-program/
Validated-Products-and-Modules

[76]https://sectools.org/tool/nessus/

[77]https://sectools.org/tool/openvas/

- **Requirement 11.3 – Internal Penetration Tests and Segmentation Tests**

  - Confirming the integrity and effectiveness of the external network layers and network segmentation

    - *CREST PTMA*[78]

- **Requirement 11.4 – Intrusion Detection/Prevention**

  - Alerting on all internal systems

    - SNORT[79]

    - Suricata[80]

    - BRO IDS[81]

- **Requirement 11.5 – Change Detection**

  - Alerting to notify any potential unauthorized changes made to internal systems

    - *OpenDLP*[82]

- **Requirement 12 – People Management**

  - Maintaining a security culture for all personnel responsible for the management of (or with access to) the internal systems and payment card data

---

[78]www.crest-approved.org/2018/07/20/penetration-testing-maturity-assessment-tools/index.html

[79]www.snort.org/

[80]https://suricata-ids.org/

[81]https://sourceforge.net/projects/bro-tools/

[82]https://code.google.com/archive/p/opendlp/

Physical Security

This section "Requirement 9" is often the most frequently misunderstood and underappreciated component of any defensive strategy. If an attacker is able to gain access to the supporting IT systems and networks, Media (Paper, Voice/Video recordings, Backups, etc.), or Point-of-Sale (POS)/PTS devices, they may be able to cause just as much damage as they could via a logical compromise.

TechTarget defines Physical Security as:

Physical security is the protection of personnel, hardware, software, networks and data from physical actions and events that could cause serious loss or damage to an enterprise, agency or institution. This includes protection from fire, flood, natural disasters, burglary, theft, vandalism and terrorism.

- Imagine the potential impact of an unknown actor plugging in a rogue device.

Wi-Fi Pineapple[83]	Signal Owl[84]

Acts as a hotspot honeypot, useful in man-in-the-middle-style Internet attacks	A simple payload-based signals intelligence platform with a unique design for discreet planting or mobile operations on any engagement

(*continued*)

---

[83]https://shop.hak5.org/products/wifi-pineapple
[84]https://shop.hak5.org/products/signal-owl

USB Rubber Ducky[85]	Shark Jack[86]

A keystroke injection tool disguised as a generic flash drive	A portable network attack and automation tool for pentesters and systems administrators designed to enable social engineering engagements and opportunistic wired network auditing
LAN Turtle[87]	Packet Squirrel[88]

A covert Systems Administration and Penetration Testing tool providing stealth remote access, network intelligence gathering, and man-in-the-middle surveillance capabilities through a simple graphic shell	An ethernet multi-tool designed to give you covert remote access, painless packet captures, and secure VPN connections with the flip of a switch

- A thief gaining unauthorized access to a building and walking off with half a dozen laptops (containing a full day of data that has not been backed up)

- An unknown actor being able to steal a stack of paperwork, containing hundreds of payment card data, in clear text (e.g., Receipts)

---

[85]https://shop.hak5.org/products/usb-rubber-ducky-deluxe
[86]https://shop.hak5.org/products/shark-jack
[87]https://shop.hak5.org/products/lan-turtle
[88]https://shop.hak5.org/products/packet-squirrel

- An attacker tampering with the ATM or PTS device

ATM Physical Skimming[89]	PTS Physical Skimming[90]

Consequently, it is essential that access to the supporting IT systems, payment devices, and payment processing environments is protected by sufficient physical security and access restrictions to ensure that only approved personnel (based upon strict role-based access controls) can access them.

The access control measures need to effectively restrict access against individuals, so that in the event of an incident persons entering the restricted areas are identifiable – in support of any follow-up investigations. In order to achieve this, it is essential that the access control measures are supported by additional measures to validate the person entering at a specific date/time (e.g., Visitor Log, CCTV, Individual PIN, Key Register, etc.). Remember that a CCTV system should be capable of distinguishing an individual rather than just capturing a low-resolution image.

Once an appropriate level of physical defensive measures has been applied (based upon the potential impact and aggregated values) and audit trails maintained, it is important to ensure that all media and payment devices are strictly controlled, with all end-of-life systems being securely destroyed/disposed of, when no longer required. The maintenance of "In Life" payment systems includes PTS devices, as per the PCI SSC-approved PTS device list.[91]

---

[89]www.atmatom.com/protecting-atms-from-rising-card-fraud/
[90]www.troab.com/important-things-must-know-paying-credit-card-prevent-fraud/
[91]www.pcisecuritystandards.org/assessors_and_solutions/pin_transaction_devices

PP1000sec

Hardware #: V09 Firmware #: 1.0 Applic #:	4-60181	3.x	PED	30 Apr 2020

Figure 4-13. *Approved PTS Device*

- BLANCCO Secure Erasure[92]

Resilience

This is a component that is not covered by the PCI DSS controls framework. However, for any business that relies on the processing of such data to remain profitable, ensuring that the support resources remain resilient makes for common sense and has become a key requirement of various data privacy legislations.

What Is Resilience?

Resilience is defined by Dictionary.com[93] as:

The power or ability to return to the original form, position, etc., after being bent, compressed, or stretched; elasticity.

The ability to recover readily from illness, depression, adversity, or the like; buoyancy.

- How quickly are you able to bounce back from an event, which might not necessarily involve the payment card data but may involve the unavailability of the support technologies or personnel?

- Do you have effective Disaster Recovery and Business Continuity contingencies related to your payment card operations?

---

[92]www.blancco.com/

[93]www.dictionary.com/browse/resilience

Recommendations

Avoid thinking of your data privacy, cyber security, information security, and resilience efforts as isolated elements within your business and try to work in harmony with the various key stakeholders from each of these domain areas to ensure that you understand how each area complements each other to safeguard the confidentiality, integrity, availability, and authenticity (CIAA) of your most valued business systems and sensitive data types.

Gain an understanding of the critical data paths (data flows) for your business, identifying their points of entry and egress into your infrastructure and all the network systems that they will interact with, or those connected systems/applications that could potentially have an impact on these critical data paths. Document your findings in appropriate network and data flow diagrams that are periodically reviewed for accuracy and currency.

Failure to understand your various business critical data paths and supporting systems may result in something getting overlooked and resulting in the potential for attacker exploitation, which could lead to a compromised network/system or data breach.

Conclusion

Changes to the way that your attackers work and data protection requirements mean that your business needs to appreciate the integrated approach that is needed for the effective protection of your critical business systems, processes, and data assets. Failure to do so can potentially open the door for opportunist attackers (either internal or external), who are continually seeking to exploit neglected and unloved infrastructures or processes that they are able to profit from.

All your supporting business systems, networks, and processes should be able to be identified and tagged against the domain that they are supporting. The results of which should enable you to provide greater assurance for both compliance and the reduction of business risk perspectives and will also enable you to identify any common failings (or positive practices) that may apply across all domain areas.

Key Takeaways

The maintenance of an integrated strategy takes teamwork, where each person with supporting responsibilities understands how their role complements and supports and could have an impact on another person's responsibility.

Effective strategies require continual communications and assurance activities, so that the opportunities for exploitation are kept to a minimum.

> ***Visibility of the supporting IT systems, teamwork, and assurance activities is at the core of any integrated strategy.***

Do you understand how the network systems are connected and how the data flows through your business infrastructure?

Do you know the full extent of your consumers' points of interaction?

Do you understand the adjoining resources that may be used to impact the consumers' journey?

Have you securely configured all the supporting IT assets?

Do have a prioritized update/remediation process based upon the category of the IT asset (e.g., External, Payment card transmission/storage/processing, etc.)?

Do you have established and mature assurance processes?

Does your monitoring enable you to rapidly identify and respond to unusual activity?

Do your logical and physical access controls adequately restrict access to the IT assets, supporting your payment processes, based upon a legitimate right of access?

In the event of an incident, do you have sufficient audit trails?

Do all personnel, with access, understand the safeguarding rules?

Risks

Maintaining an integrated Cyber/InfoSec strategy is essential for the protection of your "Crown Jewels" (Sensitive Data). However, like any integrated strategy, it is essential that this is achieved as part of a team effort. Otherwise, actions/tacks will be missed, potentially opening up opportunities for the attackers.

Do you understand the full extent of the IT assets, connections, and data flows?

Have you categorized your IT assets based upon their potential impact?

Are all changes to the cardholder date environment subject to formal approval?

Are all your supporting IT assets securely configured (based on industry guidelines) to reduce the opportunity for attackers to circumvent your defenses?

Do you minimize data storage, avoiding ad hoc duplication and storage of payment card data/personal data? – the greater the volume, the greater the risk.

Are you able to confirm that sensitive data transmitted from the "Vault" is moved out under armed guard (encrypted) to avoid interception?

Are you continually updating your dynamic environment, prioritized based upon the potential risk?

Vulnerability × Threat × Impact

Is access strictly controlled?

*Are you able to quickly identify and respond to the **ABNORMAL**?*

CHAPTER 5

The Importance of Risk Management

Figure 5-1. *Risk Assessment Practice*

Bearing in mind that you cannot completely eliminate risk *(especially when the "Human Factor" and Supplier Management is involved),* the importance of risk management, within your PCI DSS compliance program, becomes increasingly relevant to your business.

113

© Jim Seaman 2020
J. Seaman, *PCI DSS*, https://doi.org/10.1007/978-1-4842-5808-8_5

This is probably the most misunderstood aspect of most Cyber/InfoSec strategies, especially within the PCI DSS integrated framework.

Why is this?

In traditional control frameworks, such as the ISO/IEC 27001:2013 controls framework, the application of Annex A controls is applied to mitigate identified risks. However, within the Payment Card Industry Data Security Standard (PCI DSS) integrated controls framework, there is an understanding that the catalogue of controls is all that is required to ensure that the payment card processes are secure.

Unfortunately, this is not correct. The Payment Card Industry Security Standards Council (PCI SSC) have provided you with a catalogue of baseline security controls, which under the current version includes the control requirement for carrying out annual risk assessments. Employing the NIST SP800-30, r1,[1] principles, the annual risk assessment should include the following steps:

1. **Categorize**

   In addition to the baseline PCI DSS security controls, identify any additional threats, events, vulnerabilities, or predisposed conditions that are not being mitigated, *for example:*

   Man-in-the-Middle Magecart attacks[2] for an SAQ A eligible e-commerce merchant. In this style of attack, the attacker hijacks the customer journey from the out-of-scope web page, prior to being redirected to the third-party payment service provider's (PSP's) secure card payment interface. As a result, the attacker is able to carry out clandestine harvesting of the customer's card payment details, without needing to compromise the in-scope environment.

2. **Select**

   Having identified potential additional risks, not covered by the existing PCI DSS controls, identify potential additional security controls for your organizational information systems and environments of operation. This should include a number of options to help mitigate any identified risks/threats, *for example:*

---

[1]https://nvlpubs.nist.gov/nistpubs/Legacy/SP/nistspecialpublication800-30r1.pdf
[2]www.hornetsecurity.com/en/security-information/formjacking/

In the case of the Magecart attacks

- *Carrying out web application testing for JavaScript/Code injection vulnerabilities for the out-of-scope web pages, along the customer's journey*

- *Procuring the services of a third-party service to monitor the entire external web digital footprint (e.g., Cequence Security,[3] Cyber Rescue Alliance Security Scorecard[4])*

- *Bringing the out-of-scope web pages into scope (potential to impact)*

3. **Implement**

   Additional control measures are required to help mitigate against these identified risks, *for example:*

   In the case of the Magecart-style attacks, ensuring that any such vulnerabilities on the out-of-scope web pages are remediated to ensure the integrity of the redirection process cannot be undermined

4. **Assess**

   The effectiveness of the identified, additional, mitigation controls are assessed and documented, *for example:*

   In the aforementioned attack vector, suggested mitigation controls help to demonstrate the inherent risk scores (before mitigation) and residual risk scores (post mitigation) – Impact × Probability.

5. **Authorize**

   Any additional risk mitigation activities should be aligned to the business's risk appetite. Therefore, the results of any risk assessment should be documented allowing the business to make an informed choice on the best course of action for their business, *for example:*

   In the case of a "Formjacking[5]" risk, as per the Magecart threat, your appropriate business's risk owner should then be responsible for choosing.

---

[3]www.cequence.ai/

[4]https://securityscorecard.com/

[5]https://hackersonlineclub.com/formjacking/

6. **Monitor**

    By its very nature, the payment card information systems threats
    are dynamic by their very nature and need to be subject to
    continual monitoring to ensure

    - The security controls remain effective

    - Any changes to the environment or supporting system do not
      impact

    - Compliance with the appropriate legal, regulatory, policies, and
      procedures remains extant

    *For example, in relation to the "Formjacking" risk, you need to
    ensure that the chosen risk mitigation approach remains effective
    and aligned with your business's risk appetite criteria.*

In addition to identifying and assessing any risks that are not being mitigated by your
PCI DSS compliance program, you need to carry out risk assessments against your PCI
DSS controls. Remember that these are the minimum baseline security controls, but
they may not be aligned with your business's risk appetite levels. Consequently, you may
choose to enhance the existing controls to ensure that they are more appropriate to your
business expectations.

As parents, we understand and appreciate the importance of the risk assessment and
risk management process and ensure that these concepts are articulated to our children.
For example, what parent does not educate their children how to safely cross a road,
through the application of risk assessment and mitigation principles?

- **Threat**

  - Serious injury or death

- **Risk**

  - Being hit by a large vehicle or a vehicle travelling at speed

- **Control**

  - Safely cross the road.

- **Method**

  - Choose the most appropriate option.

- **Performance Standard and Specifications**

  - Green Cross Code[6]

    - THINK!

    - STOP!

    - USE YOUR EYES AND EARS!

    - WAIT UNTIL IT IS SAFE TO CROSS!

    - LOOK AND LISTEN!

    - ARRIVE ALIVE!

- **Risk Assessment**

  - Assess any additional impact and probability factors for each available option, for example:

    - Lighting conditions

    - Weather conditions

    - Road surface

    - Appropriate footwear

    - Road width

    - Speed limit

    - Volume of traffic

    - Type of traffic

    - Crossing location

    - Obstructions

    - Injuries

---

[6]www.sptraininguk.com/green-cross-code/

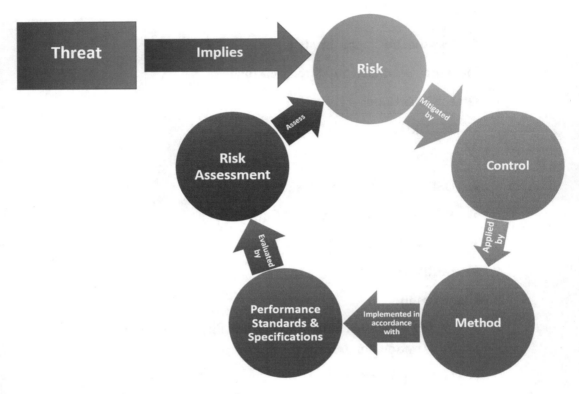

Figure 5-2. *Risk Assessment Cycle*

However, having taught them the safe way of crossing the road, parents encourage the children to seek alternative/safer options that the child may feel more comfortable with *(e.g., A bridge, Pedestrian crossing, choosing a safer crossing point, etc.)*.

Consequently, much like parents/schools are teaching children, your business needs to consider the pros and cons of the baseline PCI DSS security controls and to consider whether based upon the specific threats to your payment card processing systems and environments and to not be solely reliant on the PCI DSS controls being appropriate defensive measures, for example:

1. Let's have a look at the growing threat to e-Commerce business operations from the Magecart Group.[7] You have transferred the

---

[7]www.riskiq.com/research/inside-magecart/?utm_campaign=search_magecart&utm_source=
google&utm_medium=cpc&utm_content=inside_magecart&gclid=CjwKCAiAgqDxBRBTEiwA59eEN4
PiqV_SVdvzVcE8ak-AtxYzE1q2HdBTYv6pB-mNXof9DLZGZCZdEBoCwjwQAvD_BwE

responsibility of processing your customers' payment card data to a PCI DSS compliant third-party service provider, reducing your risk *(through the use of a crossing supervisor/crossing patrol officer, lollipop man/lady)* and becoming eligible for the completion of an SAQ A[8] (circa 22 controls). However, this risk assessment only deals with the risk of "crossing the road" and does not make any considerations of the dangers associated with being vulnerable to the dangers that could occur while you are stood on the sidewalk/footpath *(e.g., runaway vehicle)*.

> In the case of the Magecart Group, they will seek to exploit vulnerabilities within the out-of-scope web pages, within your customers' journey to the payment interface, to carry out a man-in-the-middle attack.

2. Your business takes the decision to use their customers' primary account numbers for the unique identifier for the customers' accounts.

   What are the implications for this?

   - *Printed on all paper correspondence?*

   - *Spoken during all telephone interactions?*

   - *Used to validate customers for online account resets?*

---

[8]www.pcisecuritystandards.org/documents/PCI-DSS-v3_2_1-SAQ-A.pdf?agreement=true&time=1579685825026

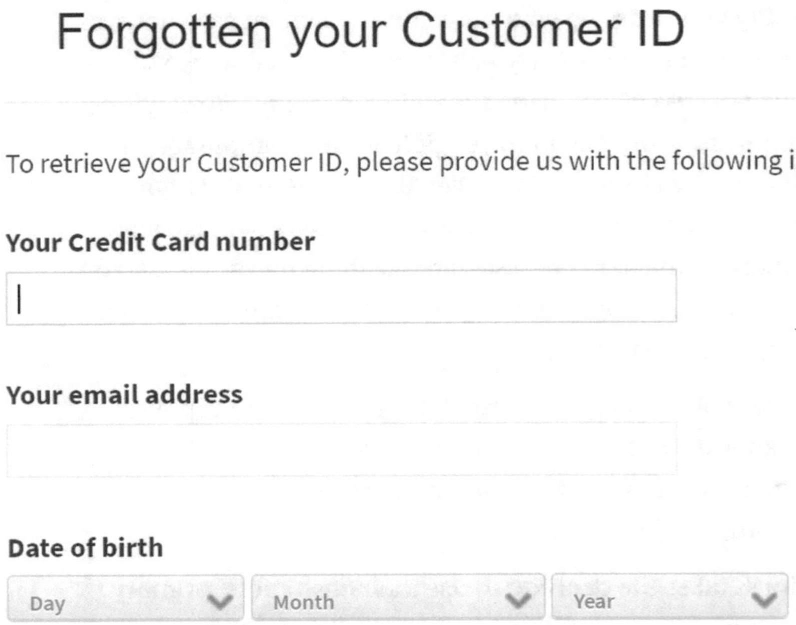

Forgotten your Customer ID

To retrieve your Customer ID, please provide us with the following information.

Your Credit Card number

Your email address

Date of birth

| Day | Month | Year |

Figure 5-3. *Payment Card Number Verification*

Introduction

The ENISA EU Agency for Cyber security publishes PCI DSS in their risk management section of their web site,[9] confirming that they are in agreement that PCI DSS is a catalogue of baseline security control developed to mitigate the risks to payment card processes. Consequently, it is important to develop an understanding of effective risk management practices.

What Is a Risk Assessment?

In PCI DSS, v3.2.1, there are six main control areas that integrate with one another to form the risk assessment process:

- 6.1. Vulnerability Risk Identification

- 11.2 Quarterly Vulnerability Scanning

---

[9]www.enisa.europa.eu/topics/threat-risk-management/risk-management/current-risk/
laws-regulation/corporate-governance/pci-dss

- 11.3. Penetration Testing

- 12.2. Risk Assessment

- 12.6. Formal Security Awareness

- 12.10. Incident Response

Each of these controls is complementary to each other and supports the risk assessment process. However, every PCI DSS control is a risk mitigation control and should be incorporated into the development of suitable risk assessment scenarios.

Synopsys[10] defines a security risk assessment as

The identification, assessment, and implementation of key security controls in applications and systems. It also focuses on preventing application and systems security defects and vulnerabilities.

SANS[11] provides further clarification of the core areas of the risk assessment process that you should be including in the development of your risk assessment practices:

- Scope

- Data Collection

- Analysis of Policies and Procedures

- Threat Analysis

- Vulnerability Analysis

- Correlation and assessment of Risk Acceptability

Background

I was first introduced to formal Security Risk Management practices during my attendance of the RAF Police's 10-week residential Counter Intelligence course, in 2002, through the application of the Royal Air Force's Air Publication 3085 (Risk Management in the RAF) and the supporting Air Publication 3085A (tactics, techniques, and protocols (TTPs) for

---

[10]www.synopsys.com/glossary/what-is-security-risk-assessment.html

[11]www.sans.org/reading-room/whitepapers/auditing/overview-threat-risk-assessment-76

Risk Management in the RAF). These publications outlined the expectations for effective risk management, including the four Ts model[12] of risk treatment:

• **T**erminate risk	*Altering processes or practices to eliminate risk completely.*
• **T**reat risk	*Controlling risk through actions that reduce the likelihood of the risk occurring or minimize its impact prior to its occurrence.*
• **T**olerate risk	*No action is taken to mitigate or reduce a risk (it still needs to be monitored).*
• **T**ransfer risk	*Assigning an individual, group, or third party to be responsible for the risk.*

During my further studies in Risk Management (a module Loughborough University's Security Management MSc[13] and ISACA's Certified Information Security Manager (CISM[14]) and certified in risk and information systems control (CRISC[15])), the same treatment options are presented but using different synonyms, which are not as easy to readily recall:

- Avoid

- Mitigate

- Accept

- Transfer

Consequently, I still tend to favor the use of the four Ts model of Risk Treatment.

Before you can carry out an effective risk assessment, you need to ensure that you have developed sufficient risk scenarios[16] for your various processes that support your payment card processes to ensure that an appropriate level of risk has been assessed for the effective protection of your payment card processing, based upon the balance of the risk elements for your business:

$$\textbf{Business Risk} \ = \ \text{Vulnerability} \times \text{Threat} \times \text{Impact}$$

---

[12]www.skillcast.com/blog/10-things-you-should-do-to-improve-risk-management-at-work

[13]www.lboro.ac.uk/students/programme-specifications/2013/business-and-economics/postgraduate/name-56595-en.html

[14]www.isaca.org/Certification/Documents/CISM-Certification-Overview_bro_eng_0519.pdf

[15]www.isaca.org/Certification/Documents/CRISC-Certification-Overview_bro_eng_0519.pdf

[16]www.isaca.org/Knowledge-Center/Research/ResearchDeliverables/Pages/Risk-Scenarios-Using-COBIT-5-for-Risk.aspx

Appropriate risk assessments should be based upon realistic, business aligned scenarios. Such scenarios should be based upon input on your specific business processes that may impact your payment card operations.

Within the current version of PCI DSS (v3.2.1), the guidance column provides extensive context on the threats and risks that these controls have been designed to mitigate against.

PCI DSS Requirements	Testing Procedure	Guidance

Figure 5-4. PCI DSS Threat and Risk Guidance

Note:

The PCI SSC have intimated that risk will have a greater importance with the release of the next version of the PCI DSS integrated controls framework:

Goals for PCI DSS v4.0

The 12 core PCI DSS requirements are not expected to fundamentally change with PCI DSS v4.0, as these are still the critical foundation for securing payment card data. However, based on feedback received, PCI SSC is evaluating how to evolve the standard to accommodate changes in technology, risk mitigation techniques, and the threat landscape. PCI SSC is also looking at ways to introduce greater flexibility to support organizations using a broad range of controls and methods to meet security objectives.

Key high-level goals for PCI DSS v4.0 are

Ensure the standard continues to meet the security needs of the payments industry.

Add flexibility and support of additional methodologies to achieve security.

Promote security as a continuous process.

Enhance validation methods and procedures.

Scenario Development

The starting point for carrying out effective risk assessments in order to satisfy the existing PCI DSS risk control requirements (e.g., Do the firewall rulesets prevent unauthorized network traffic flows (are ANY/ANY rules prohibited? Are any identified vulnerabilities risk ranked based upon both the industry best practices (e.g., Exploit DB,[17] NVD,[18] CVE,[19] CVSS,[20] etc.) and local considerations?)) and expectations[21] is the creation of appropriate risk/threat scenarios, upon which you can develop risk assessments, identify mitigation controls, and develop aligned incident response plans.

Appropriate scenarios need to be developed so that they are appropriate, credible, and plausible for your organization.

Think Like an Attacker

Your attackers will spend time planning and evaluating your corporate environment, so that they can define, validate, and formalize their best attack options. Consequently, it is essential that you apply the same approach in helping to identify your defenses and formalize your risk assessment scenarios.

To effectively achieve this, before creating your scenarios, you need to spend time planning for the scenario development, so that you understand the assets that are to be included in the scenario, the perceived threats/threat actors, and the personnel that might be impacted by the scenario.

---

[17]www.exploit-db.com/

[18]https://nvd.nist.gov/

[19]https://cve.mitre.org/cve/

[20]www.first.org/cvss/v3.1/user-guide

[21]www.pcisecuritystandards.org/documents/PCI_DSS_Risk_Assmt_Guidelines_v1.pdf

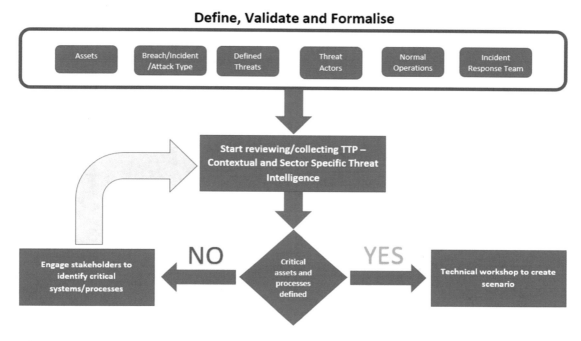

Figure 5-5. Scenario Preparation[22]

Having completed the planning phase, you can then start your technical workshop to create plausible risk assessment scenarios, in order to further develop your defensive capabilities and to assist you in articulating the risks to your business leaders.

Reviewing and applying the MITRE Att&ck resources,[23] you should apply the attackers' known tactics, techniques, and protocols (TTPs) to help create suitable risk/threat scenarios for your organization, based upon defined steps that should be followed:

1. Select target.

   • Critical Asset (Process, System, Users)

2. Review and identify potential threat actors for the target.

   • Threat attack library (TAL)

---

[22]Source: Cyber Management Alliance (www.cm-alliance.com)
[23]https://attack.mitre.org/

3.   Identify possible tactics[24] of the threat actors.

4.   Informally map tactics to the cyber kill chain[25]/cognitive attack loop[26] process.

5.   Review and apply techniques.[27]

6.   Review, validate, and apply techniques and procedures.

7.   Review, Evaluate, and Validate.

   • Past security assessments.

   • Audit findings.

   • Known vulnerabilities in systems, remaining unpatched.

8.   Confirm sufficient data to create a viable scenario.

   • Yes – Continue to step 9.

   • No – Return to step 2.

9.   Review and formally map[28] against the cyber kill chain/cognitive attack loop process.

10.   Formally map existing security controls against the five Ds of Defense (Deter, Detect, Delay, Deny, and Defend).[29]

11.   Review effectiveness of the existing controls and check with audit team.

   • Configure and optimize.

   • Identify any missing controls and describe their role in addressing the threats.

12.   Confirm scenario and create business case for any additional controls.

---

[24]https://attack.mitre.org/tactics/enterprise/

[25]www.bulletproof.co.uk/blog/what-is-the-cyber-kill-chain

[26]www.carbonblack.com/2019/07/31/introducing-the-cognitive-attack-loop-and-the-3-phases-of-cybercriminal-behavior/

[27]https://attack.mitre.org/techniques/pre/

[28]www.varonis.com/blog/mitre-attck-framework-complete-guide/

[29]https://alamom.com/5defense/

13.   Confirm scenario and complete risk scenario worksheet.

14.   Share and discuss risk scenario worksheet with stakeholders and incident response team.

15.   Enhance risk scenario based upon any feedback received.

Risk Scenarios

Well-prepared risk scenarios help create realistic and business-relevant descriptions of events that could have a real impact *(both positive and negative)* on your business and something that your business should be prepared for. By involving a variety of stakeholders, from across your business, you will help ensure that both the top-down *(analysis of the current and most relevant and probable business risks)* and the bottom-up *(employing generic risk scenarios to define a suite of business relevant and customizable scenarios (a starting point for discussion))* approaches. Each scenario should be linked to your real business risks and be prioritized against your most critical business processes/systems.

- ***Documenting the "What If" question***

ISACAs have created a very helpful toolkit[30] to support your development of risk scenarios that are specific to your organization, as well as providing you with over 50 example risk scenarios. Each scenario incorporates the five key areas that your key stakeholders would need to understand, so that they can make an informed decision as to whether this scenario is being effectively managed within their risk appetite/tolerance.

---

[30]www.isaca.org/Knowledge-Center/Research/Documents/Risk-Scenarios-Toolkit_tkt_ Eng_0914.zip

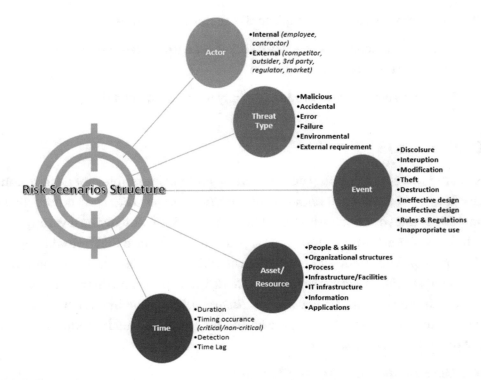

Figure 5-6. *Risk Scenarios Structure*

Embedding effective risk scenarios as part of your enterprise risk management practices has considerable benefits. However, their creation must ensure that this is based on suitable representation of realistic, unbiased, and reliable content to provide assurance to senior management that they are making risk decisions based upon good quality information. This will aid management's ability to identify, analyze, and respond to risks that are pertinent to their business areas of responsibility. Consequently, the scenarios need to incorporate the following characteristics:

- **Relevance**

  Provide meaningful information, appropriate to the factors that are relevant to your business.

- **Consistency**

  Each scenario should be compelling in itself based upon the credibility and completeness of the content.

- **Plausibility**

    Ensure that they are believable and realistic to your organization.

- **Likelihood**

    To some extent, there must be a higher chance of the scenario occurring.

- **Currency**

    Ensure that the scenarios reflect current threats to your business type.

The following data is an example of a completed Risk Scenario worksheet[31] based upon an e-Commerce retailer.

Risk Scenario
Risk Scenario Title: Formjacking Attack
Risk Scenario Category 16: Logical Attack on e-Commerce operations
Risk Scenario A vulnerability in a web page, in the earlier steps of the customer journey, allows an attacker to inject malicious code into an out-of-scope web page. However, this web page is part of the customer's e-Commerce journey. Consequently, although the e-Commerce operation has been fully outsourced, so that all payment card details are entered through a PCI DSS compliant payment service provider (PSP) interface, the vulnerability in out-of-scope business web pages presents an association to the PSP interface. This enables the potential for an attacker to exploit the "out-of-scope" web pages to carry out a man-in-the-middle (MITM) attack, where the customer's journey is diverted through their systems before getting to the PSP. As a result, the customer remains unaware that the attacker is carrying out clandestine harvesting of their personal and payment card information being entered into the PSP interface.

(continued)

---

[31]Adapted from ISACA, COBIT 5 for Risk, USA, 2013, www.isaca.org/cobit, pp. 243-244.

Risk Scenario
Risk Scenario Components

Threat Type The nature of the event	✓ **Malicious** ☐ **Accidental** ☐ **Error** ☐ **Failure** ☐ **Natural** ☐ **External requirement**
Actor Who or what triggers the threat that exploits a vulnerability?	☐ **Internal** ✓ **External** ☐ **Human** ☐ **Non-human**
Event Something happens that was not supposed to happen, something does not happen that was supposed to happen, or a change in circumstances. Events always have causes and usually have consequences. A consequence is the outcome of an event and has an impact on objectives.	✓ **Disclosure** ☐ **Interruption** ✓ **Modification** ✓ **Theft** ☐ **Destruction** ☐ **Ineffective design** ☐ **Ineffective execution** ☐ **Rules and regulations** ☐ **Inappropriate use**

Risk Scenario	
Asset An asset is something of either tangible or intangible value that is worth protecting, including people, systems, infrastructure, finances, and reputation.	☐ **Process** ☐ **People and Skills** ☐ **Organizational Structure** ☐ **Physical Infrastructure** ✓ **IT Infrastructure** ✓ **Information** ✓ **Applications**
Resource A resource is anything that helps to achieve a goal.	✓ **Process** ✓ **People and Skills** ☐ **Organizational Structure** ☐ **Physical Infrastructure** ✓ **IT Infrastructure** ✓ **Information** ✓ **Applications**
Time	**Timing Duration** ☐ Non-Critical ✓ Critical ☐ Extended **Detection Time** ☐ Short ✓ Moderate ☐ Instant **Lag** ☐ Slow ✓ Moderate ✓ Immediate ☐ Delayed

Risk Type

The nature of this malicious act enables an attacker to exploit vulnerabilities in the corporation's web site to steal customer sensitive information.

Risk Type	P/S	Risk Description
IT Benefit/Value Enablement		**N/A**

(continued)

Risk Scenario		
IT Program and Project Delivery		**N/A**
IT Operations and Service Delivery	**P**	**Security Problems**
	P	**Breach of Data Privacy Regulations**
	S	**Breach of PCI DSS compliance**
Possible Risk Responses		
Terminate	N/A	
Tolerate	The Board makes the decision that no attacker would be interested in attacking the customer journeys.	
Transfer	Procure the additional services of a third party to monitor the "out-of-scope" web pages.	
Treat	Include all "out-of-scope" corporate web sites into the PCI DSS scope, ensuring that all applicable PCI DSS controls are applied.	
Risk Mitigation		
Principles, Policies, and Frameworks Enabler		

Reference	Contribution to Response	Effect on Frequency	Effect on Impact	Essential Control
Information Security Policy	Outline information security arrangements for the protection of payment card data	**HIGH**	**HIGH**	**YES**
Data Privacy Policy	Outline the data handling rules for safeguarding personal data	**HIGH**	**HIGH**	**YES**
Secure Development policies and procedures	Detail the software development consequences for the insecure software development impact on the information security policy	**HIGH**	**HIGH**	**YES**

Risk Scenario					
Secure Software Development principles	Information security requirements are embedded within the software development practices	**HIGH**	**HIGH**	**YES**	
Process Enabler					
Reference		Title Description	Governance and Management Practices	Effect on Frequency	Effect on Impact	Essential Control
NIST CSF	PCI DSS					
ID.AM-2	2.4 12.3.7	Software platforms and applications within the organization are inventoried.	Identify all web page interfaces and connections.	**MEDIUM**	**HIGH**	**YES**
I.D.AM-5	12.2	Resources (e.g., hardware, devices, data, time, and software) are prioritized based on their classification, criticality, and business value.	Identify potential web site interfaces that could impact e-Commerce operations.	**LOW**	**HIGH**	**YES**
PR.DS-6	11.5	Integrity checking mechanisms are used to verify software, firmware, and information integrity.	Monitor web page integrity.	**MEDIUM**	**LOW**	**YES**

(continued)

Risk Scenario						
PR.DS-7	6.4.1 6.4.2	The development and testing environment(s) are separate from the production environment.	Secure Software development practices.	**MEDIUM**	**MEDIUM**	**YES**
DE.CM-7	10.1 10.6.1 11.5 12.10.5	Monitoring for unauthorized personnel, connections, devices, and software is performed.	Monitor web page changes.	**MEDIUM**	**MEDIUM**	**YES**
PR.IP-2	6.3 6.4 6.5 6.7	A Software Development Life Cycle to manage systems is implemented.	Apply secure software development and testing principles.	**MEDIUM**	**HIGH**	**YES**
ID.RA-2	6.1	Cyber threat intelligence and vulnerability information is received from information-sharing forums and sources.	Identify potential web attack interfaces.	**MEDIUM**	**HIGH**	**YES**
ID.RA-4	6.1	Potential business impacts and likelihoods are identified.	Identify risks with vulnerabilities on out-of-scope web interfaces.	**MEDIUM**	**HIGH**	**YES**

Risk Scenario						
PR.IP-12	6.1 6.2	A vulnerability management plan is developed and implemented.	Apply timely identification and remediation of vulnerabilities.	**LOW**	**HIGH**	**YES**
RS.AN-5	6.1 6.2	Processes are established to receive, analyze, and respond to vulnerabilities disclosed to the organization from internal and external sources (e.g., internal testing, security bulletins, or security researchers).	Vulnerabilities are identified and prioritized based on potential impact.	**MEDIUM**	**HIGH**	**YES**
RS.MI-3	6.1 6.2 10.63 11.2 11.5.1 12.5.2 12.10	Newly identified vulnerabilities are mitigated or documented as accepted risks.	Vulnerabilities are identified, risk assessed, and prioritized based on potential impact.	**MEDIUM**	**HIGH**	**YES**

(*continued*)

Risk Scenario				
Organizational Structures Enabler				
Reference	**Contribution to Response**	**Effect on Frequency**	**Effect on Impact**	**Essential Control**
Information Security Manager	Implement security measures	HIGH	HIGH	YES
Data Privacy Officer	Implement data privacy measures	HIGH	HIGH	YES
Service Manager	In case attacks are successful, help manage the response	LOW	HIGH	YES
SCRUM Manager	Design security measures	HIGH	HIGH	YES
Culture, Ethics, and Behavior Enabler				
Reference	**Contribution to Response**	**Effect on Frequency**	**Effect on Impact**	**Essential Control**
PCI DSS secure development practices are part of BAU.	Prevent web application attacks	HIGH	LOW	YES
Developers respect the importance of secure web development practices.	Prevent web application attacks	HIGH	LOW	YES
Stakeholders are aware of how to identify and respond to threats.	Prevent web application attacks	MEDIUM	HIGH	YES

Risk Scenario				
Information Enabler				
Reference	**Contribution to Response**	**Effect on Frequency**	**Effect on Impact**	**Essential Control**
Threat information reports	Intelligence reports on web-based attacks	**HIGH**	**MEDIUM**	**YES**
Monitoring reports	Identify attack attempts, threat events, etc.	**MEDIUM**	**HIGH**	**YES**
Services, Infrastructure, and Applications Enabler				
Reference	**Contribution to Response**	**Effect on Frequency**	**Effect on Impact**	**Essential Control**
Web application testing and monitoring	Identify weaknesses	**HIGH**	**LOW**	**YES**
Monitoring and alert services	Timely notification of potential threats	**LOW**	**HIGH**	**YES**
People, Skills, and Competencies Enabler				
Reference	**Contribution to Response**	**Effect on Frequency**	**Effect on Impact**	**Essential Control**
PCI DSS security skills	Prevent and reduce the impact of web-based attacks	**HIGH**	**HIGH**	**YES**
Secure Software Development skills	Maintain secure software development practices	**HIGH**	**HIGH**	**YES**

(continued)

Risk Scenario
Key Risk Indicators (KRIs) Related to IT Goals
<ul><li>Percentage of critical business processes, IT services, and IT-enabled business programs covered by the risk assessment</li><li>No. of significant IT-related incidents that were not identified in the risk assessment</li><li>Percentage of corporate risk assessments included IT-related risk</li><li>Frequency of update of the risk profile</li><li>No. of security incidents causing financial loss, business disruption, or reputational damage</li><li>No. of IT services with outstanding security requirements</li><li>Frequency of security assessments against latest standards and guidelines</li></ul>
Key Risk Indicators (KRIs) Related to Process Goals
<ul><li>Percentage of critical operational event types covered by automated detection systems</li><li>No. external facing business systems not covered by the business continuity plan/incident response plan</li><li>No. of out-of-scope web pages that could potentially impact the in-scope environment</li><li>No. of vulnerabilities discovered on out-of-scope web pages</li><li>Percentage of periodic testing of external digital public-facing web pages</li><li>No. of incidents relating to unauthorized access to information</li></ul>

The use of scenario development can be seen being used by NASA in support of their Technical Risk Management process.

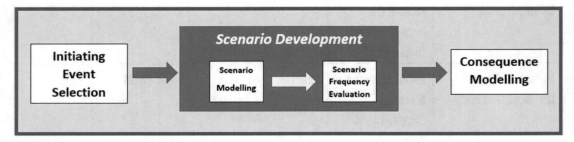

Figure 5-7. *NASA Scenario Development Process*[32]

---

[32]www.nasa.gov/seh/6-4-technical-risk-management

Risk Assessment Process

Having created your suite of appropriate and credible risk assessment scenarios, you are then able to start applying your risk assessment processes to ensure that the risks are effectively articulated to Senior Management. This will ensure that any risks remain within your businesses risk tolerances/appetites and will ensure that senior management have sufficient data to make informed risk decisions and ensuring that this answers their "So What?" questions in regard to any identified risks (Vulnerability × Threat × Impact).

Remember, your Senior Management have got to where they are in their careers because they are good at doing business and not because they are risk or security experts. Consequently, you need to ensure that only relevant/critical risks are communicated to them for their attention and that these messages are articulated in a manner that is concise and presented in a way that is easy for them to understand *(avoid the unnecessary use of technical or Cyber/InfoSec specific terminologies)*.

Try using concise methodologies to effectively articulate the results of your risk assessments, such as

   FAIR (Factor Analysis of Information Risk)

   BRA (Binary Risk Analysis)

   CIS RAM (Center for Internet Security Risk Assessment Method)

   DoD RMF (Risk Management Framework)

Whichever risk assessment process you decide to apply, it needs to be consistently applied across your business. For example, both the NIST SP800-30, r1,[33] and FAIR employ four distinct steps to their risk assessment processes.

---

[33]https://nvlpubs.nist.gov/nistpubs/Legacy/SP/nistspecialpublication800-30r1.pdf

Stage	NIST SP800-30 r1	FAIR
1	**Prepare for assessment** • Derived from Organizational Risk Frame	**Identify scenario components** • Identify the asset at risk • Identify the threat community under consideration
2	**Conduct assessment** • Identify Threat Sources and Events • Identify Vulnerabilities and Predisposing Conditions • Determine Likelihood of Occurrence • Determine Magnitude of Impact • Determine Risk	**Evaluate loss event frequency (LEF)** • Estimate the probable threat event frequency (TEF) • Estimate the threat capability (TCap) • Estimate control strength (CS) • Derive Vulnerability (Vuln) • Derive loss event frequency (LEF)
3	**Communicate results**	**Evaluate probable loss magnitude (PLM)** • Estimate worst case loss • Estimate probable loss magnitude (PLM)
4	**Maintain assessment**	**Derive and articulate risk**

PCI DSS does not stipulate the risk assessment methodology that you apply to support your risk management process, only that you have a formalized and consistent approach that is reviewed on an annual basis. The most difficult part of the risk assessment process is being able to articulate and communicate this in a manner that means something to your senior management, for example:

- **PCAN** (Problem, Cause, Answers, and Net Benefits)

- **BSC** (Balanced Score Cards)[34]

- **KRI** (Key Risk Indicator) Heat Maps/Matrices[35]

- **Risk Dashboard**[36]

---

[34]http://iia.org.au/sf_docs/default-source/technical-resources/2018-whitepapers/iia-whitepaper_balanced-scorecard-reporting.pdf?sfvrsn=2

[35]https://riskmanagementguru.com/risk-matrices-pros-cons-and-alternatives.html/

[36]https://acuityrm.com/platform

Reality Bites

As you can well imagine, having had an extremely challenging and rewarding career in the RAF Police, I have received considerable exposure to risk assessments and the applicability of new policies and procedures as the result of risk assessments.

As well as creating pre-deployment training scenarios based upon known enemy tactics, the RAF needed to keep their training current to ensure that personnel were fully aware of the countermeasures that needed to be applied. Although some scenarios could have been imagined using in house, there were some external influences from events that helped forge new scenarios, for example:

- In between my deployments to Afghanistan, the policies needed to be changed to reflect the prohibition of the use personal mobile telephones when deployed into the country. Why? There had been incidents of families/loved ones receiving malicious calls from unknown actors, who had stated that they had captured their husband/wife and were going to harm/kill them. This caused unnecessary distress for the families/loved ones, at home, and caused dangerous distractions for the deployed personnel. Clearly, the local mobile telephone network had been compromised, enabling the interception of communications to aid malicious call making.

- During pre-deployment training for deployment to Iraq, I received training into the newly developed protective countermeasures that had been developed to protect patrols from the new insurgent tactics use of an enhanced improvised explosive device (IED), where the insurgents would use metal pipes/paint tins to make explosive formed projectiles (EFPs)[37]. These devices were designed to focus a smaller explosive charge into a projectile that could penetrate the semi-armored skin of military patrol vehicles, whereas the traditional IED needed larger explosives to have the equivalent impact on their target.

[37]https://laststandonzombieisland.com/2013/08/30/explosively-formed-penetrators-for-dummies/

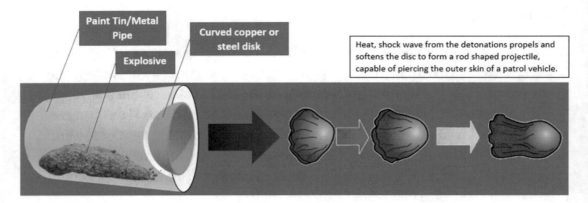

Figure 5-8. *EFP*

- During a deployment in Oman, providing security support to Operation Enduring Freedom's[38] air operations, I was suddenly tasked with carrying out an operational risk assessment for the short-notice deployment of 15 RAF Police personnel into Kabul. I had been requested to lead a team to provide Air Transport Security and Air Marshal support to the RAF Hercules detachment. They had been tasked with providing air transportation for Afghan local nationals' pilgrimage from Kabul to Mecca.

  This was a high-risk task that needed comprehensive identification of potential threats, risk analysis, and treatment to ensure that the crew, passengers, and aircraft were transported safely and securely.

  - *Part of the risk treatment included a business justification for the commandeering and redeploying a mobile X-ray machine that has been loaded onto a freight aircraft bound for return to the United Kingdom.*

In the corporate environment, the threat may not be as significant as that related to the potential loss of lives, but the enemies are as present, and the risks to your business remain high. Consequently, having an established and integrated approach to risk

---

[38]https://edition.cnn.com/2013/10/28/world/operation-enduring-freedom-fast-facts/index.html

assessment continues to represent a vital component of safeguarding your card payment and critical operations from harm, for example:

- In the event of an outage, caused through a third-party system as a service (SaaS) provider's management of a critical system, causing a significant impact on the ability of a Bank's customers to access their bank accounts or make any payments through their Bank credit card. As a consequence, the Regulators demanded a formal risk assessment, within a very short timescale, to outline how the organization was going to manage this risk and minimize the impact on their customers.

- *Overseeing a hurriedly put together risk assessment workshop with the IT team members, I was able to formulate a risk treatment plan that provided the Chief Information Officer with a number of viable risk options. As a consequence, they were able to make an informed decision on the most suitable option for the organization and to present this formal risk assessment and treatment plan to satisfy the Regulators demands.*

Recommendations

Consider the potential advantages of integrating the six main PCI DSS control areas that are associated with risk assessment to act as the catalyst for the development of appropriate risk scenarios:

- Use the results of quarterly vulnerability scanning to create plausible risk assessment scenarios.

- Use the results of your monitoring/alerting practices to help create plausible risk assessment scenarios.

- Use the results of the annual penetration testing to create plausible risk assessment scenarios.

- Use the risk assessment scenarios as contributions for the incident response playbooks and annual security incident response testing.

- Engage with your third-party suppliers to ensure that the risk scenarios incorporate any transferred risks.

- Ensure that the risk assessment is done as part of a cohesive team effort using a well-practiced formal risk assessment process that draws input from team members across various business departments.

Conclusion

Many businesses increasingly regard the risk assessment control (12.2) as an isolated *"tick box"* requirement. However, the reality is that having an effective risk assessment process is essential that the application of your baseline catalogue of PCI DSS controls remains effective, to ensure that senior management understand the inherent risks that still remain despite the maintenance of PCI DSS and to ensure that you have an effective risk management process that can quickly adapt, and respond, to different scenarios *(learning from new threats and incidents within your industry).*

Risk assessment should be applied to your assurance activities and emerging business processes, as well as against newly identified threats. Failure to develop effective risk assessment practices can significantly increase your potential for suffering a system compromise or data breach.

The transfer of responsibilities to a third party (e.g., Payment Service Provider, Data Center (Physical Security), Cloud provider (Infrastructure), etc.) does not absolve you of the need to employ suitable vendor management practices.[39]

For further reading on this, check out James Broder and Gene Tucker's book,[40]where they add further clarification on the criticality that your risk processes provide in securing your payment card operations, business critical systems, and sensitive data operations, as well as being a component of your PCI DSS compliance program.

Key Takeaways

Risk assessment is engrained throughout the PCI DSS integrated controls framework and, as a result, should be at the forefront of your compliance programs.

---

[39]www.isaca.org/Knowledge-Center/Research/ResearchDeliverables/Pages/Vendor-Management-Using-COBIT5.aspx

[40]Broder, J. and Tucker, E. (2012). *Risk Analysis and the Security Survey*. Waltham, MA: Butterworth-Heinemann.

PCI DSS is a catalogue of baseline security controls that are developed and maintained by the PCI SSC to assist you in minimizing the risks associated to your payment card business operations.

However, when carrying out any assurance work on the PCI DSS controls, you should understand the risks that these controls have been designed to mitigate against.

Risk assessments should be developed using input from threat intelligence and vulnerability resources to help create plausible and accepted scenarios, involving input from various representations across various business departments.

The risk assessment process needs to be formalized and consistent to provide senior management with concise and simple risk messages (avoiding lengthy, technical, or Cyber/InfoSec narratives).

Does your business understand the "Green Cross Code"?

Do you employ a team approach to risk assessment?

Do you understand the threats and risks that a specific PCI DSS control is designed to mitigate?

Are you wireless defensive controls marked as being not applicable, because you don't use wireless technologies?

If these controls are deemed to be N/A, how are you mitigating against the use of rogue wireless devices?

How do you clearly articulate any identified critical risks to Senior Management?

Risks

Failure to identify and analyze new and existing risks, to be communicated back to the business, may expose your business to well-known threats.

In addition, your business will be poorly prepared to respond to both well-known and newly identified threats.

Effective risk practices require the application of the five Ps:

Prior

Planning

Prevents

Poor

Performance

Poor performance can undermine your compliance efforts and your ability to apply an effective security incident response process. As a consequence, your risk of a system compromise or data breach may significantly increase.

Ask yourself:

Do I have a formalized risk assessment process?

Is my risk assessment process consistent across the business and involving widespread departmental representation?

Do I employ an integrated approach to risk assessment scenario development?

Are my scenarios kept current and relevant developed from threat intelligence inputs that are relevant to your industry?

Do I apply risk assessment against well-known and emerging threats?

Are risks identified and analyzed in a timely manner, with the results communicated to senior management?

Does my risk assessment output contribute to the security incident response playbooks?

CHAPTER 6

Risk Management vs. Compliance – The Differentiator

Although the current version of the PCI DSS integrated security controls framework incorporates the requirement for entities to implement an annual risk assessment process, where critical assets, threats, and vulnerabilities are identified and the results analyzed and formally documented, this is often seen as a one of tick box control within their compliance program.

By restricting this to only risk assessing your PCI DSS environment, you reduce your options for better safeguarding your payment card processes and operations.

Think of it like the analogy of trying to cross the road   By only considering a risk assessment against the implemented PCI DSS security controls, you are restricting yourself to the practice of navigating the crossing of the road to the "Stop, Look, and Listen" rules. However, if you were to apply the wider remit of Risk Management, you are provided with sufficient data to be able to make informed decisions on the other options you may wish to consider treating this risk:

Is there a nearby bridge that I could use to go over the traffic?

Can I choose to stop the traffic using a pedestrian crossing?

Is there a Crossing Guard, Lollypop Man/Lady, Crosswalk Assistant, or School Road Assistant?

© Jim Seaman 2020
J. Seaman, *PCI DSS*, https://doi.org/10.1007/978-1-4842-5808-8_6

Failure to think wider than the risk assessment could mean that you have to wait far longer for a safe point to navigate through busy, speeding traffic. This could lead to you becoming impatient and making unsafe decisions to cross when it is too risky to do so.

In truth, the Risk Assessment process is only a small element of the Risk Management process and, by incorporating and embedding the entire risk management process into your PCI DSS compliance, will help you enhance your ability to make informed decisions on the effective risk treatment of your payment card processes and supporting systems, rather than being solely reliant on the PCI DSS catalogue of security controls.

This is clearly visible in SRMAM's[1] Risk Management overview diagrams.

---

[1]www.srmam.com/

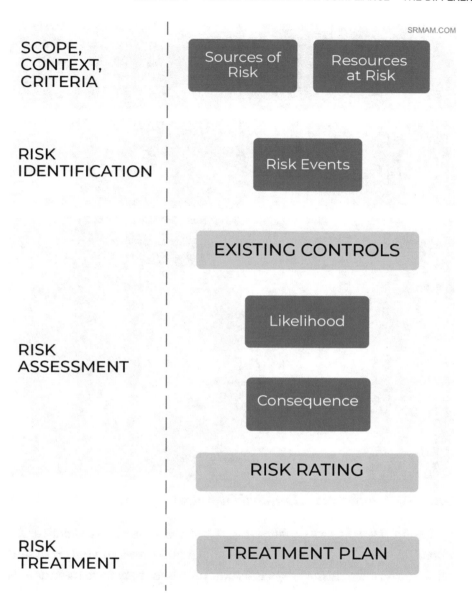

Figure 6-1. *Risk Detailed High-Level Overview*

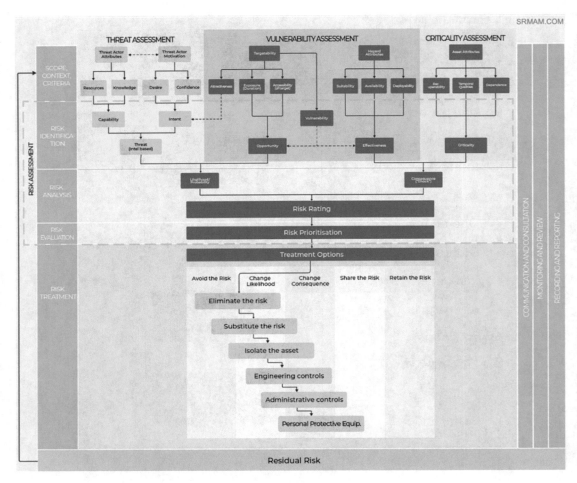

Figure 6-2. *Risk Management Detailed Overview*

Consequently, if you were to integrate your 12.2 risk assessment practices for PCI DSS compliance into your overall risk management processes, you may well find that risks pertaining to critical business systems and processes may have treatment options that will help enhance the defenses of your in-scope systems and processes.

By having an enterprise-wide security risk management process (PCI DSS incorporated within), you enhance the incorporation of the risk assessment element of your PCI DSS compliance into business-as-usual (BAU) operations and enhance making PCI DSS compliance a business enabler *(often this can be regarded as being the fifth T of risk management – Take the opportunity).*

Using a corporate approach to Risk Management, you will categorize and define all your assets and resources, based upon their criticality, and potential impact to the business. These can then be grouped or tagged to make them easily recognizable and prioritize based upon their potential value to your business, for example:

- **Categories**
  - PCI DSS Scope
  - Intangible
  - Tangible
  - Operational
  - Utilities
  - Personnel
  - Infrastructure
- **Asset Groups**
  - Employees and Contractors
  - Visitors
  - Brand and Reputation
  - Finances
  - Buildings and Equipment
  - Technology Asset

Why not use the simple "PIPER" mnemonic to help you with categorizing your business assets?

Table 6-1. *PIPER Mnemonic*

PIPER		
• **P**eople	Staff	
	Contractors	
	Stakeholders	
	Visitors	
	Suppliers	
• **I**nformation	Payment card data	
	Intellectual	
	Customer personal data records	
	Employee personal data	
• **P**roperty	Buildings	
	Data Centers	
	Equipment	
	Communications Technology	
• **E**conomic	Revenue and Income	
	Capital	
	Contingent capital (e.g., Cyber insurance)	
• **R**eputation	Brand	
	Media coverage	
	Social media	

Introduction

It is important to understand the differences between a data privacy and security program and a PCI DSS compliance program. An effective data privacy and security program has its main focus on risk managing the threats through the application of effective mitigation controls, whereas a typical PCI DSS compliance program *(PCI DSS v3.2.1)* has a focus on the control's management. This can lead to a narrowed vision with all the effort being made to only meet the minimum control requirements, as per your *(or the QSA's)* interpretations of the controls. An overview of the differing perspectives can be seen in Figure 6-3.

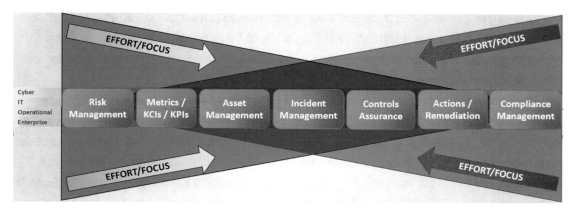

Figure 6-3. *Risk Management vs. Compliance*

The term compliance creates in peoples' minds of businesses being pressed into achieving and maintaining compliance against the PCI DSS. As a result, organizations are often seen to result in a "Tick Box," minimum effort needed to achieve PCI DSS compliance. However, in regard to the changing threats of cyber-crime and data privacy regulations, is it time for the industry to consider stopping to use the term compliance?

"The act of obeying an order, rule, or request[2]"

Data processing has become an integral part of modern business operations, so why are companies so reluctant to invest in ensuring that adequate protection and employee awareness is established?

In the United Kingdom, all drivers are legally required to have their vehicles subject to an annual safety check (a.k.a. an MOT). If this vehicle was a significant part of your business, would you consider only relying on your annual MOT to ensure that your motor vehicle remains compliant to with the road safety requirements?

- *Imagine that you are doing an average of 20,000 miles between MOT checks, when the average life of a tire is 36,000–45,000 miles!*

---

[2]https://dictionary.cambridge.org/dictionary/english/compliance

Despite the fact that reliance on payment card data operations has become an increasingly important part of the business, organizations still favor doing the bare minimum needed to pass their annual PCI DSS MOT and do not appreciate the importance of carrying out frequent checks and maintenance using suitably skilled and experienced mechanics. In the United Kingdom, to be licensed to drive a vehicle on the public highway, the learner drivers need to be able to show a proficiency in carrying out basic vehicle safety checks.[3]

However, it is important to remember that the reason for the changes to the data privacy regulations came as a result of a lack of confidence the consumers had in the way businesses respect and safeguard their personal data, and this continues to be at the forefront of consumers' minds. Consequently, if you are a business that relies on their customers entrusting them with their payment card data, in exchange for the purchase of goods or services, PCI DSS should be regarded as the starting point for the safeguarding of your customers' payment card data. Additionally, the principles of the PCI DSS catalogue of controls can be a great resource to help you safeguard your consumers' personal data processing operations.

PCI DSS Is Not a Legal Requirement...
...But Should Be a Business Requirement?

Much like other information security standards and frameworks (e.g., COBIT 2019, NIST Cyber Security Framework, ISO/IEC 27001:2013, etc.), PCI DSS is not a legal requirement. However, you should make it a business requirement as the Information Commissioner's Office[4] have stated that, in the event of a breach, they will consider the effectiveness of the PCI DSS technical and organizational controls to help safeguard personal data.

---

[3]www.gov.uk/government/publications/car-show-me-tell-me-vehicle-safety-questions/car-show-me-tell-me-vehicle-safety-questions

[4]https://ico.org.uk/for-organisations/guide-to-data-protection/guide-to-the-general-data-protection-regulation-gdpr/security/

If you are processing payment card data, you are obliged to comply with the Payment Card Industry Data Security Standard ⬀. The PCI-DSS outlines a number of specific technical and organisational measures that the payment card industry considers applicable whenever such data is being processed.

Although compliance with the PCI-DSS is not necessarily equivalent to compliance with the GDPR's security principle, if you process card data and suffer a personal data breach, the ICO will consider the extent to which you have put in place measures that PCI-DSS requires particularly if the breach related to a lack of a particular control or process mandated by the standard.

Figure 6-4. *Extract from ICO*

Consequently, if your business wants to do right by your consumers, you should prioritize the risk management of your payment card and personal data processing operations as an integral part of your organization and to ensure that you are effectively applying the PCI DSS controls to mitigate both the external and internal threats to your payment card data operations.

Cyber criminals are opportunists who seek to exploit vulnerabilities that are presented to them. As a result, your PCI DSS program should be risk focused looking at the following perspectives:

Vulnerabilities × Threats × Impacts

With a decreasing rate of businesses that are managing to maintaining PCI DSS compliance (most companies struggle to meet the Payment Card Industry Data Security Standard (PCI DSS), the set of regulations created to keep credit and debit card data secure, with just 52% in compliance, down from 55% in 2017) and an increasing rate of cases of identity theft and payment card breaches, isn't it time for your business to embrace PCI DSS as part of your organization's risk management practices?

Concept

Rather than regarding the protection of your consumers' payment card information as a mandatory obligation, look at this as being a business investment to ensure that your most critical business systems and operations are secured to a level that your business feels comfortable with *(Risk Appetite, Risk Tolerance, etc.)*.

Within your business, you will have a number of critical data paths (e.g., Intellectual Property, Customer data, Account information, Marketing, etc.), and for the payment card industry, these are termed as payment channels[5] (e.g., e-Commerce, mail order telephone order (MOTO), face to face, mobile, etc.). It is essential that these critical data paths be appropriately risk managed and protected by a company-wide security strategy, with the payment channels (involving payment card) having the PCI DSS security controls applied against them.

Essentially, you are likely to have a hierarchy of different critical data paths where you may choose to use a single data security controls framework or a "mix and match" suite of data security controls framework to ensure that your business has a suitable defensive profile, for example:

- **Corporate Governance**

  - COBIT 2019[6]

- **Cyber Resiliency**

  - NIST SP 800-160, v2[7]

- **Public-facing, Internet-facing, business operations**

  - CIS 20 Critical Security Controls, v7.1[8]

- **MOTO and e-Commerce**

  - PCI DSS, v3.2.1[9]

---

[5]https://blog.pcisecuritystandards.org/securing-emerging-payment-channels
[6]www.isaca.org/cobit/pages/default.aspx
[7]https://csrc.nist.gov/publications/detail/sp/800-160/vol-2/final
[8]www.cisecurity.org/controls/cis-controls-list/
[9]www.pcisecuritystandards.org/documents/PCI_DSS_v3-2-1.pdf?agreement=true&t ime=1579004557174

- **Financial data**

    - Sarbanes-Oxley Act 2002 (SOX)[10]

- **Health Information**

    - Health Insurance Portability and Accountability Act 1996 (HIPPA)[11]

- **Manufacturing systems**

    - NIST SP800-82, r2[12]

- **Customer Personal Data Records**

    - ISO/IEC 27701:2019[13]

    - NIST Privacy Framework[14]

- **Company Sensitive Data Records**

    - ISO/IEC 27001:2013[15]

- **Securing Cloud Services**

    - ISO/IEC 27017:2015[16]

- **Personal Data Processing in Public Clouds**

    - ISO/IEC 27018:2019[17]

- **External Audit: Third-Party/Supplier Assurance**[18]

    - NIST Cyber Security Framework, v1.1[19]

---

[10]www.soxlaw.com/

[11]www.hhs.gov/hipaa/index.html

[12]https://nvlpubs.nist.gov/nistpubs/SpecialPublications/NIST.SP.800-82r2.pdf

[13]www.iso.org/standard/71670.html

[14]www.nist.gov/privacy-framework

[15]www.iso.org/standard/54534.html

[16]www.iso.org/standard/43757.html

[17]www.iso.org/standard/76559.html

[18]www.prevalent.net/compliance/nist-sp-800-53r4-and-nist-csf-v1-1-compliance/

[19]www.nist.gov/cyberframework

Each of these controls frameworks will have commonalities and need to be mapped against each other to ensure that there are no duplication of efforts and to ensure that a single common control[20] can be applied, where the control requirement is applied against multiple critical data paths. Without this, you will increase the potential for confusion and misinterpretation of the rules that apply to specific business operations.

Just the data privacy and security frameworks are complicated enough, without considering any other industry controls frameworks that may provide additional assurance and potential benefits to your business, for example:

- **Corporate Risk Management**

  - ISO 31000:2018[21]

- **Occupational Health and Safety**

  - ISO 45001:2018[22]

- **Quality Management**

  - ISO/IEC 9000[23]

Whichever standards or controls frameworks you are mandated, or choose, to apply, you need to ensure that they are effectively being applied to reduce your inherent risks to an acceptable level and that they can provide both continued assurance to your key stakeholders and any evidence needed for your compliance requirements.

In addition, it is important to remember that your data privacy and security programs are heavily reliant on the "Human Factor" and, as such, it is almost inevitable that mistakes will happen. Therefore, it is important that your various security controls frameworks can be periodically tracked and monitored against their effectiveness to reduce your business's inherent risks.

It is interesting to see that the Canadian Government have introduced the concept of Baseline Security Controls[24] as a recommended way for Canadian businesses to enhance their security profiles.

---

[20]https://commoncontrolshub.com/

[21]www.iso.org/iso-31000-risk-management.html

[22]www.iso.org/standard/63787.html

[23]www.iso.org/iso-9001-quality-management.html

[24]https://cyber.gc.ca/en/introduction-baseline-controls

In the case event of an event, system compromise, or data breach, how much support will your various controls programs provide to your business and how can these programs deliver the assurance expectations of your key stakeholders?

How Is This Achieved?

Measuring the effectiveness of your numerous controls should not be limited to a linear response (In Place/Not In Place) and especially not when you are measuring the effectiveness of a process. Therefore, it is beneficial that the "Human Factor" is measured based on the perceived maturity[25] of the process.

Periodic risk and control effectiveness reporting should be produced in the form of Information Security performance metrics[26] (e.g., key risk indicators (KRIs) and key performance indicators (KPIs)) to ensure that the key decision-makers are fully apprised of any issues that may potentially impact your business operations and to ensure that timely intervention and investment can be actioned.

Table 6-2. *Vehicle Warning Lights*

Think of it like the warning lights on your motor vehicle….
Anti-Lock Brake Warning 
Braking System Warning 

(*continued*)

---

[25]https://cmmiinstitute.com/pm
[26]https://nvlpubs.nist.gov/nistpubs/Legacy/SP/nistspecialpublication800-55r1.pdf

Table 6-2. (*continued*)

Think of it like the warning lights on your motor vehicle….

Low Fuel Warning

Low Oil Warning

Engine Warning

Seatbelt Warning

Low Coolant Warning

- Much the same as your data privacy and security strategies, these warning lights remain invisible until they need to illuminate to warn you that you may have an issue that needs to be investigated.
- Without these KPI/KRI warning lights, you will remain oblivious to the potential risks or dangers that require further investigation.
- If your vehicle has automated monitoring, why would you not consider doing the same for your business?

The integration of your various controls should be aligned with your corporation's risk management framework and, ideally, managed within a centralized risk solution, enabling appropriate access for the business managers and key stakeholders to instantly access the "State of the Nation" data that is of concern to them.

However, it is important to note that this can also be achieved through a more manual and labor-intensive collation of numerous spreadsheets, presentations, and documents.

When considering the advantages and disadvantages of using a commercial of the shelf (COTS) solution vs. a more manual approach, it is important to remember to create a business case. This will ensure that your organization appreciates the potential advantages or resources disadvantages associated with the automated vs. manual (in-house) options that are available to the business.

Qualitative vs. Quantitative Risk Assessment

Additionally, you will need to decide on whether you will present the results of your risk assessments as Qualitative or Qualitative risk assessments.

Qualitative Risk Assessments

The qualitative risk assessment is the most common form of risk assessment.

Through the use of ordinal rating scales (e.g., 1–5) or assigning relative ratings (high, medium, low or red, yellow, green), various risks can be plotted on a heat map with Likelihood (or Probability) on one axis and the impact on the other.

Where the risks are placed in a qualitative assessment is inherently subjective and makes the prioritization of risks extremely difficult. For example, if you have ten red (5 x 5) risks, which is the most urgent? In addition, a qualitative approach does not provide a systemic approach to aggregate risks.

Finally, these risk assessments tend to be drawn toward worst case loss scenarios, based upon the specific values that are available, as opposed to assigning a value from a scale.

Quantitative Risk Assessments

Qualitative risk assessments utilize knowledge and experience to determine the risk probability, while a quantitative risk assessment relies on objective, measurable data to provide insights into your risk management process.

A quantitative risk assessment gives you the data you need to accurately predict future outcome and helps strengthen your risk management strategy moving forward by communicating to you any contingency you need to properly address a risk to your satisfaction.

As long as the information you have is dependable, a quantitative risk assessment can create more realistic targets than a qualitative assessment.

Risk Appetite/Tolerance

It is important that your business defines the acceptable risk appetites/tolerance[27] across the different hierarchy levels within your organization. Where the perceived risks (post risk assessment) are within a business manager's appetite/tolerance, they are permitted to sign off a suitable risk treatment option. However, where this exceeds their risk appetite/tolerance, it must be escalated for more senior sign off.

Case Studies

At the outset of my career in Cyber/InfoSec and Risk, in 2002, I was fortunate to have significant exposure to the benefits of the use of a centralized risk management solution. The RAF employed a multi-tiered risk hierarchy, where the risk was recorded and monitored at three levels:

- Unit/Establishment

- Regional

- Command

---

[27]www.theirm.org/what-we-say/thought-leadership/risk-appetite-and-tolerance/

Each of these risks was recorded through a single, centralized, risk management platform (SAPPHIRE[28]) to provide a consolidated view of their risks.

Having completed my 22-year career in the RAF Police, with the last decade being in Cyber/InfoSec and Risk roles, I transitioned into the corporate environment with an appointment as a third-party/supplier security assurance consultant in a Financial Services company. An integral part of this role also included the management of the ISO/IEC 27001:2005 certification for the organization's Internet banking offering. This introduced me to my first COTS risk solution (Acuity's STREAM[29]) to help manage and monitor the effectiveness of the ISO/IEC 27001 security controls and to assist with the annual certification efforts.

At the same time, the business had been trying to implement a baseline security controls framework to ensure that each of the organization's departments was allocated a suite of suitable security controls. The security controls were selected from a master catalogue of security controls, compiled from various industry security controls frameworks (e.g., PCI DSS, COBIT 4.1, ISO 27001, etc.), and agreed with the appropriate stakeholders. However, the business had been unable to identify a suitable COTS product that could deliver what they had been seeking. That was until I had identified that they already had access to such a solution – STREAM.

Consequently, I was promoted and appointed into the baseline security controls (BCM) Manager role to oversee and implement the project so that they could have tailored compliance views at departmental and business channels (Blue, Red, and Purple (combined)). Just 6 months later, I had implemented a fully functioning solution to help the business demonstrate a consolidated view of the BSCs. Unfortunately, what they failed to incorporate was the integration of risk management into their BSC project.

A few years later, while working as a PCI qualified security assessor (QSA), I once again recognized the potential benefits such a solution could provide to my clients, who were struggling to maintain a comprehensive view of the PCI DSS programs and who were seeking to enhance their payment card security profile. The vendor was extremely happy to work with me in the development of their PCI DSS module and, as a result, I was able to utilize their product to help automate my assessment process.

---

[28]www.fujitsu.com/fts/Images/sapphire.pdf
[29]https://acuityrm.com/platform

With this experience in mind, I thought I would include a couple of hypothetical case studies *(one manual and one automated)* to help demonstrate the potential benefits to your business of using such a solution to enhance your data privacy and security strategies, to provide a consolidated risk and compliance view of your organization.

Case Study 1: Telephone-Based Payments Risk Balance Case

Many organizations will attempt to manage and articulate their risks *(both PCI DSS and Business)* through the use of an in-house manual process, employing a mix of spreadsheets, documents, and presentations. Therefore, the first of my example case studies has been developed to show how this might be presented to show an informed choice has been made by senior management *(where the levels have exceeded risk appetites)*.

ABC Corporation are concerned with the risks from their Call/Contact Center operations and are seeking to risk manage this as part of their PCI DSS program.

They have chosen to document their risk management process using a manual process, consisting of three components:

- **Part A:** This is the opportunity for the business to articulate the identified and to present the potential risk treatment options that are available.

- **Part B:** Here the Information Security/Risk specialists have their inputs. This may result in the specialists disagreeing with the business departments' preferred course of action (CoA).

- **Part C:** This is the executive sign off, where they have considered all the facts presented to them and chose the option that they are most comfortable with.

Table 6-3 provides an example of how this might look.

Table 6-3. Business Risk Case Example

Part A

Section 1: Completion by Submitting Business Department

Submitted By	Signature	Joe Bloggs
	Name	Joe Bloggs
	Job Title	Call Center Manager
	Company	ABC Corporation
	Dates	April 01, 2020
Detail	The business is concerned that the Call/Contact Center is susceptible to the threat from a trusted employer/ contractor stealing customer payment card information, or from customer payment card data being breached, as the result of a compromised network *(as the Call Agents' systems reside on a flat network)*.	
Assets at Risk	Call Center systems and associated customer payment card data	
The Risk	• Insider	
	• Technology	
The Reason the Risk Exists	Customers are required to speak their payment card data to the receiving Call Agents, who then manually enter the details into the payment application via their network-connected PCs. As a result, the payment card data is passed through the voice over Internet protocol (VOIP) system, call recordings, and the Call Agents. Each of which presents a potential threat vector for the business.	
Impact Statement	A large-scale breach of the customers' data would present a considerable reputational, financial, and regulatory impact.	

(continued)

Table 6-3. (*continued*)

Part A	
Duration of Risk	The Call Center is operational 24/7, 365 days a year.
Task	To identify the best option that will reduce the risk to within tolerances, be the most manageable, and provide the best return on investment (ROI) for the business
Worst Case Scenario	A large-scale breach (*e.g., 500,000*) of customers' personal data and payment card information
Policy	• Information Security Policy • Data Privacy Policy
➤ **Mitigation:**	Identify the available mitigating options. Discuss the RBC with the RM and obtain clear direction; if the RM has indicated that they wish to Treat a risk, provide suitable courses of action (CoA) that result in treating the risk.
CoA 1	**Tolerate**	Require the Call Center shift managers to remain vigilant and to periodically train Call Agents of the policies and processes.
	Advantages	Minimal cost and resource impact to the business
	Disadvantages	Although this does partially address the insider risk, it does not address the technology risk associated with the potential risk from a compromised network, VOIP risk, or payment card data storage (*call recordings*) risk.

(continued)

CoA 2	Treat	Apply the full weight of the controls from the SAQ D *(Circa 354 controls)*.
	Advantages	Ensure that a full array of mitigation controls are applied from the PCI DSS controls catalogue.
	Disadvantages	This is extremely resources and cost intensive and difficult to manage and maintain.
CoA 3	Treat	Apply to the criteria for the eligibility of an SAQ C *(circa 155 controls)*:
		• Payment application system and an Internet connection on the same device and/or same local area network (LAN).
		• Segment/Isolate the payment application system/Internet device from other out-of-scope systems on the network.
		• The physical location of the POS environment is not connected to other premises or locations, and any LAN is for a single location only.
		Avoid the electronic storage of cardholder, including call recordings.
	Advantages	Reduces the compliance burden and enhances the security through the silo of the Call Center systems and the removal of call recordings
	Disadvantages	Extremely difficult to achieve, requiring significant network architecture and process changes

(continued)

Table 6-3. (*continued*)

Part A

CoA 4	Treat	Apply to the criteria for the eligibility of the SAQ C/VT (*circa 88 controls*): • Only payment processing is via a virtual payment terminal, accessed by an Internet-connected web browser. • The virtual payment terminal solution is provided and hosted by a PCI DSS-validated third-party service provider. • Call Agents only access the PCI DSS-compliant virtual payment terminal solution via a computer that is isolated in a single location and is not connected to other locations or systems within the environment. • Prohibit the installation of software that enables cardholder data to be stored. • Prohibit the attachment of hardware devices that are used to capture or store cardholder data. • Prohibit the receipt or transmission of electronic cardholder data through any channels. • Prohibit the storage of cardholder data.
	Advantages	Significantly reduces the compliance burden and enhances the security through the silo of the Call Center systems and removes the transmission and storage of electronic cardholder data
	Disadvantages	The business systems become extremely limited in their functionality.

(*continued*)

CoA 5:	
Transfer/ Terminate	Remove the need for any systems or Call Agents to interact with any payment cardholder data, using third-party service provider's dual-tone multi-frequency (DTMF) solution (*e.g., GCI Com's Cloud IVR*[30]). This aligns to the eligibility to complete an SAQ A (*circa 22 controls (only five of which are applicable)*): • Only card-not-present (e-commerce or mail/telephone order) transactions. • All processing of cardholder data is entirely outsourced to PCI DSS-validated third-party service providers. • No electronic storage, processing, or transmission of any cardholder data on your systems or premises, but relying solely on a third party(s) to handle all these functions. Confirmation that all third parties handling storage, processing, and/or transmission of cardholder data are PCI DSS compliant.
Advantages	Significantly reduces the risk and the burden of the Call Center's requirement to process customers' cardholder data
Disadvantages	The Call Center operations need to be adjusted to accommodate the new business processes. Some personal data may still need to be processed; however, the high-risk number-based information (e.g., National Insurance, Date of Birth, etc.) can be replaced with DTMF.
CoA 6	
Terminate	Remove the requirement to interact with any customer cardholder data.
Advantages	Completely removes the PCI DSS burden and associated risks
Disadvantages	The interaction with personal data (*non-cardholder data*) may still be required, which may still need to be secured in line with local data privacy requirements. The elimination of all cardholder data processing may not be possible.

(continued)

[30]www.gcicom.net/Our-Services/Unified-Communications/GCI-Contact-Centre/Cloud-IVR

Table 6-3. *(continued)*

Part A

Section 2: Recommendation and Business Unit's Decision

➤ **Risk Appetite:** Only complete Section 2 if the risk is within Business Department's delegated Risk Appetite; RBCs relating to InfoSec are passed directly to the Security Steering/Risk Committee. If the risk is beyond the Business Department's delegated Risk Appetite, complete and forward the RBC to the Security Steering/Risk Committee who will pass it to the relevant Risk Owner.

➤ **Risk Advisor Recommendation:** Make a recommendation with supporting comment. Identify similar risks and provide comment on compliance with previous decision conditions.

Recommended CoA *(if applicable)*	**CoA 5**	It is recommended CoA 5 be accepted for the following reasons: • Has minimal impact on the business operations while significantly reducing the associated risks • Considerably minimizes the PCI DSS compliance burden on the business
	Signature	*Joe Bloggs*
	Name	Joe Bloggs
	Job Title	Call Center Manager
	Company	ABC Corporation
	Date	April 01, 2020
Within Risk Appetite?	**Yes/No**	No
		Within risk tolerances, the Business Manager is authorized to carry out the risk assessment decision. *If outside the formal risk appetite levels, this must be escalated to include Part B.*

(continued)

Part B

Section 1: Information Security Input

InfoSec Recommendation	Agree with CoA 5	
Signature	*Jimmy Jones*	
	Name	Jimmy Jones
	Job Title	CISO
	Company	ABC Corporation
	Date	April 12, 2020
Risk ID of similar risks/RBC (if applicable)	1.	2.	3.
Compliance with previous Decision Conditions (If Extension Request)		

(continued)

Table 6-3. (*continued*)

Part B

Section 2: Security Steering/Risk Committee Decision

Agree with the recommended CoA, as all other options are too resource and cost intensive.

When balancing the resource and costs of outsourcing vs. the resource and costs of developing and maintaining an in-house operations, outsourcing presents the most significant ROI.

Signature	*Tom Mann*
Name	**Tom Mann**
Job Title	**Risk Chair**
Company	**ABC Corporation**
Date	**April 08, 2020**

Decision Review Date: **April 01, 2021**

Section 3: Risk Assessment

5 × 5 Risk Heat Map

(*continued*)

Part B

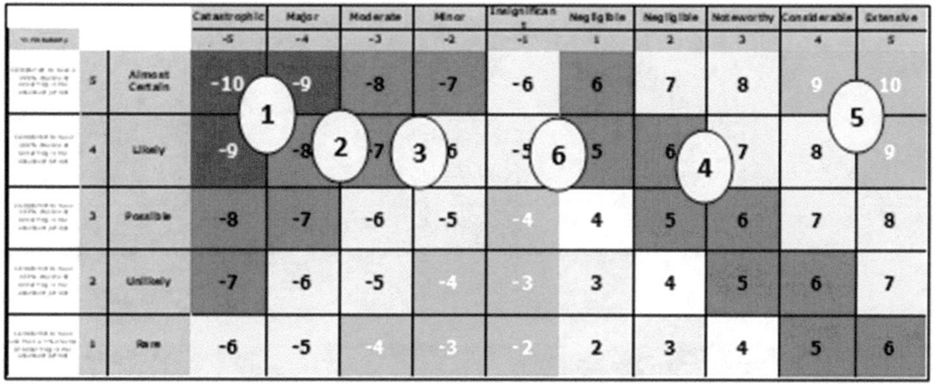

Figure 6-5. Risk Heat Map

(continued)

Table 6-3. (*continued*)

Part B

	Management of Negative Risks		Management of Positive Risks
Extreme (E)	Immediate action by Executive management and detailed planning	EXTREME (E)	Amazing opportunity requiring immediate action by the Executive
HIGH (H)	High risk, senior management attention needed	HIGH (H)	Strong or valuable opportunity that requires senior management attention
MEDIUM (M)	Management responsibility must be specified	MEDIUM (M)	Some added value. Might be worth considering
LOW (L)	Managed by routine procedures	LOW (L)	Little added value. Managed by routine procedures

Figure 6-6. *Legend*

(*continued*)

174

Part B

	Negative Consequence ◄────────────────────────					Positive Consequence ────────────────────────►				
CAPABILITY	Protracted unavailability of critical skills or personnel that has a catastrophic impact on outcomes	Unavailability of critical skills or personnel that has a major impact	Unavailability of core skills that substantially affects services	Minor adverse impact on organizational capability	Minor skills reduction at individual or workgroup level	Minor skills improvement at individual or workgroup level	Minor improvement to organizational capability	Noticeable enhancement in core skills affecting services	Major enhancement to critical skills or personnel capability	Extensive improvement critical skills and organizational capability
FINANCES	>200% adverse impact on the organisations profit or operations budget	>100% adverse impact on the organisations profit or operations budget	>50% adverse impact on the organisations profit or operating budget	>10% adverse impact on the organisations profit or operating budget	<10% adverse impact on the organisation's profit or operating budget	<10% improvement in the organisation's profit or operating budget	>10% improvement in the organizations profit or operating budget	>50% improvement in the organizations profit or operating budget	>100% improvement in the organizations profit or operating budget, revenue, cost	>200% improvement in the organizations profit or operating budget
PEOPLE	Multiple fatalities	Fatality or multiple major injuries	Hospitalisation required due to serious injury	Absences from work for up to a week, possibly requiring medical treatment	A 'near miss' or minor injury	Minimal health improvement or reduction in injury or first aid treatment	Minor improvement in safety, health and wellness	Significant improvement in safety, health and wellness	Major improvement in safety, health and wellness	Extensive organization wide improvement in safety, health and wellness
INFORMATION	Catastrophic compromise of sensitive or classified information pertaining to key organizational objectives	Major compromise of sensitive or classified information pertaining to key organizational objectives	Moderate compromise of sensitive or classified information	Minor compromise of sensitive information sensitive	Compromise of information otherwise available in the public domain	Acquire information that is available in the public domain	Acquire or improve safeguards for business intelligence including information sensitive to internal or sub-unit interests	Acquire business intelligence or improve safeguards to sensitive information which impacts the organization	Acquire significant business intelligence or improve safeguards for critical information (eg: sensitive to national interests or registered intellectual property)	Allows the organization to acquire or improve safeguards to information of the highest value
PROPERTY	Catastrophic impact on organizational assets (>75% of assets/value)	Major impact on organizational assets (51% to 75% of assets/value)	Moderate impact on organizational assets (26% to 50% of assets/value)	Minor impact on organizational assets (26% to 25% of assets/value)	Insignificant adverse impact to organizational assets (<2%)	Insignificant positive impact to organizational assets (<2%)	Minor positive impact on organizational assets (2% to 25% of assets/value)	Moderate positive impact on organizational assets (26% to 50% of assets/value)	Major positive impact on organizational assets (51% to 75% of assets/value)	Extensive positive impact on organizational assets (>75% of assets/value)
BRAND/REPUTATION	Royal Commission, Parliamentary inquiry or sustained adverse national/international media	Intense public, political and media scrutiny Eg: front page headlines, TV, etc	Scrutiny by Executive, internal committees, auditors, ASIC etc	Adverse local mention in media. Quickly forgotten. Self-improvement review required	Some positive local media attention or increase in brand value	Some positive local media attention or increase in brand value	Positive media exposure at the local level or in industry/client circles	Some benefit to brand value or positive regional media exposure	Significant benefit to brand value or positive national media attention	Significant and quantifiable increase in brand value or sustained positive national/international media attention
SYSTEMS	Critical business failure, preventing core activities from being performed which threatens the survival of the organization or project	Breakdown of key business performance, business process delays, create service delays, client dissatisfaction, costs, legislative breaches	Reduced performance such that targets are not met requiring significant review or changed ways of operations	Business delays and/or quality which be dealt with at operational level	Minimal impact on non core business operations which can be dealt with by routine operations	Minimal benefit to core operations	Some improvement in business processes (eg: reduced delays, efficiencies, systems, quality)	An impact on business resulting in enhanced performance that increases achievement of objectives	Considerable and quantifiable enhancement of key processes (Eg: faster service, improved client satisfaction, increased revenue, cost reduction)	Extensive improvement to critical business activities which delivers quantifiable improvement to core activities and achievement of objectives
OBJECTIVES	Increased barriers or failure of strategy, likely to cause catastrophic impact on outcomes or strategies objectives	Major adverse impact on outcomes or strategies	Moderate adverse impact on organizational outcomes or strategies	Some adverse impact on organizational outcomes or strategies but can be managed by routine procedures	Minimal impact on organizational outcomes or strategies	Minimal benefit to outcomes or strategies	Some improvement to outcomes or strategies	Moderate improvement in organizational outcomes	Considerable improvement in organisational outcomes or strategies in support of objectives	Extensive improvement in organisational outcomes or strategies in support of objectives

Figure 6-7. Risk Matrix

(continued)

175

Table 6-3. *(continued)*

Part B

Impact Statements	Impact Prior Mitigation (R,A,Y,G)	Impact Post Mitigation[31] (R,A,Y,G)
Confidentiality:		
Integrity:		
Availability:		
Business:		
Reputation:		

Source(s)

- Mitre Att&ck
- QSA Recommendation
- 2013 Target breach investigation

Threat Assessment

Attackers are increasingly seeking opportunities to move laterally across corporate networks from untrusted to trusted environments.

Personnel authorized access to the cardholder data environment, or to cardholder data, could compromise the network or steal the cardholder data.

(continued)

---

[31]Impact post mitigation referees to the recommended CoA.

Part B

| **Within Risk Appetite?** | **Yes/No** | No |

Within risk tolerances, the InfoSec/Security Committee is authorized to carry out the risk assessment decision.

If outside the formal risk appetite levels, this must be escalated to include Part C.

Part C

Section 4: Risk Owner's Statement

Risk Owner's
Recommendation *(if applicable)*

I conquer with the decision to pursue CoA 5.

Signature   *Robert Hill*

Name   Robert Hill

Job Title   Risk Director

Company   ABC Corporation

Date   April 14, 2020

Case Study 2: Enhanced PCI DSS Program Through Integration into Enterprise Risk Management (ERM)

Notwithstanding the PCI DSS compliance program, ABC Corporation have recognized the benefits of incorporating the risk management of their payment card operations into a single, centralized, and cohesive risk management program.

In order to achieve this more effectively, they have implemented the use of a COTS Risk Management product to help them provide an aggregated risk view of the perceived risks to the business and to provide a degree of automation of some of the associated action requirements.

The potential benefits and ROI include

- Help create a more risk-focused culture for the organization

- Provide standardized risk reporting

- Improved focus and perspective on risk

- Support of effective coordination of your regulatory and compliance matters

- Improved efficient use of resources

- Estimated time savings = $36,000 per annum[32]

Figures 6-8 to 6-25 show an array of interfaces that you might get from an effective and easy-to-use ERM solution.

---

[32]Net Cost of Time Saved *(e.g., (1680 hours per annum (10 users) @ $200 per hour (average) – Cost of Investment ($150,000))* / Cost of Investment (e.g., $150,000 per annum) × 100.

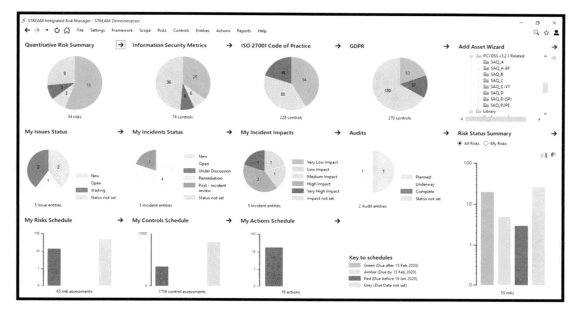

Figure 6-8. *Consolidated Views of KPIs/KRIs*

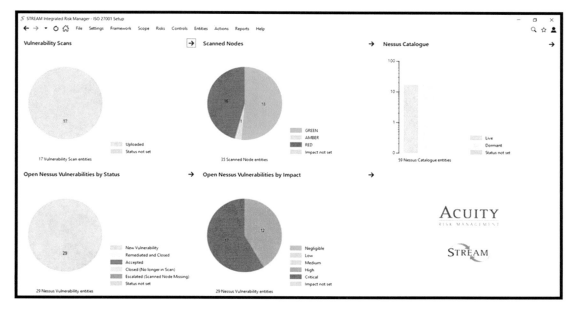

Figure 6-9. *A Consolidated View of the Critical Assets and Vulnerabilities*

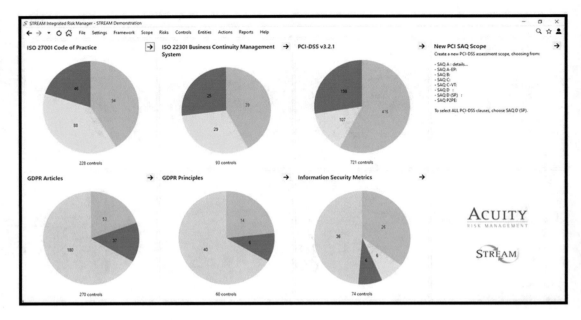

Figure 6-10. *Greater Governance*

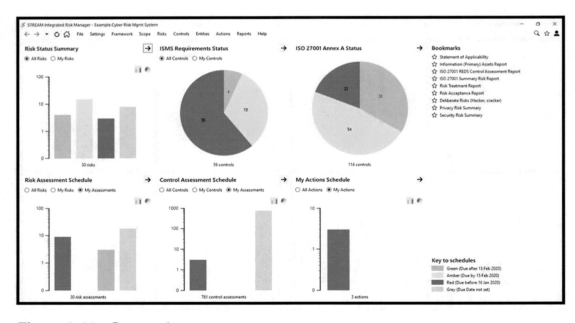

Figure 6-11. *Greater Assurance*

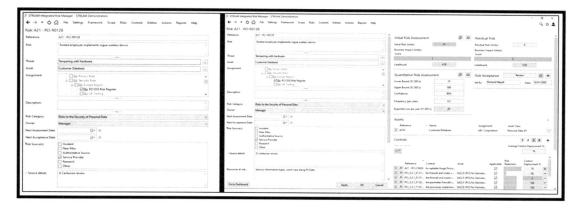

Figure 6-12. *Records of Risk Decisions*

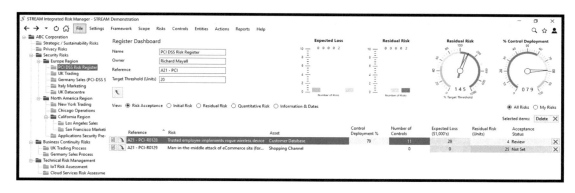

Figure 6-13. *Enterprise Risk Dashboards*

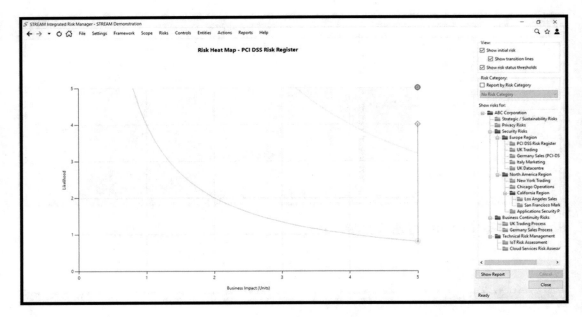

Figure 6-14. *Risk Heat Maps*

Figure 6-15. *Automated Task Scheduling*

Figure 6-16. *Controls Status Tracking*

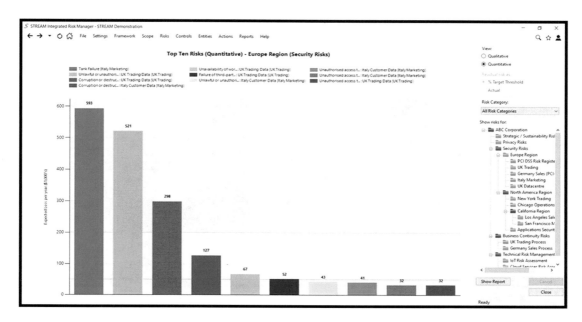

Figure 6-17. *Prioritization of Identified Risks*

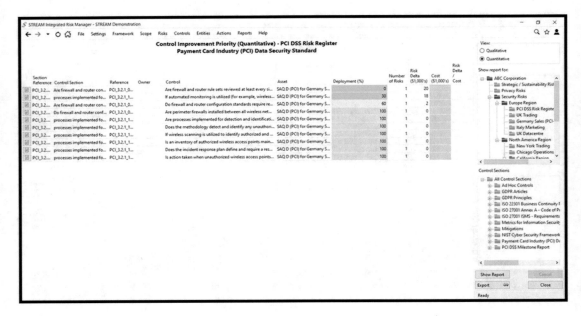

Figure 6-18. *Control Improvement Priority/ROI Reporting*

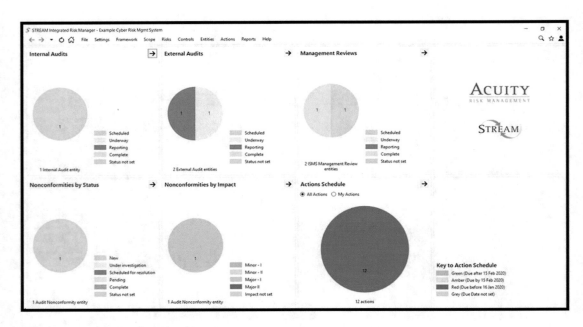

Figure 6-19. *Audit Tracking*

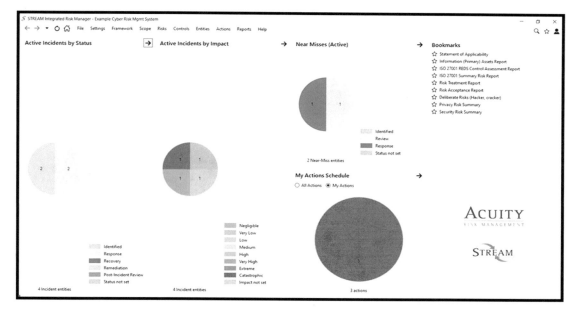

Figure 6-20. *Incident Tracking*

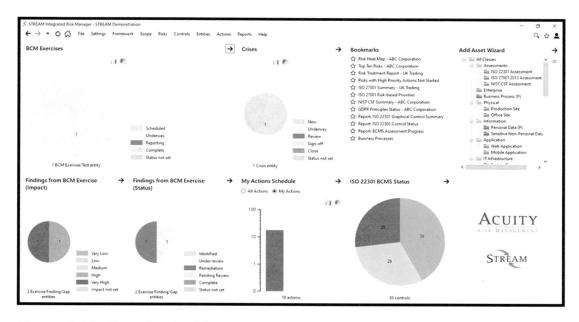

Figure 6-21. *Exercise Tracking*

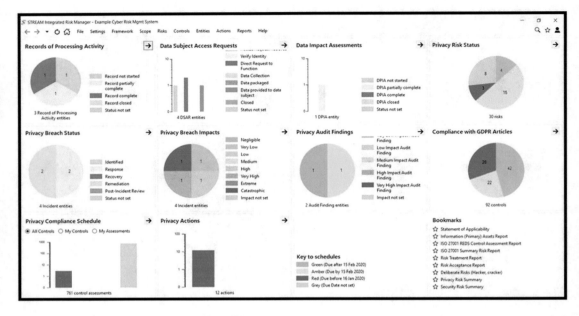

Figure 6-22. *Data Privacy Tracking*

Additionally, the ABC company was able to utilize the flexibility and functionality to help identify the different assessment control types to assist in the creation of an effective internal audit schedule and in support of the annual validation of compliance.

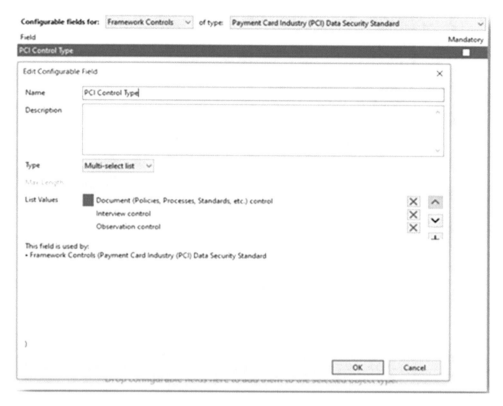

Figure 6-23. *PCI DSS Control Types*

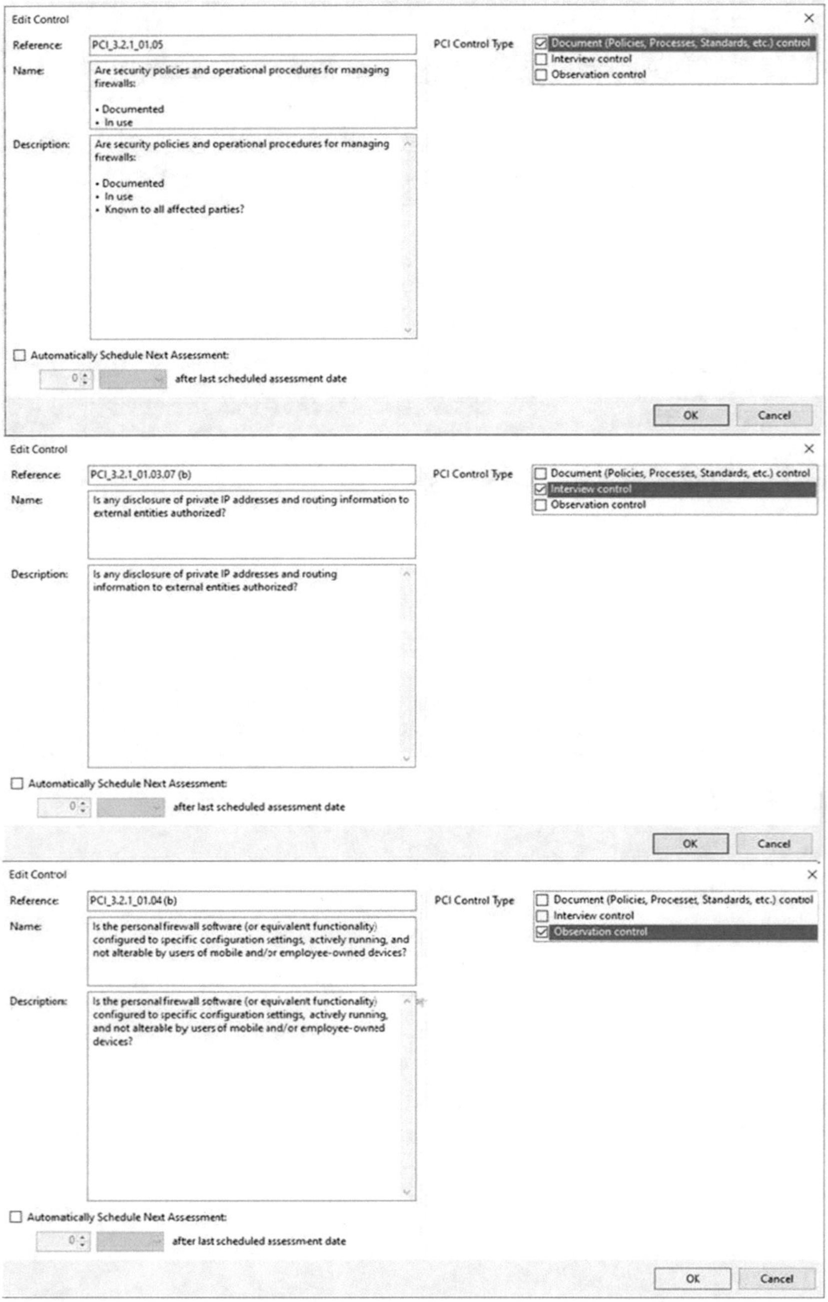

Figure 6-24. *PCI DSS Control Framework*

Figure 6-25. *PCI DSS Control Reporting*

As a consequence of the successful implementation of a suitable governance, risk, and compliance (GRC) solution across the organization, ABC Corporation could instantly provide consolidated views of the risks and controls statuses, appropriate for the individual concerned (e.g., Board Member, Key Stakeholder, Stakeholder, etc.), had integrated their PCI DSS compliance efforts, and, in the event of a data breach, could instantly provide the regulators with a "State of the Nation" overview of the affected business area of operation.

Reality Bites

I came to really appreciate the value of amalgamating Threat Management, Risk Management, Vulnerability Management, and Incident Management in support of proactive defense, when I was carrying out a threat assessment of a Royal Air Force establishment, as part of my duties on Counter Intelligence Operations. The threat actors had changed from the domestic terrorist to that of the international terrorist.

Consequently, following the terrorist attacks carried out in Mumbai, in 2008, I applied the same tactics and timeline[33] to this establishment, as it too had a shoreline.

---

[33]www.aljazeera.com/news/asia/2008/11/2008112874353615247.html

Figure 6-26. *Shorelined RAF Establishment*

Figure 6-27. *Traditional Defenses Focused on the Land Attack Vectors*

Traditionally, the defenses had been focused on land-based attacks. However, by applying the Mumbai attack tactics, techniques, and protocols (TTPs), it was quickly revealed that the existing defenses would be extremely vulnerable to these changing boat-borne attack tactics as employed by these new threat actors. The predicted result being that the existing defenses would have been caught completely by surprise and would have been annihilated within 20 minutes of the attackers landing on the shoreline of the RAF establishment.

Consequently, overlooking the boat-borne threat was escalated as being a considerable risk to the establishment, and I was tasked to complete threat assessments against all other RAF establishments that had a shoreline. The results of which were recorded in the local, regional, and command risk registers *(within SAPPHIRE)*.

Recommendations

Consider the benefits of changing your focus and efforts from being a purely compliance-focused approach to a risk-focused approach and evaluate the potential benefits of identifying your threats, vulnerabilities, and impacts as applicable to your organization's most valued business operations/processes and critical data assets.

Review your existing risk assessment/management processes and consider the potential process efficiency improvements and improved governance/assurance capabilities that may ensue from the implementation of an ERP solution for the consolidation of all your business and compliance risks and controls frameworks tracking.

Consider the benefits of providing periodic KRIs/KPIs back to the business, so as to alleviate the common misunderstanding and provide visibility to your Key Stakeholders:

"Cyber/InfoSec is extremely expensive and invisible. Just where does the investment go?"

Note   Don't wait until it goes wrong when it becomes very visible and becomes even more costly!

If you are an organization that does not need to annually validate their compliance to an Acquirer or Card Brand, consider how efficiently you would be able to provide evidence to the Regulators in the event of suffering a data breach.

Conclusion

The threat to your business operations is an ever-evolving risk, and there is a distinct difference between being compliant and having mitigated all your identified risks to your most critical assets/business processes. Failure to apply a proactive approach to reducing your business risk and adopting a minimal effort compliance-based approach increases the potential of your business systems/networks being compromised. This, in turn, could allow your opportunist attackers to impact your critical (non-pci dss) systems or to leverage these out-of-scope systems to impact the in-scope systems (e.g., British Airways man-in-the-middle (MITM) attack[34]).

Think of your data privacy and security program the same way as you might look at your motor vehicle. You should be getting timely warnings from the entire vehicle's critical components and not be purely focused on the protection of the driver/passenger environments.

Looking at your business risks as a consolidated view will help you develop additional outer defenses that will envelope your inner PCI DSS rings of defense.

Key Takeaways

It is extremely important to appreciate the differences between Risk Management, Compliance, and remaining Secure.

Your compliance efforts should be an output from your business's Risk Management, and audit practices ensure that effective mitigating security controls have been implemented and remain in effect for the protection of your most valuable business assets, as well as your customer payment card operations.

PCI DSS controls are the minimum baseline controls needed for the protection of cardholder data environments/operations. However, additional controls should be considered based upon new/evolving threats, vulnerabilities, and impacts.

A holistic approach to the defense of the business's critical operations and assets should be seen as an integral part of your organization, and regular reporting should be made available to your key stakeholders.

---

[34]www.bbc.co.uk/news/technology-45446529

The continual protection of your organization's critical data should be regarded as being business CRITICAL!

> *Do you employ a minimal effort to achieving and maintaining PCI DSS compliance?*
>
> *Have you layered your PCI DSS environment within your other defensive efforts?*
>
> *Do your Key Stakeholders actively understand the business risk profile?*
>
> *Are you prepared for a system compromise/data breach?*
>
> *How much support will your risk management practice provide to you in the event of a breach?*
>
> *Could you be more proactive?*

Risks

Criminals are opportunists who are continually on the hunt for poor practices which enable them to gain a foothold into their target environments.

Your attackers have three key drivers:

Inquisitiveness

Challenge

Reward *(Financial or Kudos)*

Ask yourself:

- *Am I solely reliant on the PCI DSS controls to safeguard my customers' payment card data?*

- *Am I content with the visibility of my data privacy and security program?*

- *Are my Key Stakeholders receiving (or able to access) regular updates on the risks to the business and the effectiveness of the mitigation controls to ensure that an appropriate level of governance is in place?*

- *Do I receive regular threat intelligence feeds that help me enhance my defensive profile?*

- *Do I have effective risk management practices?*

- *Have I implemented additional mitigation controls?*

- *Do I use a multitude of mitigation controls from industry security sources, security specialist recommendations, or locally created defensive controls?*

- *Is there a holistic view of the risks and compliance statuses to ensure informed decision-making and timely intervention can be achieved?*

- *Is data privacy and security regarded as a business investment or a business burden?*

- *How supportive are the organization's stakeholders?*

CHAPTER 7

PCI DSS Applicability

PCI DSS Overview

The Payment Card Data Security Standard (PCI DSS) has been designed to be the benchmark standard for the protection of cardholder data and applies to any business IT system or business operation that is involved in the storage, processing, or transmission of this type of sensitive data. The successful application and implementation of the PCI DSS control sets against the card payment operations makes it more difficult for the attackers to steal such data and, as such, provides greater assurance to the Card Brands, Issuers, and Acquirers and ultimately helps protect the consumers from payment card fraud. However, the criminals are opportunists seeking to exploit the misinterpretation/misapplication of the PCI DSS controls, poorly managed PCI DSS oversight, bad practices, or poor risk management processes.

Frequently, PCI DSS compliance is treated as annual "tick box" audit; however, this is far from reality where PCI DSS should be treated more like having the responsibility for owning and running courier, road haulage, or taxi services. The vehicles need to undergo annual "roadworthiness" checks but, additionally, the vehicle owner must ensure that the vehicle remains safe, well maintained, and operated safely and their contents remain secure from the point of pickup to delivery. Think of the consumers' payment card data as being precious cargo or family members' and a business IT infrastructure as being the transport vehicles, supporting a paid-for service or supplied goods.

© Jim Seaman 2020
J. Seaman, *PCI DSS*, https://doi.org/10.1007/978-1-4842-5808-8_7

MOT Test Certificate   VOSA

Vehicle & Operator Services Agency

Advisory Information

Advisory Items
001 Nearside front Shock absorber has a light misting of oil
[2.7.3]

002 O/s drive shaft oil seal leaking

MOT Test Number

Make

Model

Colour
RED

Issuer's name

Signature of Issuer

Expiry Date
JUNE 28th 2016
(SIXTEEN)

Additional Information
To preserve the anniversary of the expiry date the earliest you
can present your vehicle for test is 29/05/2016

Vehicle Registration Mark

Vehicle Identification Number

Country of Registration
GB

Test Class
IV

Odometer Reading and History
17/06/2015: 85451
18/06/2014: 76401
26/06/2013: 67545
27/06/2012: 57371

Issued
17/06/2015 12:20

Inspection Authority

Test Station

An executive agency of the
Department for
Transport

About this document
1 This document is a receipt style certificate telling you that an MOT Test pass result has
been recorded on The Vehicle & Operator Services Agency's (VOSA's) database of MOT
Test results; this may be verified at www.direct.gov.uk/yourmotcheck
2 A test certificate relates only to the condition of the components examined at the time of
test. It does not confirm the vehicle will remain roadworthy for the validity of the certificate.
3 Check carefully that the details are correct.
4 Whilst advisory items listed above do not constitute MOT failure items they are drawn to
your attention for advice only.
5 For further information about this document please visit www.direct.gov.uk/mot or
contact VOSA on 0300 123 9000*.
*Your call may be monitored or recorded for lawful purposes.

***Figure 7-1.** Annual Independent Inspection*

***Figure 7-2.** Maintenance Checks*

Figure 7-3. *Insecure Operations*

Figure 7-4. *Careless Operations*

Introduction

The heart of PCI DSS compliance is to ensure that all payment card data is adequately protected, ensuring that all supporting systems and personnel provide for the secure processing, storage, and transmission. Failure to ensure that all elements associated with your payment card operations are aligned with their applicable PCI DSS controls, increases the potential risk for malicious or accidental actions leading to a breach or loss of your customers' payment card information.

Consequently, to understand the applicability, it is essential that you understand what payment card data looks like and that you can identify such data within your environment, starting with the initial points of receipt through to all the areas of residence, copied data, shared data, and final disposal, without which you will find it extremely difficult to ensure that all your customers' payment card data is sufficiently protected.

The Precious Cargo

It is extremely helpful to treat your payment card as precious cargo and to understand what contributes to payment card data and to be able to differentiate between the two categories of payment data types (Category 1 and Category 2).

The following sections aim to deconstruct the content of a payment card, so that you will better understand how the payment card data is pieced together. This will give you a greater understanding on why the criminals seek any opportunity to gain unauthorized access to any pieces of payment card data so that they can then gather these together to reconstruct them into a single valid payment card.

Structure of a Payment Card

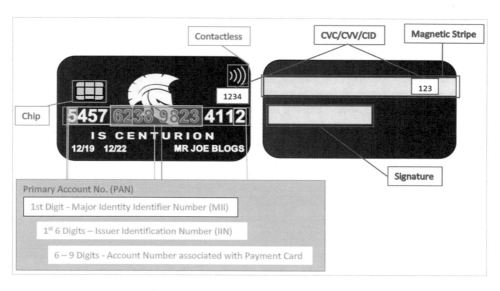

Figure 7-5. *Payment Card Overview*

Precious Cargo Categories

The two categories of data types are as follows:

- The "long number" for the card *(typically, 15 or 16 digits in length)*, which is referred to as the Primary Account Number (PAN)

- The Sensitive Authentication Data (SAD)

Precious Cargo	
Category 1:	**Category 2:**
Cardholder Data (CHD)	**Sensitive Authentication Data (SAD)**
• PAN • Cardholder Name • Expiration Date • Service Code	• Full track data (magnetic stripe or equivalent chip data) • CAV2/CVC2/CVV2/CID • PINs/PIN blocks

Front of Payment Card Breakdown

The front of the payment card is commonly where you will find the category 1 datasets. However, there are some card issuers that have started to locate the category 1 data on the rear of the payment card. An example of the front of the card can be seen in Figure 7-5 and consists of the following components.

Primary Account Number (PAN)	*When looking at the full bank card number, the first digit identifies the card issuer's industry, while the first six digits collectively identify the specific institution which issued the card. The remainder of the 16 (or 15, in some cases) digits make up the cardholder's account number, including one or more check digits, also called a "checksum." A checksum represents the sum of a formula that helps determine if the credit card number is actually valid.*

5457 6238 9823 4112

Major Identifier No. (MII)	*The MII identifies the category or type of institution which issued the card. Visa- and Mastercard-branded cards.*

MII Digit Value	Issuer Category
0	ISO/TC 68 Assignment
1	Airline cards
2	Airlines cards (and other future industry assignments)
3	Travel and Entertainment Cards
4	Banking and Financial Cards
5	Banking and Financial Cards
6	Merchandising and Financial Cards
7	Gas Cards, Other Future Industry Assignments

(continued)

| 8 | Healthcare Cards, Telecommunications, Other Future Industry Assignments |
| 9 | For Use by National Standards Bodies |

5457 6238 9823 4112

Issuer Identification No. *The IIN provides merchants with a lot of other information besides just the issuing entity. For example, when a cardholder enters their card details for an online transaction, just these first few digits tell the retailer:*

- *The name, address, and phone number of the bank funds will be transferred from*
- *The card brand (Visa, Mastercard, American Express, etc.)*
- *What type of card it is (debit, credit, prepaid, etc.)?*
- *What level the card is (black, platinum, business)?*
- *Whether the issuer is in the same country as the device used in the transaction.*
- *Whether the address provided by the cardholder matches the one on file.*
- *Finally, the IIN allows merchants to accept multiple forms of payment and speed up the overall processing.*

(continued)

Examples of the IIN format for the most widely used card brands	**Visa**	4****
	MasterCard	51**** or 55****
	American Express (AMEX)	34**** or 37****
	Discover Card	6011, 622126-622925, 644-649, 65
	JCB	3528–3589

5457 6238 9823 4112

Account No. associated with payment card	*The following 6–9 digits represent a unique bank account number. (Note: The bank account number of a customer but the account number assigned to a credit account).*

5457 6238 9823 4112

Checksum	*This digit is mathematically determined based on all the other digits and is used to minimize the risk associated with human error, when manually inputting the "long card number." This enables a checksum verification using the Luhn algorithm (MOD-10 mathematics). Using the checksum against the IS Centurion payment card, shown earlier, confirms that this is not a valid "long number."*

2x		2x		2x		2x		2x		2x		2x		2x			
5	4	5	7	6	2	3	8	9	8	2	3	4	1	1	X		
2x5=10		2x5=10		2x6=12		2x3=6		2x9=18		2x2=4		2x4=8		2x1=2			
(1+0)	1x4	1	1x7	(1+2)	1x2=2	6	1x8=8	(1+8)	1x8=8	4	1x3=3	8	1x1=1	2	Row SUM	=34
	4		7		2		8		8		3		1		Row SUM	=33
																=67

(continued)

- To calculate the check digit

  - Multiply every even-position digit (when counted from the right) in the number by two. If the result is a two-digit number, then add these digits together to make a single digit (this is called the digital root).
  - To this total, we then add every odd-position digit.

- This will result in a total (in our example =67).

  - The check digit is what number needs to be added to this total to make the next multiple of 10. In this case, **3** will need to be added to make **70**.

- The correct check digit for this fictitious number is **3**.

Not 2, as seen in Figure 7-5.

5457 6238 9823 4112

Cardholder Name	*The person to whom the card has been issued*
Expiration Date	Typically, 3–4 years from the date of issue *(Note: Upon renewal of a payment card, the PAN may remain the same.)*

Rear of Payment Card Breakdown

Commonly, card issuers will locate the magnetic stripe on the rear of the payment card, along with the signature strip and CVV *(except for American Express cards, where the CVV are the four digits located on the front of the payment card).*

Figure 7-6 shows the breakdown of the category 1 and 2 data types contained within the magnetic stripe.

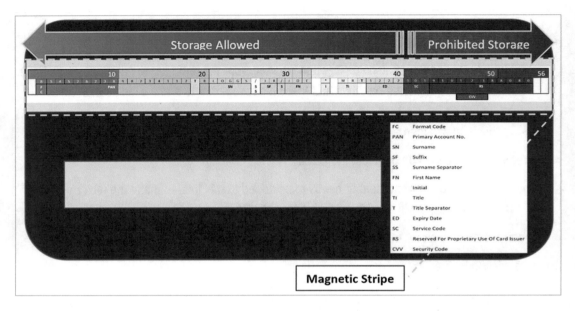

Figure 7-6. *Track 1–Track 2 Data*

Service Code   *Three- or four-digit value in the magnetic stripe that follows the expiration date of the payment card on the track data. It is used for various things such as defining service attributes, differentiating between international and national interchange, or identifying usage restrictions.*

Full track data   *As shown in Figure 7-6, the full track data is divided into track 1 and track 2, with the storage of track 2 (post authorization) being prohibited, as this contains the SAD relating to the payment card.*

• Up to 79 characters

| **Security Code** | *The Card Verification Code (CVC) is the three- or four-digit "Security Code" (sometimes referred to as the Card Verification Value (CVV) or Card Identification Number (CID)[1]):* |

CAV2	*Card Authentication Value 2 (JCB payment cards)*
CAV2	*Mastercard*
CID	*American Express*
CID2	*Discover*
CVV2	*Visa*

These are generated by a CVV algorithm and are used to authenticate payment cards. To generate or calculate the three-digit CVV, the algorithm requires the following:

- *Primary Account Number (PAN)*
- *Four-digit Expiration Date*
- *A pair of Data Encryption Standard (DES keys) (Code Verification Keys (CVKs))*
- *Three-digit Service Code*

Note: This algorithm is only known to the bank and not for any person or organization.

Consequently, because of the aggregated value, it is only permitted for issuers and their supporting companies to store SAD but only if

- *There is a justified reason for doing so*
- *The SAD is stored securely*

Personal Identification Number (PIN)/PIN Blocks

If an organization fails to protect their consumers' PIN/PIN blocks, they are gifting the criminals the keys associated with any stolen payment card details. Suddenly, the criminals have the "free reign" to clone payment cards and to go on a spending spree, using the credit of the affected consumers.

---

[1]Note: On some payment cards, these can be three or five digits and can be located on the front of the card.

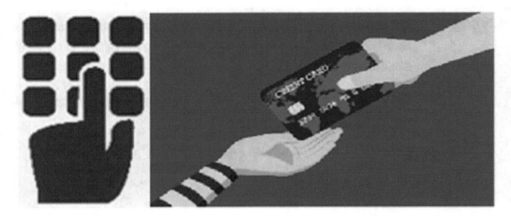

Figure 7-7. *Gifting Away CHD*

CHD Storage

The storage of CHD is permitted; however, it is recommended that the Keep It Simple Solution is applied:

"In general, no payment card data should ever be stored unless it's necessary to meet the needs of the business.

Avoid the unnecessary storage, if this can be avoided, and keep all storage to the absolute minimum needed.

Once the CHD is no longer needed, securely dispose of the CHD."

"PCI DSS does not prevent a business to store category 1 payment card data.

However, PCI DSS is the de facto security benchmark for the protection of **cardholder** *data and must be applied to the various payment card data lifecycles."*

Accessing Applicability

Now that you have an appreciation of what type of data makes your business applicable to the PCI DSS, it is essential to trace the journey of the data, so as to identify the extent of the environments that need to be aligned.

Tracing the journey starts at the point of origin (where the consumers' payment card data is entrusted to you), right through to its final secure disposal/destruction and including any local reproductions/duplications that are taken from your main data vaults (e.g., local spreadsheets, tables, etc.), and to include any third parties that may come into contact with such data assets.

Unfortunately, you may have fallen into the trap of only looking at the card payment operations and have omitted to include the associated systems, interfaces, suppliers, personnel, and business operations.

For example, what happens to the PANs, which, for convenience, are given a duplicated use as being their account number?

- Printed in full on monthly account statements?

- Added to correspondence?

- Used as a means to carry out online password resets?

Figure 7-8. *Web Page Using Full PAN Entry*

Consequently, it is essential that for any PCI DSS compliance efforts all applicable interfaces, storage locations, and connected systems/applications are identified in order to identify all potential avenues, which may not have been secured but could be advantageous for the criminal to exploit.

Identify all your "Nooks and Crannies," where CHD may be residing!

Recent data breaches, such as the Magecart Group[2] and Mastercard,[3] have demonstrated that today's criminals will seek any opportunity to exploit poor security practices. Additionally, criminals have turned data theft into an extremely profitable professional and are even known to have created online business-style models[4] to achieve this very goal.

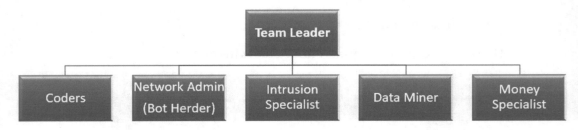

Figure 7-9. *Criminal Gang Hierarchy*

The Future

Consumers are increasingly looking for more convenient and technology-based ways of paying for goods and services, as can be seen in the illustration in Figure 7-10. Consequently, opportunist thieves will seek to exploit poor CHD practices and the poor baselining of CHD operations against the PCI DSS controls framework.

As a result, it has never been more important to understand how PCI DSS may apply to your business and to ensure that you are looking after all the consumers' cash – not just the notes.

---

[2]https://threatpost.com/magecart-ecommerce-card-skimming-bonanza/147765/

[3]www.finextra.com/newsarticle/34310/mastercard-loyalty-programme-customers-hit-by-data-leak

[4]www.ncsc.gov.uk/news/ncsc-publishes-new-report-criminal-online-activity

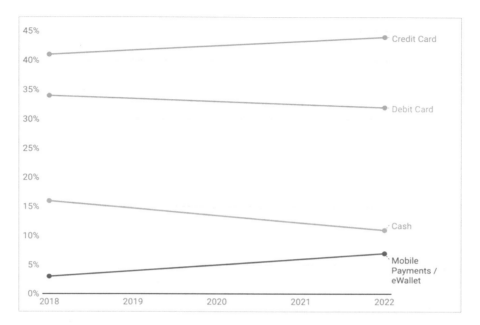

Figure 7-10. *Payment Trends[5]*

In fact, payment card data inclusive of the SAD is known[6] to sell on the "Black Market" for 80% more than without ($110–$220 per card). This makes this treasure hunt a very profitable venture for today's modern criminal, seeking to make a living from an organization's carelessness.

Take care of all the loose change!

---

[5]www.merchantsavvy.co.uk/mobile-payment-stats-trends/

[6]https://krebsonsecurity.com/2019/10/briansclub-hack-rescues-26m-stolen-cards/

Key Takeaways

PCI DSS applies to any business that directly, or indirectly, relies on the processing storage or transmission of payment card data. At the heart of any PCI DSS program should be the focus on safeguarding the cardholder data and its supporting environment. Therefore, these become applicable areas for PCI DSS and need to be maintained for compliance against their applicable controls, whether as a fully in-house, partially outsourced, or entirely outsourced.

Any employee, third party, or IT systems that interacts with such data (electronic, spoken, paper, etc.) or that could impact such operations becomes into scope.

It is important to understand the type of cardholder data storage that is permitted to be stored and how valuable this type of data is for the criminals.

For example, Mail Order, Telephone Order (MOTO)

Customer speaking provides CHD via their telephone (spoken).

Receiving Voice Over Internet Protocol (VOIP) system – In-Scope.

Receiving Call Agent – In-Scope.

Call Agent types CHD into Third Party payment application via network-connected business PC – PC, Network, and payment application are In-Scope.

Calls are recorded for training and monitoring – In-Scope (Note: Call recordings will include the prohibited SAD).

Ancillary personnel (e.g., Cleaners, Building Maintenance, etc.) who have authorized access to the Call Center – In-Scope.

Risks

Today's criminals have one thing in common; they are opportunists who prey on the weakest. Therefore, they will seek every opportunity to exploit poorly configured systems, poor practices, or poorly scoped environments (allowing them to circumvent defenses).

PCI DSS is the primary benchmark, ensuring that businesses have a reference suite of controls to layer the defenses around these valued datasets.

Consequently, if you are a business that relies on any form of CHD, then PCI DSS applies to you and will be a target for the criminals.

Transferring the responsibility, by outsourcing to a third party, does not eliminate the accountability for you as a business.

Ask yourself:

- *Do I know all the interfaces, systems, third parties, and personnel who interact (or could come into contact with CHD)?*

- *Do my PCI DSS compliance efforts include all the environments where CHD could be intercepted?*

- *Are all these environments having the PCI DSS benchmark applied to them?*

- *If not, could I be leaving myself open to the criminals?*

- *Could I be making a false declaration of compliance?*

CHAPTER 8

De-scoping the Scoping Risk

Scoping means[1]

> *The PCI DSS security requirements apply to all system components included in or connected to the cardholder data environment. The cardholder data environment (CDE) is comprised of people, processes and technologies that store, process, or transmit cardholder data or sensitive authentication data. "System components" include network devices, servers, computing devices, and applications.*

—PCI DSS v3.2.1,[2] p. 10

Although de-scoping your CDE from your non-CDE is highly recommended, it is not currently a mandated requirement. However, if you should decide to reduce your PCI DSS burden and the associated risks, it is essential that you understand the effectiveness of any scoping efforts.

As well as reducing your PCI DSS compliance burden, an effectively scoped environment will help reduce the potential risk from an attacker breaching your out-of-scope environment and moving laterally[3] until they identify a hole in your CDE defenses or leveraging a weakness of connected third parties (Island Hopping[4]) to gain unauthorized access to your CDE.

---

[1]www.pcisecuritystandards.org/documents/Guidance-PCI-DSS-Scoping-and-Segmentation_v1.pdf

[2]www.pcisecuritystandards.org/document_library

[3]https://awakesecurity.com/glossary/lateral-movement/

[4]www.itpro.co.uk/cyber-attacks/33200/what-is-island-hopping

© Jim Seaman 2020
J. Seaman, *PCI DSS*, https://doi.org/10.1007/978-1-4842-5808-8_8

Traditionally in the military, they would have two entirely separate and isolated environments – **RED** (subject to stringent control) for the highly sensitive operations *(Top Secret and Secret)* and **BLACK** for the less sensitive operations *(Confidential and Restricted).*

For example, within a military base (**BLACK**), there could be a highly sensitive center of operations (**RED**), providing critical support services to military operations around the globe. Due to the sensitivity and criticality of these operations, it has its own suite of mitigation controls (e.g., separate access controls, secure rooms, security cabinets, CCTV, alarms, security checks, etc.). Access to this facility is strictly limited based upon specific need to know and need to access requirements. Just because personnel have the right to access the **BLACK** does not give them the automatic right to gain access to the **RED**.

The **RED** was further enhanced through the application of additional mitigation controls that were applied for the defense of the **BLACK**.

Figure 8-1. *Secure Enclave Within a Military Base*

It is unlikely that your business will have the desire or budget to build military grade defenses by dedicating an entirely separate and isolated environment. However, similar principles can be applied to your business through the use of segmentation. Think of your CDE as being **RED** assets, any out-of-scope assets as being **BLACK** assets, and any that set within a buffer zone as being **BROWN** assets. As well as having identified and documented all your **RED** and **BLACK** assets, it is important to ensure that any potential impacting **BROWN** assets are identified, **for example, Network and Systems.**

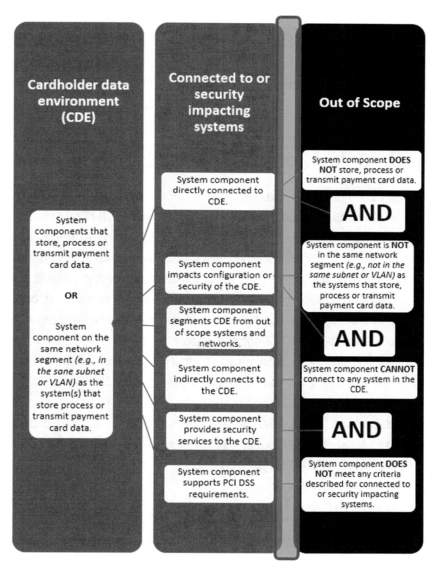

Figure 8-2. *Network De-scoping*

Understandably, there needs to be a clear delineation area between the **RED** and **BLACK** assets for you to consider these to be out-of-scope for your PCI DSS program and that this does not only apply to networks and systems but also your third parties *(e.g., VPN entry/egress connections, within an infrastructure as a service (IAAS) provider)*, infrastructure *(e.g., open plan offices, where payment card operations are carried out)*, and personnel *(e.g., maintenance personnel with access to all areas of the business)*.

Remember, as the entity, you are responsible for ensuring that the de-scoping of your environment is accurate and there is not potential "muddying of the waters" by omitting assets that could be leveraged by an attacker against your CDE.

Introduction

Despite the fact that segmenting your network is not compulsory, it can de-scope your compliance obligations and make things easier. "In-scope" (RED Zone) is any IT systems that are involved in the processing, storage, or transmission of cardholder data (CHD) or any IT systems that can impact these systems. Therefore, with a "Flat Network" everything would be brought into scope, making things extremely difficult. However, given that today's cyber-attackers are constantly seeking opportunities to compromise corporate networks and to create a persistent, hidden presence within the network (exploiting weakness in the "Out-of-Scope" environments (BLACK zone) to enable them to undermine a RED Zone. Take, for example, the Citrix data breach which was thought to have been perpetrated by Iranian hackers in a group called IRIDIUM[5] and who are believed to have remained undetected for 10 years.

Other exploitations of "Out-Of-Scope" environments were seen in 2018, by the Magecart Group's[6] Man-In-The-Middle (MITM)[7]-style attacks where they seamlessly changed the customers' experience/journey:

---

[5]http://techtictok.com/tag/iridium-hacker-group/
[6]www.bleepingcomputer.com/news/security/automated-magecart-campaign-hits-over-960-breached-stores/
[7]https://pciramblings.com/2019/08/06/pci-ssc-online-skimming-blog-post/

- **British Airways**[8]

- **Ticketmaster**[9]

- **Newegg**[10]

If an organization chooses to de-scope their environment (creating a bordering "Badlands"), does this increase the opportunity for the cyber-attacker and as a result the risk? With all the defenses being focused on the cardholder data environment (CDE) and not on the adjacent BLACK zone within a corporate zone, could this present an opportunity for the cyber-attackers to create a staging ground?

Lessons Learned from History

These types of incidents are not new and are not the only occasions that attackers have managed to compromise an environment, using the out-of-scope areas. Take, for instance, in 2013, when the 15-year-old Russian hacker that managed to compromise Target's[11] CDE, through the "piggy-backing" onto the connection from a third-party air conditioning company's network connection.

Looking further back into history, the City of Troy[12] suffered a similar fate to their physical security defenses around 1200 BC, when their outer defenses were compromised after a clandestine army was wheeled inside. This enabled a refreshed enemy to launch an offensive from inside the perimeter, leaving the Troy army little time to respond and react.

---

[8]https://managingrisktogether.orx.org/sites/default/files/downloads/2019/01/british-airways-suffers-data-breach-compromising-information-over-429-000-customer-cards.pdf

[9]https://securityboulevard.com/2019/01/ticketmaster-and-fastbooking-hacked-lessons-learned/

[10]https://techcrunch.com/2018/09/19/newegg-credit-card-data-breach/

[11]https://arxiv.org/pdf/1701.04940.pdf

[12]www.livescience.com/38191-ancient-troy.html

Figure 8-3. *City of Troy*

When de-scoping your PCI DSS scope, it is extremely important to apply the lessons from history and the military, so that you understand and apply the principles of having concentrated security controls *(using the PCI DSS controls framework)* on your **RED** environment but without neglecting the need to protect your **BLACK** environments *(perhaps through the use of a separate security controls framework, e.g., NIST CSF[13] or CIS 20 CSC[14]).*

You would validate that your CDE is secure through the accurate validation of the de-scoping of the environment (**RED**) and to validate that this environment is protected and assessed against the PCI DSS controls framework. Additional defensive layers would be applied to the outer environment (**BLACK**) through the application and validation of a secondary controls framework. Where controls are commonly applied across the **BLACK** and **RED**, the default defensive control would be the more robust control.

Thinking Like the Enemy

The attackers are now employing either the traditional "Cyber Kill Chain"[15] or the "Cognitive Attack Loop"[16] approaches, where their first step is to carry out recon and to establish potential opportunities *(this may include the seamless redirection of the customers' journey).*

---

[13]www.nist.gov/cyberframework

[14]www.cisecurity.org/controls/cis-controls-list/

[15]www.lockheedmartin.com/en-us/capabilities/cyber/cyber-kill-chain.html

[16]www.carbonblack.com/2019/09/09/introducing-the-cognitive-attack-loop-and-its-3-phases/

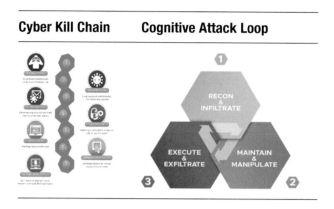

The Way Forward

It is important to treat the de-scoping as an opportunity to decrease the complexities of PCI DSS compliance and to make things more difficult for the opportunist attackers. Treat the "Out-of-Scope" environment as additional layers of defense for "wannabe" intruders. Think of your network and web infrastructure along the lines of a Bank's Branch/Store, where a stranger is prevented from walking straight in off the street to directly access the contents of the safe or safety deposit box:

1. **Perimeter Door Access**

2. **Foyer area**

3. **Counter Access Control**

4. **Safe Access Control**

5. **Safety Deposit Box Access**

> **Note**   At each point of access, personnel are monitored, and the access filtered, based upon their authorized need to know and their need to gain entry to these restricted zones. Any attempts for an attacker to divert the customers' journey would be prevented by ensuring that the supporting layers are adequately protected (e.g., The bank foyer is a protected environment, ensuring that customers cannot be redirected to a fake branch/counter or ATM machine).

Reality Bites

An equivalent example would be in the case of the Landry's data breach,[17] where their point-to-point (P2P)[18] technology (**RED**) was undermined when their employees mistakenly swiped customers' payment cards on devices used to enter kitchen and bar orders (**RED/BROWN/BLACK**), which are different devices than the point-of-sale terminals used for payment processing. Clearly Landry's had recognized the benefits of de-scoping their payment card operations but did not consider the potential impact the out-of-scope systems would potentially have on their business.

However, Landry's are not the only restaurant business to have had their point-of-sale (POS) systems compromised by opportunist attackers in 2019.[19]

Dates Affected	Business Impacted	Details
2019	Landry's	Landry's, the parent company of over 600 restaurants, casinos, and hotels, including Bubba Gump Shrimp, Joe's Crab Shack, M Grille, and Rainforest Cafe, reported that they detected unauthorized access to the network supporting their payment processing systems between March and October of 2019.
2019	Wawa	Over 800 of Wawa's convenience stores had POS malware planted in their systems that went undetected for 8 months. The malware is said to have harvested payment information, like names, card numbers, and expiration dates.
2019	Catch Hospitality	Catch NYC, Catch Steakhouse, and Catch Rooftop disclosed the presence of POS malware in their systems between March and October of 2019 that searched for track data, which could include cardholder and card information.

(continued)

[17]www.landrysinc.com/CreditNotice/

[18]www.pcisecuritystandards.org/assessors_and_solutions/
 point_to_point_encryption_solutions

[19]https://upserve.com/restaurant-insider/pos-data-breaches/

Dates Affected	Business Impacted	Details
2019	DoorDash	In September the company announced that a breach – which occurred on May 4 and affected users who created accounts before April 5, 2018 – affected 4.9 million customers, delivery workers, and merchants who had information stolen by hackers including names, email and delivery addresses, order history, phone numbers, and passwords.
2019	Checkers and Rally's	Malware planted by hackers collected credit card information from systems at over 100 locations. Almost 15% of locations were compromised from software that was installed in September of 2018.
2019	Mudshark Brewing Company and Other Arizona restaurants	An investigation of "suspicious activity" led to the uncovering of dozens of Arizona restaurants having data breaches that may have compromised customers' personal information.

Yet another victim of the Magecart-style attacks, Macy's online[20] (www.macys.com) was also the victim of a man-in-the-middle attack. The attackers had injected malicious code into an out-of-scope (**BLACK**) web page in the customers' e-Commerce journey.

As you can see in Figure 8-4, Macy's has a large and complex digital web-based footprint.

---

[20]www.documentcloud.org/documents/6552530-MACY-S-NOTICE-OF-DATA-BREACH.html

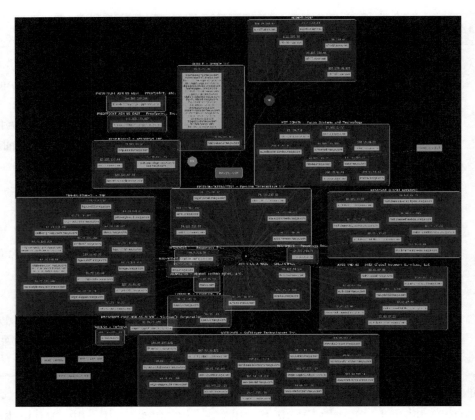

Figure 8-4. *Macys.com Topology – DNS Dumpster*

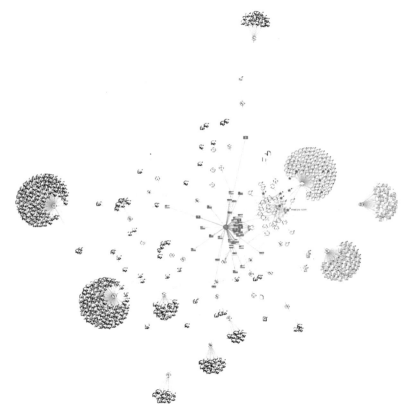

Figure 8-5. *Macys.com – VirusTotal*

Consequently, the attackers were able to divert the customers' journey through their infrastructure, enabling them to carry out harvesting of the customers' payment card input into the in-scope (**RED**) e-Commerce interface. Although the vulnerable out-of-scope web page was not directly involved in the processing, storage, or transmission of payment card data, it was involved in the journey to hand over to the secure payment interface. Therefore, the attackers were unable to compromise the in-scope (**RED**) interface so had taken the opportunity to exploit vulnerabilities to the adjoining web pages.

Macy's has complex web interfaces, the greater the need to fortify both your in-scope (**RED**) and out-of-scope (**BLACK**) environments to help reduce the adjoining web pages from turning a muddy **BROWN** color.

Recommendations

Ensure that your asset inventory is categorized in a manner that easily shows your in-scope **RED** assets (*e.g., Critical Asset Inventory*), as well as documenting any other assets within your business (*e.g., Business Asset Inventory*).

An example of such an approach can be seen in ISACA's Open PCI Scoping Toolkit.[21]

Cat 1a.	Devices that store, process, or transmit cardholder data
Cat 1b.	Devices that do not store, process, or transmit cardholder data, but are "infected by" Category 1a devices due to the absence of controlled access or isolation
Cat 2a	System components which, through controlled access, provide security services (e.g., authentication) to a Category 1 device
Cat 2b	System components which, through controlled access, can initiate an inbound connection to a Category 1 device
Cat 2c	System components which, through controlled access, can only receive a connection from a Category 1 device (i.e., cannot initiate a connection). Category 2x System components which, through indirect and controlled access, have the ability to administer Category 1 devices **Note: Category 2x devices have no direct access to/from Category 1 devices.**
Cat 2x	System components which, through indirect and controlled access, have the ability to administer Category 1 devices **Note: Category 2x devices have no direct access to/from Category 1 devices.**
Cat 3	System components do not store, process, or transmit cardholder data and are isolated from and do not provide any services to any Category 1 device.

Having identified and categorized your business assets based upon their criticality, it is then extremely important to visualize their interactions and connections.

This is achieved through the use of asset inventory aligned to Data Flow and Network Diagrams. Think of these as being like State/County and City/Town/District maps.

---

[21]www.isaca.org/Groups/Professional-English/pci-compliance/GroupDocuments/ OpenPCIScopingToolkit.pdf

High-Level Overview

This provides an overview of all your business assets (e.g., State view), as well as the location of the CDE.

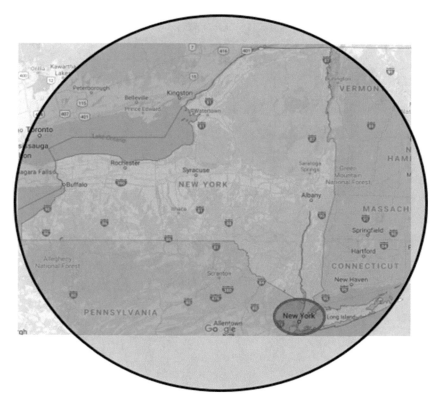

Figure 8-6. *New York State*

Detailed-Level Overview

This shows the critical assets and their associated connections within the CDE. As a consequence, any **BLACK** assets that may be interacting, connected to, or have a potential impact on the **RED** would become **BROWN** and would need to be investigated further.

Figure 8-7. *New York City*

This approach will help you confirm how accurately you have scoped your PCI DSS and help identify any potential **BROWN** assets that could impact your business if neglected or overlooked.

As part of your penetration and segmentation testing, these supporting documents should be periodically reviewed and be provided to the personnel who will carry out the penetration/segmentation testing.

Remember that the identification and maintenance of your scoping should not be limited to your network and systems infrastructure and it remains just as important to extend this process to your physical and applications environments.

For example, in regard to your applications, it is highly recommended that you consider the incorporation of the following:

- Maintain a complete list of your applications inventory.

- Identify where these applications hosted in your network.

- Identify the architecture of the applications including programming language, database type used, authentication, and authorization controls.

- Identify the encryption used for secure communications.

- Identify the encryption used in the application and database.

Start by thinking of your business as being completely flat and with everything being interconnected in some way. Much like a flat network, everything is in-scope and needs some form of protection from malicious attackers (both internal and external); however, the amount of protective measures you apply is dependent on the aggregated value of the services that they provide. As you identify the assets and their connections, you should color code them based upon their potential risk/importance to your business. These color-coded assets should then be articulated onto your supporting network and data flow diagrams.

Your identified systems that support your payment card operations are high risk and must be protected using the PCI DSS integrated controls framework, while any other business critical assets should also be protected against any known threats. Although you only need to ensure that your payment card environment is compliant with the PCI DSS integrated control framework, you should consider the additional benefits of fortifying your environments outside the scope of your PCI DSS program.

For example, consider

- The implications of Maersk incident, where their business systems (non-PCI DSS) were impacted by the NotPetya vulnerability[22]

- The potential impact on your company brand/reputation if a vulnerability in your web interfaces (non-PCI DSS) were to be subjected to digital graffiti or defacement[23]

---

[22]www.wired.com/story/notpetya-cyberattack-ukraine-russia-code-crashed-the-world/
[23]https://blog.radware.com/security/attack-types-and-vectors/2019/09/
defacements-the-digital-graffiti-of-the-internet/

Conclusion

You cannot protect what you do not know, so it is essential that you identify, categorize, and catalogue all of your assets and the results recorded in your asset inventories, network diagrams, and data flow diagrams. This should be your starting point for both your PCI DSS compliance obligations and for the effective application of mitigation measures.

Any changes to your business environments should be reflected in the updates to your supporting documents. Failure to do this effectively could provide your attackers with the opportunity that they are looking for, and wouldn't you rather understand the risks to your business assets before those risks are made a reality?

Attackers are known for carrying out reconnaissance of their victims to ensure that they have a full and accurate inventory and understanding of the critical data paths. Therefore, if your attackers are doing this, why shouldn't you be doing the same?

Accurate scoping is heavily reliant on good asset management which is a key component of an effective data privacy and security strategy. However, the criticality of this element is often underappreciated with businesses failing to understand the extent of their assets and their interconnections and not even including network and data flow diagrams' maintenance as a key business responsibility.

Whether for PCI DSS compliance or for the protection of your business, this is just commonsense and is priceless activity for your business and for the security of your most valuable data and business critical systems.

Key Takeaways

De-scoping can make an organization's compliance efforts easier by helping simplify the extent of the environment requiring the application of the PCI DSS controls framework. However, the scoping efforts must be validated and (once validated) managed to ensure that there are no assets (deemed out-of-scope) that can undermine the protection of the in-scope CHD.

Do not wait between audit/assessment checks to validate that any changes to the PCI DSS have not undermined the "Scope."

Can insecure coding on a web interface enable unauthorized access into the supporting corporate network?

*Can a vulnerability in a **BLACK** (Out-of-Scope) web page be used to redirect the customers' journey through their environment before being returned to the **RED** zone?*

Have you confirmed and documented the in-scope assets and do they match up to the supporting network and data flow diagrams?

*Do your network and data flow diagrams show the interconnections between the **RED** (In-Scope) and **BLACK** (Out-of-Scope) environments?*

When carrying out segmentation testing, have you considered all points where the lines could become blurred?

*If you are relying on systems hosted by a third party, do they provide you with confirmation that their environments are suitably isolated from your **RED** zone?*

- *Does your scoping include the identification of the IT systems, Buildings, Rooms, and authorized personnel?*

- *Can you identify a clear demarcation between the RED and BLACK zones?*

- *Have you established a "Buffer Zone" between the RED and BLACK zones?*

Risks

It is important to look at your PCI DSS scope from the view of a potential attacker and to consider the potential benefits for risk reduction through the application of additional defensive controls for the early detection and response to incursions into the **RED** zone via the **BLACK** zone. Poor segmentation and scope validation provide the attackers the potential opportunities to exploit these **BROWN** zones.

Ask yourself:

- *Is the scoping exercise accurate?*

- *Do I maintain effective asset inventories?*

- *Are my asset inventories used to create my network and data flow diagrams?*

- *Are my network and data flows restricted to the **RED** zone only?*

- *Do I have a visualization of both the "State" and the "City"?*

- *Can I easily identify any demarcation points?*

- *Is this being done to simplify compliance or to reduce the associated risks?*

- *Do I understand the segmentation perspective for any third-party-hosted environments?*

- *Have the third parties provided sufficient reassurance that their **RED** and **BLACK** zones are sufficiently isolated?*

- *Should I add additional protective controls to the "Buffer Zone" within the **BLACK** zone?*

- *As a Service Provider, am I satisfied that I am sufficiently safeguarding their RED zone from unauthorized incursions? If so, can I provide appropriate evidence to my client so that they remain reassured?*

CHAPTER 9

An Introduction to the PCI DSS Controls Framework

Brief History of PCI DSS

Prior to 2004,[1] the various Card Brands (Visa, Mastercard, American Express, JCB, and Discover) had already introduced their own security controls frameworks. However, if you were a business trying to align to these standards, life could be extremely disparate, without a single controls framework to follow. Consequently, in 2005 the Payment Card Industry Security Standards Council (PCI SSC)[2] were tasked to develop a standardized controls framework, which would articulate how businesses could best protect customers' payment card transactions.

As you can see in Figures 9-1 to 9-4, this was well timed and aligned to the increased growth of online shopping, the consumer use of payment cards, and, of course, the criminals' increasing trend to Internet-related crime.

---

[1] https://searchsecurity.techtarget.com/feature/The-history-of-the-PCI-DSS-standard-A-visual-timeline
[2] www.pcisecuritystandards.org/

© Jim Seaman 2020
J. Seaman, *PCI DSS*, https://doi.org/10.1007/978-1-4842-5808-8_9

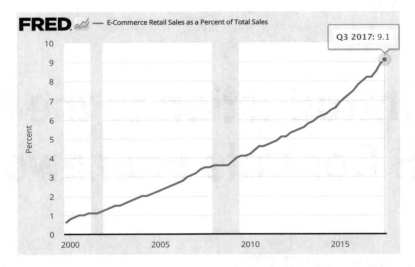

Figure 9-1. *E-commerce Spending Trends[3]*

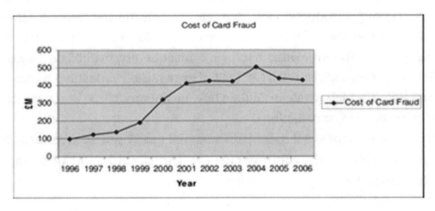

Figure 9-2. *Payment Card Fraud Trends*

---

[3]https://growthhackers.com/articles/what-is-the-future-of-ecommerce-in-2018-and-beyond-10-trends-transforming-how-we-shop-online

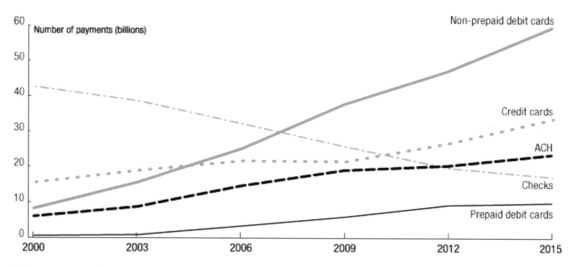

Figure 9-3. *Consumer Payment Card Use Trends[4]*

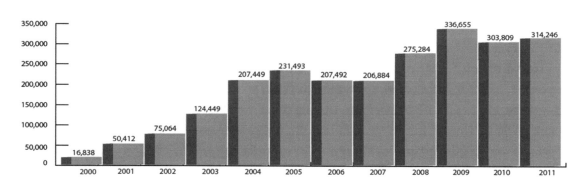

Figure 9-4. *Internet-Related Crime Trends[5]*

The mandated application of PCI DSS for all businesses with payment card operations is only a contractual obligation. Adherence to this contractual obligation is currently policed by the Acquiring Banks for Merchants and by the Card Brands for high-risk Service Providers.

Failure to achieve PCI DSS compliance may result in breach of contract fines or, in rare occasions, the removal of the right to have payment card operations. Remember that it is in the interest of both the Card Brands and the Acquiring banks for businesses to process purchases through payment cards – perhaps a risk they are willing to take!

---

[4]www.federalreserve.gov/paymentsystems/2016-noncash-payments.htm
[5]www.infosecisland.com/blogview/21329-IC3-2011-Internet-Crime-Report.html

However, in contrast, the evolving global data privacy legislations require personal data to be securely processed, and payment card data is deemed to be a component of personal data. Therefore, in-scope for legislative and regulatory compliance and in the event of a data breach will be subject to a regulatory investigation.

However, until the regulators make the requirement for PCI DSS compliance to be a legal requirement for all payment card business operations to be compliant with PCI DSS, the business perception of its importance will always be limited. As a result, there is not a common security baseline that will be applied across all businesses, and this will then continue to present a lucrative hunting ground for the criminals.

"Without PCI DSS, it was open season for the criminals!"

My Life Before PCI DSS

I was first introduced to the PCI DSS controls framework, in early 2012, and successfully completed my Payment Card Industry Qualified Security Assessor (PCI QSA) course in early 2013.

However, long before this, I had gleaned a comprehensive understanding and exposure to Cyber/InfoSec best practices through an extremely rewarding and lucrative 22-year career as an RAF Policeman. During this time I had been employed on various security-related appointments which culminated in the final decade of my military service being employed to provide specialist security support to mission-critical assets (both in the United Kingdom and on deployed overseas operations) working in Counter Intelligence (CI) and RAF Police Special Branch operations. This furnished me with the fortune of having been exposed to numerous "real life" examples, which are directly relatable to specific controls requirements from the PCI DSS controls framework.

The benchmark for becoming an RAF Police CI specialist was the ability to successfully complete a 10-week residential RAF Police CI course. This course consisted of 6-week *theory (covering all the domain areas from the Joint Service Publication 440 (JSP 440) – Defence Manual of Security)*:

- Two weeks of investigative interviewing
- Two weeks of practical assessments (putting the theory into practice)
- Weekly progression exams

- A final theory exam that needs to be passed before progressing onto the practical assessment phase of the course

The content of the JSP 440 consisted of approximately 2500 pages of guidance, across three volumes, that needed to be theoretically understood and practically applied in order to become the "Instant expert, just add water."

Volume 1:   The principles of protective security, the responsibilities of those concerned with applying them, and physical security policy.

Volume 2:   Personnel security policy including the vetting system, line manager responsibility and travel security.

Volume 3:   Guidance and policy on the security of Communications and Information Systems (CIS).

Figure 9-5. *Content Areas from JSP 440*

I am extremely passionate and driven in my chosen career path due, in part, to the fact that approximately 5 weeks into my CI course, I suffered the tragic loss of my father dying suddenly. On the very same day that the hospital had discovered two cancerous tumors was the day that he died.

Unfortunately, from the time that I received notification that he was seriously ill in hospital to the time that it took me to get back, he had already died. Added to this, I had been informed that to continue on my CI course I would need to return to the RAF Police school to sit the final theory exam *(This was just 6 days later (the morning after my dad's funeral))*. Failure to do so would have resulted in my needing to start the course all over again from scratch. Inspired in the knowledge that my dad would have wanted me to continue, I returned to complete the CI course.

Having successfully completed the course, my first appointment was as the IT and Information Security specialist for an RAF base whose mission was to train the pilots of the future. This role required that I provide CI and computer security support, so it was not long before I was returning to the RAF Police School, in order to complete the computer security (CompSy) level 1 (2 weeks) and CompSy 2 (3 weeks) courses.

Although the CompSy courses provided me with a fundamental understanding of computer security, I identified that I could further benefit from having a greater technical knowledge and thus enrolled myself on a "Computing" higher national diploma (HND) course, delivered over 2 years of evening classes.

During my 10 years of working as a CI operative, I was extremely fortunate to have been selected for some extremely challenging and rewarding appointments, including two appointments as Unit Counterintelligence specialist and two appointments on regional CI Operations (Central UK and Scotland and Northern UK Regions).

Yes, as part of the CI Operations roles, this included providing Field Intelligence and Security support to military assets while deployed into hostile environments.[6] *This proved to provide invaluable opportunities to apply effective practices, often under high-pressure conditions.*

> **Counter-Intelligence Activity.**
> Counter-intelligence activity can make a significant input to force protection and operations security. Primary activities are liaison, investigations, casework, screening of locally employed civilians and intelligence collection.39 Liaison is conducted to obtain and corroborate information, develop sources of information and foster both goodwill and understanding. Investigations are conducted into the activities of an adversary and into personnel security matters. Counter-intelligence casework may exploit opportunities to develop greater understanding of security threats or weakness. Investigations and casework may employ interviews, record checks, technical measures, computer forensics, covert search and covert passive surveillance to develop understanding. Counterintelligence activities require a high degree of integration with intelligence staff.
>
> **Counter-Intelligence Analysis.**
> Counter-intelligence analysis is the fusion of multi-source information and intelligence on hostile intelligence services, terrorists, extremists and other groups or individuals. It also includes the analysis of the effectiveness of security measures and counter-intelligence operations.
>
> **Counter-Intelligence Advice.**
> Counter-intelligence staffs are responsible for advising commanders on the effectiveness of countermeasures and variation in the threat.

Figure 9-6. *Extract from Joint Doctrine Publication 2-00*

---

[6]https://assets.publishing.service.gov.uk/government/uploads/system/uploads/ attachment_data/file/311572/20110830_jdp2_00_ed3_with_change1.pdf

Additionally, life on Counter Intelligence duties[7] proved to be far more complex than just aligning to the various domains of the JSP 440 (Volumes I, II, and III (circa 2500 pages) and brought into play numerous other JSPs and Air Publications (Risk Management, Aviation Security, Governance, etc.), for example:

- Air publication 3085 and 3085A: Risk Management in the RAF

- JSP (Joint Service Publication) 525: Corporate Governance and Risk Management

Toward the end of my military career, I prepared myself for a transition to the corporate sector by successfully completing a Master of Science (MSc) in "Security Management" at Loughborough University.

My Life Living with PCI DSS

Two months into my first appointment within the corporate world, I was selected as the Baseline Security Controls manager, responsible for the successful implementation of a Baseline Security Controls framework. This project first introduced me to the implementation of a suite of industry security controls (ISO 27002, PCI DSS, COBIT 4.1), which were to be aligned to various departments within a financial services institution. This proved to be an extremely useful experience, as the need for detailed cross-mapping helped me understand the similarities and commonalities of different frameworks.

Sequentially to this, I sought to transfer my knowledge gained through the RAF Police for a globally recognized industry information security course and successfully self-studied to become ISACA Certified Information Security Management (CISM) qualified.

My second appointment, within the corporate world, was to join a small Cyber/ InfoSec consultancy team for an organization that provided network security services, penetration testing, and professional consultancy services (including QSA).[8] This began my journey into the development of a comprehensive understanding of the PCI DSS controls framework.

---

[7]https://assets.publishing.service.gov.uk/government/uploads/system/uploads/ attachment_data/file/311572/20110830_jdp2_00_ed3_with_change1.pdf
[8]www.professionalsecurity.co.uk/news/interviews/cyber-reserve-unit/

However, after almost 5 years working as a QSA, I started to become a little disillusioned with the payment card industry's (PCI's) tick box approach and the inconsistencies with the interpretation of the standard.

Here are a couple of examples:

1. On one occasion, I had my advice overruled by one of the card brands. I had been carrying out a gap assessment for a client who was a Service Provider, providing printing services for financial institutions. Part of this service included the printing of account statement, which included the full PAN in clear text *(as this was used as the customers' account information)* which was then posted out, in bulk, via standard post.

    Consequently, owing to the known threat that criminals will intercept the post to steal PANs and PINs,[9] I advised the client that they should try to avoid printing out the full PAN *(not possible)* or to apply PCI DSS control 9.6.2 *(sending media by trackable means, rather through standard post)* to help mitigate this risk.

    The client objected, based upon the potential cost implications, and asked that I escalate the incident to the Card Brands. Approximately, 3 months later I received an extremely disappointing response from the Card Brands who contradicted my advice, stating that *(due to the cost implications)* this control does not apply to Financial Institutions.

2. While working with a Financial Institution, to help them align their Acquirer payment card operations of their business with PCI DSS, we were trying to understand and identify the extent of their scope. This was proving to be extremely difficult, as their systems that supported their in-scope systems were heavily entwined with their other payment card operations. Applying the concept that PCI DSS applies to any IT system that directly processes, transmits, or stores *(or any IT systems that could impact)*,

---

[9]www.usnews.com/news/best-states/new-jersey/articles/2019-12-19/ ex-postal-worker-admits-taking-bribes-to-steal-credit-cards

as you can imagine as we started to identify and visualize the environment, the scope started to significantly grow.

The discussions with the Card Brands resulted in their advice that it was important to remember that the Financial Institution did not need to be PCI DSS compliant *(thankfully, this is a message that has appeared to have changed[10])* so any in-scope systems that were deemed to be severely intertwined with any out-of-scope systems could be deemed as being out-of-scope.

3. I had been carrying out a gap assessment for a UK-based business, during which their US-based sister company had approximately a dozen of their customer payment cards breached. Consequently, the UK client had asked if I would be willing to go out to the United States to carry out a formal assessment of their sister company, following their remediation efforts. Initial discussions were made with their Acquirer to confirm what they would deem to be acceptable. Being that the client was a small business and only processed a small volume of payment cards, it was agreed that they would accept an onsite completion of a version 2.0, self-assessment questionnaire (SAQ) C by a QSA.

The client was happy with this proposal and asked if I would be willing to go out to the United States to complete this assessment. I was happy to oblige but advised them that they might be better served by engaging with a local QSA company, so as to avoid unnecessary additional travel and accommodation costs.

Several weeks later, I was tasked to go out to the United States to carry out the formal onsite assessment of the sister company. The reason being that despite the fact that their Acquirer had stated they were happy with the QSA completing a SAQ, every QSA Company had appeared to have seen the dollar signs and would only quote for the time-consuming and lengthy completion of a full-blown report on compliance (RoC).

---

[10]https://globalrisk.mastercard.com/wp-content/uploads/2019/06/Q2-2019-PCI-Quarterly-Newsletter.pdf

4.   During another engagement, I was tasked to deliver a 10-day engagement to provide a PCI DSS assessment for a US marketing company, providing services to some large, well-known US retailers.

Previously, the client had been sold a number of security tools and policy templates to help support their PCI DSS compliance efforts and were now apparently ready for their assessment. On arrival, at the client site, I commenced with the planning and preparation phase of the engagement by asking the question

"So, describe to me how your business is involved with payment card data?"

The reply:

"We don't! Our clients have asked us to become PCI DSS compliant!"

As a consequence, as the result of the salesperson just selling them the requested service without confirming the requirements, the client had incurred unnecessary expense. I ended up delivering them an alternative effective data privacy and security strategy to provide the assurance that their clients were seeking.

PCI DSS Structure

Despite my becoming disillusioned with the PCI and choosing to move away, one thing that I have never become disillusioned with is the PCI DSS controls framework and how effectively it is layered to create an integrated approach for the protection of card payment channels. Unfortunately, the very complexity of the framework distracts from the effectiveness of the framework. The PCI DSS integrated controls are an extremely payment card–specific framework, and when successfully understood and implemented, this can be exceptionally effective in the safeguarding of a business's payment card operations. Additionally, the PCI DSS integrated framework is particularly prescriptive which sometimes leads to organizations adopting an extremely lineal/check box/audit-style approach.

It is important to remember that this is specifically designed for the protection of payment card data. However, these principles and approaches can be suitably adapted to help protect other types of sensitive data assets.

With a long-standing career of working in high-tempo/high-risk and hostile environments to provide comprehensive frontline security investigations and successfully interpreting/implementing numerous security controls frameworks *(along with hundreds of PCI DSS assessments)*, I have come to appreciate the value of businesses correctly aligning with the PCI DSS controls in the mitigation of their risks.

Rather than looking at the PCI DSS controls in isolation, it is better to look at using the PCI DSS controls framework to help answer your "So What?" question and for you to understand the intent and the potential impact on the other layers of the PCI DSS model.

PCI DSS: 6 Goals, 12 Requirements

As I write this book, the PCI Security Standards Council (PCI SSC) are looking to update the PCI DSS to version 4.0. However, the basic model will remain (6 Goals supported by 12 Requirements). Therefore, rather than delve into the complexities, at the control level, this chapter will provide an overview of the intent of the model, and the readers should familiarize themselves with the specific controls that support their particular requirement by visiting the PCI SSC web site.[11]

Requirement 1
•   1.1.......
o   1.1.1.......
•   1.2.......
o   1.2.1......
•   1.3......
o   1.3.1.....
•   1.4......
o   1.4.1......
•   1.5......

Figure 9-7. *PCI DSS Control Structure*

---

[11]`www.pcisecuritystandards.org/document_library`

Goals

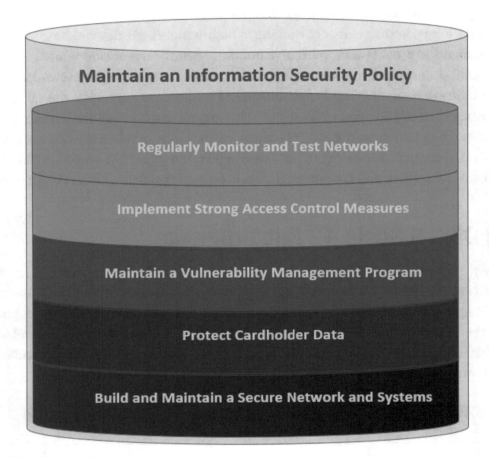

Figure 9-8. *PCI DSS Six Goals*

6. 3 Ps: People, Policies, and Processes *(Maintain a Policy That Addresses Information Security for All Personnel)*

Within the PCI DSS controls frameworks, this is the final goal. However, in reality this should be the primary goal of any compliance efforts – ensuring that all the following is in place:

- Personnel understand the importance of protecting card data processing operations.

- The rules that must be adhered to are fully understood.

- Their roles and responsibilities in achieving/maintaining this.

- Ensuring that their knowledge and skills are maintained for the supporting function that they supply.

- Effective supplier management is established to provide suitable assurance for any supporting outsourced services.

- Being able to rapidly identify and respond to actions that could lead to compromise or responding and containing actual compromises of your payment card environments.

- Periodic internal testing to ensure policies and processes are being adhered to.

Documentation, Documentation, Documentation

There is a common misunderstanding that for PCI DSS compliance there needs to be "War and Peace"-sized policies and procedures.

This is incorrect. Nowhere in the PCI DSS controls framework does it mandate the need for lengthy documentation. In fact, the shorter and more concise the policy and procedures can be, the easier it is for personnel to understand and comply with.

PCI DSS is your benchmark, and, as such, to help you identify the PCI DSS controls that apply to your payment card operations, the PCI SSC have helpfully produced a range of payment channel–aligned Self-Assessment Questionnaires (SAQs). These provide all the expected controls that they would expect to be applied to the SAQ-specific payment channels, as described in the "Before You Begin" Section.

Before You Begin

SAQ C has been developed to address requirements applicable to merchants whose payment application systems (for example, point-of-sale systems) are connected to the Internet (for example, via DSL, cable modem, etc.).

SAQ C merchants process cardholder data via a point-of-sale (POS) system or other payment application systems connected to the Internet, do not store cardholder data on any computer system, and may be either brick-and-mortar (card-present) or mail/telephone-order (card-not-present) merchants.

SAQ C merchants confirm that, for this payment channel:

Figure 9-9. *Extract from SAQ C*

Reality Bites

The policies are essential for setting the "tone at the top" and can be easily undermined by Senior Management. One such incident occurred, during the mid-2000s, when the UK Government decided to implement extensive defense cuts. This led to the disbandment of a long-standing Air Squadron *(established in World War I)* and the subsequent closure of an RAF airbase. Members of this squadron were specialists and had spent all their careers at this single airbase *(some having served more than 20 years)* and were now to be made redundant.

Clearly this resulted in some disaffected airmen/women and one such individual took it upon themselves to inform the UK Prime Minister of the huge error they were making. Consequently, they took a highly sensitive document and, using the highly sensitive fax machine, faxed a copy of the document to the Prime Minister's highly sensitive fax machine.

The document had been sent to the UK Prime Minister using a secure communication's channel. However, the UK Prime Minister's fax machine was located in their secretary's office and the document was retrieved by their secretary. The secretary was security cleared to the appropriate level but did not meet the "Need to Know" requirements. This was in breach of the Station Standing Orders.

Consequently, regional CI operations personnel were tasked to carry out a security incident investigation into this breach of policy. However, the investigation could not find the offending individual guilty of any breach of policy, after it transpired that the Station Commander (Policy Owner) had verbally instructed the individual to send the document in this manner.

Secure Architecture (Build and Maintain a Secure Network)

Having aligned your payment channels to the applicable controls, now is the time to visualize and harden the supporting IT systems which support the CHD life cycles from the point of origin, right through to the secure disposal/destruction (after the legitimacy for retention has ended).

By the very nature, IT systems (Servers, Databases, Switches, Routers, Firewalls, etc.) are supplied in an insecure state.

Therefore, these systems need to be linked together and locked down to ensure that they are secured (eliminating any unnecessary functionality) and to prevent unauthorized network traffic being able to pass between the network zones.

In the event that your network gets breached, a layered and secure architecture will help apply the 5 Ds of Defense:

- **Deter**
- **Detect**
- **Delay**
- **Deny**
- **Defend**

Layered Defenses

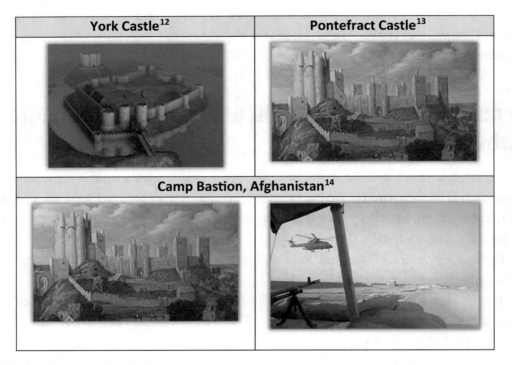

Figure 9-10. *Secure Architecture*

Although PCI DSS does not prohibit the use of "Flat Networks," the very fact that PCI DSS applies to any systems that process, store, or transmit CHD (or any systems that could impact these systems) makes achieving PCI DSS considerably more difficult.

The concept of layered defenses has been seen to be extremely effective for the physical defenses to control who was permitted to go where, and this can be seen being successfully applied in castle structures, as well as in modern military defenses.

Given today's threats to cardholder data, the benefits of a layered architecture have proven itself for centuries. However, in today's data technology environments, there is a need to be mindful of rogue devices providing alternative access routes – rather than a direct attack through the main entrances (firewalls).

---

[12]www.twcenter.net/forums/showthread.php?575311-The-Dukedom-of-York-York-Castle-York
[13]www.pontefractheritagegroup.org.uk/page2.html
[14]www.bbc.co.uk/news/world-19635544#panel7

Identify and Manage IT Assets

7. Application	Human to computer interactions	
	Where applications access the network services	Website requests content Content returned in the requested format
6. Presentation	Presents the data in a usable format and in which data encryption happens	Encryption Compression Translation
5. Session	Maintains connections	
	Controls Ports & Sessions	Communication sessions
4. Transport	Transmits data using transmission protocols, including TCP & UDP	Segmentation Transport Reassemble
3. Network	Appoints the physical path that the data will follow	Packet creation Transport Packet assemble
2. Datalink	Structures the format of the data on the network	Frame creation Transport Transfer frames between network nodes
1. Physical	Transmits raw bit streams	Sending cable Bitstream *(01010000 01000011 01001001 00100000 01000100 01010011 01010011)* Receiving cable

Figure 9-11. *Seven-Layer OSI Model*

Having identified all the people involved in supporting the payment channels, the next crucial step is to accurately identify and manage the IT assets involved in the processing, transmission, and storage of the consumers' CHD.

All the identified IT assets, across the entirety of the Open System Interconnection (OSI) seven-layer network reference model,[15] need to be securely configured to ensure that any attacks are unable to circumvent the protective measure applied at the software layers through the manipulation of the hardware layers.

---

[15]www.w3schools.in/cyber-security/osi-security-layers-and-their-significance/

Traffic Control

Traffic Filtering (Between Untrusted and Trusted Zones)

Figure 9-12. *World War II Internal Access Control*

Figure 9-13. *TSA Security Checkpoint*

We all know that the safest and most secure business operations are those that are permanently locked and which prohibit any access. Unfortunately, this model does not work in the PCI DSS environments as businesses are heavily reliant on the processing and storage of CHD. Consequently, the traffic needs to be strictly controlled – checking the authority for all network traffic ingress/egress. In the physical environment, this is established by the issuance of access cards/fob/keys (based upon their role) or access control lists:

"If your name is not down, you're not coming in!"

An example would be to ensure that your firewalls and routers have their rulesets configured to implicitly deny, so as to prevent any traffic that is not specifically recognized from passing between your untrusted and your trusted network environments.

Just having the rights to enter an environment should not automatically elevate their rights to transit anywhere. Traffic flow access needs to be filtered based upon legitimate access needs.

For example, when travelling, the purchase of a "Boarding Card" does not allow you uncontrolled access to anywhere within the airport architecture. The same should be applied to networks supporting payment channels.

Reality Bites

Every military establishment applies these principles. For example, Camp Bastion was the size of the UK city of Reading (approximately 61 km^2) and employed multiple internally segmented (trusted) areas, where access was strictly limited based upon legitimate needs to access, with an external perimeter access control (external firewall) where all access was subject to explicit checks, before transiting through the 1.5 km long De-militarized zone (DMZ).

After transiting through the DMZ, the traffic was then faced with more security checks, searches, validation, and approval (at the inner access control) before being granted access to the inner sanctum. However, it did not stop there, as further access restrictions were applied to the more sensitive inner sanctums.

During a 6-month CIFT deployment, my team encountered over 550 reportable security incidents that were identified through the monitoring of these points of access/egress.

Secure by Design/Secured by Default

Network assets are sold in an open (unlocked) and vulnerable state, as they are designed to be functional. It is essential that all unnecessary settings are disabled so that only essential settings are enabled for the specific service they are providing.

This includes changing default passwords, closing unnecessary ports/protocols, disabling insecure settings, and disabling all surplus services.

Reality Bites

During my role as a station CI operative, I was responsible for the management of an extensive library of physical security cabinets. The purpose of these security containers was to provide secure storage facilities for highly sensitive hardcopy data and media, with locking mechanisms that enabled the restriction of access to only authorized personnel, and their use was strictly restricted for the sole purpose of the secure storage of this media and it was prohibited for using these containers to support additional purposes *(e.g., Storing valuable and attractive items or cash)*. These security containers were provided with either Manifoil combination locks (MCL) or Mersey-style locking mechanisms.

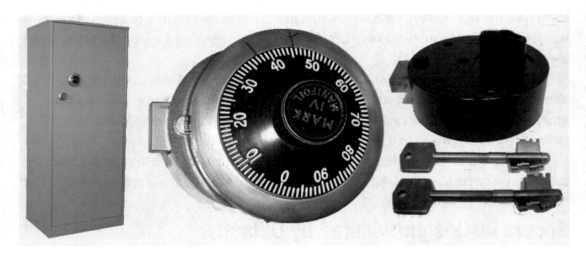

Figure 9-14. *Sy Container and MCL and Mersey-Style Locks*

For ease of use, newly issued security containers were set to the manufacturer's setting and, when being stored, need to be set to a unique setting that was only to be known by CI personnel.

When being stored or issued out for use, it may be more convenient to leave the setting on the manufacturer's combination. However, this makes the setting susceptible to compromise or misuse *(The same applies to any assets supporting the payment card operations)*. Additionally, on return from use, it is important that the security combinations are reset to the establishment's unique setting or returned to manufacturer's setting before reuse or disposal.

After recently taking over the responsibilities, I was carrying out a review of my inventory of security containers, only to discover that the previous incumbent had failed to effectively manage the return of these assets. I discovered that approximately half a dozen of these security containers had been secured, without being reset to the unique configuration setting. As a consequence, I was unable to gain authorized access to confirm that these were empty or to reissue them for use and needed to procure the services of a locksmith to brute force access *(rendering the assets as scrap)* to ensure that no sensitive data/media remained within.

Another recent example is the online dating site "Heyyo" was breached[16] after they left their Elasticsearch server without any password protections (the default setting). This led to the leaking of the private information (e.g., messages, photos, sexual preferences, occupations, etc.) of over 70,000 registered users worldwide. Such a vulnerability may not be discovered as part of your quarterly vulnerability scans and should be addressed as part of the implementation, ensuring that all assets are benchmarked against industry security configuration standards *(e.g., CIS Benchmarks[17])*.

I would highly recommend incorporating security configuration checks into your vulnerability management practices using (where possible) automated tools *(e.g., Titania Nipper[18]/PAWS,[19] CIS CAT,[20] etc.)*.

---

[16]www.forbes.com/sites/nicolemartin1/2019/09/27/another-dating-app-has-leaked-users-data/#501853c67da6

[17]www.cisecurity.org/cis-hardened-image-list/

[18]www.titania.com/products/nipper/?utm_term=titania%20nipper&utm_source=adwords&utm_campaign=titania+brand+ppc&utm_medium=ppc&hsa_acc=2787898520&hsa_tgt=kwd-782740145036&hsa_ver=3&hsa_grp=76079675036&hsa_ad=361430641582&hsa_src=g&hsa_kw=titania%20nipper&hsa_mt=e&hsa_cam=2058213049&hsa_net=adwords&gclid=cj0kcqiasbrxbrdparisaannz_odpq3zxxotchilexggv77l_s0dfa5u9q2cqcfujk-yk1kpsuznygoaaoooealw_wcb

[19]www.titania.com/products/paws/

[20]https://learn.cisecurity.org/cis-cat-lite

Secure Data at Rest and in Transit (Protect Cardholder Data)

THINK: SECURING THE VAULT   THINK: CASH IN TRANSIT

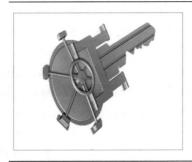 

The first consideration here is to decide whether there is a need for the persistent storage of CHD or are there other measures that can be applied to further reduce the risks and burden associated with having to maintain a vault, for example:

- Transferring the risk through the use of PCI DSS-compliant Payment Service Providers

    - *Securely redirecting, or using an embedded iFrame, to ensure that all customers' payment card details go through a PCI DSS-compliant third-party Service Provider's interface (no business systems or personnel interaction with payment card data – fully outsourced).*

- Terminating the risk through the use of Dual-Tone Multi-Frequency (DTMF) technologies

    - *Your consumers enter their CHD via their own phone keypad, rather than needing to be passed verbally to a call agent and then manually entered into the application via the business IT system interface (no business systems or personnel interaction with payment card data – fully outsourced).*

- Treating the risk through encryption or tokenization. In the event that the vault gets compromised, the keys needed to unlock and the system needed to untokenized the CHD are completely independent and protected.

    - All customers' payment card data operations are carried out in house and the payment card data is securely stored (in a vault), protected by encryption (kept under lock and key). The use of encryption makes the stored payment card data useless in the event of a compromise. However, this is heavily reliant of good key management practices.

    - *Customers' payment card information is exchanged for tokenized data (carried out by a third party) to ensure that only tokenized payment card data is processed by the business systems, supporting the payment card operations.*

Within your trusted network, it is currently permitted for an organization to move the CHD unencrypted *(This may well change with the release of v.4.0)*. However, at any point that an organization needs to move it across a public-facing environment, this needs to be kept under lock and key.

Reality Bites

Having issued out the security containers for use, each one had their locks re-configured to unique settings that were only known to authorized personnel. However, in my role as the station CI operative, I had the responsibility to securely manage the rotation of their supporting keys and combination changes and to securely store the duplicates.

I did not have a need to access these duplicates, so they were securely sealed and securely stored in a separate security container, away from the in-use security containers.

Periodically, I would manage the mustering and changing of the keys and combinations and respond to potential compromises. Additionally, in the event of a compromised key, forgotten combination, or in the event of the need for emergencies, I would be responsible for ensuring that safe and secure changes were made.

All these combination and key management procedures were essential for the maintenance of the integrity of the security containers and to ensure that the enclosed highly sensitive data assets retained their confidentiality, integrity, and availability (CIA).

This principle is similar to that needed to meet the compliance requirements for safeguarded stored payment card data through the application of encryption.

Secure Maintenance (Maintain a Vulnerability Management Program)

Vulnerability and Patch Management	Change Management	Secure Development Operations

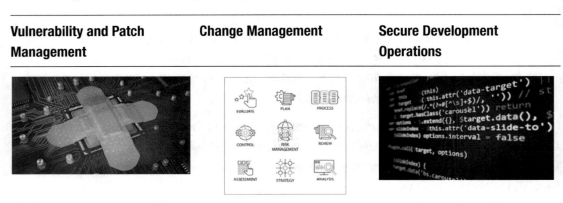

This is all about keeping the vehicle roadworthy and making sure that any new vulnerabilities and updates are effectively risk managed so that they are identified, prioritized, and treated, within a timely manner, before they can be exploited.

In addition, any changes need to be documented and risk assessed for the potential impact to make the change and the options for rolling back the change, in the event that it has an adverse impact on operations. Any significant changes may lead to additional testing to ensure that the changes do not undermine the integrity of the supporting systems and software.

Finally, the supporting hardware requires software applications (both internal and external) which need to be risk managed and tested so that any coding imperfections cannot lead to exploitation, or circumvention, by an attacker.

Reality Bites

During my two CIFT deployments to Afghanistan, the results of effective vulnerability management were clearly in evidence. During my first deployment to support the operations at Kandahar airport, as part of the Force Protection Wing, we would carry out off-base patrols using modified soft skin or "Snatch" Land Rovers.

Figure 9-15. *Soft-Skinned and Snatch Land Rovers*

While in the Air Terminal, at RAF Brize Norton, waiting to board our aircraft to Kandahar to take over from the duties from the existing Force Protection deployment (51 Sqn RAF Regiment), we learned of the death of Senior Aircraftman (SAC) Bridge.[21]

---

[21]www.gov.uk/government/fatalities/senior-aircraftman-christopher-bridge-51-squadron-royal-air-force-regiment-killed-in-afghanistan

While carrying out off-base patrols of the external perimeter, their patrol had driven over an improvised explosive device (IED) with SAC Bridge taking the direct brunt of the explosion. Consequently, we spent the next 6 months faced with this real threat.

The insurgents continued to successfully employ and develop similar tactics against the coalition forces, but, fortunately, the MOD responded to the vulnerabilities of using soft-skinned patrol vehicles, the insurgent threat of the use of IEDs, and the real impact of this presented by developing and using more appropriate vehicles. Consequently, less than 2 years later, on my next CIFT deployment, we had access to more appropriate patrol vehicles, such as the Jackal (shown in Figure 9-16).

Figure 9-16. *Foxhound Armored Patrol Vehicle*

The same principle should be applied to your vulnerability management program to ensure that you are effectively managing your environment to ensure that any new identified vulnerabilities and threats are being appropriately managed and that you do not introduce known vulnerabilities. All this is formally documented and controlled through your change management processes to ensure that you have assessed the potential risks, assessed the impact, and understand your potential rollback options *(in the event that the changes are ineffective).*

Gate Keeping *(Implement Strong Access Control Measures)*

Logical Access Restriction	Physical Access Restriction

There is an aggregated risk that must be mitigated through stringent access control measures to ensure that access is restricted based upon strict need to know and strict need at access requirements. Personnel must only be granted access to the physical and logical Card Data Environment (CDE) based upon business legitimate needs, and such personnel must ensure that they keep their access credentials secure and do not share their access with anyone else.

Maintaining strict access, with each access being able to be associated with a specific individual, is essential in support of effective monitoring and incident response.

The careless use of access controls can weaken the integrity of the defenses, with unauthorized personnel being able to interact with components in the CDE and, thus, increase the potential for compromised systems and data theft.

Reality Bites

There will always be a need to allow authorized access to your CDE and the payment card data. This requirement brings with it a considerable increased risk to your operations and needs to be strictly controlled so that only confirmed and authorized access is granted.

During deployments to hostile environments, it was commonly known for the insurgents to carry out both brute force *(suicide attacks)* and clandestine (masquerading as coalition personnel). For example, the insurgents would frequently carry out attacks and ambushes or seek to gain unauthorized entry, dressed as members of the Afghan nation police (ANP) or Afghan national army (ANA).

While on CIFT deployed operations, we received intelligence of a hidden cache of ANA uniforms which we were able to confiscate and to help prevent their use in future insurgent activities.

Consequently, it is extremely important that your personnel understand the need for robust access controls and that you are able to quickly identify ABNORMAL activities, which could be attributed to malicious use of an approved user account *(e.g., Attempts to elevate account privileges)* and to strictly control the number of POWER USER accounts, which if compromised could cause considerable damage to your business.

Routine Assurance (Regularly Monitor and Test Networks)

Monitor and Detect

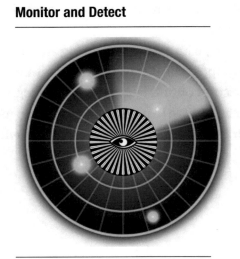

This is compartmentalized into two sections:

Part 1: This is your early warning and alerting component of the PCI DSS controls framework, and it relies on the aforementioned areas having been correctly configured and implemented, so that an organization can easily identify and respond to investigate suspicious activities associated to the CDE and personnel with authorized access.

Note   Under v3.2.1, the following requirements are listed under Part 2 of this particular section.

- Use the strategic placement of Intrusion Detection Systems (IDS)/Intrusion Prevention Systems (IPS) to detect and prevent unauthorized incursions into the CDE.

- Employ change detection technologies to provide alerts against any changes to the supporting network and systems.

Part 2: Consider this to be your routine internal and external patrols, checking for exploitable weaknesses. This involves the mandatory routine testing of the CDE to provide assurance that the CDE remains to be secure.

Testing includes

- Mandatory testing/physical inspections to detect rogue devices

  - Rogue personnel with authorized access may choose to connect rogue devices in order to bypass the defenses, for example, creating a Wi-Fi connection (N.B. Applicable whether or not the CDE has Wi-Fi infrastructure).

- Mandatory vulnerability scanning and confirmation of effective and timely remediation on internal and external facing IT systems

  - Additional scanning may be required after a significant change has occurred.

- Mandatory intrusion (penetration) and web application testing to validate that no exploitable vulnerabilities remain on internal or external facing IT systems

  - Additional testing may be required after a significant change has occurred.

Note   Under v.3.2.1 Web Application testing is included in the Secure
Development Operations and is separate to the penetration testing requirement.

- Network and Systems Segmentation testing

Reality Bites

During deployments into hostile environments, the importance of effective monitoring
and testing was abundantly apparent. However, it became increasingly clear that the
insurgents were doing exactly the same.

While carrying out security patrols of the internal zone, adjacent to the external
perimeter fence *(stretching for 15 km)*, the dog patrols needed to be covertly deployed
to enable the protection of a more condensed region around a weapon storage facility.
The morning following one of the nightly patrols, the area upwind and outside of my
internal patrol area had been compromised. The opportunist insurgents had cut through
the perimeter fence and broken into an isolated storage building, stealing some low-
value items. It is likely that these insurgents had spent many hours, days, or months
monitoring our patrol activities.

Figure 9-17. *Patrol Dog "Snap" (a.k.a. "The Hound of Basrahville"[22])*

Your attackers will test your "rules of engagement"[23] (RoE) and understand what your NORMAL activities look like. This will help them develop their skills to improve their chances of evading detection and to successfully compromise your network and

---

[22]www.mirror.co.uk/news/uk-news/the-hound-of-basraville-561573

[23]www.businessdictionary.com/definition/rules-of-engagement.html

sensitive data assets. Remember that not every attacker's activities are intended to compromise or steal your data and that a great deal of their actions can be part of their reconnaissance and testing of your business environment.

During a CIFT tour in Afghanistan, I experienced the insurgents carrying out exactly the same tactics approach. On one occasion, the external main access point observed a lone female walking directly toward them, across an expansive, arid, and isolated desert landscape. This lone female was wearing open-toed casual sandals *(not suitable for many miles of hiking across this hostile terrain)*, with a shawl covering her arms crossed across her body, head down, and muttering in a non-local language *(neither Pashto or Dari)*. Despite escalating challenges for her to halt, she continued walking directly toward the perimeter security post – everything you might associated with the actions of a suicide bomber.

Fortunately, the CIFT interpreter was able to speak five languages and recognized that this lone female's mutterings *(translated as "I'm going to Mecca")* were in Urdu *(a language native to Northern Pakistan – over 900 km),* and we were able to de-escalate the situation before it got out of hand. Further investigations with the ANP identified the lone female to have mental health issues, who had been picked up and transported from Northern Pakistan by persons unknown, dropped off adjacent to the military base, and she was told that Mecca was in the direction of the base.

It is extremely likely that the insurgents were observing from a distance and were using this lone vulnerable female to test our RoEs.

If your attackers have recognized the importance of monitoring and testing your activities, then should you not be doing the same to identify their **ABNORMAL** activities?

PCI DSS 12 Requirements

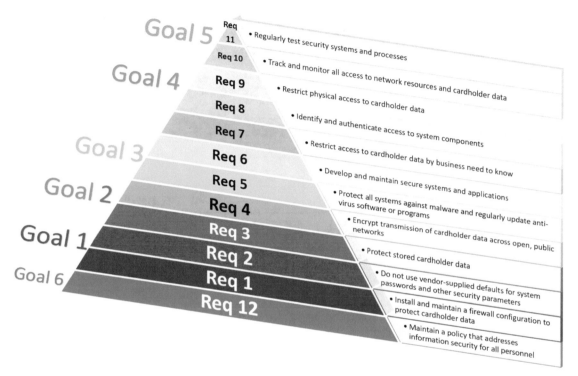

Figure 9-18. *Breakdown of PCI DSS 12 Requirements*

Introduction

Note   This is based upon the content of the current version of PCI DSS (v3.2.1).

This is an area of the standard which are frequently overlooked, but when seeking to understand the objective and intent of a particular requirement, it is essential that you understand the section title, as well as the adjoining explanatory notes for each control, sub-control, and so on.

Goal Title: Lorem ipsum dolor sit amet, consectetur adipiscing elit

Requirement No. **   Ut enim ad minim veniam, quis nostrud exercitation ullamco laboris nisi ut aliquip ex ea commodo consequat

Narrative text describing the objective of the requirement...

PCI DSS Requirement	Testing Procedures	Guidance
1.1	Testing requirements	Narrative text explaining the intent of the control.
1.1.1	Testing requirements	Narrative text explaining the intent of the control.
1.1.2	Testing requirements	Narrative text explaining the intent of the control.
1.1.3	Testing requirements	Narrative text explaining the intent of the control.
1.1.4	Testing requirements	Narrative text explaining the intent of the control.
1.1.5	Testing requirements	Narrative text explaining the intent of the control.
1.1.6	Testing requirements	Narrative text explaining the intent of the control.
1.1.7	Testing requirements	Narrative text explaining the intent of the control.
1.2	Testing requirements	Narrative text explaining the intent of the control.

Figure 9-19. *PCI DSS Control Structure*

Using this content, I will summarize the objectives and intent of each requirement area. However, this will likely change with the release of version 4.0, so you should familiarize yourself with these areas and make note of any changes that may have been introduced.

Additionally, the PCI SSC will provide a "Summary of Changes" document on their web site.[24]

Requirement 12: 3 Ps (People, Policies, and Processes)

Although this is placed at the end of the PCI DSS controls framework, this is at the heart of any compliance efforts. Often PCI DSS relies on a single point of failure, where the program falls down when an individual is unavailable. PCI DSS is an integrated controls framework and, as such, embraces the military concept of personnel resilience, where an individual was expected to know the role of a rank above and a rank below. Such a concept can be seen being demonstrated by Mel Gibson in the helicopter training scene in the film *We Were Soldiers*.[25]

Figure 9-20. *We Were Soldiers – Helicopter Drills*

To effectively achieve this requirement, you need military-style approach, having well-drilled teams, a collaborative approach, and senior management and leadership support. Consequently, all personnel supporting the PCI DSS program should fully

---

[24]www.pcisecuritystandards.org/document_library
[25]www.imdb.com/title/tt0277434/

understand their roles and responsibilities as outlined to them in their policies and procedures (As per v3.2.1):

- Information Security Policy

- Risk Assessments

- Acceptable Usage Policy

- Responsibility, Accountability, Consulted, Informed (RACI) Matrix

- Roles and Responsibilities, Job Descriptions, and so on

- Security Awareness Training

- Security Vetting

- Supplier Management

- Incident Response

- Internal Audit

Requirement 1: Layering the Network

Filtering traffic as it passes between trusted and internal network zones, ensuring that the firewalls and routers (or their equivalent) are appropriately configured. These act as the "Gate Keepers" to prevent transmissions, that do not adhere to specific security criteria, and also identifying/preventing the connection of rogue/unauthorized devices (*including wireless*). Either of which could compromise the layered network defenses.

Understanding the network topology is essential, and each system component must be identified and visualized in network diagrams to show both the Cardholder Data Environment (CDE) and the delineation of this from the non-CDE. Additionally, the Data Flow Diagram will further visualize the interaction of these CDE systems with CHD.

Any changes to the network should be subject to the change management process, so as to identify the potential impact and rollback options. Remember, the impact decision is essential as this will identify the potential for this being a "Significant Change," which will invoke additional measures (*vulnerability scanning, penetration testing, etc.*) to confirm that this change has not impacted the integrity of the environment.

All systems identified in the network diagram must correlate with an inventory (as part of requirement 2).

Figure 9-21. *Layered Defenses*[26]

Figure 9-22. *De-militarized Zone (DMZ) – 1.5 km*

---

[26]https://atwar.blogs.nytimes.com/2010/05/26/the-poo-pond/

Figure 9-23. *Filtered Access*[27]

[27]www.raf.mod.uk/our-organisation/force-protection/news/raf-leeming-based-34-
squadron-raf-regiment-returns-to-cyprus/

268

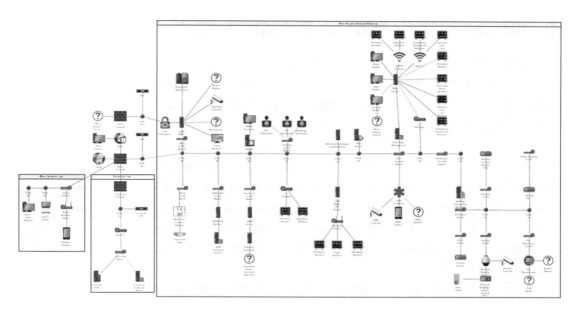

Figure 9-24. *CSET[28] Created Network Diagram*

[28]www.us-cert.gov/ncas/current-activity/2019/11/04/cset-version-92-now-available

Requirement 2: Secure by Design/Default

In the event that your network gets compromised, this is essential for reducing the available attack surfaces for the attacker by removing unnecessary services, functionality, and user accounts and by changing insecure vendor default settings on supporting system components.

Additionally, this includes the requirement to maintain an up-to-date asset inventory. I would recommend that you include a listing of their End-of-Life/End-of-Support dates, as this will help you prepare for the inevitable time that you need to change out a system component. Effective preparations can help make this practice more time and cost efficient, by timing these changes to coincide with your annual or quarterly testing requirements and also at a time when it will be less impactive on the business.

When implementing a new infrastructure, it is essential that this asset is introduced so that it complements and does not impact the integrity of any existing security measures. At the heart of any changes of developments made should be the potential security consideration needed to ensure that the assets are "locked down," as part of the design and development, to prevent the potential for misuse/abuse. For example, when designing the infrastructure upgrades for the main entrance to a deployed operation base (Figure 9-25), ensuring it was secured by default/design was a key consideration during the planning phase.

Figure 9-25. *Secure by Default/Design*[29]

Requirement 3: The Vault

In the event that you need to store CHD (or with a legitimate need) Sensitive Authentication Data (SAD), this requirement is designed to minimize the impact of an attacker managing to compromise your network and system components to gain unauthorized access to your data stores.

In order to effectively reduce the risk, it is essential that data retention is kept to an absolute minimum and the retained data is saved in a manner that the attacker is unable to profit from these data stores, for example, Encryption, Tokenization (with effective supporting practices), and so on.

Remember, gaining unauthorized access to the vault and being able to unlock the safety deposit boxes is the criminals' Return On Investment (ROI), enabling them

---

[29]www.army-technology.com/contractors/infrastructure/hesco/

to exploit these details for their gain. In 2019, the Ponemon Institute[30] estimated the average cost of a data breach to be at **$150 per record** (Globally) or **$242 per record** (United States).

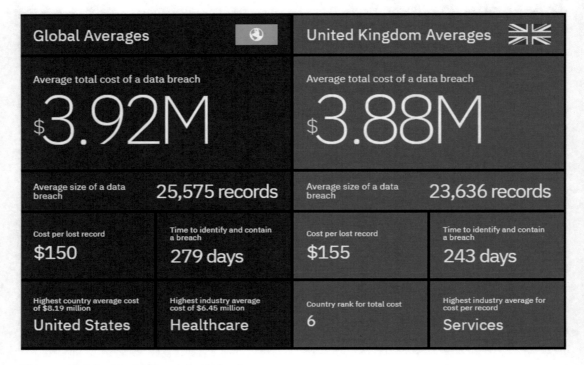

Figure 9-26. *Data Breach Calculator*

Therefore, the retention of surplus data or unnecessary data may prove to be a risk that when assessed could exceed your tolerances and which could be better risk managed:

- **T**reat: Encryption and Key Management – Limited Storage

- **T**erminate: No CHD usage – No storage

- **T**ransfer: PCI DSS Compliant Third-Party Services (e.g., Tokenization, Payment Service Providers (PSP), Dual-Tone Multi-Frequency (DTMF), etc.) – No storage

- **T**olerate: After effective application of PCI DSS, requirement 3 controls – Limited storage

---

[30]www.ibm.com/security/data-breach

Much like your CDE storage environments, within a deployed operation base, there was a need to have further enhanced secure enclaves, where the most valued assets are securely housed. Figure 9-27 shows an example of a secure enclave, within a deployed operation, with heightened and more robust security controls and with everything held under lock and key.

Figure 9-27. *Secure Vault*

Requirement 4: Secure in Motion

Much like "Cash In Transit," there will be a need to move CHD from the vault from one secure location to another. Consequently, just like the Banks when they move money, you need to ensure that the CHD remains under lock and key when transiting over public-facing environments. This includes

- Internet
- Mobile (Wireless, Bluetooth, Cellular, Text, Instant Message, Chat, Radio and Satellite comms)

- Virtual Private Networks

- Email

When moving your payment card data out into public environments, ensure that it is adequately protected and kept under lock and key *(encrypted)* while being transported.

This will help mitigate the risks presented from your convoys being ambushed while in flight.

Figure 9-28. *Secure in Motion*

Requirement 5: Entry Search

Think of this like having a digital explosives and ammunitions search (AES) dog asset, seeking to identify and detect suspicious "payloads" on visitors to your establishment *(think effective malware detection software)*. The search asset needs to be in place and able to detect foreign objects, which could do harm to your network, before they are able to initiate. Criminals are constantly evolving the malware strains, so it is essential that the search asset remains updated and is tested to ensure that it remains an effective asset.

Figure 9-29. *Malware Detection*

Requirement 6: Build and Maintain

Ensure that all security vulnerabilities are mitigated against, in a timely manner, based upon their criticalities, helping prevent attacker's ability to use known vulnerabilities to gain privileged access to systems.

Additionally, the development of software must be carried out securely so as to ensure that no known vulnerabilities are introduced to the environment through poor software development practices.

All changes must be managed, so as to document the supporting risk-based decisions made (e.g., Impact, Rollback options, etc.).

Requirement 7: Role-Based Restrictions

Ensure critical data can only be accessed by authorized personnel, systems, and processes based upon the strict need to know/need to access requirements for their role.

This applies to both logical and physical entry control practices. In Figure 9-30, you can see an example of the ANA restricting access to their encampment (Camp Shorabak), which was located within the confines of Camp Bastion. Despite the fact that members of the RAF Police and United States Marine Corps needed to gain access to their enclave, access had to be granted based upon specific role-based requirements.

Figure 9-30. *Role-Based Checks*

"Sir, please do not confuse your rank with my authority!"

Requirement 8: Logical Entry Control

Having created a secure environment, it is essential that in the event of an incident, the actions of an authorized individual can be identified against a specific person. Therefore, personnel need to be assigned a unique identification (ID) for each person with access, making them accountable for their actions. In the event they are involved in breach of company policies.

Consequently, each individual should be assigned their own strong access credentials, which are never shared and are only known to themselves. Logical access restrictions can be further enhanced through the use of additional defensive measures (Multi-Factor Authentication (MFA)), which requires another "independent" factor to authenticate the user.

This applies to any individual with authorized access *(based upon a (role-based) legitimate requirement)* to any system that supports the card payment operations.

Requirement 9: Physical Entry Control

Not all attacks occur in the IT systems, and opportunist attackers will seek to profit from gaining physical access to the systems and media that contain CHD or support the payment card operations.

Gaining access to a data center presents an aggregated risk, while stealing unencrypted backup tapes, call recordings, or paperwork can prove to be equally profitable to an attacker. Additionally, criminals are well known for tampering/replacing PIN Transaction Security (PTS)[31] devices to skim the CHD of your consumers.

Imagine the damage that an unsupervised cleaner, engineer, or rogue employee could do to your CDE in the event that they are able to physically social engineer their way to gain unauthorized access to the payment card systems.

For example, a "trusted" Call Center employee is blackmailed to plug in a number of $30 wireless keyloggers to harvest each and every key stroke made during the processing of consumers' card payments.

Figure 9-31. *$30 USB Keylogger*

---

[31]www.pcisecuritystandards.org/assessors_and_solutions/pin_transaction_devices

Requirement 10: Monitor and Detect

Having all requirements 1–9 and 12 in place, it is critical for effective monitoring to be in place so as to ensure that you are able to identify and respond to malicious or unapproved activities. Such actions need to be evidentially collected so as to help identify the potential "Root Cause" – affected systems, location, time, user account, and so on.

Effective monitoring should identify the stages of a potential attack and assist in your incident response, potentially preventing unauthorized access to the "Vault," "Supporting Systems", and "Layered Network."

Under version 3.2.1, the following control areas are included in requirement 11. However, I believe that these are more appropriately placed in this monitoring and detection section:

- Intrusion Detection/Prevention

- Change Detection

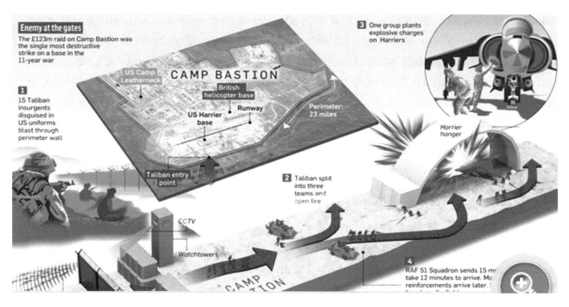

Figure 9-32. *Monitor for the ABNORMAL*

"Detecting the **ABNORMAL** from the NORMAL!"

Requirement 11: Assurance Testing

Think of this section as having periodic internal and external patrols to provide independent assurance that all requirements 1–10 and 12 are still active and effectively safeguarding your payment card operations, seeking to identify poor practices, poor configurations, or exploitable vulnerabilities:

- Rogue Wireless Access devices (circumvent the network defenses to create a "backdoor")

- Internal network vulnerabilities

- Perimeter network vulnerabilities

- Intrusion testing

- Secure Silo testing

- Web Application testing *(relocated from requirement 6)*

Testing your environment should be considered through the eyes of your attacker, seeking to identify potential exploitation opportunities. Remember that your attackers can originate from both outside and inside your corporate environment. Consequently, the testing should look at the perimeter (network and Web), your untrusted environment, and your trusted environment, confirm the effectiveness of any isolated internal network areas, and test both the network and application layers of your environment. Essential to the effectiveness of testing engagements is to work closely with your testers to confirm the accuracy of the scope of each engagement.

One area that is currently not included in the current version is the concept of security testing the "Human Factor" – otherwise known as Physical Penetration Testing (Social Engineering).[32]

Having tested your environment, it is critical that you can remediate any failings in a timely manner before they have the potential to impact your business and, most importantly, before your enemies have the ability to exploit them.

Your quarterly vulnerability scanning can be likened to the internal and external patrols that would help identify potential weaknesses in the infrastructure that could provide opportunities for exploitation *(e.g., ajar doors and windows)*.

---

[32]www.elsevier.com/books/social-engineering-penetration-testing/
watson/978-0-12-420124-8

Figure 9-33. *Internal Patrols (Within the Perimeter)*

Figure 9-34. *External Patrols (Outside the Perimeter)*

The vulnerability scans differ from your penetration and segmentation testing, in that you are looking to dig deeper into your vulnerabilities to see whether by acting like an attacker, you are able to further manipulate to allow additional exploitation *(e.g., plying open a door/window, picking the lock, etc.)*.

Think of it as being the difference between looking for visible weaknesses (vulnerability scanning) and acting like an attacker to manipulate additional exploitation opportunities (penetration testing).

Your penetration testing efforts will apply the known tactics, techniques, and protocols (TTPs) that are employed by your attackers. Consequently, you should ensure that your testing includes the following:

External   With average dwell times[33] on external network layers of **184 days**, it is extremely important that you can identify and remediate your vulnerabilities that can be leveraged by your attackers.

Internal   With average dwell times of **50.5** days, it is essential that you can identify and remediate any exploitable vulnerabilities that could be exploited by an attacker who manages to breach your perimeter.

It is important to ensure that the testing employs a defined methodology to ensure that it includes the testing of the Network *(OSI Layer 3)* and Application *(OSI Layer 7)* layers.

Conclusion

The PCI DSS Controls Framework has been designed to provide you with an integrated structure, where changes to the earlier requirements could have an impact on the subsequent layers.

Changes need to be carefully managed, so as to align with the other dependencies.

Have you implemented the three Ps, where the Personnel understand their roles and responsibilities and the Policies and Procedures that apply to them?

Do you have a layered network?

Are your "Firewall Rules" effectively filtering the network traffic?

Have you identified and documented the systems that support the payment card operations?

Are these systems "locked down" to prevent misuse?

Has data retention been limited based upon strict business needs?

Is all CHD moving outside the CDE done so under lock and key?

---

[33]https://content.fireeye.com/m-trends

Are all vulnerabilities remediated against, within a timely manner, based upon the potential risk to prevent exploitation by an attacker?

Do you have a formal change management process?

Is all in-house software developed securely, so as to ensure that known vulnerabilities are not introduced to the environment?

Is access strictly limited?

*Can you easily detect and rapidly respond to the presence of the **ABNORMAL**?*

Do your testing activities provide suitable levels of assurance?

Risks

The risks associated with each requirement are further explored in Chapter 6.

CHAPTER 10

Payment Channel Attack Vectors

Criminals are predators, seeking any opportunities to exploit bad practices or poorly configured, or managed, systems. Increasingly, consumers are seeking to use more convenient, efficient, and quicker ways to purchase goods or services. In response to this demand, businesses are turning to new technologies to meet customer expectations.

Such technology has advanced at such a pace, with payments being able to be made instantly, without even a need for any contact. Increasing technological advancements have served to create a distanced shopping experience:

- The customer making the purchase online has little, or no, concept of what happens during the payment process or how insecure the process might be.

- The businesses receiving the payment have little, or no, understanding of their customers' payment card journeys or a true concept of the actual value and activeness of their payment process is to criminals.

While businesses have embraced new technological advances to deliver an enhanced customer experience, the criminals are doing likewise in order to exploit insecurely developed or poorly protected technologies for their monetary gain.

© Jim Seaman 2020
J. Seaman, *PCI DSS*, https://doi.org/10.1007/978-1-4842-5808-8_10

Prior to the increased attractiveness of simply using a payment card, or payment card-enabled technology, to pay for goods or services, the consumers would need to go to their bank and either withdraw the money from the Automated Teller Machine (ATM) or for larger amounts go into the branch to request the monies needed. The reality of carrying $5000 in notes rather than just having a payment card in your wallet/purse makes the risk more real for both the consumer *(handing over)* and the business *(receiving)*. Having paid for the goods or services, the business receiving would then need to securely retain this, along with other sums, until the amount exceeds their risk appetite and they feel the need to safely deposit their monies into their bank.

As a consequence of this distancing between the potential value of a payment card and payment card-enabled technology, criminals are gaining significant returns for relatively low effort, often being perceived as a victimless crime!

Working on behalf of the Card Brands (Mastercard, Visa, American Express, JCB, and Discover), the Payment Card Industry Security Standards Council (PCI SSC)[1] maintain a suite of security controls (Payment Card Industry Data Security Standards (PCI DSS)), designed to help mitigate against the threats to all methods of taking payment card purchases.

Introduction

Despite the fact that the PCI DSS has been continually evolving over the past 15 years, the volume of payment card theft/fraud/data breaches continues to grow and the number of businesses that manage to maintain PCI DSS compliance continues to decrease.

---

[1]www.pcisecuritystandards.org/

Payment Card Breach Trends[2]   **PCI DSS Compliance Trends[3]**

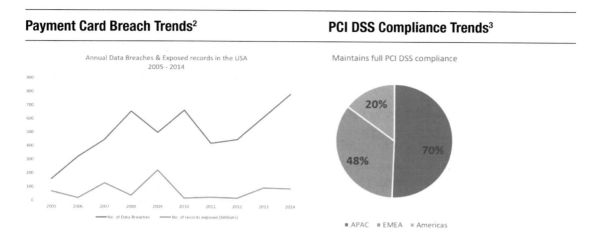

With a ratio of just 1:5 businesses in the Americas managing to maintain their annual compliance obligations, the attraction for criminals becomes abundantly clear.

Unfortunately, despite all the efforts of the Card Brands and the PCI SSC to provide a bespoke controls framework for the Payment Card Industry, the complexities of different payment channels make maintaining a secure environment even more difficult. However, it is important to remember that the PCI DSS controls are only applicable to your business information systems, networks, infrastructure, and personnel. How the consumer safeguards their environment and systems is not applicable until you are entrusted with their payment card information.

Therefore, when seeking to fortify your payment card business operations through the use of the PCI DSS controls framework, it is important to start by looking at each point of interaction as a separate entity and to identify the potential risks that are associated with these methods of interface (a.k.a. Payment Channels). Helpfully, the PCI SSC have already done some of this for you through the creation of separate payment channel-aligned Self-Assessment Questionnaires.

This concept is similar to that applied by the National Institute of Standards and Technology (NIST),[4] who have created a master catalogue of security controls (NIST SP800-53, R4[5]). This master catalogue is then used as their reference for the creation of specific risk mitigation guidance.

---

[2]https://digitalguardian.com/blog/history-data-breaches
[3]https://enterprise.verizon.com/resources/reports/2019-payment-security-fullreport-bl-global.pdf
[4]www.nist.gov
[5]https://nvlpubs.nist.gov/nistpubs/SpecialPublications/NIST.SP.800-53r4.pdf

All of the following NIST guidance are aligned with controls within the PCI DSS framework:

- **NIST SP800-18, Rev 1:** *Guide for Developing Security Plans for Federal Information Systems*[6]

- **NIST SP800-37, Rev 2:** *Risk Management Framework for Information Systems and Organizations: A System Life Cycle Approach for Security and Privacy*[7]

- **NIST SP800-39:** *Managing Information Security Risk: Organization, Mission, and Information System View*[8]

- **NIST SP800-40, Rev 3:** *Guide to Enterprise Patch Management Technologies*[9]

- **NIST SP800-41, Rev 1:** *Guidelines on Firewalls and Firewall Policy*[10]

- **NIST SP800-70, Rev 4:** *National Checklist Program for IT Products: Guidelines for Checklist Users and Developers*[11]

- **NIST SP800-77:** *Guide to IPsec VPNs*[12]

- **NIST SP800-83, Rev 1:** *Guide to Malware Incident Prevention and Handling for Desktops and Laptops*[13]

- **NIST SP800-92:** *Guide to Computer Security Log Management*[14]

- **NIST SP800-153:** *Guidelines for Securing Wireless Local Area Networks (WLANs)*[15]

---

[6]https://csrc.nist.gov/publications/detail/sp/800-18/rev-1/final
[7]https://csrc.nist.gov/publications/detail/sp/800-37/rev-2/final
[8]https://csrc.nist.gov/publications/detail/sp/800-39/final
[9]https://csrc.nist.gov/publications/detail/sp/800-40/rev-3/final
[10]https://csrc.nist.gov/publications/detail/sp/800-41/rev-1/final
[11]https://csrc.nist.gov/publications/detail/sp/800-70/rev-4/final
[12]https://csrc.nist.gov/publications/detail/sp/800-77/final
[13]https://csrc.nist.gov/publications/detail/sp/800-83/rev-1/final
[14]https://csrc.nist.gov/publications/detail/sp/800-92/final
[15]https://csrc.nist.gov/publications/detail/sp/800-153/final

For example, *you are an organization that is looking to mitigate the risks to your Manufacturing IT systems.*

SP800-53, R4: Security and Privacy Controls for Federal Information Systems and Organizations[16]	SP800-82: Guide to Industrial Control Systems (ICS) Security[17]	PCI DSS v3.2.1
Control Families	• Access Control (AC)	• Requirement 7
AC – Access Control;	• Awareness and Training (AT)	• Requirement 8
AU – Audit and Accountability;	• Audit and Accountability (AU)	• Requirement 10
AT – Awareness and Training;	• Security Assessment and Authorization (CA)	Requirement 12.10
CM – Configuration Management;	• Contingency Planning (CP)	• Requirement 12.6
CP – Contingency Planning;	• Configuration Management (CM)	• Requirement 2
IA – Identification and Authentication;	• Identification and Authentication (IA)	• Requirement 8.7
IR – Incident Response;	• Incident Response (IR)	• Requirement 12.10
MA – Maintenance;	• Maintenance (MA)	• Requirement 9.5/9.6
MP – Media Protection;	• Media Protection (MP)	• Requirement 9
PS – Personnel Security;	• Physical and Environmental Protection (PE)	• Requirement 12.2
PE – Physical and Environmental Protection;	• Planning (PL)	• Requirement 11
PL – Planning;	• Personnel Security (PS)	• Requirement 1
PM – Program Management;	• Risk Assessment (RA)	• Requirement 4
RA – Risk Assessment;	• System and Services Acquisition (SA)	• Requirement 5
CA – Security Assessment and Authorization;	• System and Communications (SC)	• Requirement 6
SC – System and Communications Protection;	• System and Information Integrity (SI)	
SI – System and Information Integrity;	• Program Management (PM)	
SA – System and Services Acquisition		

---

[16]https://nvd.nist.gov/800-53/Rev4

[17]https://nvlpubs.nist.gov/nistpubs/SpecialPublications/NIST.SP.800-82r2.pdf

The NIST suite of controls are compartmentalized into family groups and are prioritized based upon their perceived importance:

Total of 170 High-Impact Controls[18]

Table 10-1. *Access Control (AC) High-Impact Controls*

No.	Control	Priority	High
AC-1	ACCESS CONTROL POLICY AND PROCEDURES	P1	AC-1
AC-2	ACCOUNT MANAGEMENT	P1	AC-2 (1) (2) (3) (4) (5) (11) (12) (13)
AC-3	ACCESS ENFORCEMENT	P1	AC-3
AC-4	INFORMATION FLOW ENFORCEMENT	P1	AC-4
AC-5	SEPARATION OF DUTIES	P1	AC-5
AC-6	LEAST PRIVILEGE	P1	AC-6 (1) (2) (3) (5) (9) (10)
AC-7	UNSUCCESSFUL LOGON ATTEMPTS	P2	AC-7
AC-8	SYSTEM USE NOTIFICATION	P1	AC-8
AC-10	CONCURRENT SESSION CONTROL	P3	AC-10
AC-11	SESSION LOCK	P3	AC-11 (1)
AC-12	SESSION TERMINATION	P2	AC-12
AC-14	PERMITTED ACTIONS WITHOUT IDENTIFICATION OR AUTHENTICATION	P3	AC-14
AC-17	REMOTE ACCESS	P1	AC-17 (1) (2) (3) (4)
AC-18	WIRELESS ACCESS	P1	AC-18 (1) (4) (5)
AC-19	ACCESS CONTROL FOR MOBILE DEVICES	P1	AC-19 (5)
AC-20	USE OF EXTERNAL INFORMATION SYSTEMS	P1	AC-20 (1) (2)
AC-21	INFORMATION SHARING	P2	AC-21
AC-22	PUBLICLY ACCESSIBLE CONTENT	P3	AC-22

---

[18]https://nvd.nist.gov/800-53/Rev4/impact/HIGH

Additionally, NIST provide an extremely useful supporting guidance document to help explain how the controls from the catalogue should be assessed:

- **NIST SP800-53A, Rev 4:** Assessing Security and Privacy Controls in Federal Information Systems and Organizations: Building Effective Assessment Plans[19]

This is a very helpful aid to help you understand what is expected when assessing the effectiveness of your controls *(either by yourself or with a Qualified Security Assessor (QSA)).*

Under PCI DSS version 3.2.1, the PCI SSC have identified and grouped the applicable controls into shortened SAQs, based upon the perceived risks associated with these business operations, for example:

Card Not Present

E-commerce

- **SAQ A: Fully Outsourced** – No business systems or personal interaction with Cardholder Data

    - *Circa 22 controls*

- **SAQ A-EP**: Partially Outsourced E-commerce Merchants Using a Third-Party Web site for Payment Processing

    - *Circa 148 controls*

- **SAQ C**: Merchants with Payment Application Systems Connected to the Internet – **No Electronic Cardholder Data Storage**

    - *Circa 108 controls*

- **SAQ D-Merchants**: All other SAQ-Eligible Merchants

    For example, Application Programmable Interface (API) enabled e-Commerce

    - *Circa 332 controls*

---

[19]https://csrc.nist.gov/publications/detail/sp/800-53a/rev-4/final

Telephone-Based (a.k.a. Mail Order Telephone Order)

- **SAQ C-VT**: Merchants with Web-Based Virtual Payment Terminals – **No Electronic Cardholder Data Storage**

  - *Circa 66 controls*

Card Present

Face to Face

- **SAQ P2PE**: Merchants using Hardware Payment Terminals in a PCI SSC-Listed P2PE Solution Only – **No Electronic Cardholder Data Storage**

  - *Circa 24 controls*

- **SAQ B**: Merchants with Only Imprint Machines or Only Standalone, Dial-out Terminals – **No Electronic Cardholder Data Storage**

  - *Circa 38 controls*

- **SAQ B-IP**: Merchants with Standalone, IP-Connected PTS Point-of-Interaction (POI) Terminals – **No Electronic Cardholder Data Storage**

  - *Circa 64 controls*

- **SAQ D-Service Providers**: SAQ-Eligible Service Providers

  For example, Provision and Management of Automated Teller Machines (ATMs)

  - *Circa 362 controls*

Eligibility for completion of the shortened SAQs must meet the criteria outlined in the "**Before You Start**" section of the SAQ, and any electronic storage *(Localized spreadsheets, CCTV recording, Telephone recordings, System Logs, etc.)* of cardholder data makes you ineligible for the shortened SAQs and you will need to be assessed against the SAQ D controls (circa 332 controls.).

If you are a business that provides services to Merchants, you will need to use the SAQ D-Service Providers (SAQ D-SP), which includes additional specific Service

Provider controls. However, it might be that your offered service aligns to one of the shortened SAQs. In this case it might be that you validate your company against the shortened SAQ plus the Service Provider controls on the SAQ D-SP.

Important Reminder   Higher risk Merchants and Service Providers are ineligible for completion of the SAQ and must have their compliance independently validated through an onsite assessment, conducted by a PCI SSC-verified Qualified Security Assessor (QSA), and compiled into the Report On Compliance (ROC) and the supporting Attestation Of Compliance (AOC).

Note   Completed ROCs should be securely retained for 3 years *(as supporting evidence, in the case of suffering a data breach)*, and these should not be provided as proof of evidence *(owing to sensitive contents)*.

The AOCs should be the only documentation needed to prove your PCI DSS compliance status.

However, just like any effective defensive strategy, before simply applying the suite of controls, first it is important to assess the potential impact on your business operations (e.g., critical systems that are difficult to update, external facing and sensitive data processing systems, etc.). Having identified the importance and potential impact on each system, it is then important to understand the applicable and potential attack vectors that could be leveraged against your payment card business operations.

Understanding your attack vectors is essential in helping you understand the importance of the mitigation controls (a.k.a. Threat Intelligence[20]).

> *Threat intelligence is evidence-based knowledge, including context, mechanisms, indicators, implications, and action-oriented advice about an existing or emerging menace or hazard to assets. This intelligence can be used to inform decisions regarding the subject's response to that menace or hazard.*

> —Gartner

---

[20]www.gartner.com/en/documents/2487216/definition-threat-intelligence

Think of it as playing a competitive sport and researching the set plays of your competitor. In order to be able to effectively defend against them, you need to have knowledge of their "Set Plays." The same applies when trying to proactively defend your business from compromise or data loss.

There are multiple sources of information that are available to you. However, you need to ensure that these various sources of information are refined and made relevant to your business, rather than just being a dump of raw information.

Turning information into actionable intelligence

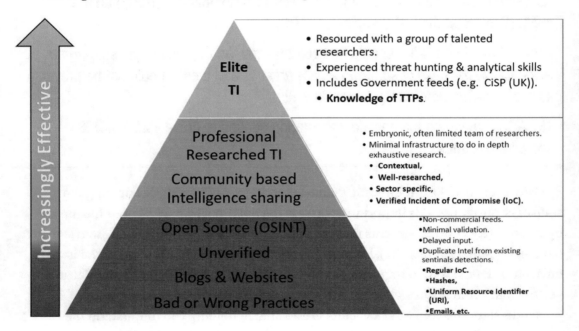

Figure 10-1. *CM-Alliance TI Pyramid*

- How well do you know your enemy?

- How aligned are your security tools to your identified and known threats?

- Does your defensive strategy adapt to the changing TTPs of your attackers?

Card Not Present (CNP) Attack Vectors

The increased use of online digital shopping has provided significant consumer convenience, with purchases being able to be made with a simple click (or swipe) on their Internet-connected devices.

Figure 10-2. *E-commerce*

As much as the Internet-connected digital advances has distanced the consumer from the shop, the criminal has been distanced from the victim. Consequently, attackers increasingly regard CNP attacks as being victimless crimes, with no apparent regard for the consequences of their actions.

This is well-known psychological consequence of using the Internet and can be demonstrated in the "Trolley/Train/Tram Experiment":[21]

- **Scenario 1**

  A runaway Trolley/Train/Tram is hurtling down the tracks, directly toward the path of five railways workers. You have to make the decision whether to pull an adjacent switch or divert the runaway along another track. However, on the diverted route, there is a lone worker who will be killed.

  - Do you pull the switch to divert the runaway?

    - *Sacrifice 1 to save 5.*

- **Scenario 2**

  A runaway Trolley/Train/Tram is hurtling down the tracks, directly toward five rail workers. You have to make the decision whether to push a single person from a bridge (to their certain death) into the path of the runaway to derail it and save the lives of five rail workers.

  - Do you push the person into the path of the runaway?

    - *Sacrifice 1 to save 5.*

Table 10-2. *The Runaway Trolley Conundrum*

Scenario 1[22]	Scenario 2[23]

[21]https://towardsdatascience.com/trolley-problem-isnt-theoretical-2fa92be4b050
[22]https://images.app.goo.gl/XtdRY8Ponz4ZWBf49
[23]https://images.app.goo.gl/75tkS3uTBkPy46ye6

This distancing effect, provided by the Internet, presents significantly differing attacking intent, ranging from the amateur hacker to the state-sponsored and organized criminal groups. The amateur (have a go) hackers may have distanced themselves from the potential damage they are having on their victim and, as such, may not be attacking you for financial gain. However, their actions could inadvertently provide opportunities for criminals to profit from, for example, making stolen data available on the dark Web or bragging about the vulnerabilities that they have found within your corporate network or web applications.

Traditionally, attackers would seek to exploit vulnerabilities in the network infrastructures. However, the changing face of web-based business means that increasingly the Web and email have become alternative avenues of attack.

An attacker is only limited by their imagination and the types of attack are continually enhanced and changed. Therefore, the following are a representation of some of the types of attacks, and it is essential that you maintain an understanding of the attacker's tactics, techniques, and protocols (TTPs) using some of the available resources:

- Security Threat Intelligence Services[24]

- Mitre Att&ck[25]

- US-CERT CISA[26]

- Exploit.db[27]

"Payload" Delivery Attacks

If a criminal is unable to gain unauthorized access to a corporate network via traditional methods, they will seek other approaches. One such way is through the exploitation of human nature, where they are able to use the data freely available on social media to craft emails, containing malicious payloads, which entice the recipients to read and download the email.

---

[24]www.gartner.com/reviews/market/security-threat-intelligence-services
[25]https://attack.mitre.org/
[26]www.us-cert.gov/
[27]www.exploit-db.com/

The development of malicious emails is becoming increasingly difficult to identify, as criminals are developing increasingly well-crafted and sophisticated emails. No longer are they the traditional, poorly written emails relating to your lately departed long lost Uncle.

> - **Phishing.**
> "Phishing is a form of fraud in which an attacker masquerades as a reputable entity or person in email or other communication channels. The attacker uses phishing emails to distribute malicious links or attachments that can perform a variety of functions, including the extraction of login credentials or account information from victims".
> - **Spear Phishing.**
> Spear phishing is an email spoofing attack that targets a specific organization or individual, seeking unauthorized access to sensitive information. Spear phishing attempts are not typically initiated by random hackers, but are more likely to be conducted by perpetrators out for financial gain, trade secrets or military information.
> - **Whaling Attack (Whale Phishing).**
> A whaling attack, also known as whaling phishing or a whaling phishing attack, is a specific type of phishing attack that targets high-profile employees, such as the CEO or CFO, in order to steal sensitive information from a company, as those that hold higher positions within the company typically have complete access to sensitive data. In many whaling phishing attacks, the attacker's goal is to manipulate the victim into authorizing high-value wire transfers to the attacker.
>
> Source: https://searchsecurity.techtarget.com/

Among the known Spear Phishing-style tactics, the most common are

- **Spear Phishing Attachment**

  The use of malware attached to an email. In this scenario, adversaries attach a file to the spear phishing email and normally rely upon End User Execution to gain execution.

- **Spear Phishing Link**

  The use of links to download malware contained in email, instead of attaching malicious files to the email itself, to avoid defenses that may inspect email attachments

- **Spear Phishing via Service**

  The use of third-party services rather than directly via enterprise email channels. The attacker builds rapport with a target via social media, then sends content to a personal webmail service that the target uses on their work computer.

  - This allows an adversary to bypass some email restrictions on the work account, and the target is more likely to open the file since it's something they were expecting.

  - If the payload doesn't work as expected, the adversary can continue normal communications and troubleshoot with the target on how to get it working.

Unfortunately, employees and consumers fail to recognize the importance the criminals place on carrying out "hostile reconnaissance" on their targets, and as a result, people can be far too complacent with the type of data they make freely available to their enemies:

Social Media Intelligence Gathering Tools

Facebook

- Facebook scanner

- Socmint

- Lookup ID

- FindMyFbid

- Facebook JSON Search

- LikeAlyzer

- Face Live

- Who posted what?

- ExtractFace

Twitter

- Twitter search home
- Twitter advanced search page
- Twitter Deck
- All My Tweets
- Trendsmap
- Foller
- First Tweet
- Social bearing
- Twicsy
- Follower wonk
- Sleeping Time
- Simple Twitter Profile Analyzer (Python script)
- Tag board
- Tinfoleak
- Spoonbill
- Export Tweet

LinkedIn

- Searching LinkedIn using Google custom search
- Recently Updated Profiles
- LinkedIn Contact Extractor
- LinkedIn Résumés
- LinkedIn People Finder (International)

Instagram

- Iconosquare

- Picodash

- ToFo

Reddit

- Mostly Harmless

- redditarchive

- Reddit Enhancement Suite

- Reddit investigator

- Reddit metrics

- atomiks

- SnoopSnoo

- Reddit Comment Search

Any of these resources can be used to create an air of enhanced credibility for a malicious email, which have been designed to create an urgency or desire to access the contents of the email. These are the attackers' opportunity to create a remote access point or deliver malicious software, all to undermine or bypass the existing defensive measures. These tactics are nothing new, when during the siege of the City of Troy the Greek commander Odysseus is believed to have conceived the very first "Trojan Horse"[28] style of attack.

Following 10 years of unsuccessful attempts to breach the City of Troy's defenses, the Greek Army left an attractive wooden horse as a gift to the residents of Troy. Once the "gift" had been wheeled through to the heart of the city, the gift remained dormant until the quiet of the night when it delivered its clandestine payload – the enemy!

---

[28]`www.nationalgeographic.org/thisday/apr24/fall-troy/`

A fresh Greek Army then attacked from within and were able to undermine the defenses, allowing additional unauthorized access for further armies to attack.

Once inside a target user's email inbox, the attacker has access to a wealth of data *(through numerous messages, application account resets, etc.)*, which proves to be a valuable resource for further reconnaissance, data harvesting, and attack planning.

CNP Perimeter Attacks

The very nature of CNP business operations requires your organization to make a public interface available, so as to enable your consumers to buy goods or services from you. However, by making this interface available to your customers, you are also making it available to your attackers.

As well as attempting to circumvent the existing security defenses, through the exploitation of your user's weaknesses, the attackers will seek to identify potential infiltration opportunities that are presented by poorly managed or configured external/public-facing network infrastructures. Consequently, your attackers will start by carrying out extensive reconnaissance of your perimeter. The attacker's reconnaissance will target the supporting network layer, as well as the web application interface.

Perimeter Network Attacks

The easiest gateway into your supporting network infrastructure is via unused/insecure Services,[29] Protocols,[30] or Ports[31] *(easily identified through a simple scan)* or poorly configured firewall/router ruleset filtering *(allowing uncontrolled traffic flows)*. Other perimeter-style attacks include External Remote Services.

- **External Remote Services**

  Exploiting external remote services (e.g., VPN, Citrix, etc.) to gain initial access and/or persist within a network

---

[29]www.owasp.org/index.php/Top_10_2014-I3_Insecure_Network_Services
[30]www.newnettechnologies.com/downloads/NNT-Open-Port-Hardening-Guide.pdf
[31]www.speedguide.net/ports.php?filter=risk

- Access to Valid Accounts to use the service is often a requirement, which could be obtained through credential pharming or by obtaining the credentials from users after compromising the enterprise network.

- Access to remote services may be used as part of Redundant Access during an operation.

- For example, Pwned[32] accounts

- **Hardware Additions**

  Attackers gaining physical access to an environment can introduce computer accessories, computers, or networking hardware into a system or network that can be used as a vector to gain access.

  - Numerous commercial and open source products[33] are readily available that provide various functionalities, for example:

    - Passive network tapping

    - Man-in-the middle encryption breaking

    - Keystroke injection

    - Kernel memory reading via DMA

    - Wireless access points

  - Replication Through Removable Media

    Attackers may utilize disconnected or air-gapped networks, using malware copied to removable media and taking advantage of Autorun features to gain unauthorized access to systems.

  - When the media is inserted into a system and executes

    - In the case of Lateral Movement, this may occur through modification of executable files stored on removable media or by copying malware and renaming it to look like a legitimate file to trick users into executing it on a separate system.

---

[32]https://haveibeenpwned.com/

[33]https://shop.hak5.org/

- In the case of Initial Access, this may occur through manual manipulation of the media, modification of systems used to initially format the media, or modification to the media's firmware itself.

- **Valid Accounts**

  Attackers steal the credentials of a specific user or service account using Credential Access techniques or capture credentials earlier in their reconnaissance process through social engineering for means of gaining Initial Access.

  - Accounts that an adversary may use can fall into three categories:

    - **Default**

      Default accounts are those that are built into an OS such as Guest or Administrator account on Windows systems or default factory/provider set accounts on other types of systems, software, or devices.

    - Default accounts are also not limited to Guest and Administrator on client machines; they also include accounts that are preset for equipment such as network devices and computer applications whether they are internal, open source, or COTS.

      - Appliances that come preset with a username and password combination pose a serious threat to organizations that do not change it post installation, as they are easy targets for an adversary.

    - **Local**

      Local accounts are those configured by an organization for use by users, remote support, services, or for administration on a single system or service.

    - **Domain accounts**

      Domain accounts are those managed by Active Directory Domain Services where access and permissions are configured across systems and services that are part of that domain. Domain accounts can cover users, administrators, and services.

Compromised credentials may be used to bypass access controls placed on various resources on systems within the network and may even be used for persistent access to remote systems and externally available services, such as VPNs, Outlook Web Access, and remote desktop. Compromised credentials may also grant an adversary increased privilege to specific systems or access to restricted areas of the network.

- Attackers may choose not to use malware or tools in conjunction with the legitimate access those credentials provide to make it harder to detect their presence.

Perimeter Web Attacks

Historically, web interfaces were developed for the presentation of information. However, the world of web-based business has changed significantly over the past 15 years, and now the Web has become far more consumer interactive. As a result, web-based attacks have become a preferred choice for the attackers seeking alternative options to gain unauthorized access to data and the supporting network infrastructures. Such tactics include

- **Drive by compromises**

  An attacker gains access to a system through a user visiting a web site over the normal course of browsing. In this style of attack, the user's web browser is typically targeted for exploitation, but attackers may also use compromised web sites for non-exploitation behavior, for example:

  - Acquiring application access tokens

    Multiple ways of delivering exploit code to a browser exist, including

  - A legitimate web site is compromised where attackers have injected some form of malicious code, for example:

    - JavaScript

    - iFrames

    - Cross-site scripting

- Using malicious paid-for advertising provides built-in web application interfaces, which are used to insert any other kind of object, and that can be used to display web content or contain a script that executes on the visiting client, for example:

  - Forum posts

  - Comments

  - Other user controllable web content

  Typically, the attackers' web sites are targeted against a specific community, where the goal is to compromise a specific user or set of users based on a shared interest.

- A strategic web compromise

- Watering hole attack

- Exploit Public-Facing Applications

  An attacker uses software, data, or commands to take advantage of a vulnerability in an Internet-facing computer system or program in order to cause unintended or unanticipated behavior, for example:

  - Coding bugs

  - Coding glitches

  - Design vulnerabilities

These applications are often web sites, but can include databases and any other applications with Internet accessible open sockets (e.g., Web servers and related services).

Card Present (CP) Attack Vectors

As per the title "Card Present," this involves payments being made while the cardholder owner is present at the time of the purchase and where they provide their own payment card using a Point-Of-Interaction (POI)/PIN Transaction Security (PTS)/Point-Of-Sale (POS)/Pretty Damn Quick (PDQ) device or using a payment card as a method of authentication, in order to withdraw funds from a "Hole in the Wall" (ATM).

POI/PTS/POS/PDQ Device   **ATM**

Usually, this would be a store (e.g., Shop, Gas/Fuel Station, Supermarket, Bar/Public House, Restaurant, Sports Stadium, Hotel, etc.) or an ATM provided in convenient locations for the consumer, typically in public areas (e.g., Shopping Malls/Centers, High Street, Local Bank, etc.).

Frequently, the importance of these devices is often misunderstood and underappreciated. However, this is not the case for the criminals who have understood that these are extremely valuable targets, being that they are hardware, software, and even network-connected devices. As a result, this significantly increases their attack options based upon their specific objectives. For instance, consider the reasons to attack an ATM. These are not always just brute force attacks[34] from your traditional criminals but are also the target of cyber criminals,[35] where they seek to exploit more system/software vulnerabilities for financial gain or to gain unauthorized access to the supporting Local Area Network (LAN), thus enabling the ability for lateral movement.

There has been a significant increase of attacks on these types of devices.

---

[34]www.finextra.com/newsarticle/34886/abn-amro-shuts-down-half-of-its-atm-estate-in-response-to-escalating-violence

[35]www.upguard.com/blog/biggest-threat-to-atm-security-is-misconfiguration

EUROPEAN PAYMENT TERMINAL CRIME STATISTICS - SUMMARY						
Terminal Related Fraud Attacks	**2014**	**2015**	**2016**	**2017**	**2018**	**% +/- 17/18**
Total reported Incidents	15,702	18,738	23,588	20,971	13,511	-36%
Total reported losses	€280m	€327m	€332m	€353m	€247m	-30%
ATM Related Physical Attacks	**2014**	**2015**	**2016**	**2017**	**2018**	**% +/- 17/18**
Total reported Incidents	1,980	2,657	2,974	3,584	4,549	+27%
Total reported losses	€27m	€49m	€49m	€31m	€36m	+16%
ATM Malware & Logical Attacks	**2014**	**2015**	**2016**	**2017**	**2018**	**% +/- 17/18**
Total reported Incidents	51	15	58	192	157	-18%%
Total reported losses	€1.2m	€0.74m	€0.46m	€1.52m	€0.45m	-70%
Source: European Association for Secure Transactions (EAST)						

Figure 10-3. *European Payment Terminal Crime Report*[36]

ATM Attacks

Being that ATMs need to be available for the convenience of consumers' access, they are made available for public access. This free access makes them an increasingly viable target for criminals. If the criminals can get access to the terminal or supporting network infrastructure, they are seen as being an easy target.

Consequently, most banks have transferred this increasing risk and have outsourced the provision of an ATM service for their consumers. However, this does not transfer all of their compliance obligations, as they need to fulfill their third-party management obligations while ensuring that the physical security of the terminal is maintained and periodic checks are carried out.

Here are some examples of the types of ATM attacks, which need to have appropriate risk mitigation controls applied:

- **Brute Force**

    This is the most basic of attacks, where the criminals physically attack the surround physical infrastructure to gain unauthorized physical access (e.g., Ram Raid[37] or ATM Burglary[38]) to the

---

[36]www.association-secure-transactions.eu/east-publishes-european-fraud-update-1-2019/

[37]www.thisismoney.co.uk/money/news/article-7244023/How-surge-ram-raids-ATMs-fuelling-race-axe-cash.html

[38]www.wired.com/2017/04/hackers-emptying-atms-drill-15-worth-gear/

terminal. Remembering that an ATM is an IT system attached to a cash vault, the target of this style of attack is the cash vault and with the attached IT system becoming the collateral damage for the attack. Post attack, it is essential that the IT system, in-scope for PCI DSS, has not had its integrity compromised.

- **Physical Skimming**[39]

  Freely available on the Dark Web, criminals can purchase Physical Skimming devices that are simply attached to the ATM. The purpose of such devices is to illegally harvest the consumers' payment card data.

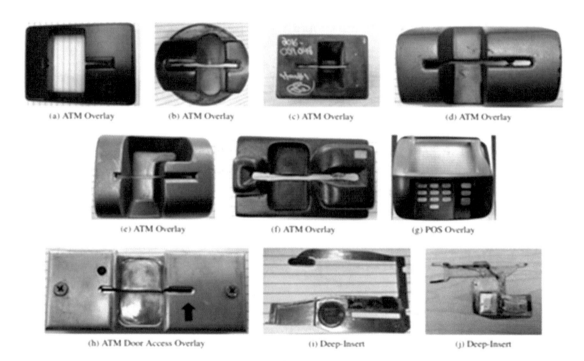

Figure 10-4. *Ten ATM Skimming Overlay Devices*[40]

---

[39]https://krebsonsecurity.com/tag/atm-skimmers/

[40]https://blog.acolyer.org/2018/09/03/fear-the-reaper-characterization-and-fast-detection-of-card-skimmers/

- **Malware attacks**[41]

  The ATM attack vectors are a good example where PCI DSS can support "Out-of-Scope" considerations. If you look at the "Jackpotting"[42] attack, the criminals are not seeking to steal payment card data but to introduce malware to the ATM *(in essence, a computer-connected electronic cash vault)* to illegally withdraw cash from consumer bank accounts.

- **Network attacks**[43]

  Increasingly we are seeing cases where the cyber-attacks have used vulnerabilities in the network-connected ATMs to enable cyber hackers (e.g., APT-37, The Lazarus Group[44]) to gain unauthorized access to the supporting corporate network for their financial gain.

POI/PTS/POS/PDQ Device Attacks

The styles of attacks[45] that are carried out against POI devices are very similar to the ATM-style attacks (e.g., Physical Skimming,[46] Malware,[47] Network,[48] etc.). However, unlike the ATM-style attacks, POI devices produce ancillary paper media which contain payment card data (full or partial) – Receipts, which are valuable to the criminals (as they seek to piece together their jigsaw puzzles), and being portable devices, they are easier to be tampered with or exchanged for bogus skimming devices.

---

[41]www.association-secure-transactions.eu/tag/atm-malware/

[42]www.paymentscardsandmobile.com/threat-actors-demonstrate-persistent-interest-in-atm-malware/

[43]www.wired.com/story/north-korean-hacker-group-apt37/

[44]https://attack.mitre.org/groups/G0032/

[45]www.blackhat.com/docs/us-16/materials/us-16-Valtman-Breaking-Payment-Points-of-Interaction.pdf

[46]www.pcisecuritystandards.org/documents/Skimming%20Prevention%20BP%20for%20Merchants%20Sept2014.pdf

[47]https://krebsonsecurity.com/2014/07/sandwich-chain-jimmy-johns-investigating-breach-claims/

[48]https://rambleed.com/

Consequently, the hardware devices need to be subject to periodic integrity checks against an asset inventory and hardware life-cycle management,[49] and all receipts securely managed to ensure the integrity of the POIs.

Associated Problems

Unfortunately, there can be conflicts between PCI DSS and the business objectives to support the maintenance of good customer service and crime reduction. Frequently, the POI environments will be subject to Closed Circuit Television (CCTV) surveillance in support of customer compliant investigations and in support of crime reduction efforts.

If you are using CCTV, you will be wanting to ensure that the imagery is clear enough to identify individuals, as per the goal of having CCTV monitoring. However, if the recordings overlook the POI devices, you may be recording the Payment Card details and Personal Identification Number (PIN) (a.k.a. Sensitive Authentication Data (SAD)), as the payments are being made.

Remember

- PCI DSS applies to any storage, transmission, or processing of cardholder data.

- The storage of SAD is prohibited under PCI DSS.

Consequently, the digital recordings could be a valuable target for the criminals, and the storage systems (and any connected systems) would become part of your PCI DSS scope.

Ongoing Research

Researchers, such as the Computer Laboratory, University of Cambridge, UK, are continually identifying vulnerabilities[50] and innovative ways to exploit POI devices:[51]

- **EMV PIN verification "wedge" vulnerability**

---

[49]www.pcisecuritystandards.org/assessors_and_solutions/pin_transaction_devices
[50]www.cl.cam.ac.uk/research/security/banking/ped/
[51]www.cl.cam.ac.uk/~osc22/docs/preplay_oakland14.pdf

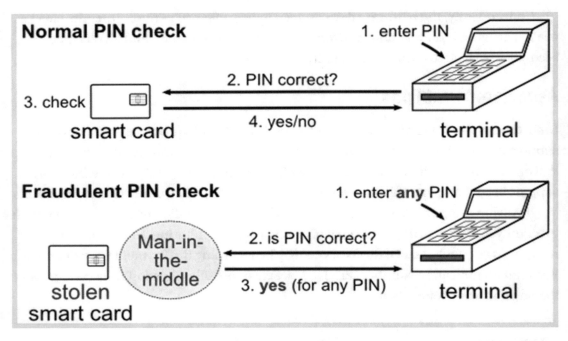

Figure 10-5. *Cambridge University Research*[52]

- **Chip Authentication Program (CAP) vulnerabilities**

- **PIN Entry Device (PED) vulnerabilities**

- **Chip and PIN (EMV) relay attacks**

- **Tamper resistance of Chip and PIN (EMV) terminals**

- **Chip and PIN (EMV) Interceptor**

This shows the risks associated with these devices and the importance of safeguarding these devices from opportunist criminals. Consequently, it is essential that you maintain an inventory of your physical POS/PTS assets *(as well as all your other assets that support your payment processes)* and ensure that you periodically review your asset inventories and ensure that their end-of-life(EoL)/end-of-support (EoS) dates are recorded within the inventory. For PTS devices, you should consult the PCI SSC's web site.[53]

---

[52]www.cl.cam.ac.uk/research/security/banking/

[53]www.pcisecuritystandards.org/assessors_and_solutions/pin_transaction_devices

Third-Party Attack Vectors

Increasingly, if an attacker is unable to directly target an organization, they will seek to identify associated company relationships, where they can exploit vulnerabilities/poor practices of a third party in order to gain lateral movement or access to the data of their primary targets:

- **Supply Chain Compromises**

  Supply chain compromise is the manipulation of products or product delivery mechanisms prior to receipt by a final consumer for the purpose of data or system compromise.

  Attacks on your Supply chains can take place at any stage including

  - Manipulation of development tools

  - Manipulation of a development environment

  - Manipulation of source code repositories (public or private)

  - Manipulation of source code in open source dependencies

  - Manipulation of software update/distribution mechanisms

  - Compromised/infected system images

  - Replacement of legitimate software with modified versions

  - Sales of modified/counterfeit products to legitimate distributors

  - Shipment interdiction

  While supply chain compromises can impact any component of hardware or software, attackers will often focus on using malicious additions to legitimate software, within the software distribution or update channels.

  The distribution of malicious software can be distributed to a broad set of consumers but only move on to additional tactics on specific victims or to specific individuals.

- Extra caution should be applied when considering the use of popular open source projects, as these may have been targeted for the delivery of malicious software.

  - Only use authorized/approved software from reputable sources.

- **Trusted Relationships**

  Attackers seek to gain unauthorized access through trusted third-party relationship, exploiting existing connections, which may not be protected or are subject to less scrutiny than standard mechanisms of gaining access to a network.

  It is common for businesses to allow elevated access to second- or third-party external providers, in support of the management internal systems, as well as cloud-based environments, for example:

  - IT services contractors

  - Managed security providers

  - Infrastructure contractors

Third-party access should be treated in exactly the same manner as all other access management procedures, ensuring that all access requests are approved and based on strict restrictions, against specific role requirements, and all third-party access is subject to periodic reviews (confirm that the access remains appropriate).

Recommendations

Whether you are designing your own defensive strategy or reducing the risks of successful attacks being perpetrated against your payment channels, it is essential that you understand your specific threat actor TTPs and ensure that you have incorporated some level of Threat Intelligence[54] into your vulnerability management process.

This will enable you to better understand the kinetic (external) and non-kinetic (internal), both traditional and non-traditional, that are relevant to your organization.

---

[54]www.crest-approved.org/wp-content/uploads/CREST-Cyber-Threat-Intelligence.pdf

Traditional	Non-traditional

• Terrorism[55]
    • *Direct target*
    • *Collateral Damage*
	• Environmental
	    • Fire
	    • Flood

• Industrial Espionage[56]	• Theft
• Sabotage[57]	• Loss
• Subversion[58]	• Accidental
• Organized Crime[59]	

Throughout my career, I have seen the value (at first hand) of having a proactive approach to vulnerability management, where effective risk mitigations are driven by the maintenance of an up-to-date understanding of the TTPs that might be used against you and being able to rapidly identify and mitigate any associated vulnerabilities.

For example, during my appointments on Counter-Terrorism or Counter Intelligence duties, there was continual gathering and inter-departmental sharing of intelligence. This intelligence was then analyzed and converted into defensive measures (e.g., Actions on) to be applied for the protection of high-value/mission-critical military assets (a.k.a. Intelligence Led Policing[60] and Security).

The reality is that in today's digitally connected business environments, the threat is ever present and is expanding on a daily basis. Consequently, you may have the firm believe that your type of business is not of value to an attacker. That is no longer true, as you might be easy pickings for an attacker, and once they have a persistent presence, they may well be able to develop you into a viable target.

---

[55]www.rms.com/blog/2019/11/13/cyberterrorism-a-risk-assessment/

[56]https://interestingengineering.com/industrial-espionage-is-nothing-new-explore-what-it-is-and-its-history

[57]www.resolver.com/blog/top-4-risks-security-teams/

[58]www.bloomberg.com/news/articles/2019-11-10/russia-s-growing-subversion-risks-conflict-u-k-official-says

[59]www.ncsc.gov.uk/news/ncsc-publishes-new-report-criminal-online-activity

[60]https://onlinedegrees.sandiego.edu/what-is-intelligence-led-policing/

Therefore, it is essential that you familiarize yourself with the current and any emerging attacker TTPs and apply them to your organization. This will help your monitoring team identify such actions being applied to your business environment.

Additionally, ensure that you apply Threat Intelligence assessments to your third-party due diligence activities and ensure that any third-party connections are subject to segmentation testing. Remember, if any third parties have a remote access function, you need to confirm that they (as well as yourself) have a secure termination point and that they do not inadvertently present an unauthorized access opportunity.

Stage 1

- Through a compromised email account, a small number of employees receive a malicious phishing email.

  - One employee clicks the attached link and enters their Office 365 credentials into a bogus Office 365 login page. On clicking return, an error page is presented. The employee fails to report this and carries on their everyday duties.

  - One month later, 2 minutes after logging out of their Office 365 account, unknown attackers log in and use this account to spend the next 4 hours to send out hundreds of spurious, malicious emails.

    - Post-incident countermeasures included sending out communications to all recipients of the malicious emails.

Stage 2

- During stage 1, the attackers had gained sufficient intelligence to confirm this manufacturing company as being a potentially viable target.

- The senior executives were the targets of Spear Phishing emails, specifically crafted to lure the recipients into compromising their Office 365 credentials. Three of these accounts were created and used to send out urgent communications to the payment clerk, requesting that they make an urgent invoice payment to one of their suppliers. The communications came through a variety of Office 365 communication channels (from the three senior executives) and stressing that failure to make the payment would have a significant impact on the business and its relations with the supplier.

- Of course, this was criminals, seeking to defraud the organization out of thousands of dollars.

- Fortunately, the payment clerk noticed something out of the ordinary and contacted one of these senior executives to confirm the validity of the communications.

This particular attack involved a 12-month period of dormancy between stages 1 and 2. However, the reality is that this was a simple style of attack which only required patience and the exploitation of the employees. The truth is that this will have been just one of many attacks that will have been carried out simultaneously.

The reality of this incident was that had they had received and acted upon the threat intelligence related to the use of Office 365,[61] they could have implemented conditional access mitigation measures. However, this had been a decision made by the Chief Information Officer (CIO) and the IT Director to enhance the business office products and without any consideration for the perceived risks associated with the change to this new cloud technology.

Reality Bites

Threats to your business can be from both deliberate attackers targeting your business but often overlooked is the potential impact and damage that can be caused from an accidental or negligent action by one of your employees or a contractor.

It is well known that the military deployments into Iraq and Afghanistan would receive a high number of insurgent attacks. However, the potential risk of negligent actions from visiting drivers created as much of a threat of injury or death to the coalition service personnel residing within the relative safety of the deployed operating bases.

---

[61]www.scmagazineuk.com/scams-use-false-alerts-target-office-365-users-admins/
  article/1591914

For example, each and every day the bases would receive essential supplies that were needed to maintain effective operations. This was something that needed to be risk managed, so as to allow the deliveries to continue without causing unnecessary risks to the persons within.

Now imagine the scenario where a local national delivery driver, bringing in their fully loaded 5–6 axle artic truck *(44 tons),* is discovered, during the entry search, to be in possession of a large amount of Afghan Skunk.[62] The CIFT are tasked to carry out a risk assessment as to whether it was safe for this driver to drive their heavily loaded vehicle onto the base while potentially under the influence of this drug.

During the investigation, the driver initially protested that they had no knowledge of how that item could have come to have been hidden in the cab of their vehicle. However, this slowly changed to them accepting that it was theirs and that their job was extremely monotonous. They then confessed to being occasional users and admitting that they had been smoking it while they were waiting in the vehicle queue to enter the base *(less than 1 hour earlier).*

The result was that the Afghan Skunk was confiscated and destroyed, and the vehicle was allowed entry to deliver the supplies but without the driver driving it.

Or how about the unnecessary risks of an unsafely loaded supply vehicle being allowed entry to the base? The local understanding of what might be safe was a far different view to ours.

---

[62]https://weedmaps.com/strains/afghan-skunk-afghani-skunk

Figure 10-6. *"Safety First"*

Conclusion

PCI DSS should never be seen as a "Tick Box" solution but more as a suite of baseline security controls that have been developed to help mitigate the known risks associated with the 12 PCI DSS requirements.

Criminals are creatures of habit and will use well-known TTPs that they've either successfully used previously or which are known to have been successfully used by some of the peer groups. Consequently, it is essential that you keep your knowledge of TTPs current and ensure that this is included as an enhancement into your vulnerability management process.

This is especially important to consider when making any changes or introducing new technologies to your corporate environments.

Utilizing threat intelligence can help you ensure that you are proactively mitigating the new and evolving risks to your business (a.k.a. Intelligence Led Security). The criminals are continually developing and refining their TTPs rather than waiting to align their TTP updates with the changes to PCI DSS.

Waiting for the PCI DSS controls framework to be updated or waiting for that annual assessment may prove too late for your organization.

Key Takeaways

PCI DSS is a suite of integrated security controls designed to mitigate the risks associated with the 12 requirements. However, an effective security defense strategy needs to consider the specific Tactics, Techniques, and Protocols (TTPs) that are known to be used against your payment channels.

Being solely reliant on a "Tick Box" approach to the application of PCI DSS may help you achieve your annual compliance obligations, but can still leave you vulnerable to compromised infrastructures or bad practices.

Consequently, a mature PCI DSS program can still be vulnerable without the integration of intelligence-led security (Threat Intelligence) into your vulnerability management process.

Remember: Risk = Vulnerability × Threat × Impact

- *If you have network connected systems, are your teams familiar with the TTPs employed by the attackers to compromise this infrastructure and enable them unauthorized access to the corporate network or sensitive data?*

- *Have you restricted traffic flows, services, ports, and protocols to prevent misuse or unauthorized access and prevent lateral movement across the corporate network?*

- *Have you securely configured the supporting systems against the commonly used TTPs?*

- *Do you check test your web interfaces against known threats?*

- *Do you include segmentation testing reviews of your third-party connections?*

- *Does your penetration testing include aspects of intelligence-led security?*

Risks

Criminals are ever present and constantly on the prowl, seeking to employ their favorite "Tools of the Trade."

Consequently, it is essential that your teams are trained and made aware of the Tactics, Techniques, and Protocols (TTPs) that are known to be used by your potential attackers.

No matter the type of business, consider yourself to be under threat of criminal interest.

Essential to your PCI DSS program is understanding the threats to your payment channels, supporting infrastructures, processes, and personnel.

PCI DSS compliance is the minimum benchmark, and you may wish to choose to apply enhancements to the existing controls, for example:

- *Monthly vulnerability identification, remediation, and updates on external/web-facing systems*

- *A program of regular security awareness training*

- *A dedicated formal internal and third-party audit program*

- *Physical checks of rogue devices plugged into receiving PCs*

CHAPTER 11

Compliance – A Team Effort

Throughout my 22-year career in the RAF Police, I was continually reminded of the importance the concept of teamwork plays in developing and maintaining effective defenses.

Be this in the form of me providing the first line of defense *(providing covert nightly security patrols of the perimeter fence delineation between the Badlands in Basra, Iraq (Working as a team of two dog units (one on foot and one in mobile support-driving in complete darkness to avoid detection)))* right through to working as the counter intelligence field team (CIFT) component of a deployed Force Protection regiment, in Afghanistan – each and every role was an essential component of the defensive efforts and was heavily reliant on the personnel receiving the initial level of training to deliver their roles and responsibilities and continuing a high level of investment in continual training, to meet the ever-evolving and demanding challenges of the assignments.

However, since entering the corporate environment, I have rarely observed businesses appreciate the need to invest in the development and maintenance of cohesive team approaches to effectively defend their realms. In contrast, many organizations appear to under invest in training and team building of their defensive units and with many working in conflict against each other – almost in a state of blame gaming, rather than as a cohesive unit.

This is probably the single most important element of the PCI DSS integrated framework. Unfortunately *(much like other industry security standards/frameworks)*, the current version of the standard does not articulate its importance for reducing the risks associated with poorly integrated processes (a.k.a. Teamwork). This chapter will explain the reason for my approach of making requirement 1 the layer that underlies all the others.

© Jim Seaman 2020
J. Seaman, *PCI DSS*, https://doi.org/10.1007/978-1-4842-5808-8_11

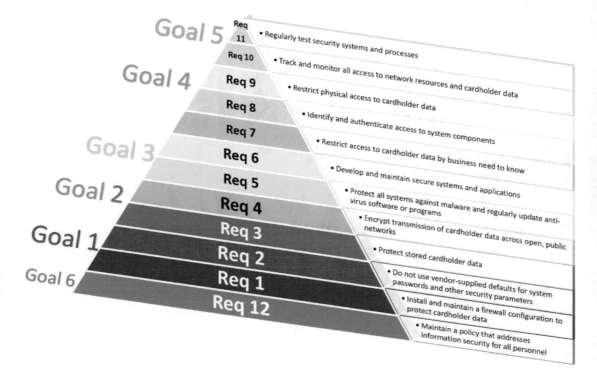

Figure 11-1. Requirements' Pyramid

This approach is designed to be complementary to, and should not be confused with, the Payment Card Industry Security Standards Council's (PCI SSC's) prioritized approach,[1] which prioritizes the controls in order of milestones, based upon the perceived risks:

1. Remove sensitive authentication data and limit data retention.

2. Protect systems and networks and be prepared to respond to a system breach.

3. Secure payment card applications.

4. Monitor and control access to your systems.

5. Protect stored cardholder data.

6. Finalize remaining compliance efforts and ensure all controls are in place.

---

[1]www.pcisecuritystandards.org/documents/Prioritized-Approach-for-PCI-DSS-v3_2_1.pdf ?agreement=true&time=1577538686226

Any effective Data Privacy and Security program is heavily reliant on the human factor; however, businesses still too often regard compliance as being IT systems focused. Unfortunately, this reluctance to invest into the people skills can significantly increase the risks of something going wrong, which could lead to a compromised system or data breach. In recent reports[2] the human factor was cited as being the cause of between **67%** and **90%** of all security incidents.

In reality, the human factor is more likely to be the **100%** causal reason behind every compromised system, incorrect transmission, or data breach.

How can this be?

It is difficult to find a single reported data breach where the human factor has not had an influence on the cause of security incident. Let's take a look at some of the notable events from 2019:

1. **Adobe Inc**[3]

   - *Poorly configured Elasticsearch database – **7.5 million** compromised records*

2. **Canva**[4]

   - *On discovery of the attack, Canva immediately took action to fix the cause of the breach (exposed data included usernames, email addresses, and encrypted passwords, which were salted and hashed with the bcrypt algorithm). However, this action did not prevent the unauthorized access to and exfiltration of customers' sensitive data – **139 million** compromised records.*

3. **Capital One**[5]

   - *An Amazon Web Services third-party contractor carried out the deliberate extraction of data stored on Amazon's servers – **106 million** compromised records.*

---

[2] www.csoonline.com/article/3504813/the-human-factor-of-cyber-security.html
[3] www.comparitech.com/blog/information-security/7-million-adobe-creative-cloud-accounts-exposed-to-the-public/
[4] www.zdnet.com/article/australian-tech-unicorn-canva-suffers-security-breach/
[5] https://edition.cnn.com/2019/07/29/business/capital-one-data-breach/index.html

4. **DoorDash**[6]

- *Poor security controls allowed a hacker to gain unauthorized access to customers' data – **4.9 million** compromised records.*

5. **First American Corporation**[7]

- *Insecure by design in one of its production applications, enabled the unauthorized access and exfiltration of sensitive data – **885 million** compromised records.*

6. **JustDial**[8]

- *Four unprotected application program interfaces (APIs) had enabled a hacker to gain unauthorized access to steal customers' sensitive data – reported to be **100 million** compromised records.*

7. **Mobile TeleSystems (MTS)**[9]

- *During a handover of a data folder, an unnamed third party failed to follow their company's business processes, security policies, and their personal responsibility to protect the sensitive data – **100 million (1.7 Tb)** compromised records.*

8. **Truecaller**[10]

- *Despite the reports of millions of customer records (all with Truecaller ID apps) being available for sale,[11] Truecaller have denied that their database has been breached. However, they have confirmed that they have discovered evidence of employees carrying out "data scraping[12]" – reported to be between **100 and 300 million** compromised records.*

---

[6]https://techcrunch.com/2019/09/26/doordash-data-breach/

[7]https://techcrunch.com/2019/09/26/doordash-data-breach/

[8]https://economictimes.indiatimes.com/tech/internet/data-breach-at-justdial-leaks-100-million-user-details/articleshow/68930607.cms

[9]www.upguard.com/breaches/mts-nokia-telecom-inventory-data-exposure

[10]https://analyticsindiamag.com/data-breach-truecaller-exposes-indian-users-data-shows-cracks-in-cyber-security-infrastructure/

[11]www.bankinfosecurity.asia/researcher-data-leaked-for-300-million-truecaller-users-a-12519

[12]www.techopedia.com/definition/33132/data-scraping

9. **Zynga**[13]

   - *A poorly configured social mobile game enabled the unauthorized access to a connected database – **218 million** compromised records.*

10. **Westpac**[14]

    - *Failure to identify and respond quickly to a brute force attack on a payment platform (PayID) enabled the hacker to compromise customer details before containment was established – **98,000** (of 100,000) compromised records.*

It is reported that in the first six months of 2019, a total of **4.1 billion** records were compromised[15] and with the global average cost of a data breach estimated at **$3.92 million**[16] and with an average cost of $150 per compromised record, this becomes an ever-increasing risk to today's digital/Internet-connected businesses. Consequently, it is essential that businesses adopt a team approach to their compliance efforts, ensuring that adequate investment is made to ensure that the team members (game players) have and maintain sufficient motor skills/knowledge to effectively develop and maintain the systems integrity while being able to rapidly respond to unusual events or incidents.

The maintenance of an effective compliance program has very similar similarities to the maintenance of a competitive team sport (e.g., American Football, Baseball, Basketball, Cricket, Football (Soccer), Ice Hockey, Rugby League, Rugby Union, Volleyball, Water Polo, etc.). Consequently, any organization seeking to develop and mature their compliance programs should look at applying some lessons from their favorite team sport.

---

[13]https://venturebeat.com/2019/09/30/words-with-friends-player-data-allegedly-stolen-for-218-million-users/

[14]https://finance.nine.com.au/business-news/westpac-data-breach-100000-australian-customers-at-risk/84c91581-90b6-464e-9137-a2d973492614

[15]www.forbes.com/sites/daveywinder/2019/08/20/data-breaches-expose-41-billion-records-in-first-six-months-of-2019/#71077994bd54

[16]www.ibm.com/security/data-breach?cm_mmc=0Social_Blog-_-Security_Optimize+the+Security+Program-_-WW_WW-_-CODB2019Blog_ov70891&cm_mmca1=000000NJ&cm_mmca2=10000253&_ga=2.155608443.1344017930.1577447996-405938945.1575975888&cm_mc_uid=69077084300315759758876&cm_mc_sid_50200000=52560441577447996051&cm_mc_sid_52640000=74762651577447996076

Such an approach should make the compliance program more effective and enjoyable, whilst significantly increasing the skill levels and, thus, considerably decrease the potential risk of a compromise system/network or data breach?

Introduction

Despite the ever-present numbers of data breaches,[17] since 2005, both the Governments and Businesses have been slow to respond and the statistics for businesses continue to grow.

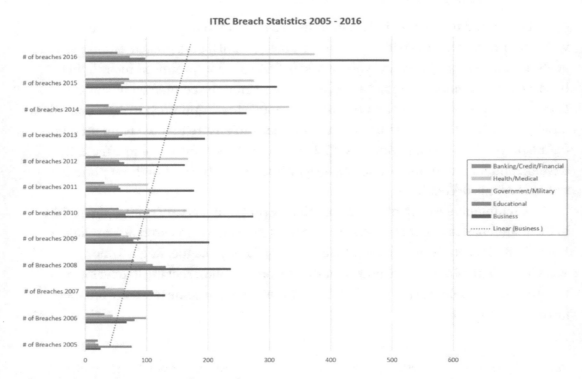

Figure 11-2. *Data Breach Trends*

---

[17]www.idtheftcenter.org/images/breach/Overview2005to2016Finalv2.pdf

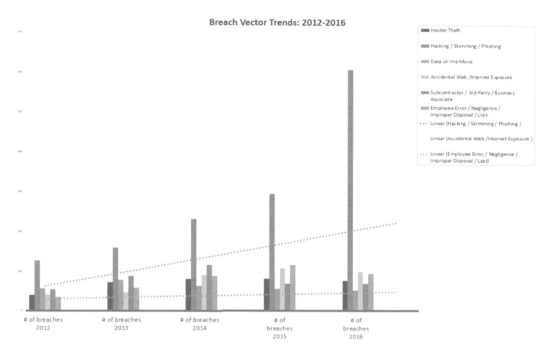

Figure 11-3. *Breach Vectors*

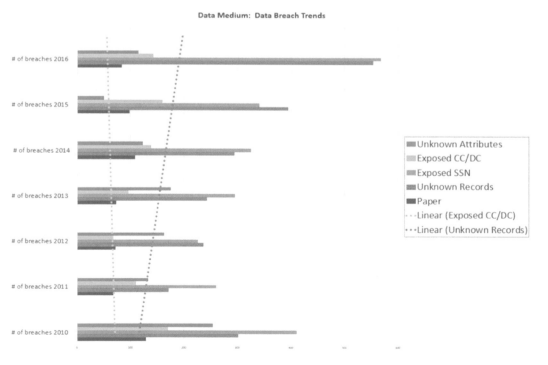

Figure 11-4. *Data Types*

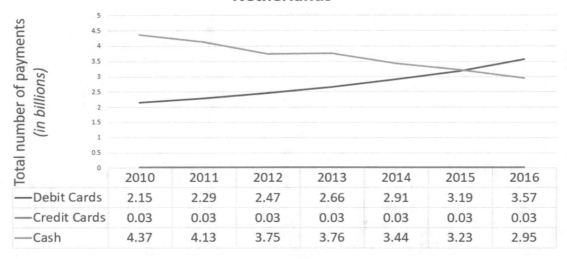

	2010	2011	2012	2013	2014	2015	2016
—Debit Cards	2.15	2.29	2.47	2.66	2.91	3.19	3.57
—Credit Cards	0.03	0.03	0.03	0.03	0.03	0.03	0.03
—Cash	4.37	4.13	3.75	3.76	3.44	3.23	2.95

Figure 11-5. *Cash vs. Payment Card – Volume*

On the positive side, despite a considerable increase in the volume of Credit Card (CC)- and Debit Card (DC)-based payments[18] *(aligned with the first significant update to the PCI DSS (v2.0, 2010)[19])*, the number of data breaches involving payment card data appears to have decreased.

This could be an indication of the impact the continued development of the PCI DSS controls framework is having on reducing the associated risks.

The next significant change to the PCI DSS controls framework came with the introduction of version 3.0[20] in 2015. The major change that was introduced here was the introduction of making PCI DSS compliance a Business-As-Usual (BAU) part of your business. However, much like any Data Privacy and Security program, this needs to be a team effort following the business "Game Plan."

---

[18]www.dnb.nl/binaries/From%20cash%20to%20cards_tcm46-372117.pdf
[19]www.pcisecuritystandards.org/documents/webinar_101116_no_builds_standards_2.0.pdf
[20]www.pcisecuritystandards.org/pdfs/PCIDSS.pdf

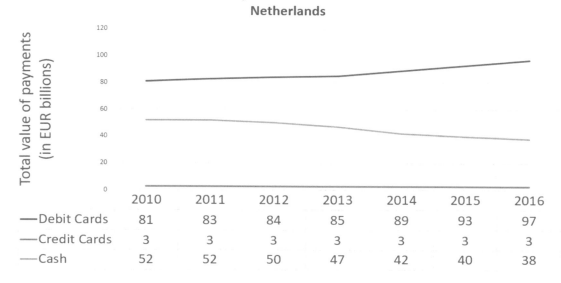

Figure 11-6. *Cash vs. Payment Cards – Value*

	2010	2011	2012	2013	2014	2015	2016
—Debit Cards	81	83	84	85	89	93	97
—Credit Cards	3	3	3	3	3	3	3
—Cash	52	52	50	47	42	40	38

It's All in the Game

Whether you have been a coach/player in a team sport at a professional level, or just as an amateur level, or just a spectator of your country/local team sports club, you will already have an appreciation of the value of having a well-practiced, cohesive team.

You cannot imagine a team winning the league *(or even a match)* without having extensively practiced the skills needed, the set/player combination plays, or understanding the specific threats of the opposition.

The same applies to your Data Privacy and Security program. However, the investment in teamwork and maintaining the skill levels is often underappreciated, leading to compliance becoming a minimal compliance effort.

If you were to compare the efforts of your Data Privacy and Security program to that of a team sport, where might your team effort be comparable to?

- Full-time Professional team

- Part-time Semi-Professional team

- Local amateur social team

- Secondary/High School team

- Primary School team

- Pre-School team

Team Structure

If you look at the team sport clubs that you might coach/play or support, you will see a clear team structure where specific roles are filled by personnel with specific skillsets and experiences. All these players come together with one specific goal – to win matches. To achieve this, the senior management of the club needs to be supportive of the coaching staff, while the players need to be focused during the coaches' training session.

A successful sports club does not expect to win matches by doing the absolute minimum. Long before the season commences, the club's senior management, coach, and support staff will have carried out extensive planning and preparations for the forthcoming season. Much of this work begins long before the fixture lists are announced.

For instance, if you take a look at my local professional Super League club (Castleford Rugby League Football Club (RLFC)), they commenced their pre-season training in November 2019[21] in preparation for their 2020 season. Yet, their 2019 season did not finish until September 26, 2019,[22] and their first Super League fixture for 2020 is not scheduled until February 02, 2020,[23] with an away match with the newly promoted Toronto Wolfpack.

Not long after the previous season had come to a close, the club and coaching staff will already have been making plans for the following season, for example:

- **October 2019**: The Club looks to sign a specialist half back to replace the outgoing Luke Gale.[24]

- **October 2019**: The Club's retail outlets plan for the arrival of the 2020 team kit, to be sold in advance of the 2020 season.

---

[21]www.pontefractandcastlefordexpress.co.uk/sport/rugby-league/castleford-tigers-report-back-pre-season-ready-train-differently-972187

[22]www.bbc.co.uk/sport/rugby-league/teams/castleford/scores-fixtures/2019-09

[23]https://castlefordtigers.com/fixtures.php

[24]https://castlefordtigers.com/article.php?id=6653

- **October 2019**: The Club's coach formulates pre-season training plan. This needs to be planned in conjunction with the conditioning staff, so as to complement each other – rather than be in conflict.

- **November 2019**: Conditioning staff prepare pre-season conditioning programs.

- **November 2019**: The Club, Coaching staff, and players refresh their knowledge of the rules,[25] relevant to their position, as part of their pre-season training.

- **November 2019**: Club and Coach seek to arrange suitable pre-season friendly games[26] in support of the pre-season training plans.

- **December 2019**: The Club, Coaching staff, and players familiarize themselves with any rule changes that are being introduced for the 2020 season.[27]

- **December 2019**: The Club consider their options for the half back pairing to Luke Gale's replacement, following the departure of Jamie Ellis.[28]

- **January 2019**: The Club's administrative teams commence planning for the team's needs for the forthcoming season.

This is just a small example list of what may be involved in ensuring the club remains successful or not. All of these actions/plans need to be well planned so that they work integrally to one another, needing extensive communication and agreement between the interdependent departments. For example, the merchandising department needs to work in conjunction with the retail outlets to ensure that there are sufficient display spaces within their stores in order to optimize the sales opportunities.

How does your PCI DSS team planning look in comparison?

---

[25]www.rugby-league.com/flipbooks/2019-operational-rules-tiers-1-3/mobile/index.html
[26]https://castlefordtigers.com/article.php?id=6721
[27]www.rugby-league.com/article/56064/shot-clock-adjustments-for--season
[28]https://castlefordtigers.com/article.php?id=6703

Rugby League Game Play

Imagine the structure of a typical game of Rugby League and you will see a great deal of similarities between your PCI DSS compliance and the sport of Rugby League *(Remember, these similarities can be seen in most team sports and it is not limited to just Rugby League).*

The objective of a successful Rugby League club is to win matches; this is achieved through the effective movement of the ball, through retaining possession *(storage)*, passing (in a backward motion) between players *(processing),* and kicking *(transmission)* to get the ball across the opposition's try line or over and between the opposition's goal posts to be rewarded with a score (Try = 4 points; Conversion = 2 points; Field Goal = 1 point). This can only be done within a maximum six-try tally and with the maximum distance needing to be travelled being 7616 m^2 to 8296 m^2, and all being done within the spirit of the rules of Rugby League.[29]

Meanwhile, the opposition is seeking opportunities to prevent you from being rewarded, through gaining more possession than you, so as to ensure that they make more reward than their opposition.

Each attacking and defending Rugby League player has their own differing skills and specializations, which have been integrated together through extensive training and coaching staff game plans. The successful application of these skills, training, communication, and teamwork helps ensure success for the better prepared and drilled teams.

Note   The attackers have recognized the value of working as part of a team, so why aren't businesses doing likewise?

Poor application and planning often results in poor on-field execution which leads to lost possession and continual loss of matches. This, in turn, leads to demoralization of the losing team's supporters, which results in a lack of trust in the supporting spectators. This results in a reduced volume of spectators and gate receipts, leading to a reduction in profits.

Typically, a poorly performing team will return a small number of dedicated supporters *(perhaps 33.3%)*, while another 33.3% will return when they can see a remarkable improvement (e.g., new signings, coaches, won games, etc.). However, after a long run of defeats, it is likely that the remaining third of supporters may become so disillusioned that

---

[29]https://support.skybet.com/s/article/Rugby-League-Rules

they will never return to the club *(perhaps preferring to watch it on television, instead, or even changing their allegiances).* These lost spectators need to be replaced by new spectators.

The same effect can be seen in the payment card industry, with businesses suffering significant data breaches being affected in similar ways:[30]

- **83% of consumers** will stop spending with a business for several months in the immediate aftermath of a security breach or a hack.

- **Over a fifth (21%) of consumers** will never return to a brand or a business post breach.

How long can your business cope with such significantly reduced "Gate Receipts"?

Take, for example, the impact the 2013 hack had on Target, with a reported cost of **$300 Million.**[31] They lost a considerable number of customers' records, having had 70 million of their customers impacted and 40 million payment card records compromised. Imagine the impact of a loss of **58.1 Million** customers or **33.2 Million** payment card purchases. Consequently, Target have made significant investments into the enhancement of the Data Privacy and Security program.[32]

Consequently, before you suffer those fumbled, dropped passes or poorly placed kicks that cost your organization its reputation, is it not better to invest in the team development?

Team Player Development

Much like the development required to build and maintain a professional rugby league team, an effective PCI DSS compliance program requires the right specialist for the right role and with each specialist having proportionate training to develop and maintain their skill/knowledge levels.

In a professional rugby league side, they will spend each, and every, week carrying out strength, weakness, opportunities, and threat (SWOT) analysis of the members of the team against the upcoming competitions. Even though these players might have been playing for over a decade, the coaching staff still seek any prospects to gain the upper hand against their opponents. However, in business, there is a tendency to regard

---

[30]www.securitymagazine.com/articles/89501-avoid-a-business-following-breach-and-21-never-return

[31]www.thesslstore.com/blog/2013-target-data-breach-settled/

[32]www.welivesecurity.com/2018/12/18/target-targeted-five-years-breach-shook-cybersecurity/

their Data Privacy and Security programs as being isolated responsibilities, with limited consideration for the potential impact on other supporting roles.

Imagine the chaos that might ensue if a rugby league team were to attempt the same approach:

- During the game, the attacking side are in possession and are on the fifth tackle. The half back receives the ball, in the center of the pitch, and decides to kick the ball into the opposition's corner. The intention was for their center or winger to rush up on the kicked ball, to put pressure on the receiving opponent, or to regather the ball and go over to score a try. However, at the point that the half back kicks the ball, the center and winger are in front of them and are in an offside[33] position and must give the receiving opponent 10 meters, unless, of course, the half back was to run ahead of their team players before kicking the ball. Even though one of the responsibilities of the half back might be to kick well-placed kicks, they need to be mindful of their support players to ensure that a team effort is applied.

Figure 11-7. *Well-Placed Kick*

---

[33]www.rugby-league.com/the_rfl/rules/laws_of_the_game/offside

Now imagine your PCI DSS compliance program. Your IT team understand the criticality of their public-facing supporting IT systems. However, they fail to inform the vulnerability management specialist, and, thus, a medium-rated vulnerability on a critical public-facing system is deemed to be a lower priority for remediation and is left vulnerable for a period of 90 days. Prior to remediation, the opposition *(hackers)* pounce on the opportunity to pick up this mistake and successfully breach the defensive line *(compromise the network)* to score a try over your goal line *(steal data)*. Alternatively, they fail to include the IT asset owner of a public-facing critical asset that was identified as having a critical vulnerability. As a result, the critical update remains untreated and vulnerable to exploitation.

Sounds Unrealistic?

I'm sure that Equifax[34] thought the same, until their lack of a team approach became the cause of their security breach. This simple error resulted in the failure to patch its network after being alerted in March 2017 to a critical security vulnerability (CVE-2017-5638[35] – The Jakarta Multipart parser in Apache Struts 2 2.3.x before 2.3.32 and 2.5.x before 2.5.10.1[36]) affecting its ACIS database. This database handled inquiries from consumers about their personal credit data, enabling the attacker to gain unauthorized access and to steal **148 million** customer records *(credit card numbers of approximately 209,000 consumers)* and resulted in a reported settlement figure of **$700 million**. Their security team had carried out their responsibility of communicating the rule that all critical vulnerabilities affecting critical systems must be updated within 48 hours *(kicked the ball)*. However, they had failed to identify whether the IT asset owner was aware that you were about to *kick the ball* and were left unaware that they were in an *offside position* (failed to notify). This allowed their opponents the opportunity of an *extra 10 meters to pick up and run with the ball* (exploit the vulnerability).

In the case of the Equifax breach, members of their coaching team (chief information officer (CIO) and the chief information security officer (CISO)) appear to have been deemed culpable for the lack of a team effort within their Data Privacy and Security

---

[34]https://republicans-oversight.house.gov/wp-content/uploads/2018/12/Equifax-Report.pdf

[35]www.exploit-db.com/search?cve=2017-5638

[36]https://nvd.nist.gov/vuln/detail/CVE-2017-5638

program. Following the cyber-attack (May through July of 2017) and the public announcement of the data breach (September 8, 2017), Equifax announced (September 15, 2017) that with immediate effect "personnel changes" were being made, with the CIO, CISO, and chief executive officer retiring.[37]

Each member of the professional rugby league team needs to have a general understanding of the "rules of the game" and must possess a standard skill competency to have been selected for the team. However, each player may have more specialist knowledge, skills, or experiences that make them more suitable for a particular field position. In addition to the 13 players, the coach needs to select four suitable interchanges, who can be timely impact players and who can be as effective as the players they may need to replace. Consequently, some standout players may be those that may be called upon to be effective in multiple positions *(Utility Players)*, deputizing if the primary player is not available, for example:

- **Jason Flowers**[38]

  A former professional rugby league footballer who played in the 1990s and 2000s and has coached in the 2010s

  - He played at representative level for Scotland and at club level for Redhill ARLFC (in Airedale, Castleford), the Castleford (Tigers), Halifax, and the Salford City Reds.

    - Primarily as a fullback, but also at wing, center, or second row

- **Ian Smales**[39]

  A former professional rugby league footballer who played in the 1980s and 1990s

  - He played at representative level for Great Britain (non-Test matches), and Yorkshire, and at club level for Lock Lane ARLFC, Featherstone Rovers, Castleford Tigers, and Hunslet Hawks.

    - Played as a winger, center, stand-off, second-row, or loose forward

---

[37]www.bankinfosecurity.com/after-mega-breach-at-equifax-ceo-richard-smith-out-a-10335

[38]www.loverugbyleague.com/stats/players/Jason-Flowers-/

[39]www.rugbyleagueproject.org/players/ian-smales/summary.html

In order to make the teams more effective, it is vital that the club and coaching staff support the development of complementary "Team Tactics" that can be applied to effectively defend against the tactics, techniques, and protocols (TTPS) of their opposition *(Threat Intelligence[40])*. As a result, the coaching staff will be continually reviewing the games of their opponents and developing multiple "Playbooks." These will then have defensive countermeasures developed and be extensively practiced during team practices.

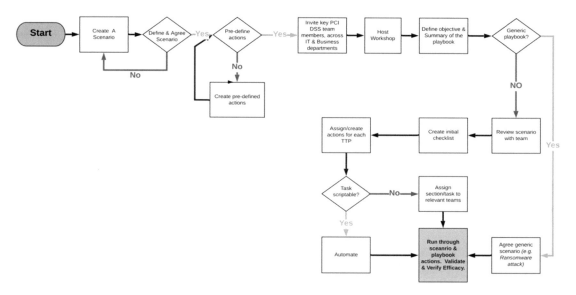

Figure 11-8. *Creating a "Playbook"*

---

[40]https://whatis.techtarget.com/definition/threat-intelligence-cyber-threat-intelligence

Initial Access	Execution	Persistence	Privilege Escalation	Defense Evasion	Credential Access	Discovery	Lateral Movement	Collection	Command And Control	Exfiltration	Impact
Drive-by Compromise	AppleScript	.bash_profile and .bashrc	Access Token Manipulation	Access Token Manipulation	Account Manipulation	Account Discovery	AppleScript	Audio Capture	Commonly Used Port	Automated Exfiltration	Account Access Removal
Exploit Public-Facing Application	CMSTP	Accessibility Features	Accessibility Features	Binary Padding	Bash History	Application Window Discovery	Application Deployment Software	Automated Collection	Communication Through Removable Media	Data Compressed	Data Destruction
External Remote Services	Command-Line Interface	Account Manipulation	AppCert DLLs	BITS Jobs	Brute Force	Browser Bookmark Discovery	Component Object Model and Distributed COM	Clipboard Data	Connection Proxy	Data Encrypted	Data Encrypted for Impact
Hardware Additions	Compiled HTML File	AppCert DLLs	AppInit DLLs	Bypass User Account Control	Credential Dumping	Domain Trust Discovery	Exploitation of Remote Services	Data from Information	Custom Command and Control Protocol	Data Transfer Size Limits	Defacement
Replication Through Removable Media	Component Object Model and Distributed COM	AppInit DLLs	Application Shimming	Clear Command History	Credentials from Web Browsers	File and Directory Discovery	Internal Spearphishing	Data from Local System	Custom Cryptographic Protocol	Exfiltration Over Alternative Protocol	Disk Content Wipe
Spearphishing Attachment	Control Panel Items	Application Shimming	Bypass User Account Control	CMSTP	Credentials in Files	Network Service Scanning	Logon Scripts	Data from Network Shared Drive	Data Encoding	Exfiltration Over Command and Control Channel	Disk Structure Wipe
Spearphishing Link	Dynamic Data Exchange	Authentication Package	DLL Search Order Hijacking	Code Signing	Credentials in Registry	Network Share Discovery	Pass the Hash	Data from Removable Media	Data Obfuscation	Exfiltration Over Other Network	Endpoint Denial of Service
Spearphishing via Service	Execution through API	BITS Jobs	Dylib Hijacking	Compile After Delivery	Exploitation for Credential Access	Network Sniffing	Pass the Ticket	Data Staged	Domain Fronting	Exfiltration Over Physical Medium	Firmware Corruption
Supply Chain Compromise	Execution through Module Load	Bootkit	Elevated Execution with Prompt	Compiled HTML File	Forced Authentication	Password Policy Discovery	Remote Desktop Protocol	Email Collection	Domain Generation Algorithms	Scheduled Transfer	Inhibit System Recovery
Trusted Relationship	Exploitation for Client Execution	Browser Extensions	Emond	Component Firmware	Hooking	Peripheral Device Discovery	Remote File Copy	Input Capture	Fallback Channels		Network Denial of Service
Valid Accounts	Graphical User Interface	Change Default File Association	Exploitation for Privilege Escalation	Component Object Model Hijacking	Input Capture	Permission Groups Discovery	Remote Services	Man in the Browser	Multi-hop Proxy		Resource Hijacking
	InstallUtil	Component Firmware	Extra Window Memory Injection	Connection Proxy	Input Prompt	Process Discovery	Replication Through Removable Media	Screen Capture	Multi-Stage Channels		Runtime Data Manipulation
	Launchctl	Component Object Model Hijacking	File System Permissions	Control Panel Items	Kerberoasting	Query Registry	Shared Webroot	Video Capture	Multiband Communication		Service Stop
	Local Job Scheduling	Create Account	Hooking	DCShadow	Keychain	Remote System Discovery	SSH Hijacking		Multilayer Encryption		Stored Data Manipulation
	LSASS Driver	DLL Search Order Hijacking	Image File Execution Options Injection	Deobfuscate/Decode Files or Information	LLMNR/NBT-NS Poisoning and Relay	Security Software Discovery	Taint Shared Content		Port Knocking		System Shutdown/Reboot
	Mshta	Dylib Hijacking	Launch Daemon	Disabling Security Tools	Network Sniffing	Software Discovery	Third-party Software		Remote Access Tools		Transmitted Data Manipulation
	PowerShell	Emond	New Service	DLL Search Order Hijacking	Password Filter DLL	System Information Discovery	Windows Admin Shares		Remote File Copy		
	Regsvcs/Regasm	External Remote Services	Parent PID Spoofing	DLL Side-Loading	Private Keys	System Network Configuration Discovery	Windows Remote Management		Standard Application Layer Protocol		
	Regsvr32	File System Permissions	Path Interception	Execution Guardrails	Securityd Memory	System Network Connections			Standard Cryptographic Protocol		
	Rundll32	Hidden Files and Directories	Plist Modification	Exploitation for Defense Evasion	Steal Web Session Cookie	System Owner/User Discovery			Standard Non-Application Layer Protocol		

Figure 11-9. *Tactics, Techniques, and Protocols (TTPs)*[41]

Applying "Team Tactics" to Win the PCI DSS Compliance Game

Okay, so hopefully you will now have an appreciation for the value of a cohesive team-based approach to managing your PCI DSS compliance efforts and, thus, reducing the potential opportunities for your opponents to profit from your mistakes.

In the current version of the PCI DSS controls framework (v3.2.1), the "Team Tactics" is partially addressed through the concluding controls of each requirement and throughout requirement 12:

- Requirement-specific supporting policies and operational procedures management

- Security policy management

- Risk management

- Acceptable Usage policy management

- Defined information security responsibilities for all personnel

- Assignment of information security management responsibilities

---

[41]https://mitre-attack.github.io/attack-navigator/enterprise/

- Security Education management

- Security vetting management

- Vendor management

- Incident response management

- Internal audit management

Unfortunately, in its current format, the PCI DSS controls framework aligns to support isolated departmental responsibilities and does not require "team tactics" to be developed and applied.

In fairness, even the more structured three lines of defense (3LOD) model[42] can often be seen being misapplied in heavily regulated industries (e.g., Financial Services). However, such a model would be most effective when applied to your PCI DSS compliance efforts.

Figure 11-10. *3LOD Model*

1LOD

Under the 1LOD, operational management has ownership, responsibility, and accountability for directly assessing, controlling, and mitigating risks.

---

[42]www.coso.org/Documents/COSO-2015-3LOD.pdf

2LOD

The 2LOD consists of activities covered by several components of internal governance (compliance, risk management, quality, IT, and other control departments).

- This LOD monitors and facilitates the implementation of effective risk management practices by operational management and assists the risk owners in reporting adequate risk-related information up and down the organization.

3LOD

Internal audit forms the organization's 3LOD. An independent internal audit function will, through a risk-based approach to its work, provide assurance to the organization's board of directors and senior management.

- This assurance will cover how effectively the organization assesses and manages its risks and will include assurance on the effectiveness of the 1LOD and 2LOD.

  - It encompasses all elements of an institution's risk management framework (from risk identification, risk assessment and response, to communication of risk-related information) and all categories of organizational objectives: strategic, ethical, operational, reporting, and compliance.

The need for a teamwork-based approach has been alluded to, within Appendix A3 of the existing PCI DSS controls framework (v3.2.1), where the Card Brands require greater assurance from the organizations, they deem to be Designated Entities Supplemental Validation (DESV):

- **A3.1 Implement a PCI DSS compliance program.**

  - Executive management are responsible for the protection of cardholder data and a PCI DSS compliance program.

  - Establish a formal PCI DSS compliance program.

- Define and formally assign PCI DSS compliance roles and responsibilities.

- Establish an up-to-date PCI DSS and InfoSec formal training program.

For example, develop a cohesive and holistic compliance, which includes the need for

- *The establishment of a PCI DSS security working group/committee to work in support of the PCI DSS compliance program*

- *Periodic PCI DSS security working group/committee meetings to discuss matters, risks, or issues pertaining to the PCI DSS compliance program*

- *Annotation of a PCI DSS controls responsible, accountable, consulted, informed (RACI) matrix*

- *Periodic general security awareness for all personnel*

- *Periodic PCI DSS-specific payment card security and awareness training*

- *Role specific on the job training*

- **A3.2 Document and validate PCI DSS scope.**

  - Periodically document and confirm the accuracy of PCI DSS scope.

  - Risk assess all changes to systems or networks for any potential impact on the PCI DSS scope.

  - Post changes: Verify any changes against the relevant PCI DSS requirements.

  - Risk assessment of any organizational changes for any potential impact on the PCI DSS scope.

  - Periodic segmentation testing to validate PCI DSS scope.

  - Periodic data discovery audits.

  - Clear text monitoring for unauthorized transmissions.

For example, develop a cohesive change management approach to ensure that all changes to the environment are subject to change management approval:

- *Discussion and approval for any significant changes.*

  - *All changes are documented.*

  - *All changes are risk assessed and rollback considerations made.*

- **A3.3 Validate PCI DSS is incorporated into business-as-usual (BAU) activities.**

  - Monitor and respond to any critical security control failures.

  - Establish system and software life-cycle management.

  - Establish periodic internal auditing.

  For example, develop a cohesive compliance status and performance process:

  - *Periodic key risk indicators (KPIs) and key performance indicators are submitted to the PCI DSS security working group/committee.*

  - *The results of the audit program are presented to the PCI DSS security working group/committee for discussion.*

- **A3.4 Control and manage logical access to the cardholder data environment.**

  - Conduct periodic reviews of in-scope standard and privileged user accounts.

  For example, develop a cohesive access management process, which includes the need for

  - *Formal access management practices, where all new and removed accounts are recorded and periodically reviewed by the PCI DSS security working group/committee*

- **A3.5 Identify and respond to suspicious events.**

  - Establish a methodology to rapidly identify and respond to ABNORMAL activities based upon known TTPs.

For example, develop a cohesive and holistic monitoring and incident response process, which includes the need for

- *The monitoring and incident response teams work together as a unit.*

- *The monitoring and incident response teams receive periodic on-the-job training.*

- *A library of scenarios is created and periodically practiced.*

- *A **BLUE** Team and **RED** Team style approach[43] is embedded into the business.*

- *The penetration testing teams deliver periodic awareness training to the monitoring and incident response team members.*

Although not currently included in the main PCI DSS controls framework, it is extremely likely that elements of a team-based approach will be included in the next release of PCI DSS (v4.0). However, even if it is not added to any updates, it is important to remember that the PCI DSS controls frameworks are your MINIMUM requirements and you should seek to develop a team-based approach, where each team is fully supportive of each other and becomes habitualized into communicating with each other.

Reality Bites

The growing reliance on data processing technologies in business increases the potential for the misuse of this data and supporting data processing systems. This, in turn, makes this a more attractive element to the criminal fraternity. However, the volume of suitably experienced, trained, and skilled Cyber/InfoSec professionals falls short of what is required to meet the business demands. A recent study,[44] by the ISC,[2] revealed that there was an estimated shortfall of **4.07 million** professionals that are needed to safeguard today's businesses.

---

[43]https://csrc.nist.gov/Glossary/Term/Red-Team-Blue-Team-Approach
[44]www.isc2.org/-/media/ISC2/Research/2019-Cybersecurity-Workforce-Study/ISC2-Cybersecurity-Workforce-Study-2019.ashx?la=en&hash=D087F6468B4991E0BEFFC017BC1ADF 59CD5A2EF7

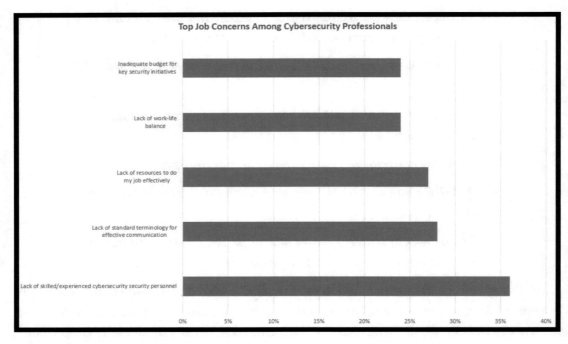

Figure 11-11. *Skills Gaps*

Consequently, successful companies need to address this Cyber/InfoSec cognizance[45] risk through a combination of procuring the services of suitably skilled and experienced individuals to help mentor and train internal resources. In the meantime, the lack of Cyber/InfoSec savvy personnel across the various departments needs to be documented and articulated to Senior Management. Remember, Cyber/InfoSec involves far more than just the technologies and your greatest risk is presented by your "Human Firewall."

> *I really think that if we change our own approach and thinking about what we have available to us, that is what will unlock our ability to truly excel in security.*
> *It's a perspectives exercise.*
> *What would it look like if abundance were the reality and not resource constraint?*

> —Greg York, Vice President, Tribune Media, SecureWorld Chicago

---

[45]https://reader.elsevier.com/reader/sd/pii/S2405896319320191?token=EE47B90DD9613CB
690648BF0B18D20BBE7A34AD6535E6016803E3EE97F372D970D52CA1AFEE06FB2C85D802032B54843

Military Lessons Applied

Ever since I joined the Royal Air Force, I have been fortunate enough to have been taught the value of investing in the people. Throughout my 22-year service, I was the recipient of a variety of trainings. This included trade-specific development, as well as generic and situational training needs. Additionally, as I progressed through my career, I was expected to mentor and train up non-Cyber/InfoSec specialists to help extend the reach of the embedded security culture.

It is extremely common for non-RAF personnel to assume that the effectiveness of the RAF is limited to just the pilots, aircrew, and aircraft engineers. However, this is far from being the truth, and even an attack on the operations supply chain can severely impact operations, for example:

- In the late 2000s, the MOD was crippled when all the supporting IT systems became infected with the Conficker virus.[46]

- During overseas deployments, it was extremely common for the insurgents to attack the military logistics convoys.[47]

Right from the outset of my military career, I was introduced to the concept of training and team building, commencing with 6-week general service training at RAF Swinderby, as part of Sgt Fosbury's 5 Flight, following which I was sent to RAF St. Athan to complete 2 weeks of driver training. Eight weeks later, I was then eligible to commence my RAF Police trade training course.

My trade training course involved a 7-week "Blues" course (Police training), followed by a 6-week "Greens" course (level 7 Infantry training (Special Weapons Protection)) and an 8-week Police Dog-handling course – 21 weeks of trade training at RAF Newton.

Following over 6 months of training, after my attestation into the Royal Air Force, I was finally qualified to be posted to my first operational role – an RAF Police Dog handler, at RAF Brize Norton. However, the training did not stop there. No, as well as the mandatory annual Nuclear, Biological, and Chemical (NBC), Fire awareness, First Aid training and weapons safety refresher training (L1A1 self-loading rifle, L2A3 Sterling Machine Gun, and L9A1 Browning self-loading pistol, L85A1 and L885A2 conversions), and practical exercises (TACEVAL, MAXEVAL, MINEVAL, and OPEVAL), I had weekly continuation training and nighttime dog training exercises.

---

[46]www.theregister.co.uk/2009/01/20/mod_malware_still_going_strong/

[47]http://content.time.com/time/world/article/0,8599,1928899,00.html

Figure 11-12. *Military Weapons*

Much like the weapons safety refresher training, my nighttime airfield patrol companion was considered to be a weapon. A very effective weapon is the military patrol dog (as long as they are continually trained *(a.k.a. a furry, 42-toothed furry Exocet)*). Imagine a weapon system that can detect the scent of an intruder from up to a kilometer away, with the ability to travel at around 30 mph,[48] moving up and around obstacles, and with the biting pressure of around 240 *PSI (easily exceeding the 160 PSI needed to break a human femur[49])*. Consequently, each and every year the dog teams would be subjected to an annual "Efficiency" test to ensure that the dog teams remained an effective and safe unit. The top 22 dog teams in the RAF Police would then be selected for the 5 ½ day UK Trails and with the runners up being selected for Regional Trial competitions. Each year, the annual tests would be altered to meet the changing demands of the service, for example, moving toward more controllable dog assets as the result of the end of the Cold War.

---

[48]https://ihomepet.com/how-fast-can-a-german-shepherd-run/

[49]www.reference.com/science/many-pounds-pressure-needed-break-bone-40b58899df33af93

Figure 11-13. *RAF Provost Marshal's UK Dog Trails – 1992*

Figure 11-14. *Basra, Iraq – 2006*

Figure 11-15. *CIFT – Afghanistan 2007*

In addition to this essential training, I received specialist training at particular times along my military career path. This included

- Air transport security (ATSy) training

- Further trainings 1 and 2 (RAF Police management training)

- General service training 1 (GST 1)

- Intermediate management and leadership course (IMLC) training

- Counter intelligence (CI)

- Computer security 1 (CSy 1)

- Computer Security 2 (CSy 2)

- Special Branch training

- Source handling

- Combat photographer

- Off road driving

Subjects

The Threat
The Official Secrets Acts
Principles of Security
Terrorism
Counter Terrorism
Public Military Events
Security of Arms, Ammunition and Explosives
Arms Control
CI Investigations
CI Enquiries and Practices
CI Reports
Personnel Security
Suicides, Attempts and Gestures
Physical Security
Risk Management
Control of Protectively Marked Documents
Registry Procedures
Checks and Musters
Maintenance of Security Locks
Criminal Security Records Office
Waivers and Exemptions
Security Audits
Computer Security
Communications Security TEMPEST
Powers of Arrest
Evidence
Air Force Act 1955
Criminal Damage Act 1971
Search
Examination of a Scene of Crime
Finger Printing
Reporting Offences
Tape Recorded Interviews
Witness Interviewing
Practical Exercises

Figure 11-16. *Counter Intelligence Subjects*

```
┌─────────────────────────────────────────────┐
│                   Subjects                    │
│                                               │
│        Computer Principles and Concepts       │
│              How Computers Work               │
│               Operating Systems               │
│          Word Processing (MS Word)            │
│             Hardware architecture             │
│          Input, Output and Processing         │
│        Database Management and Security       │
│                                               │
│   Following successful completion of the      │
│          techniques phase,                    │
│         students receive instruction on:      │
│     Management of Computer systems in the RAF │
│            The Threats to Computers           │
│      Data Communications and Approved Circuits│
│              Personnel Security               │
│               Physical Security               │
│               Hardware Security               │
│               Software Security               │
│  Management, Command and Control and          │
│        Electronic Office Systems              │
│         Computer Emanations (TEMPEST)         │
│   Computer Registration and Accreditation     │
│                 Process                       │
│          Personal Computer Security           │
│          Security of Portable IT Systems      │
│  Contingency Planning, Standby Procedures     │
│              and Backups                      │
│       Use of Privately Owned Computers        │
│  Airborne Computers and their Ground Support  │
│              Facilities                       │
│                Risk Analysis                  │
│               IT Security Audits              │
│         Security Operating Procedures         │
│               Compusec Policy                 │
└─────────────────────────────────────────────┘
```

Figure 11-17. CSy1 Subjects

```
┌─────────────────────────────────────────────────────────────┐
│                          Subjects                             │
│                                                               │
│                     How Networks Work                         │
│                                                               │
│                Network Architecture Components                │
│                                                               │
│                        Disk Storage                           │
│                                                               │
│               Disk Diagnosis/Tools and Utilities             │
│                                                               │
│                   Data Recovery Techniques                    │
│                                                               │
│                        Data Transfer                          │
│                                                               │
│                     Intranets/Internet                        │
│                                                               │
│       Following successful completion of the techniques phase,│
│                     instruction is provided on:               │
│                                                               │
│             Security Involvement in a Computer Project        │
│                                                               │
│                 Security Operating Procedures                 │
│                                                               │
│                   Trusted Computer Bases                      │
│                                                               │
│  Information Technology Security Evaluation Criteria (ITSEC)   │
│                                                               │
│                  Modes of Secure Processing                   │
│                                                               │
│             Information Technology Security Audits            │
│                                                               │
│               Investigations of Security Breaches             │
│                                                               │
│                     Malicious Software                        │
│                                                               │
│                        IT Forensics                           │
└─────────────────────────────────────────────────────────────┘
```

Figure 11-18. *CSy2 Subjects*

Then, of course, there was the pre-deployment training for assignments into hostile environments. All personnel deploying would be required to attend mandatory training, so that they were adequately equipped for their deployment role. Being the RAF Police component of the Force Protection Wing, the training I received was considerably longer than those personnel that would be restricted to the relative safety of the deployed operating bases. The purpose of the training was to update and familiarize deploying personnel on the latest enemy TTPs and to train them in the most up-to-date mitigation practices to be applied while deployed. This training was critical for the protection of deployed personnel and assets.

This training was never expected to make them a frontline infantry specialist, but was tailored to ensure that they had a general understanding of how they were expected to react and how to identify malicious or dangerous activities.

Additionally, as part of my role as a CI operative, my duties included the delivery of up-to-date security awareness training, as part of their mandatory annual training.

As a result of the mandatory training of all personnel, there was a much-improved security culture, where personnel had a better understanding of what good practices looked like.

Further to the mandatory training, the RAF employed a series of committees, one of which was a security steering committee. This committee would be compiled of departmental representation (unit security officers (USyOs)/branch security officers (BSyOs)) from across the supporting business areas. Each month, the USyOs/BSyOs would be required to carry out security checks of their areas of responsibility and provide a report back to the unit security officer, for review, and the committee would meet on a 6-weekly basis to discuss any issues that could present an impact on the establishment's mission statement.

Clearly, the risk was far greater for the military, but the benefits of wider, more general security awareness training can only be of benefit to reduce the potential risk of accidental or negligent actions presenting opportunities for exploitation by your attackers or leading to a data breach, for example:

- **Firewall misconfiguration – Capital One**[50]

  "Paige Thompson, a former Amazon web services employee who has been arrested by the justice department, is alleged to be the hacker behind the security breach. The initial news of the breach sent the value of Capital One shares plummeting down 5.9%. The case has sparked further worries for businesses looking to move to Amazon's cloud-based system, although Capital One is understood to have been using its own web-app to access the cloud in this case. Capital One stated the issue arose due to a "firewall misconfiguration", but there are fears Ms. Thompson may have shared the data she accessed with others."

- **Misconfigured Database – Ecuador**[51]

  "The personal records of most of Ecuador's population, including children, has been left exposed online due to a misconfigured database."

---

[50]www.shlegal.com/news/data-protection-update---august-2019

[51]www.zdnet.com/article/database-leaks-data-on-most-of-ecuadors-citizens-including-6-7-million-children/

- **Unencrypted Database – MoviePass**[52]

  "The database also contained email address and some password data related to failed login attempts. We found hundreds of records containing users' email addresses and presumably incorrectly typed passwords — which was logged — in the database. We verified this by attempting to log into the app with an email address and password that didn't exist but only we knew. Our dummy email address and password appeared in the database almost immediately.

  None of the records in the database were encrypted."

- **Malware – Wawa**[53]

  "On December 10, the company found malware on the servers it uses to process payments at 'potentially all Wawa locations.'"

- **SQL Injection – Magento**[54]

  "Magento, an Adobe-owned company since 2018, released security patches for 37 security issues affecting both the commercial and open-source versions of its platform. Exploitation of the flaws can enable remote code execution, SQL injection, cross-site scripting, privilege escalation, information disclosure and spamming."

- **Password Spraying – Citrix**[55]

  "The FBI believes the technology company's network was penetrated using "password spraying," which refers to the tactic of attempting to remotely access a large number of accounts at once by using known usernames together with long lists of weak passwords, Black says.

  'Once they gained a foothold with limited access, they worked to circumvent additional layers of security.'"

---

[52]https://techcrunch.com/2019/08/20/moviepass-thousands-data-exposed-leak/

[53]https://edition.cnn.com/2019/12/19/business/wawa-credit-card-breach-trnd/index.html

[54]www.csoonline.com/article/3385525/critical-magento-sql-injection-flaw-could-be-targeted-by-hackers-soon.html

[55]www.bankinfosecurity.com/citrix-hacked-by-password-spraying-attackers-fbi-warns-a-12154

- **Insecure media disposal – Boston Globe**[56]

  "Boston Globe used recycled paper containing credit, debit card, and personal check routing information for printing and for wrapping newspaper bundles for distribution. As many as 240,000 records were potentially exposed."

Recommendations

Since leaving the RAF Police, I have seen numerous businesses that often treat security awareness training and the investment in the development of their personnel as having no return on investment (ROI) and as being a waste of time.

I have always been extremely passionate about making security awareness training relevant and available to everyone, and I am a strong believer that security is the responsibility of ALL. However, I can recall one particular organization whose chief information officer (CIO) was particularly negative in response to delivering security awareness training and was an adamant believer that any security awareness training should be limited to just their IT staff. In fact, they thought that my spending time delivering a number of onsite security awareness presentations to the shift personnel on one of their industrial/manufacturing sites and asking to investigate the potential benefits of procuring a security awareness platform to deliver security awareness training to ALL personnel was a complete waste of time.

Strange then that, the audience were extremely receptive to the training *(having previously received any security awareness training, in the previous **11 years**)*, and the procurement of the security awareness platform, and delivery of security awareness training to personnel, in Western Europe and EEMEA locations was included in their Annual Report:

"A specialist training package was purchased and rolled out to appropriate employees in Western Europe and EEMEA."

Just because you cannot see the ROI from keeping your personnel up to date with the training, they need to keep you safe and do not think the same as the aforementioned CIO. The greater the number of security aware *"eyes and ears,"* the better the chances of detecting ABNORMAL or dangerous activities that could lead to a compromised network/system or data breach.

---

[56]https://its.ucsc.edu/security/breaches.html

Think of the benefits of applying some of the lessons learned from team sports or the military in addition to meeting the minimum requirements as outlined in the PCI DSS controls framework.

Conclusion

Until there is no reliance on human beings to implement, maintain, and administer data processing systems, there will always be a greater risk to your organization. Poor practices are a primary target, and, therefore, ensuring that your personnel receive regular up-to-date awareness training and any specialist training to maintain their security awareness knowledge they need for their particular role (e.g., Secure architecture, Systems familiarization, Secure software development (OWASP), Media handling/disposal, Password management, etc.) may not provide a visible business profit, but the reality is that the cost of maintaining a high level of security awareness is far cheaper than the costs associated to poor practices – caused through a lack of understanding.

Key Takeaways

The PCI DSS security awareness requirement is your minimal baseline. If you want to enhance your security defenses and reduce the risks associated with the "Human Factor," it is essential that you consider prioritizing the need to develop an integrated security awareness program.

Senior management should be supportive and encourage the development of a suitable training program, which delivers appropriate training so that all personnel receive general security awareness training. More specialist/high-impact roles receive tailored training.

The security awareness program should be overseen by a member of senior management and be supported by a security steering committee. This will ensure that it is tailored to be an integrated approach and continues to deliver value, and the right messages, at the correct level, to create an extensive "eyes and ears" network.

An effective security awareness program is an essential component in any business, helping mitigate the "Human Factor" risks, through a cohesive and integrated model.

- *Do all your personnel fully understand and embrace their policies and procedures?*

- *Does your business easily meet the minimum security awareness requirements as outlined in requirements 6 and 12?*

- *Do you recognize the business benefits that an effective security program provides to your business?*

- *Is senior management supportive of an effective security awareness program?*

- *Are your security efforts delivered as part of a team effort?*

Risks

If you take a look at the causes of data breaches or security incidents, you will find that the majority *(if not all)* are caused by the "Human Factor."

These are the result of poor practices or malicious actions from your employees or contractors.

In order to maintain a high degree of risk mitigation of the "Human Factor," it is essential that continual awareness training is established, tailored to the potential impact of the employee's specific roles.

For example, why restrict your security awareness training to the "In-Scope" personnel? If an attacker needs to gain physical access to the premises, wouldn't it be a better defense to have everyone knowledgeable to Social Engineering TTPs?

Ask yourself:

- *Do I have a tick box (compliance) approach to security awareness?*

- *Do I have an inclusive or exclusive security awareness program?*

- *Does my security awareness program include keeping key personnel current with the latest technology trends (e.g., Do I ensure that key personnel carry out periodic vendor-specific training to ensure that they can use the security tools to their best abilities?)?*

- *Do I have an effective, holistic security culture?*

CHAPTER 12

PIE FARM – A Project Managed Approach to PCI DSS

Often PCI DSS projects can be extremely complex and will likely involve numerous employees and teams. This complexity needs to be effectively project managed, so as to provide key deliverables over defined steps.

Building a secure and robust payment card operation is very similar to trying to build a property (Payment Channels). The PCI DSS controls framework is your catalogue of components needed to build a property. However, these components cover everything needed to build anything from a bungalow to a block of flats.

Consequently, you need a methodical approach to ensure you understand what types of property you are trying to build, so that you can align with the appropriate security controls.

The PIE FARM methodology helps you formally plan and divide up the workstreams and track the progression of your compliance efforts. This helps ensure that you can avoid unnecessary wasting of time, expenses, effort, and resources.

Introduction

With the increasingly digitalized and data-heavy business dependencies, along with the ever-present criminal threats, it has never been more important for businesses to be able to embed good security practices to provide ring-fence for their most critical IT systems and processes. However, balancing the vision of the business with the expectations of a security controls framework can prove to be an extremely complex and tricky thing to

© Jim Seaman 2020
J. Seaman, *PCI DSS*, https://doi.org/10.1007/978-1-4842-5808-8_12

achieve, especially when you consider the apparent naivety and complicity of employees and business in understanding the true value of the data that they rely on.

If you think of the different types of data as being pieces of a jigsaw puzzle, you cannot piece together the whole jigsaw if you lose pieces from the box. However, if a criminal can gather together enough pieces of a jigsaw, they may be able to piece together enough of a picture to provide them with a financial gain and, of course, add to this the attackers who are just looking for the challenge of being able to gain unauthorized access to a corporation's jigsaw box. Whether the goal of the attackers is for financial gain or kudos, they need to illicitly steal pieces of the jigsaw from their box. Common to all attacks is their opportunity to exploit poor security practices.

This concept came out of a marriage between established principles from the world of Project Management and an investigative interviewing concept, called PEACE *(as employed in Counter Intelligence Security investigations and all UK Police investigators)*. While the project management principles provide the ability to align your data privacy and security strategies against defined steps, the PEACE concept provides the structured formality proven for the conduct of successful investigations.

Integrated Project Management

With PCI DSS being a detailed and systematic framework, with an interdependent layered structure, it comes as no surprise that it lends itself to the Waterfall approach. The disadvantage of the Waterfall approach is that it can leave elements lying dormant, while the previous stage has been complemented.

However, for your PCI DSS compliance project, you are able to speed up the process by embedding the sensible application of the SCRUM methodology against separate workstreams that are aligned to specific PCI DSS requirements (Slicing and Dicing).

Waterfall Method

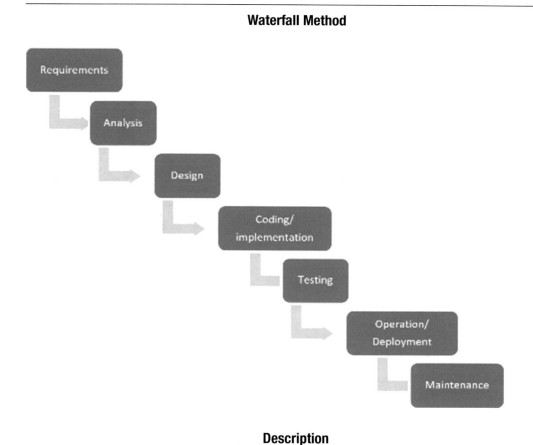

Description

This is a project management approach model where a project is completed in distinct stages before moving step by step toward ultimate release.

The big plan is made up front and then executed in a linear fashion, relying on the fact that there won't be any changes in the plan.

SCRUM Method

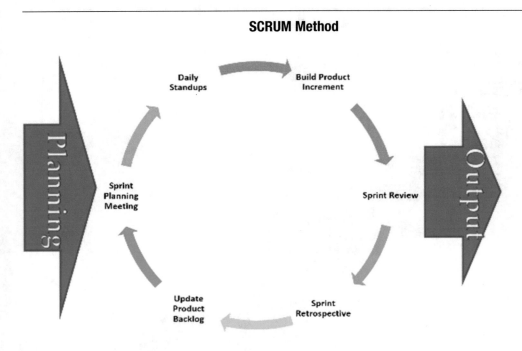

Description

The SCRUM element provides an element of flexibility using agile project management principles.

At the end of steps 1 and 2, you carry out a review of your findings. At this point, you are provided the opportunity to adjust the project and restart the step.

Consequently, this incorporates iterative and incremental practices, helping organizations deliver working software more frequently.

PEACE Framework

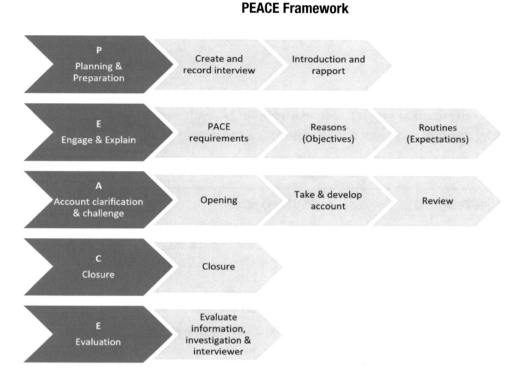

Description

Investigations are a core duty of policing, with the effective interview of victims, witnesses, and suspects being central to the success of an investigation. Consequently, interviews need to be conducted to the highest standards.

During 10 years on Counter Intelligence operations, I gained firsthand appreciation of the value of interviews that are conducted professionally and quality assured realize several benefits.

In particular, they can

- Direct an investigation and gather material, which in turn can lead to a prosecution or early release of an innocent person
- Support the prosecution case, thereby saving time, money, and resources
- Increase public confidence in the police service, particularly with witnesses and victims of crimes who come into direct contact with the police

Consequently, the principles, from the PEACE model, have been incorporated to enhance the PIE FARM approach.

Benefits

Waterfall Methodology

1. **Uses clear structure**

    In comparison to other methodologies, Waterfall focuses mostly on clearly defined steps. The structure is simple with each project going through these steps, with clearly defined checkpoints.

Waterfall Stages	Steps

Requirement gathering and documentation	• Check and Review
	  • On track – Continue
	    • Off Track – Re-Review
	  • Sign Off

System design	• Check and Review
	  • On track – Continue
	  • Off Track – Consider a return to previous step
	    • Sign Off

Implementation	• Check and Review
	  • On track – Continue
	  • Off Track – Consider a return to previous step
	    • Sign Off

Testing	• Check and Review
	  • On track – Continue
	  • Off Track – Consider a return to previous step
	    • Sign Off

Delivery/Deployment	• Check and Review
	  • On track – Continue
	  • Off Track – Consider a return to previous step
	    • Sign Off

Maintenance	• Check and Review
	  • Lesson Learned
	    • Sign Off

Teams must complete an entire step before moving onto the next one, so if there are roadblocks to completion, they're brought to light right away. Half-finished projects are less likely to get pushed aside, leaving teams with a more complete, polished project in the end.

In addition to being clear, the progression of Waterfall is intuitive. Unlike other Project Management methodologies, Waterfall does not require certifications or specific training for project managers or employees.

2. **Determines the end goal early**

    One of the defining steps of Waterfall is the ability to slice and dice up the complexities of a project; it supports the team efforts and at the outset commits to what the final product, goal, or deliverables will look like, and teams should be encouraged to stick to that commitment. For smaller projects where goals are clear, this step makes your team aware of the overall goal from the beginning, with less potential for getting lost in the details as the project moves forward.

    Unlike other methodologies, which divide projects up into individual sequential sprints, Waterfall keeps the focus on the end goal at all times. If your team has a concrete goal with a clear end date, Waterfall will eliminate the risk of getting bogged down as you work toward that goal.

3. **Transfers information well**

    Waterfall's approach is highly systematic, so it is not surprising to hear that this methodology emphasizes a clean transfer of information at each step. When applied to a PCI DSS payment channel, every new step involves a new group of people, and though that might not be the case at your company, you still should aim to document information throughout a project's life cycle. Whether you're passing projects off at each step or experience unexpected personnel changes, Waterfall prioritizes accessible information so new additions to the team can get up to speed quickly if needed.

SCRUM Framework

- Enables a quicker release of useable products

- Greater quality

- Improved productivity

- Reduced costs

- Improved flexibility (incorporating changes as they occur)

- Improved morale

- Greater satisfaction

- An improved project completion rate

PEACE Framework

- **Confidence**

  This increases the confidence in the protective services, particularly with validating proficiencies.

- **Consistent performance**

  The techniques of investigative interviewing will help achieve results in even the most unpromising circumstances.

- **Support for frontline services**

  Personnel may become nervous or get overwhelmed when being evaluated. Good investigative interview techniques will help to calm or reassure them so that they can provide an accurate account.

- **Dealing with employees/third parties**

  Do not assume that all employees want to cover things up or deliberately do things that are negligent or to do harm to the business. Some may do this inadvertently, but how the information is gathered is essential to the strength of material gathered during the assurance work.

  Remain "Open-Minded!"

Background

It is extremely rare for an organization to consider any potential security implications prior to the business already processing, storing, or transmitting sensitive data that is on the attackers' shopping list. Consequently, it is frequently the case that a company realizes the importance of securing their critical data assets long after this data has become an intrinsic part of the business and often having been carelessly copied, shared, and stored (in various guises) across their corporate network. Rather unhelpfully, the IT systems used to support the processing of this highly sought-after data is developed with usability, rather than security, in mind and is inherently insecure by its very nature.

Consequently, when the business decides to enhance the robustness of the data defenses, they often turn to the various industry security controls frameworks as their accepted baseline – however, there are numerous such frameworks available and each has its own particular strengths and weaknesses. Fortunately, for those businesses providing goods or services in exchange for payment through a debit or credit card, the de facto "go to" controls framework is the Payment Cards Industry Data Security Standard (PCI DSS).

Having been a PCI Qualified Security Assessor (QSA) for almost half a decade, I experienced at first hand numerous businesses attempt to get their various business operations and supporting IT to align with PCI DSS. During one such engagement, I was assigned to help a large financial organization to pick apart their in-scope business operations and supporting IT systems from the out-of-scope business operations and systems. I was assigned to assist them some 6 years after they had commenced their project and a mere 6 months before they had predicted that they would be ready to be independently assessed as having secured their customers' payment card data operations and to be deemed as being compliant with PCI DSS.

This was an extremely complex project, and despite them having assigned ten project leads, overseen by a project manager, it soon became clear that there had been a great deal of wasted time, effort, and resources and that without clearly defined project milestones/checkpoints they were unlikely to be able to meet their business leader's expectations. Consequently, I started to develop a project management approach to PCI DSS, which established primary and secondary markers/milestones against strategic objectives that needed to be achieved and signed off before the next milestone could be initiated.

I affectionately named this seven-stage approach PIE FARM.

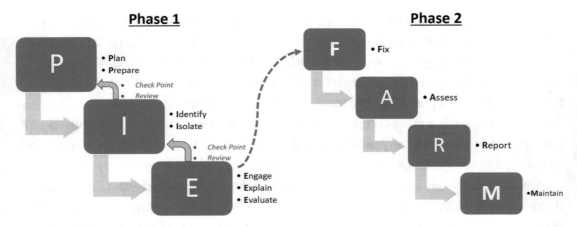

Figure 12-1. PIE FARM

PIE FARM Methodology

A methodical and stepped approach is essential to any organization with the goal of aligning their business processes and supporting IT systems to any controls framework. Fortunately, the seven-stage PIE FARM approach is security controls agnostic and is methodology that can be used for any organization wishing to align their business to a particular controls framework. In reality, most businesses will have implemented multiple controls frameworks across their organization. This is another advantage of PIE FARM; it helps identify existing policies and processes that are already in place and which may already meet the intent of their equivalent control that is to be implemented or only needing a few minor enhancements.

How to Bake Your PIE?

Phase 1 – Making your PIE

Stage 1: Plan and Prepare

Much like any project, the importance of sufficient planning and preparation is essential for the success of the project. There were two old adages that were taught to me during my 22 years of service in the RAF Police:

"Failure to Plan is Planning to Fail!"

"5 Ps:

Prior Preparation Prevents Poor Performance!"

Never has the need for stage 1 than when trying to implement an integrated Cyber/InfoSec strategy using a security controls framework. During this stage, it is essential that SMART (Specific, Measurable, Achievable, Realistic, and Timebound) objectives for the project are documented and agreed by the business. This becomes the foundation for the development of an effective Cyber/InfoSec strategy. This is the starting point where, as a team effort, the expectations of the project are established, resources allocated, funding confirmed, and senior management support obtained, for example:

- *Have you created a suitable Business Case for the PCI DSS project?*

- *As a Merchant, speaking with the Acquirer to confirm the merchant level and compliance validation expectations*

- *Confirming with the Acquirer whether they are happy to accept single SAQs for each payment channel*

  - *Waiting until both payment channels (MOTO and e-Commerce) are PCI DSS compliant shows you to be **0% compliant**. However, fix a single payment channel and your business is regarded as being **50% compliant**.*

- *Understanding your various payment channels and aligning them to their appropriate self-assessment questionnaire (SAQ)*

  - *E-commerce, fully outsourced to a PCI DSS-compliant third-party payment service provider.*

    - *SAQ A – Circa 22 controls*

  - *Mail order, telephone order (MOTO), in-house operation using a PCI DSS compliant third-party payment service provider. However, call recording is in place that electronically stores payment card data, making this ineligible for an SAQ C – 155 controls.*

    - *SAQ D – Circa 352 controls*

Remember, it's easier to roll a boulder down the hill than to try and struggle to push it up the hill.

Stage 2: Identify and Isolate

The next stage involves the identification of the differing payment channels, their data flows, inventory of connected supporting IT systems (across the network), business processes, personnel, and any outsourced services that are involved in the interaction with payment cardholder data.

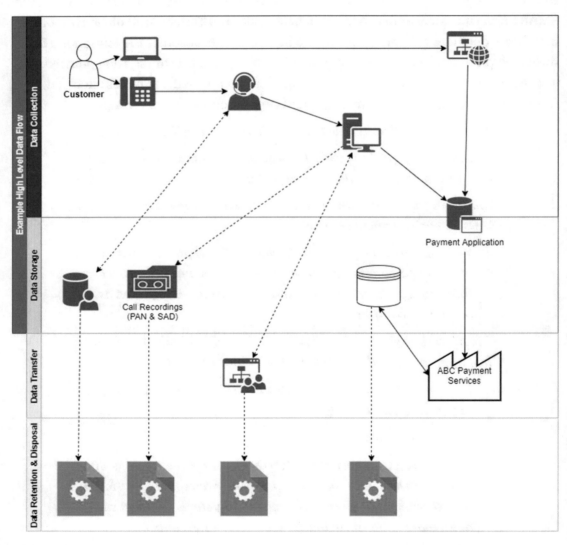

Figure 12-2. Example Data Flow Diagram (DFD)

- **This is the scope for PCI DSS!**

Having identified the scope, the next stage is to identify the applicable PCI DSS controls. Handily, the PCI Security Standards Council (PCI SSC) have provided some aides for this – in the form of the Self-Assessment Questionnaires (SAQs).

With the payment channels having been identified, in order to identify the most applicable controls, the next step is to review these payment channels against the "Before You Begin" section of the available SAQs.

- These are the PCI DSS controls that are deemed applicable to that type of payment channel. Where a payment channel does not fit into the shorter SAQs, the default is the SAQ D-Merchant or SAQ D-Service Provider (SP).

Note   *If you are a Service Provider that provides a service that aligns to one of the shorter SAQs, your default will still be the SAQ D-SP but with the applicable controls taken from the shorter SAQs, plus the Service Provider-specific controls.*

Having identified the people, applicable controls, and outsourced services (per payment channel), it is recommended that these be documented against a PCI DSS controls RACI matrix:

- **R**esponsible (R)

  - Individual responsibilities are assigned against their particular PCI DSS controls.

- **A**ccountable (A)

  - Manager that is assigned as being accountable for ensuring that their department responsibilities have been actioned effectively.

- **C**onsulted (C)

  - Stakeholders that could be impacted by the actions of another.

- **I**nformed (I)

  - Key stakeholders who provide governance and oversight of the data privacy and security strategy.

PCI DSS Control Ref	IT Support	IT Manager	IT Architect	Head of IT	InfoSec Mgr	3rd Party Supplier
1.1	(R)					(R)
1.1.1		(A)				
1.1.2			(C)			
1.1.3				(I)	(I)	

Figure 12-3. *RACI Chart*

Now that the scope and the controls have been identified, the next step is to attempt to isolate the technologies, people, and processes as PCI DSS applies to any technologies, people, and processes directly involved in the processing, storage, or transmission of cardholder data or (more importantly) anything connected to these systems which could impact the cardholder data.

- **This is the Cardholder Data Environment (CDE) – In-scope!**
- **Think......**
    - **Red Zone** – In-scope!
    - **Black Zone** – Out-of-scope!

In addition to minimizing the scope for PCI DSS, effectively layered networks and systems should help isolate the in-scope from the out-of-scope environments. This is essential to the Defense, Delay, Disruption, and Deterrence of a "wannabe" attacker while helping with the Detection of malicious activities.

5 Ds

- **Defend**
- **Delay**
- **Disrupt**
- **Deter**
- **Detect**

For example:

- *Identify all the personnel, assets, and documentation needed for each payment channel. Document these within asset inventories, network, and data flow diagrams to identify any connected environments that would need to be isolated to reduce the potential impact and scope.*

Stage 3: Engage, Explain, and Evaluate

Unlike popular belief, the ongoing maintenance of secure operations cannot be the responsibility of a handful of employees and takes teamwork. Therefore, following on from stage 2, having identified the key personnel involved in supporting the CDE, this stage starts by engaging with these stakeholders and explaining the controls that apply to their supporting job functions and the implications of their job against their applicable PCI DSS controls.

Having identified the gaps between your current state and your desired state will help provide you with some indicative costs associated with your mitigation options, which could be applied as part of your fixing step.

Next comes the evaluation of the status of any in-place systems, processes, procedures, and policies. This will readily identify any gaps or areas needing improvements and provide the foundation and priorities needed for Phase 2, for example:

- *Carry out a review of each payment channel against their applicable controls, ensuring that any processes are evaluated based upon their maturity levels.*[1]

---

[1]https://cmmiinstitute.com/learning/appraisals/levels

Capability Level 1: Initial	Maturity Level 2: Managed	Maturity Level 3: Defined	Maturity Level 4: Quantitatively Managed	Maturity Level 5 : Optimizing
Unpredictable and reactive.	**Managed on the project level.**	**Proactive, rather than reactive.**	**Measured and controlled.**	**Stable and flexible.**
Work gets completed but is often delayed and over budget.	Projects are planned, performed, measured, and controlled.	Organization-wide standards provide guidance across projects, programs, and portfolios	Organization is data-driven with quantitative performance improvement objectives that are predictable and align to meet the needs of internal and external stakeholders.	Organization is focused on continuous improvement and is built to pivot and respond to opportunity and change. The organization's stability provides a platform for agility and innovation.

Figure 12-4. *CMMI Maturity Levels*

Note   *I could have called this phase "Gap Assessment," but being a Pescatarian (although mostly leaning toward a "Plant-Based" diet, nowadays), I prefer the Acronym "**PIE FARM**" vs. the alternative "**PIG FARM**" but I shall leave that for you to choose your preference.*

Phase 1 – Complete!

Phase 2 – FARMing

Having selected your preferred choice of PIE, next comes the task of FARMing your PIE.

Stage 4: Fix

The first stage of phase 2 is to set about prioritizing the remediation of any gaps identified during phase 1. At this point, you will already have an indication of the possible costs associated with your chosen type of PIE.

This becomes a crucial part of the process, as you shop around for the best ingredients, which provide the best value for money. Remember, when shopping for ingredients for your PIE, to look at various suppliers and even ask for a sample tasting (Proof Of Concept) so that you are sure that the ingredients you are choosing complement the other ingredients that you need for your data security program.

If you are unsure, at this point, this is a good opportunity to get in a seasoned PIE maker (adviser) so that they can provide you with some timely advice, based upon their experience of successfully mixing these ingredients together. Be cautious of the individual recommendations from the vendor; obtain some independent feedback from other business experiences.

For example:

- *When reviewing the requirements to fix the gaps between the current state and the desired state of your MOTO operation, you may choose to avoid the need to store payment card data through the use of an "Auto Start/Stop" software solution (SAQ C) or to avoid any systems or call agent interaction with payment card data through the use of a dual-tone multi-frequency (DTMF) solution (SAQ A).*

Stage 5: Assess

Now comes the interesting part:

"The Taste Test!"

Do not assume that you will get it right from the very first attempt:

"Practice makes Perfect!"

To perfect the perfect PIE, you may get lucky, but you need to remain realistic to the fact that you may need to refresh your recipes or even replace some ingredients or to add some additional seasoning.

Here is where bringing in a seasoned professional could save you a great deal or time, money, and effort and speed up your efforts to fortify your data security.

Don't get me wrong; anyone should be able to follow a recipe (controls framework) and make an edible PIE!

Additionally, if you choose to bring in an independent PIE maker, make sure that you check out their credentials:

- How many PIEs have they made?

- How long have they been making PIEs?

- What certificates do they hold?

- Are they accredited/licensed?

- Are they working for a licensed PIE-making company?

- What about quality control? Do all their PIE makers make the PIEs the same way?

- Can they provide a list of satisfied customers?

- Do they have experience of working with different brands of ingredients?

- What is their specialist area (Pastry, Filling, Baking, Tasting, etc.) or are they more of a generalist?

Make sure that you choose a QSA from a PCI SSC-accredited company, as listed on the PCI SSC web site, and, most importantly, ensure that they are licensed to operate in your country of operations.

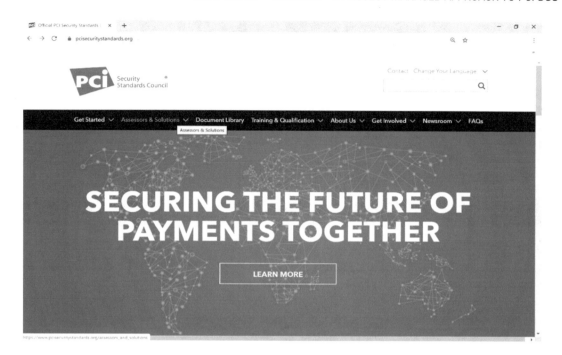

Figure 12-5. *PCI SSC Web Site*

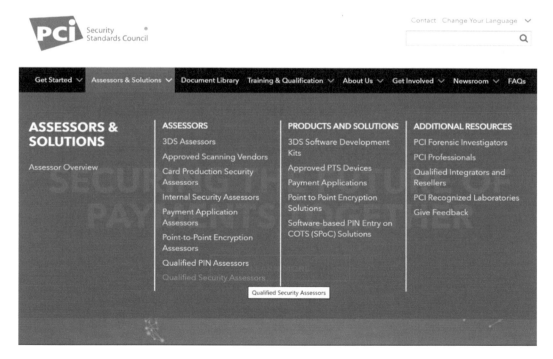

Figure 12-6. *Validation Selection*

Figure 12-7. *Validation Confirmation*

Stage 6: Report

Having created your perfect PIE (or PIEs), it's now time to get it/them quality checked. The bigger the PIE, the greater the responsibility. Under PCI DSS, the Card Brands (Visa, Mastercard, AMEX, JCB, and Discover) stipulate at what size a PIE needs to be independently checked for quality. This applies for both merchants and their service providers.

Here is an example of VISA rules.

Merchant Levels		
Level / Tier	Merchant Criteria	Validation Requirements
1	• Merchants processing over 6 million Visa transactions annually (all channels) or • Global merchants identified as Level 1 by any Visa region ··	• Annual Report on Compliance (ROC) by Qualified Security Assessor (QSA) • Quarterly network scan by Approved Scan Vendor (ASV) • Attestation of Compliance Form
2	• Merchants processing 1 million to 6 million Visa transactions annually (all channels)	• Annual Self-Assessment Questionnaire (SAQ) • Quarterly network scan by ASV • Attestation of Compliance Form
3	• Merchants processing 20,000 to 1 million Visa e-commerce transactions annually	• Annual SAQ • Quarterly network scan by ASV • Attestation of Compliance Form
4	• Merchants processing less than 20,000 Visa e-commerce transactions annually and all other merchants processing up to 1 million Visa transactions annually	• Annual SAQ recommended • Quarterly network scan by ASV, if applicable • Compliance validation requirements set by acquirer

Service Providers			
Level	All Regions	Validation Requirements	Result
1	VisaNet processors or any service provider that stores, processes and/or transmits over 300,000 transactions per year	• Annual ROC by QSA • Quarterly network scan by ASV • Attestation of Compliance Form	Included on Visa's List of PCI DSS Compliant Service Providers
2	Any service provider that stores, processes and/or transmits less than 300,000 transactions per year	• Annual SAQ • Quarterly network scan by ASV • Attestation of Compliance Form	Not included on Visa's List of PCI DSS Compliant Service Providers/Confirmation Letter of Receipt·

For those organizations baking smaller PIEs, you have the ability to carry out your own independent quality checks (self-assessment questionnaires (SAQs) and attestations of compliance (AoCs)). This can be carried out under the supervision of an experienced external consultant, by a PCI SSC-trained internal security assessor (ISA) or even by PCI DSS knowledgeable internal resource.

Note   SAQs/AoCs **DO NOT** always need to be validated by a Qualified Security Assessor (QSA). However, you may choose to employ a QSA (or seasoned PIE maker) to provide additional reassurance to the quality of the PIE you are producing for your customers.

THE CHOICE IS ALL YOURS…..!

Outside of PCI DSS, you may decide *(or not)* to choose to have your data security program independently validated against differing controls frameworks, such ISO/IEC.

In the case of ISO/IEC, I would recommend that you choose an accredited company to carry out these independent checks for the quality of your PIEs, for example:

- United Kingdom Accreditation Service (UKAS)[2]
- NSI-ASQ National Accreditation Board (ANAB)[3]

Stage 7: Maintain

Ultimately, this is equally important as another element listed earlier. The maintenance of the quality is essential to help in the continued evasion of the predators. Any changes to the PIE recipe must be carefully considered and managed based upon the potential for an increased risk of impacting the integrity and taste of the PIE. You don't want anyone stealing your recipes (Confidentiality), changing the ingredients (Integrity), or affecting your ability to produce the same consistent PIEs.

Therefore, it is essential at this phase you are able to schedule in both the mandatory quality checks and other additional checks of both the in-house and outsourced services/deliverables to provide added reassurance that throughout the year your services/deliverables are of the utmost quality, as you would expect, for example:

- Review previous assessment and apply any lessons learned.
  - Carry out additional On-The-Job training, if needed.
- Identify the quality checks you plan to do and at what date.
- Carry out quality checks using maturity levels.

---

[2]www.ukas.com/

[3]https://anab.ansi.org/

- Document the findings of these reviews.

  - Consider the potential benefits of using a suitable risk platform.[4]

- Timetable dates for quality checks.

- Identify resources needed – do you have single points of failure?

- Identify when to engage the assessor resources to ensure that the annual review is done before the last 12 month expires.

- Review previous assessment and ensure any lessons learned have been applied.

The results of this will then be included for consideration as a repeat of this cycle.

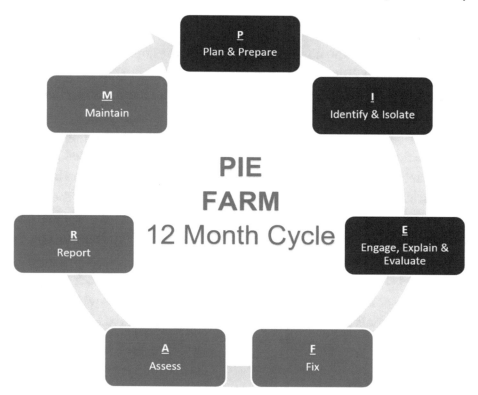

Figure 12-8. *PIE FARM Cycle*

"PCI DSS compliance is something that should be embedded into your business and not something that needs to be done just once a year!"

---

[4]https://acuityrm.com/use-benefits/control-assurance

Conclusion

PCI DSS is often seen as being a complex and high-technical subject; however, the reality is that data breaches occur because of simple mistakes. Eradicating these mistakes takes a little bit of time, effort, and investment in your employees. The mistakes begin by assuming that anyone should be able to make a PIE if they are given the ingredients and the correct recipe to follow. Unfortunately, within business that are taking customers' payment card details in payment for goods or services, there are many different variations of PIE with different types/amounts of ingredients that make up these PIEs.

For example, one of the most attractive PIEs for criminals to steal are those that rely on stored cardholder data. If the cardholder data is stored, this becomes those most difficult quality PIE to produce.

Another example (and the most simple) would be the company who solely relies on a PCI DSS-compliant Third-Party Payment Service Provider(PSP) to process their customers' payment card data: As they do not process, store, or transmit the payment card data, PCI DSS does not apply – **RIGHT?**

WRONG......! The responsibility lies with the PSP, but the accountability still lies with the company selling the goods/services, for which the payment has been made.

Failure to create the right time of PIE for your business, which can be baselined against the correct recipe and ingredients, creates the opportunities for the "Predators."

As I have mentioned earlier, if in any doubt, I would recommend that you bring in the independent services of a well-respected "PIE Maker" to help reassure you that you have interpreted the requirements correctly.

Applying good "PIE Making" principles will really help protect your reputation and ensure that you are doing the right thing by your customers, who have entrusted their payment card credentials to you in exchange for your goods/services.

Key Takeaways

Data privacy and security and, especially, PCI DSS compliance can be an extremely daunting and complex topic. However, it does not need to be if you are well prepared, employ a methodical approach, "slice n dice" your payment card operations, and ensure that you tackle this as part of a team.

PCI DSS does not tell you how to design and maintain secure card operations. However, it does provide you with a catalogue of recommended security controls, along with payment channel-aligned SAQs. Consequently, it is essential that you understand just how your business may align with any applicable SAQs.

By "Slicing and Dicing" your environment, you will be better able to prioritize your remediation efforts based upon either the risk (volume of payment cards being processed) or the ease of remediation. These can then be validated against their respective SAQs.

There are many ways of "Skinning a Cat"!

Have you engaged with your Acquiring Bank to discuss your transaction volumes?
Do you understand your payment channels?
Have you identified the assets that support each of these payment channels?
Have you identified any associated "Out-of-Scope" environments that could impact your in-scope payment channels?
Have you considered the potential benefits of the PIE FARM methodology?

Risks

Understanding your payment card environments and documenting the connectivity of these assets is essential for being able to develop a suitable approach to building appropriate infrastructures.

Failure to do so can lead to a mis-scoped environment, which could lead to an insecure system/process, which could be exploited by an opportunist attacker.

Poor project management of your data privacy and security strategies, or PCI DSS compliance efforts, can lead to time wasting, unnecessary expense, and a poor use of resources.

Ask yourself:

- *Do I understand my environment?*
- *Do I have the right resources with the relevant skills, knowledge, and experience?*
- *Does the idea of applying PCI DSS to my business fill me with fear?*
- *Do I have a team approach?*
- *Have I identified key checkpoints where progress can be reviewed and refreshed?*

- *Do I have a living business case for the project work?*

- *Do I have the timely opportunity to identify the required tools and resources needed for the PCI DSS project?*

- *Do I understand what might be the potential cost and resource implications?*

- *Can I demonstrate a project plan to the key stakeholders?*

- *Do the key stakeholders understand and support what is needed to achieve my project goals?*

CHAPTER 13

Proactive Defense

Maturing the Five Pillars of Defense

Throughout my career, I have referenced and used multiple controls frameworks and I am often asked which domains I would choose as my foundation for creating Proactive Defenses. This chapter identifies the areas of any Cyber/InfoSec strategy that I believe any business should be focusing their efforts, so as to make them less of a target for criminals. Each pillar is reliant on the pillar before it to help focus your efforts in improving your ability to identify and respond to the presence of ABNORMAL activities within your corporate environment.

Introduction

The PCI SSC have kindly provided you with a prioritized approach.[1] However, the five pillars go one further by prioritizing the common domains into those that are most important for the proactive defense of your organization. These are the foundations and should be prioritized into any Cyber/InfoSec strategy.

All too often the "Defense of the Realm" is regarded as being virtually invisible, very expensive, and providing little (or no) return on investment by the business. That is until there is a breach, when it suddenly becomes very visible and even more expensive, as you try to rebuild the confidence of both your shareholders and customers.

---

[1] `www.pcisecuritystandards.org/documents/Prioritized-Approach-for-PCI-DSS-v3_2_1.pdf ?agreement=true&time=1575031349655`

© Jim Seaman 2020
J. Seaman, *PCI DSS*, https://doi.org/10.1007/978-1-4842-5808-8_13

It is reported that **83%** of customers avoid a business, following a breach, and despite all your efforts, **21%** are gone forever.[2]

Can you avoid to lose such a large customer base?

This is where you can really start to appreciate the need for the right investment – not just for compliance but as investment to protect the trust that your customers have placed in your business.

It is important to remember that the reason for the enhancement of the EU Data Protection came as the result of a 2008 survey of EU citizens,[3] for example:

- Most European Internet users feel uneasy when transmitting their personal data over the Internet.

  - 82% of Internet users reasoned that data transmission over the Web was not sufficiently secure.

Additionally, the trend for purchases of the Internet using payment cards has significantly increased.

Consequently, it is essential that you continue to invest wisely into the effective "Defense of your Realm." Rather than just listening to the latest vendor, selling you those "Magic Beans" which will fix everything, you need to ensure that your suite of security tools provide you with the visibility you need to ensure that your "Crown Jewels" are adequately protected and, in the event of a compromise, you are able to rapidly identify and respond to potential malicious activities.

Hence, the foundation of an effective proactive defense revolves around the following five pillars:

Asset Management

- Identification
- Categorization
- Prioritization
- Linkages

---

[2]www.securitymagazine.com/articles/89501-avoid-a-business-following-breach-and-21-never-return

[3]https://ec.europa.eu/commfrontoffice/publicopinion/flash/fl_225_en.pdf

- Secure Configurations

- Life-Cycle Management

NIST have recognized the importance of having an effective IT Asset Management[4] process to complement existing asset management, security, and network systems. Much like Market Business News' Asset Management[5] definition, assets supporting critical business operations need to be effectively maintained for optimal efficiency and effectiveness across their life cycles.

Asset management refers to the management of people's assets. The term also applies to dealing with other organizations' or companies' investments. Assets include either intangible or intangible assets.

Intangible assets are things we cannot touch such as intellectual property, goodwill, financial assets, or human capital. Tangible assets, on the other hand, are things we can touch, including buildings, land, computers, and office equipment.

As a student in Counter Intelligence operations, I was taught the value of asset management within any defense strategy, and despite being hundreds of years old, the concept still rings true in the modern era. Medieval castles would be designed so that the infrastructures supported layered and segmented environments.

Consequently, it is essential that you are able to trace the data journeys, through your infrastructure, from the point of being used, right through to be securely stored, handed off to an approved third party, or securely destroyed/disposed of once the data is no longer needed.

Each of the industry security controls frameworks has prioritized Asset Management. The following data is an example.

---

[4]https://nvlpubs.nist.gov/nistpubs/SpecialPublications/NIST.SP.1800-5.pdf
[5]https://marketbusinessnews.com/financial-glossary/asset-management/

Asset Management	• **NIST CSF – ID.AM[6] (Stage 1: IDENTIFY)**
	• **ID.AM-1**
	Physical devices and systems within the organization are inventoried.
	• **ID.AM-2**
	Software platforms and applications within the organization are inventoried.
	• **ID.AM-3**
	Organizational communication and data flows are mapped.
	• **ID.AM-4**
	External information systems are catalogued.
	• **ID.AM-5**
	Resources (e.g., hardware, devices, data, time, personnel, and software) are prioritized based on their classification, criticality, and business value.
	• **ID.AM-6**
	Cyber security roles and responsibilities for the entire workforce and third-party stakeholders (e.g., suppliers, customers, partners) are established.
	• **PCI DSS[7] – Requirements**
	• 1.1.1; 1.1.2; 1.1.3; 2.4; 9.6.1; 9.9; 11.1.1; 12.2; 12.3.3; 12.3.7; 12.4, 12.5, 12.8, and 12.9
	• **CIS 20 Critical Security Controls – 1 and 2 *(Basic Controls)***
	• **CIS Control 1 – Inventory and Control of Hardware Assets[8]**
	Actively manage (inventory, track, and correct) all hardware devices on the network so that only authorized devices are given access and unauthorized and unmanaged devices are found and prevented from gaining access.

---

[6]www.nist.gov/cyberframework/framework

[7]www.pcisecuritystandards.org/document_library

[8]www.cisecurity.org/controls/inventory-and-control-of-hardware-assets/

- **CIS Control 2 – Inventory and Control of Software Assets**[9]

  Actively manage (inventory, track, and correct) all software on the network so that only authorized software is installed and can execute and that unauthorized and unmanaged software is found and prevented from installation or execution.

- **ISO/IEC 27001:2013**[10] **– A8: Asset Management**

  - **A.8.1**

    The responsibility for assets. The objective in this Annex is to identify information assets in-scope for the management system and define appropriate protection responsibilities.

  - **A.8.2**

    To ensure that information receives an appropriate level of protection in accordance with its importance to the organization (and interested parties such as customers)

    To prevent unauthorized disclosure, modification, removal, or destruction of information stored on media

- **Standards of Good Practice (SoGP) 2018**[11] **– Physical Asset Management**

  - **Principle**

    Robust, reliable hardware should only be acquired (e.g., purchased or leased) following consideration of security requirements and identification of security deficiencies.

  - **Objective**

    To ensure that hardware provides the required functionality and does not compromise the security of critical or sensitive information and systems

---

[9]www.cisecurity.org/controls/inventory-and-control-of-software-assets/
[10]www.iso.org/isoiec-27001-information-security.html
[11]www.securityforum.org/tool/the-isf-standard-good-practice-information-security-2018/

Each of these controls frameworks recommends that business prioritize Asset Management, which means identifying, cataloguing, and visualizing your assets.

Essential to effective asset management is ensuring that you are able to identify the importance of the assets to your business's objectives and goals. Categorize the assets based upon which are the most important (life support) and which could impact these systems.

This is not as easy as it sounds and may need input from various team members and certainly not limited to your IT team.

Let me give you a real-life example.

In 2002, having successfully completed my Counter Intelligence (CI) course, I was assigned my first CI job – CI Junior Non-Commissioned Officer (JNCO) for an RAF Station, whose mission statement was to

"Train the pilots of the future!"

With all this new knowledge, my first job was to put this theory into practice and to establish an effective Asset Management process that supported the mission statement.

My first port of call was to speak with the Chief Instructor, so as to ascertain how many aircraft were needed to sustain the pilot training course. Out of a fleet of 30 aircraft, 22 aircraft needed to remain serviceable. With this in mind, 22 aircraft were added to my "Critical Asset Register" and 8 aircraft were added to the "Unit Asset Register." When aircraft were deployed or became unserviceable, this would be reflected in their associated asset registers. When the available spare aircraft (from the "Unit Asset Register") started to exceed the risk tolerances, this could be escalated to Command, ensuring that we had the support to maintain the mission statement.

Failure to maintain the mission statement had the potential for serious collateral damage, with the student pilots being unable to complete their training on time and, thus, being able to move onto their specialist pilot training (e.g., Fast Jets, Transports, Helicopters, etc.). This, in turn, could have the greater potential impact to the RAF not having sufficient numbers of pilots to support the RAF's Strategy.[12]

Purpose   To deliver Air and Space Power for the United Kingdom.

Goal   Harness the full potential of our people, our aircraft, and our systems.

---

[12]www.raf.mod.uk/documents/PDF/Royal-Air-Force-Strategy/

However, that was not a problem for me as I had my Asset Management process in place and everything was running smoothly, with me being fully informed of the risks associated with any assets that might impact the mission statement.

How wrong could I have been?

A few months later, I was in the tea bar of the aircraft ground engineers, having a chat, over a coffee, with one of the support engineers. During my chat, I happened to mention my *"awesome"* Asset Management process, only for the engineer to reach under the coffee table, pull out a tatty, unzipped, tool bag. The engineer proceeded to pull out an extremely worn and dirty socket head. He proceeded to ask me whether I had listed this item in my *"awesome"* Asset Registers. I had to confess that I had not!

Imagine my shock when I learned the importance of this socket head. To remain serviceable, each of the aircraft needed to have a number of bolts torqued up to a certain pressure. This socket head turned out to be a bespoke item for the aircraft and this was their last remaining one available to the engineers, and ordering and obtaining replacements could take between 3 to 4 months.

Suddenly, I had a single "more" critical asset to add, and in case of loss or breakage, I had no replacements.

Consequently, you should ensure that you have "sliced n diced" your environment to ensure that you understand each data flow and all the assets that support it.

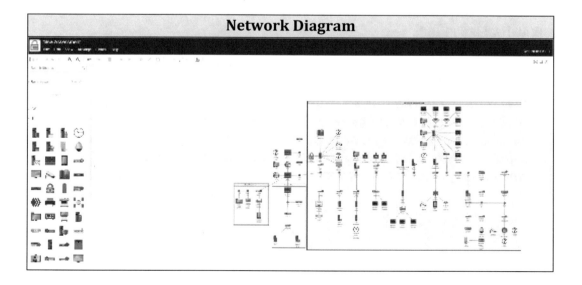

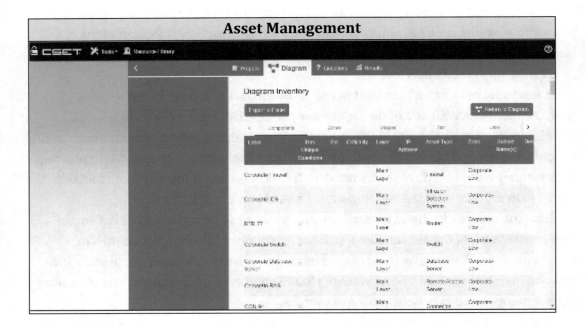

Asset Management

Note   Network Diagrams and Asset Inventory can be easily created using the National Cyber security and Communications Integration Center (NCCIC) Cyber Security Evaluation Tool.[13]

The InfoSec Institute[14] describes assets as follows:

> *In the realm of information security and information technology, an asset is anything of value to a business that is related to information services. These can take the form of a device, data or information, or even as people or software systems within the structure of a business. Anything that has value and supports the operation of a business can be considered an asset.*

---

[13]www.us-cert.gov/sites/default/files/FactSheets/NCCIC%20ICS_FactSheet_CSET_S508C.pdf

[14]https://resources.infosecinstitute.com/asset-management-guide-information-security-professionals/#gref

Note   Assets are not limited to Information Technology[15] and can come in various guises.

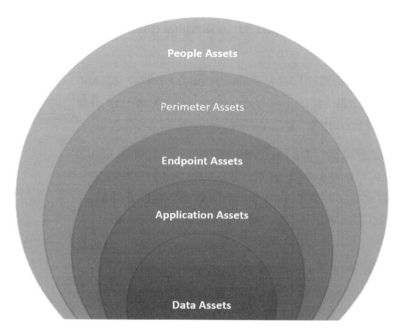

Figure 13-1. *Asset Categorization*

Vulnerability and Patch Management

- Check
- Identify
- Risk Assessment
- Prioritization
- Timely Remediation
- Confirmation
- Risk Management

---

[15]www.nccoe.nist.gov/sites/default/files/library/sp1800/fs-itam-nist-sp1800-5-draft.pdf

It is of note that following Hardware and Software Asset Management, the Center for Internet Security deems this to be the next important control.[16]

TechTarget defines Vulnerability and Patch Management as

Vulnerability management is a proactive approach to managing network security. It includes processes for

- **Checking for vulnerabilities**: This process should include regular network scanning, firewall logging, penetration testing, or use of an automated tool like a vulnerability scanner.

- **Identifying vulnerabilities**: This involves analyzing network scans and pen test results, firewall logs, or vulnerability scan results to find anomalies that suggest a malware attack or other malicious event has taken advantage of a security vulnerability or could possibly do so.

- **Verifying vulnerabilities**: This process includes ascertaining whether the identified vulnerabilities could actually be exploited on servers, applications, networks, or other systems. This also includes classifying the severity of a vulnerability and the level of risk it presents to the organization.

- **Mitigating vulnerabilities**: This is the process of figuring out how to prevent vulnerabilities from being exploited before a patch is available or in the event that there is no patch. It can involve taking the affected part of the system offline (if it's non-critical) or various other work-arounds.

- **Patching vulnerabilities**: This is the process of getting patches – usually from the vendors of the affected software or hardware – and applying them to all the affected areas in a timely way. This is sometimes an automated process, done with patch management tools. This step also includes patch testing.

---

[16]www.cisecurity.org/controls/continuous-vulnerability-management/

Having identified and categorized your assets, next comes the need to ensure that they are protected by up-to-date anti-malware software and to ensure that the assets remain protected by newly emerging vulnerabilities. Remember that an asset is more than just IT assets and all assets need to be effectively protected from new vulnerabilities. Consequently, it is essential that you have effective threat management so that you are aware of the Tactics, Techniques, and Protocols (TTPs)[17] that might be used against you. In addition to understanding the TTPS, it is essential that you identify any underlying vulnerabilities that reside within your environment that could be used against you.

Remember that once you have identified the vulnerabilities, it is vital that you risk assess the vulnerabilities against the affected asset/business process. Something that the industry deems to be a **MEDIUM**-risk vulnerability may in fact be affecting one of your business critical external public-facing assets and which you would not be comfortable with leaving there for a 90-day period. On the flip side of this, you may have identified a vulnerability that is deemed, by industry, to be a **HIGH**-risk vulnerability but which resides on an internal asset of lower value to the business. Hence, you might wish to decide (as the result of a risk assessment) to downgrade this to a **MEDIUM** risk and prioritize the remediation of the external, public-facing asset for remediation.

Having risk assessed and prioritized your remediation efforts, it is essential to re-check the vulnerability to confirm that the vulnerability has been effectively remediated against. Remember with IT assets, if you are using automated patch solutions, these are not always 100% effective, as some updates might require the asset to be rebooted for an update to be applied. Therefore, it is imperative that you carry out pre and post scan reviews to ensure that any automated patching has been effective.

Care should also be taken to ensure that Secure Software Life Cycle (Secure SLC)[18] procedures are followed to ensure that no inherent vulnerabilities are introduced, or present, within your applications.

---

[17]https://attack.mitre.org/tactics/pre/

[18]www.pcisecuritystandards.org/documents/PCI-Secure-SLC-Standard-v1_0.pdf?agreement
  =true&time=1575370558148

For example, if you are a business that has web-facing presence, you are highly likely to be vulnerable to the risks published by Open Web Application Security Project (OWASP):

- Top Most Critical Web Application Security Risks[19]

- Application Programmable Interface (API) Top 10 Risk[20]

Finally, you are likely to have "life support" assets that are extremely difficult to apply updates to and that need to be carefully risk managed, so as to apply any mitigation measures in a manner that will provide minimal disruption to the business, yet effectively reduce the opportunities for your attackers.

Here are some both IT- and non-IT-related vulnerability and patch management real-life examples.

Human Firewall

An organization was using Office 365, yet had not implemented conditional access. Consequently, employees could access their corporate Office 365 accounts from both their corporate and personal devices, via the Cloud, from anywhere in the world. Despite the fact that the criminals were known to send phishing emails[21] to compromise legitimate access credentials, the organization dismissed the vulnerability of not having additional Multi-Factor Authentication (MFA) or conditional access controls in favor of the convenience this provided to their employees. Within 1 week, this convenience was exploited by criminals to send out almost 500 spurious emails, for a 4-hour period, seeking to harvest additional credentials, much to the embarrassment of the affected organization.

This decision had not been taken as the result of a risk assessment but as the result of the CIO and IT Director's efforts to save, what they believed to be, unnecessary spending *(Protecting their bonus eligibility?).*

---

[19]www.owasp.org/images/7/72/OWASP_Top_10-2017_%28en%29.pdf.pdf

[20]www.owasp.org/index.php/OWASP_API_Security_Project

[21]www.trendmicro.com/vinfo/us/security/news/cybercrime-and-digital-threats/
compromised-office-365-accounts-used-to-send-1-5-million-email-threats-in-march

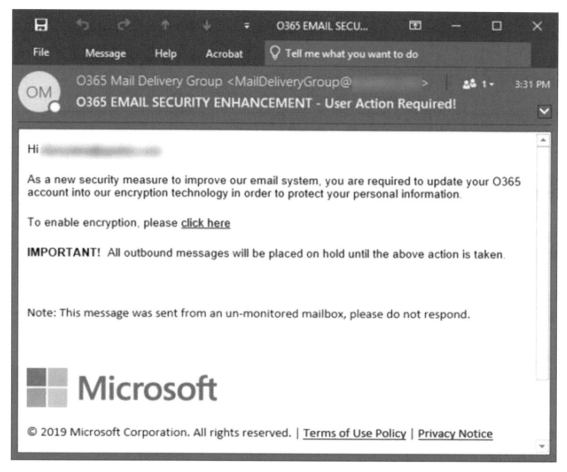

Figure 13-2. *Example Office 365 Phishing[22]*

The outcome of this incident resulted in the costly upgrade of every employee system, so as to enable additional conditional access capabilities.

Unfortunately, the time taken to remediate this vulnerability (without prioritization of the efforts) resulted in the accounts of three C-Suite members being compromised. As a result, these compromised accounts were used in the attempt to present credibility for the emergency payment of an invoice for the approximate sum of $500,000. Fortunately, the unknown attackers made a simple mistake of having the Financial Director signing of their correspondence, to the payment clerk, using their surname instead of their forename, when they were on first-name terms. However, this showed the value of the

---

[22]https://blogs.cisco.com/security/office-365-phishing-threat-of-the-month

compromised email accounts, enabling the attackers with a wealth of information to provide them with a plausible attack.

Infrastructure

During a formal onsite PCI DSS assessment, for a client, I pointed out a potential vulnerability with the Electronic Automated Access Control Systems (EAACS) that controlled access to their onsite data centers. The magnetic lock that secured the EAACS had been incorrectly fitted to the external facing door frame, meaning that anyone could (if they so wished) simply gain unauthorized access to a highly sensitive environment with the aid of a "Philips-Head/Cross-Head" screwdriver. Simply removing the magnetic backing plate from the door frame would allow them access, without the need for a telemetry card and PIN number.

Understandably, this observation caused the client to object as no other previous assessments (in the past 10 years) had ever picked this as being inappropriate. Being relatively new to the QSA company, my observation was overruled by my line manager and resulted in my being informed that PCI DSS does not require "Military Grade" security measures – "Gun emplacements!"

Fortunately, during the remaining onsite assessment, a conversation with the facilities management team revealed that this vulnerability had been previously exploited by an authorized employee, who had forgotten their access card.

As a result, all three EAACS had their magnetic locks re-sited onto the internal facing door frame.

Application

Along with hundreds of other e-Commerce organizations, British Airways,[23] Newegg,[24] and Ticketmaster[25] were the victims of the Magecart Group.[26] In all incidents, the web page adjoining to the customers' payment interface was used for a Man-In-The Middle

---

[23]www.wired.co.uk/article/british-airways-data-breach-gdpr-fine
[24]www.darkreading.com/cloud/getting-up-to-speed-on-magecart-/a/d-id/1334884
[25]https://searchsecurity.techtarget.com/answer/
Ticketmaster-breach-How-did-this-card-skimming-attack-work
[26]www.riskiq.com/blog/labs/magecart-group-4-always-advancing/

(MITM) attack. The tactics of using well-known vulnerabilities (e.g., Formjacking,[27] Clickjacking,[28] etc.) are still successfully employed today,[29] despite these being older vulnerabilities.

Network

In 2017, Equifax[30] failed to inform the asset owner that the external public-facing server that they were responsible of was missing an Apache Struts update.[31] In fact, this individual was not even a participant of their vulnerability steering committee, despite being responsible for the management of an extremely high-value asset. This resulted in the attacker being able to use Metasploit to create a remote access point, leading to the loss of the following customer records:

- 147 million names and dates of birth

- 145.5 million SSNs

- 99 million physical addresses

- 20.3 million telephone numbers

- 17.6 million email addresses

- 209,000 payment card numbers and expiration dates

Privileged Access Management (PAM)

- Identification

- Restriction against specific tasks

- Formal approval

- Change Management

- Periodic audit

---

[27]https://secureteam.co.uk/articles/what-are-formjacking-attacks/

[28]www.keycdn.com/blog/x-frame-options

[29]www.theinquirer.net/inquirer/news/3084034/macys-magecart-data-breach

[30]www.ftc.gov/system/files/documents/cases/172_3203_equifax_complaint_7-22-19.pdf

[31]www.exploit-db.com/exploits/41614

Because of the power and potential damage that can be done through the compromise of privilege user accounts, they are a number 1 target for criminals[32] and as such should be closely monitored to help in the timely identification of their misuse or unauthorized privilege escalation.[33]

TechTarget[34] defines PAM as:

Privileged access management (PAM) is the combination of tools and technology used to secure, control and monitor access to an organization's critical information and resources. Subcategories of PAM include shared access password management, privileged session management, vendor privileged access management and application access management.

Gartner[35] regards this as a high priority for organizations seeking to reduce this risk and has developed the following best practices:

- Track and Secure Every Privileged Account

- Govern and Control Access

- Record and Audit Privileged Activity

- Operationalize Privileged Tasks

Security Information and Event Management (SIEM)

- Identification

    - Critical Systems connections

    - User activities against critical systems connections

- Alignment to pillars 1, 2, and 3

---

[32]www.beyondtrust.com/blog/entry/the-5-most-cringe-worthy-privileged-data-breaches-of-2018

[33]https://attack.mitre.org/techniques/T1068/

[34]https://searchsecurity.techtarget.com/definition/privileged-access-management-PAM

[35]www.gartner.com/en/documents/3899567/
best-practices-for-privileged-access-management-through-

The purpose of an effective SIEM process is to ensure the timely identification of abnormal activities. However, to enable this, you need to have refined and matured the aforementioned pillars (1, 2, and 3). It is important to remember that your attackers are extremely unlikely to act quickly and will prefer to achieve a persistent presence within your corporate environment, taking their time to carry out clandestine reconnaissance and planning before making their move.

TechTarget[36] explains the concept of SIEM as:

Security information and event management (SIEM) is an approach to security management that combines SIM (security information management) and SEM (security event management) functions into one security management system. The acronym SIEM is pronounced "sim" with a silent e.

The underlying principles of every SIEM system is to aggregate relevant data from multiple sources, identify deviations from the norm and take appropriate action. For example, when a potential issue is detected, a SIEM might log additional information, generate an alert and instruct other security controls to stop an activity's progress.

At the most basic level, a SIEM system can be rules-based or employ a statistical correlation engine to establish relationships between event log entries. Advanced SIEMs have evolved to include user and entity behavior analytics (UEBA) and security orchestration and automated response (SOAR).

[36]https://searchsecurity.techtarget.com/definition/
security-information-and-event-management-SIEM
[37]www.zdnet.com/article/marriott-ceo-shares-post-mortem-on-last-years-hack/

Some examples of the value of having an effective SIEM process can be seen through the following incidents:

- **Marriott**[37]

- Following the acquisition of the Starwood company, Marriott inherited Remote Access Trojan (RAT)[38] and Mimikatz[39] malicious software. An abnormality was detected through the monitoring being carried out by the IBM Guardian software, which alerted Marriott to the presence of malicious activity occurring within their corporate environment. It is believed that the attackers had remained undetected for around 4 years,[40] and given the length of time, they remained undetected, and the root cause/delivery method was never identified.

- **Citrix**[41]

- Attackers gained access to the Citrix internal network through password spraying, a technique that exploits weak passwords. Once within the network, the attackers intermittently accessed and stole business documents and files from a company shared network drive that has been used to store current and historical business documents, as well as a drive associated with a web-based tool used in their consulting practice. It is reported that the attackers remained undetected for a period of 6 months.[42]

Bearing in mind the fact that criminals will attempt to remain undetected for long periods of time, maintaining secure log records covering a sufficient period of time is essential in trying to identify the actions taken by the attackers and the potential root causes.

---

[38]https://searchsecurity.techtarget.com/definition/RAT-remote-access-Trojan
[39]www.varonis.com/blog/what-is-mimikatz/
[40]https://krebsonsecurity.com/2018/11/
  marriott-data-on-500-million-guests-stolen-in-4-year-breach/
[41]www.zdnet.com/article/hackers-lurked-in-citrix-systems-for-six-months/
[42]www.bankinfosecurity.com/citrix-hackers-camped-in-tech-giants-network-for-6-
  months-a-12436

For PCI DSS compliance, the current mandatory log retention periods are **3 months immediately available** for analysis, with **at least 1 year of auditable history** *(e.g., online, archived, or restorable from backup).* Given the known TTPs of attackers remaining dormant for many months, and even years, you may want to choose longer archive retention periods.

Incident Management

- Prepare

- Detection and Analysis

- Contain, Eradicate, and Recover

- Post Incident

The concept of having in effective incident response is based on being able to identify and respond to abnormal activities occurring within your corporate environment. The ability to proactively respond is reliant on your ability to quickly identify unusual activity or activity that is in breach of the corporate policies/procedures.

It is important to be prepared and to think that it is inevitable that something will happen, whether that be a deliberate, malicious, or an accidental act, and that you need to be prepared for such an event. Remember that your Incident Management processes should not be restricted to data breaches and not also include minor events or incidents that impact your valued assets *(This could be the stumbling activities of an attacker's clandestine activities),* which would need to be subject to further investigation.

Incident Management should include multiple elements, for example, NIST SP800-61 R2:[43]

- Establishing Incident Response Capabilities

- Incident Handling

  - Planning

  - Detection and Analysis (Investigation)

---

[43]https://nvlpubs.nist.gov/nistpubs/SpecialPublications/NIST.SP.800-61r2.pdf

- • Containment, Eradication, and Recovery

- • Post-Incident activity

- Coordination and Information Sharing

The best way to look at your incident response is to align it with the concept of a burglary.

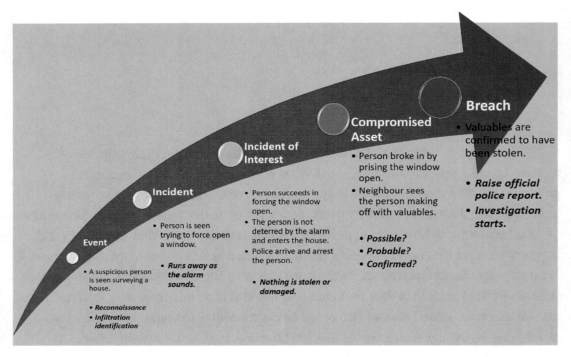

Figure 13-3. *Stages of an Incident*

In the event of a real incident occurring, the first thing that happens is your incident response team are highly likely to panic. Therefore, it is essential that extensive, continual training and familiarization against various scenarios, specific to your organization, is established.

Stages for Designing a Scenario

1. Select a critical process.

2. Review and identify likely threat actors that would attack the process.

3. Identify possible tactics[44] of the threat actors.

4. Loosely map the tactics to the kill chain[45]/cognitive attack loop[46] process.

5. Review and apply techniques.[47]

    a. *Check techniques against Cyber Analytics Repository (CAR)[48] to identify key actions and events carried out by criminals.*

6. Review, validate, and apply techniques and procedures from Threat Intelligence Reports.

7. Review, Evaluate, and Validate.

    a. *Past Security Assessments*

    b. *Audit Findings*

        i. *Known vulnerabilities in systems **NOT** patched*

8. Validate if the scenario is viable.

    a. *If not, return to step 2.*

9. Review and map against kill chain/cognitive attack loop process.

---

[44]https://attack.mitre.org/tactics/pre/

[45]www.lockheedmartin.com/en-us/capabilities/cyber/cyber-kill-chain.html

[46]www.carbonblack.com/2019/07/31/introducing-the-cognitive-attack-loop-and-the-3-phases-of-cybercriminal-behavior/

[47]https://attack.mitre.org/techniques/pre/

[48]https://car.mitre.org/

10. Map existing controls against the five Ds of resilience:

    a. **De**ter

    b. **De**tect

    c. **De**lay

    d. **De**ny

    e. **De**fend

11. Review effectiveness of existing controls and confirm with Audit Team.

12. If deemed to be effective, identify any missing controls *(enhancement)*.

    a. If ineffective, configure and optimize existing controls.

13. Describe the missing controls effectiveness in addressing the threats.

14. Confirm scenario and business case for additional controls.

15. Formally share scenario with Incident Response Team and Stakeholders.

Reality Bites

I have been fortunate *(or some might say unfortunate)* enough to have spent over 30 years being trained for and delivering incident response capabilities. I strongly believe in the value of an effective incident response capability, that despite spending 22 years in the RAF Police being trained to provide effective incident response in high-risk environments (e.g., Cold War exercises (TACEVAL, MAXEVAL, MINIVAL, etc.) and Deployed Operations into hostile environments, as well providing incident response support, as part of the second Line of Defense (2LoD) risk function, I still continue to refresh my skills and knowledge on the subject. For example, in 2019, I took the opportunity to attend two of Cyber Management Alliance's incident management courses (GCHQ-Certified Cyber Incident Planning and Response[49] and Building and Optimizing Incident Response Playbooks[50]).

How well can you identify and respond the presence of the **ABNORMAL** from the NORMAL and how much confidence do you have in the maturity[51] of your incident response process?

During my military career, everyone received a minimal level of incident response training so that ALL were deemed responsibilities for identifying the presence of potential **ABNORMAL** activities.

As an example, here is my account of a couple real-life incidents, where a minor event proved to have greater implications.

During one of my overseas deployments (Between December 2009 and May 2010), on the Counter Intelligence Field Team (CIFT), I had the responsibility for leading a team of two responsible for providing 24/7 initial incident response for every incident for a military establishment[52] *(spanning 35 km²)* with numerous military assets and around 21,000 residents (5000 UK military personnel, 2000 contractors, and around 14,000 US military personnel). As you might imagine, this was an extremely busy 6-month period with over 600 reportable and documented incidents occurring.

One such incident occurred under the cover of darkness, when an unknown local national elderly male was discovered as he attempted to climb the perimeter fence. On arrival, my colleague and I were apprised of the situation and we commenced our investigations. Our first decision was to seek medical attention for the individual and to ensure that he was well cared for, until we were confident that he was fit to be interviewed. All attempts to identify this potential intruder failed to confirm who he was, so we remained with him overnight and planned to interview him the following morning, so as to ascertain whether his intentions may have been malicious or not.

The following morning, we commenced our investigations with the now fed, watered, and refreshed unknown male. We quickly established a rapport with the elderly male, and he freely began to provide us information about himself and how he had come to be ensnarled in the perimeter defenses. However, none of the responses appeared to make any sense. Suddenly, he requested the use of some paper and a pencil.

---

[49]www.cm-alliance.com/training/cipr-cyber-incident-planning-response/

[50]www.cm-alliance.com/training/cipr-playbooks

[51]www.crest-approved.org/cyber-security-incident-response-maturity-assessment/index.html

[52]www.gov.uk/government/news/camp-bastion-doubles-in-size

Having received a piece of paper and the pencil, he started to draw while stating

"Your base commander will know what this means!"

The first paper being drawn on, the elderly male gestured for another piece of paper and then another and another. After five pieces of paper, we had possession of five identical drawings.

At the time, we surmised that the elderly male was suffering from mental illness, he was released to the local authorities and we documented the incident for our records.

Two years later, in September 2012, the Taliban breached the camp perimeter in an attack,[53] coming through the very same area where the elderly male had been caught.

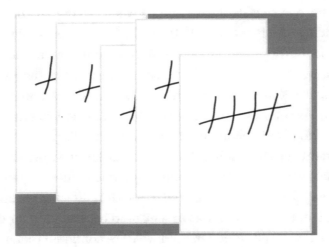

Figure 13-4. Intruder Drawing

Coincidence?

During the very same deployment, my colleague and I were tasked to investigate an incident, where a trusted local national had been caught in possession of a camera-enabled mobile telephone. The policy, at the time, was that local nations were prohibited from being in possession of any technologies while within the confines of the military base.

---

[53]www.bbc.co.uk/news/world-asia-19704620

At the commencement of the investigation, it was discovered that the offending party was deemed to be a "trusted contractor" who had, over a 5-year period, gained employment as the procurement manager for the base. Consequently, he argued that this policy was not appropriate for his role (despite him having access to a landline) and that he needed to have access to his mobile telephone to speak with his suppliers.

As part of the investigation, forensic investigation of the mobile phone revealed 13 deleted movie files of live beheadings. As a result, the perpetrator was further interviewed, where he explained that these deleted files had been previously on his mobile phone so that he could persuade local nationals that this is the reason for working for the coalition. Notwithstanding this explanation, the investigation continued with a search of the compound where he and others were accommodated. To ensure that his was included in the searches, the company's security manager was approached and asked to identify the exact location of the offender's living accommodation. As a result, the security manager pointed to an accommodation pod, which was clearly identifiable by the three satellite dishes that were mounted on its roof.

The search revealed that the individual was in possession of a workstation, and when subject to forensic examination, it was found to contain evidence of the embezzlement of $2 billion. Unfortunately, the investigation was unable to identify what had happened to the stolen money. However, it was believed that the funds could have been used to fund the Taliban and to pay their bounties.[54]

The apparently innocent can be harboring more dastardly deeds!

Recommendation

I would recommend that you use the PCI DSS Prioritized Approach if you're looking to measure the compliance status against the PCI DSS controls framework. However, I would recommend that you consider the development of an agnostic security controls foundation to help you build a robust proactive defense. This will help you ensure you can reduce the risks before adding the compliance levels.

---

[54]www.thetimes.co.uk/article/taliban-win-pound1600-bounty-for-each-nato-soldier-killed-z9thb5j389l#

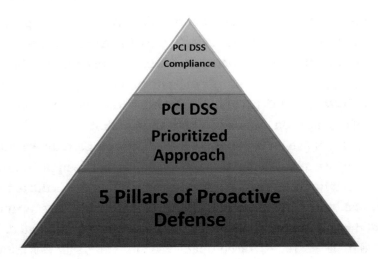

Figure 13-5. *Proactive Compliant Defenses*

Both Lockheed Martin's Kill Chain and Carbon Black's Cognitive Attack Loop identify the early stages of an attacker's TTPs. These five pillars are designed to focus on the effective identification and response to the early stages of an attack.

Conclusion

The world has moved on with far more people being technology aware and the modern criminals are increasingly turning their attention to the monetarization of personal data. However, businesses have been slow in responding to the ever-increasing threats to their data processing operations. This apparent apathy or confusion at what is required to effectively defend their realm has provided considerable opportunities for the criminals.

The application of defensive security controls needs to be aligned to your perceived threats, so as to minimize your risks and to enhance your ability to safeguard your most critical business operations and data.

Whether you need to comply with PCI DSS or are just looking at the development of a suitable integrated strategy, focusing on maturing these five pillars is a great place to start building proactive defenses.

The five pillars provide you with a prioritized conceptual approach based upon risk. Once you have matured this, you will significantly reduce your risk profile and you will have created a stable foundation on which to build your compliance model.

Key Takeaways

Creating a proactive defensive model is distinctly different to building a PCI DSS compliant environment. However, if you consider the five pillars as your foundational controls, you can rapidly enhance your security posture and make yourself less of a target to the opportunist attackers.

Having matured the five pillars, you will then be better placed to meet your compliance objectives while retaining a robust foundational level.

Being agnostic of any particular security controls framework but using the common high priorities ensures that your strategy supports a progressive program.

Rome was not built in a day.

Establish a layered approach to the creation of your defensive strategies.

- *Have you identified and categorized your assets based upon their business criticality?*

- *Do you understand the vulnerabilities and potential impact associated to your assets?*

- *Are your remediation efforts prioritized based upon risk assessments?*

- *Do you validate patching effectiveness?*

- *Do you strictly control and monitor the access of those user accounts that can do the most damage?*

- *Does your SIEM provide you with an accurate picture of NORMAL?*

- *Can you easily identify the **ABNORMAL** from the NORMAL?*

- *In the event of the **ABNORMAL**, are you prepared and able to respond so as to prevent harm to your customers' data assets or to prevent an impact to your essential business operations?*

Risks

Mitigating your risks must be prioritized and balanced against the potential impact a compromise to your critical assets will have on your business operations.

Consequently, understanding what your most important assets are to your business should be your very first consideration.

Ask yourself:

- *Do I understand the asset chain of all my connected devices, which support my most important business operations?*

- *Have I segmented my critical assets, so as to minimize the potential opportunity for an attacker to move laterally through my environment?*

- *Have my assets been categorized based upon their potential impact and importance to my organization?*

- *Have I identified and prioritized my vulnerabilities against the perceived values of these assets?*

- *Do I have a Secure SLC process?*

- *Can I easily answer the "So What?" question?*

- *Do I confirm the effectiveness of any updates/mitigation efforts?*

- *Am I effectively controlling the number of "Super User" (Privileged) accounts, so as to minimize the potential opportunity for misuse?*

- *Can I easily identify an unauthorized escalation of privileges?*

- *Can I rapidly detect and respond to the **ABNORMAL**?*

CHAPTER 14

People, People, People

The single, most difficult, component of any data security and privacy program is the people factor. The very nature of employing people increases the risk to your data processing operations. This is not because everyone wants to steal your data or that they are incompetent – far from it!

Being a successful business can be stressful, and there are times when the time pressures can lead to people taking shortcuts. Additionally, people having varying skills and abilities need to be accommodated for any successful protective security program.

Let's face it, an effective protective security program is an inconvenience to running a successful business.

Of course, it is!

The very nature of your data privacy and security controls is to make it less convenient for your attackers to steal your data or break your supporting IT systems.

Now imagine a world without any security defenses!

Without any defenses, your business becomes an easy target to attack and being "blacklisted" by the Card Brands, so that you are prohibited from taking card payments or having fewer customers because rather more of an inconvenience to your business.

Your personnel are on the front line of any effective data privacy and security program and are often the predominant cause of security breaches or system outages, all of which contribute to a degradation of consumer trust and present additional financial implications.

J. Seaman, *PCI DSS*, https://doi.org/10.1007/978-1-4842-5808-8_14

For example, let's say that you were to suffer a payment card breach as the result of a deliberate or accidental action by a trusted member of your team, what is the potential impact?

1. **Reputational damage**

   Given that payment card data is deemed as being personal data, most data privacy legislations require that your business notify the affected people and the regulators. Often this involves a public notice.

   In the case of a large breach, your business will have a lengthy period of being associated with bad security practices.

   - *Loss of consumers*

     - *1/2 of your customer base may never return.*[1]

   - *Reduced share price*

2. **Financial impact**

   Post breach, you will be required to carry out a forensic investigation to identify the root cause and will need to invest heavily in the enhancement of your security defenses.

   The Card Brands will escalate your status to that of a high-risk (level 1) entity and you will be subject to a minimum of 3-year onsite report on compliance (RoC) assessments.

   The Regulators will investigate the cause of the data breach and will administer a fine, according to the extent of the bad practices identified.

   You may be subject to private litigation being taken against you, for example:

---

[1]https://securityboulevard.com/2019/09/
businesses-can-lose-half-of-customers-after-a-data-breach-research-shows/

- Equifax[2]

- Morrisons Supermarket[3]

- British Airways[4]

- Marriott[5]

Each year the Ponemon Institute[6] provides an estimate for the average cost of a data breach.

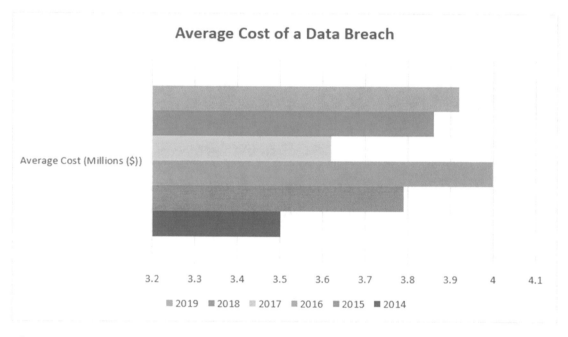

Figure 14-1. *Ponemon Institute Data Breach Costs*

[2]www.ftc.gov/enforcement/cases-proceedings/refunds/equifax-data-breach-settlement
[3]www.personneltoday.com/hr/morrisons-data-leak-implications-for-employers/
[4]www.leighday.co.uk/News/2019/October-2019/Court-gives-go-ahead-to-compensation-claim-by-Brit
[5]www.law.com/2019/05/30/marriott-data-breach-judge-puts-lawyers-on-a-fast-track/
[6]https://databreachcalculator.mybluemix.net/?_ga=2.149557686.1675720369.1575975888-405938945.1575975888&cm_mc_uid=69077084300315759758876&cm_mc_sid_50200000=71927031575975887633&cm_mc_sid_52640000=28803861575975887648

Putting this into context, this equates to an average cost of **$150 per record** breached. Adding to this the findings and recommendations outlined in Verizon's Data Breach Investigations Report (DBIR), the Security Culture is clearly a high risk and should be considered a number 1 priority.

Keep it clean.
Many breaches are a result of poor security hygiene and a lack of attention to detail. Clean up human error where possible, then establish an asset and security baseline around internet-facing assets like web servers and cloud services.

Maintain integrity.
Web application compromises now include code that can capture data entered into web forms. Consider adding file integrity monitoring on payment sites, in addition to patching operating systems and coding payment applications.

Redouble your efforts.
2FA everything. Use strong authentication on customer-facing applications, any remote access and cloud-based email. There are examples of 2FA vulnerabilities, but they don't excuse lack of implementation.

Be wary of inside jobs.
Track insider behavior by monitoring and logging access to sensitive data. Make it clear to staff just how good you are at recognizing fraudulent transactions.

Scrub packets.
Distributed denial of service (DDoS) protection is an essential control for many industries. Guard against non-malicious interruptions with continuous monitoring and capacity planning for traffic spikes.

Stay socially aware.
Social attacks are effective ways to capture credentials. Monitor email for links and executables. Give your teams ways to report potential phishing or pretexting.

Figure 14-2. *DBIR 2019 Breach Prevention Best Practices*

Unfortunately, the current version (v3.2.1) includes elements of creating a security culture but does not clearly prioritize this as being a high importance in reducing your data breach risks.

Introduction

Having observed the benefits of having a robust security culture, during a long, often challenging and rewarding military career, I am a strong advocate of focusing on the investment in your people. Until businesses no longer need people to interact with people, the people risk should be regarded as a high priority.

At the tender age of 17, I was introduced to the value of teamwork and the importance of being suitably trained for your specific roles and understanding the associated risks. As you can imagine, the Royal Air Force (RAF) is heavily reliant on the adherence to rules and procedures. Throughout my military career, I was fortunate enough to have been employed on a variety of police- and security-related roles. Before becoming an RAF Policeman, I commenced several weeks of the fundamental military training at RAF Newton. All traders entering the RAF commenced their careers with several weeks of basic military training before moving onto more specialized trade training. As a result, all RAF personnel gained an elementary understanding of the policies and procedures for a safe life in the RAF.

Following on from this, I underwent military driver training, at RAF St. Athan, before commencing my basic Police, Infantry training and Police Dog handler training courses (20 weeks) at RAF Newton.

Basically, the first 6 months of my career consisted of training courses so that I possessed the basic skills needed to be an RAF Police Dog handler.

Training did not stop there, and the remainder of my career was subject to On-the-Job training, regular continuation training, annual training, station exercises (MAXEVAL, MINIVAL, TACEVAL, Crashed Aircraft, etc.), annual testing, and further specialist trade training courses. Each course was designed to refresh the basic knowledge, to provide additional training, and to enable the opportunity of putting that learned theory into practice.

Ultimately, over time, much like a professional sports player, these skills were engrained into my very being and became as natural to me as breathing. As a result, I didn't need to refresh my memory on a particular policy or procedure needed for my particular role, and the commanders became confident in the fact that all RAF Police personnel would deliver to minimum standards.

Having a standardized approach is extremely important in the maintenance
of secure systems and the handling, processing, and storage of personal data. A
standardized approach becomes more important when you consider the impact non-
standard practices could have on interdependent data privacy and security controls.

The benefits of standardization were clearly evident with the introduction of
standard gauge tracks, as the railways began to become more interconnected. Imagine
the travel experience, for a long train journey, when each section of the track required a
change of carriage to accommodate differing widths of track *(Notwithstanding the risks
of attempting to navigate a broad gauge configured train onto a narrow-gauge track)*.

Figure 14-3. *Standardization*

Effective standardization requires the establishment of the "Tone at the Top," through the documentation of a set of rules (policies) that shall be adhered to, to ensure that safe and secure operations are maintained. In support of the policies, department managers should be responsible for ensuring that appropriate guidance (procedures) are developed and all personnel are initially trained on what is (and what is not) acceptable.

It must be made clear that any personnel making unauthorized or deliberate deviations from these rules and guidance will be subject to disciplinary action, whereas personnel making accidental deviations will require refresher training.

All supporting rules and guidance need to be clearly and concisely written so that all personnel understand the reasons why it is important for them to strictly follow them and to seek temporary dispensation, in instances where the rules cannot be applied *(subject to a documented and approved Security Risk Exemption assessment).*

Within PCI DSS requirement 12 and the final control statement for each requirement covers the requirements for effective People Management. However, there is one important omission which presents a significant risk to your business.

- **Human Resilience**

  - Do you have the capacity to have another suitable team member to deputize in the absence of one of your specialists?

  - Do you establish regular On-the-Job training to these deputies?

    - *Avoid single point of failures.*

Documentation

Figure 14-4. *Documentation*

Your supporting documentation to your Data Privacy and Security strategy will have a natural hierarchy. This is especially true with PCI DSS, where specific policies and procedures may have an impact on other control areas and where some policies are applicable to all and others are role specific.

The Document Hierarchy Tree can be seen in Figure 14-5.

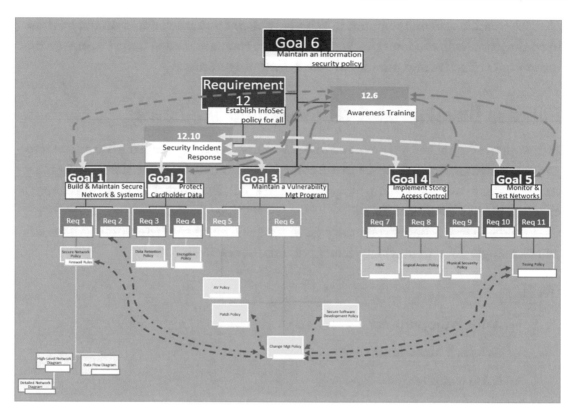

Figure 14-5. *Document Hierarchy Tree*

Your document sets should be sequential and complementary to each other
and should not act in conflict to another document within the document hierarchy.
Consequently, you may find the identification and mapping of your policies, procedures,
and supporting documents into a hierarchy tree extremely useful in ensuring that you
can trace the documents to their relevant departments and the inter-related documents.

I'm still amazed to see organizations who "Tick the Box" for compliance, by thinking
that just maintaining a suite of supporting policies and operational procedures and
making them available on their corporate intranet makes them compliant and, more
importantly, secure. Just having a new starter read and acknowledge the policies at the
start of their employment does not help when the technology changes, or they have been
employed for several years, picking up multiple bad habits along the years.

The effectiveness of your documentation is enhanced through the periodic
reminders of the dangers being mitigated by the policies/procedures and the risks to the
business, in the event of the policies/procedures not being followed.

The creation and maintenance of effective policies and procedures should be done in conjunction with the target audience, with feedback being encouraged to ensure that they remain effective and relevant to your business operations.

Policies Development *(Establishing the Laws)*

Your supporting policies do not need to be "War and Peace" and need to be relevant to your organization. Therefore, if you are considering purchasing "Out of the Box" policy templates, ask yourself how much tailoring of the policies you will need to make them a comfortable fit for your company.

Could you create better rules through the use of a number of short policy statements within a single document which clearly outlines the following?

5WH

- **W**hat is the purpose?

- **W**hy is it important?

- **W**ho it applies to?

- **W**hen it must be followed?

- **W**here is it applicable to?

- **H**ow personnel refresh their understanding and how and when to report incidents?

At a minimum the contents of your policy should clearly describe the following using simple/high-level terminologies which are easy for all the intended audience to understand:

1. **Purpose**

   First state what the purpose of the policy is.

2. **Audience**

   Define who the audience is, to whom the policies apply.

3. **Information security objectives**

   Provide agreed-on and well-defined objectives for strategy and security.

4. **Authority and access control**

    Who is the owner and approver of the policies?

5. **Data classification**

    Classification helps clarify what data is important and why.

6. **Data support and operations**

    Where the policy applies.

7. **Security awareness and behavior**

    How personnel are expected to act and the potential
    consequences for non-adherence to these rules.

8. **Responsibilities, rights, and duties of personnel**

    Who is involved and what are their responsibilities?

Remember:

- The longer and more complex that you make your policies, the
  less chance of your intended audience being able to remember it
  and the greater the chance that the readers will skip through the
  content.

- Consider tailoring the policy statement contents to suit the full
  ranges of your target audiences.

- Consider the potential benefits of using local languages
  (if applicable).

- Consider the potential benefits of supplementing your policy
  statements with a pictorial representation.

- A picture paints a thousand words.

In order to set the "Tone at the Top," your policies should be subject to periodic review and approval by senior management and a record to these changes be maintained and recorded in the policies, for example:

Version No.	Date of Review	Date of Approval	Reviewed/ Changed by	Approved by	Summary of Changes
V1.0	December 10, 2017	December 10, 2017	Information Security Manager	Finance Director	Initial release
V1.1	December 09, 2018	December 09, 2018	Information Security Manager	Finance Director	Annual Review
V1.2	December 09, 2019	December 09, 2019	Information Security Manager	Finance Director	Annual Review
V2.0	June 01, 2019	June 01, 2019	Information Security Manager	Finance Director	Changes to scope statement, following an acquisition

As you can see, the secondary digit reflects the recording of minor changes to the policies, whereas a change in the primary digit reflects a significant change to policy:

- Significant changes to a policy statement should be communicated out to all applicable personnel, and all personnel should make note of the changes that have been made.

- Personnel should be encouraged to periodically refresh their knowledge of the rules outlined within the policy statements that apply to an individual's roles and responsibilities.

In the event of an incident, as part of the post-incident reviews, it is important to include a review of any supporting policy statements. The purpose is to confirm that the policy statement remains effective and to validate whether this was a willful or negligent act.

Representative feedback should be encouraged from across the intended target audience to ensure that the content remains appropriate and relevant while clearly articulating what is needed to reduce the associated risks.

Senior Management will be accountable for the approval of the policy statements, while a security steering committee should be responsible for ensuring contributing and reviewing the content.

Requirement	Policy Statements
1	• Mobile Device
2	• Secure Systems configuration
3	• Secure Data handling, Storage, and Disposal • Encryption Key Life-cycle Management
4	• Secure transmission
5	• Anti-virus
6	• Vulnerability, Patch, and Risk Management • Change Management • Secure Software Development
7	• Access Control
8	• Access Control
9	• Physical Security • Media handling, storage, and disposal
10	• Monitoring
11	• Security Testing
12	• Information Security • Acceptable Usage • PCI DSS Charter • Security Vetting • Third-Party Management • Security Incident Response and Breach Reporting • Security Auditing

Procedures

Think of your procedures as being your "Standard Operating Procedures" (SOPs), which clearly document the steps that all personnel must adhere to.

Your SOPs are designed to be at a department level, developed to articulate the steps that everyone must follow.

The SOPs should align to the overarching policy statements, so that if all personnel are trained and strictly adhere to the appropriate process steps, they will automatically be meeting the objective of the policy statement:

- It may be that there are multiple SOPs that are associated with a single policy statement.

The department/team managers will be accountable for ensuring that the SOPs remain aligned to meet the objectives of the overarching policy statements and that the content is appropriate for their team members and that all their team members adhere to their SOPs.

Team members should be encouraged to provide feedback on the suitability of the content to their duties.

There are no formal template requirements and can be as simple as a process flow diagram.

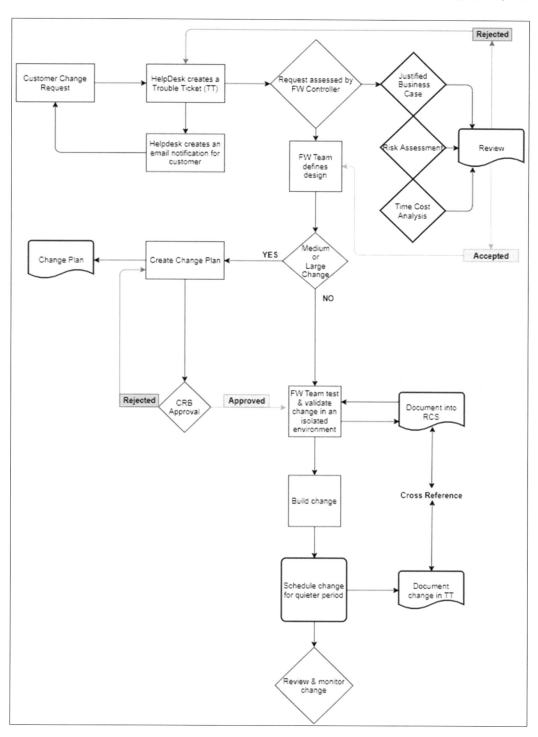

Figure 14-6. *Example Firewall Change Process Flow*

Requirement	Procedures
1	• Firewall/Router secure configuration build standards • Firewall/Router change SOPs
2	• Secure System configuration build standards • Secure System configuration build SOPs • Secure Wireless configuration build standards • Secure Wireless configuration SOPs
3	• Secure Data handling and Disposal SOPs • Key Management SOPs • *Secure key life-cycle management*
4	• Secure transmission SOPs
5	• Anti-virus SOPs
6	• Vulnerability, Patch, and Risk Management SOPs • Change Management SOPs • Secure Software Development SOPs
7	• Role-Based Access Control (RBAC) SOPs
8	• Access Control SOPs
9	• Operational Requirements (ORs) • Physical Access Control SOPs • Physical Security SOPs • Visitor SOPs • Media handling SOPs • Physical inspection SOPs
10	• Monitoring SOPs

11	• Rogue device inspection and response SOPs
	• Security testing SOPs
	   • Vulnerability detection and remediation
	   • Penetration testing
	   • Segmentation testing
	   • Alerting response

(*continued*)

Requirement	Procedures
12	• Policy reviews SOPs • Risk assessment SOPs • Security education/awareness SOPs • Security vetting SOPs • Third-party management SOPs • Security Incident SOPs

Supporting Documents

Within the PCI DSS controls framework, there is a specific supporting document that is needed to evidence that you have an appropriate formalized data privacy and security program established.

Requirement	Procedures

1	• Firewall/Router change records
	• High-Level network diagram
	   • In-scope and out-of-scope environment
	      • *Like a Country Map*
	         • *Showing location of major towns, cities, and connecting roads*
	         • *The delineation of boundaries (between trusted and untrusted)*
	• Detailed network diagram
	   • In-scope environment
	   • Like a City/Town Map
	      • Showing housing estates and street level details
	      • Detailing the connectivity of internal, in-scope, supporting systems
	• Data Flow Diagrams
	   • Identifying the support systems that are involved in the processing, storage, or transmission of payment card data (Cat A)
	   • Identifying any adjacent support systems (Cat B), which may impact the Cat A systems
	• Ping tests
	• Command Prompts
	• Asset discovery scans

(continued)

Requirement	Procedures

2	• System configuration audit reports
	• Asset inventory
	  • Cat A systems
	  • Cat B systems
	    • Aligned to network and data flow diagrams

3	• Quarterly data discovery audits • Encryption configuration audits

4	• Secure transmission audits
	  • Wireshark
	  • SSL Labs

5	• Anti-virus (AV) policy vendor documents
	• Anti-virus checks
	  • EICAR[7] testing
	  • WICAR[8] testing
	• Anti-virus audit logs.
	  • Showing records of any AV alerting.
	• Anti-virus system configurations

6	• Currently vulnerability and patch reports
	• Risk assessments
	• Change tickets
	• Network diagrams showing separation of environments
	  • Live
	  • Test
	  • Development
	• Code Review checklists
	• Internal Software security test reports
	• Annual web application test reports
	  • *Or after any significant changes*
	• Web Application Firewall logs

(continued)

---

[7]www.eicar.org/

[8]www.wicar.org/

Requirement	Procedures
7	• RBAC requests • AD Group Policy configurations
8	• Access request tickets • User account system configurations • System access configurations
9	• CCTV recordings • Electronic Automated Access Control System (EAACS) logs • Visitor • Media log • Inspection schedule • Inspection reports
10	• Audit logs • Linked audit trails • File Integrity logs • Time synchronization configurations • Secure audit storage configurations • Logs and events (minimum 12 months) • Records of investigations/analysis of suspicious events (e.g., Helpdesk tickets)

11	• Inventory of wireless enabled devices
	• Quarterly internal scan reports
	• Quarterly external scan reports
	• Follow-up post-remediation scan reports
	• Annual penetration testing
	  • *Or after any significant changes*
	• Post-remediation penetration retesting
	• Six-month segmentation testing
	• Alerting tickets
	  • *IDS/IPS*
	  • *Change Detection*

(continued)

Requirement	Procedures
12	<ul><li>Policy review/change tables</li><li>Annual policies signed acknowledgment</li><li>Responsible, Accountable, Consulted, Informed (RACI) Matrix</li><li>Job descriptions</li><li>Security Steering committee minutes</li><li>Annual training and awareness material<ul><li>*PCI DSS*</li><li>*Secure software development*</li></ul></li><li>Training attendance records</li><li>Security vetting checks</li><li>Contracts</li><li>Due diligence inspections</li><li>AoCs</li><li>PCI DSS controls RACI</li><li>Security incident playbooks</li><li>Security Incident Response Testing<ul><li>*Annually (at a minimum)*</li></ul></li><li>Post-incident/testing minutes</li><li>Security audit reports</li></ul>

Continual Security Awareness/Education

Figure 14-7. *Security Awareness Training*

The return on investment for building an effective security awareness/education program is priceless to an organization and, as such, needs "Top-Level" and senior management support and participation *(setting a good example)*.

Security should be seen as everyone's responsibility, with the more people being able to identify and report suspicious events/incidents providing an additional defensive layer to your security program.

Dependent on the size of your organization, the training investment can be tailored to suit, for example:

- **Large enterprises**

    Providing generic training modules to all your employees (in-scope and out-of-scope) through the use of a third-party vendor (KnowBe4[9]) to improve the effectiveness of the "Eyes and Ears" monitoring for the outer layers of defense

---

[9]https://info.knowbe4.com/one-on-one-demo-partners?partnerid=0010c000022xCHUAA2

433

- *This is supplementary for the PCI DSS-specific awareness training, for the "In-scope" personnel, where these employees receive refresher training on the intent of the policies and procedures that apply to their role.*

  - *Locally developed and delivered in house*

  - *Procuring the services of a security consultancy firm to deliver appropriate content*

- **Medium enterprises**

  Establishing a team of departmental security champions, who have a secondary responsibility for periodic general security awareness training

  - *This is supplementary for the PCI DSS-specific awareness training, for the "In-scope" personnel, where these employees receive refresher training on the intent of the policies and procedures that apply to their role.*

    - *Locally developed and delivered in house*

    - *Procuring the services of a security consultancy firm to deliver appropriate content*

- **Small enterprises**

  Delivery of periodic generic security awareness training to all personnel, locally developed and presented by the Information Security representative

  - *This is supplementary for the PCI DSS-specific awareness training, for the "In-scope" personnel, where these employees receive refresher training on the intent of the policies and procedures that apply to their role.*

Under the existing PCI DSS compliance requirements, you only need to deliver security awareness training on an annual basis. However, from my experience, you can significantly improve the effectiveness of your "human firewalls" through a periodic program of security awareness refresher training.

Regular and periodic refresher training is less burdensome on your personnel and is less resource intensive. In order to make your training program effective,[10] ensure that it remains relevant to your target audience and use differing methods of delivery, for example:

- Face-to-Face presentations

- Newsletters

- Posters

- Email campaigns

- Quizzes

- Intranet notices

- Videos

Consider including security best practice advice that they can use to help protect them and their families, outside of the work environment, and do not be afraid to make some sessions interactive and thought-provoking. Remember that having some real-life examples based upon your perceived threat landscape really does help convey the importance of adhering to good security practices.

Maintaining Specialist Knowledge/Skillsets

An infamous quote from Richard Branson,[11] British business magnate, investor, author, and philanthropist, has never been more prevalent in the security environment:

> *"Train people well enough so they can leave, treat them well enough so they don't want to".*

—Richard Branson

---

[10]www.forbes.com/sites/forbestechcouncil/2019/08/16/
 seven-tips-for-a-successful-security-awareness-training-program/
[11]https://swiftkickhq.com/leadership-quotes-richard-branson/

Maintaining the effectiveness of your specialist, within your scope, has never been more important. Consequently, it is extremely important that you develop bespoke training development plans, where you are able to analyze their Strengths, Weaknesses, Opportunities, and Threats (SWOT) and to identify their short-term, medium-term, and long-term goals.

Having a formal development program shows the employee that you value their support and are willing to reward them with continual development, be that specialist conferences, training courses, or time for self-development (all relevant to their roles/responsibilities).

Such a program will also help you identify potential training/development or specialist resource risk, an extremely relevant concept given the apparent shortage of security skilled personnel.[12] If you are unable to recruit the people with the right skills/knowledge, are you able to identify suitable internal candidates?

Here are examples:

- IT Desktop support candidate wishing to become a network security specialist

  - Short-term goal

    - CompTIA A+

  - Medium-term goal

    - CompTIA Network+

  - Long-term goal

    - CompTIA Security+

Do you have the resource capacity to enable a suitable deputation in the event of your primary specialist being absent for a period of time (e.g., Holiday, Maternity/Paternity, Sickness, etc.) or in the event of your primary specialist handing in their employment notice?

- If your primary specialist becomes unavailable, what impact will this present?

  - Have you carried out a risk assessment?

---

[12]www.infosecurity-magazine.com/news/cybersecurity-skills-shortage-tops/

Building an Effective Security Culture

Figure 14-8. *Building a Security Culture*

A positive Security Culture[13] should be seen as being complementary to your business rather than being a barrier. It is important that everyone is encouraged to be part of your security program and should be rewarded for good practice while being encouraged to challenge bad practices.

The challenging of bad practices is probably the most difficult part of the development of a positive Security Culture. It is not within everyone's comfort zone to directly challenge bad practices. However, they should be provided with alternative means to report suspicious activities or bad practices. If something does not feel right, your staff should not feel embarrassed at raising an alert. It's better to have been told about something and to investigate it further. Even the minor violations could be the prequel to larger violations or could identify enhancements that are needed for the continued effectiveness of the supporting policies and procedures.

Critical to an effective Security Program is the two-way engagement with your stakeholders and frontline personnel.

---

[13]www.ncsc.gov.uk/collection/you-shape-security/a-positive-security-culture

Building a positive Security Culture needs Senior Management buy in and support and a team effort, ensure that all business are represented by their various department managers (or their appointed deputies) and have the opportunity to contribute to the development of an effective security culture. Department representatives will then be the most appropriate means of cascading the good practice method, as appropriate to their departments.

Managing Change

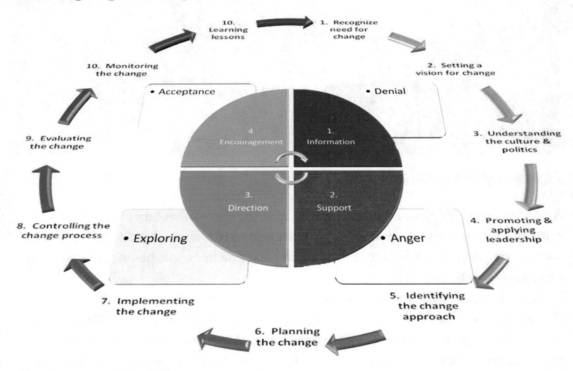

Figure 14-9. *Change Management Process*

It is quite apt that change management currently sandwiched in the center of the PCI DSS controls framework (v3.2.1), and is central to the success or failure of any data privacy and security program. Even minor changes can impact the effectiveness of the controls or present implications for other control measures.

Let's take, for example, an effective asset management process has escalated a risk associated with an in-scope system that is approaching its end-of-life/end-of-support date. As a result, the IT support team need to commence their procurement and change procedures. However, during the associated risk assessment, it was identified as a significant change, and, consequently, they need to ensure that the Information Security Manager has been notified so that they can make the arrangements for the post-installation vulnerability scan and penetration test.

Additionally, your record of changes becomes increasingly important for proactive security management *(consider the implications and potential fallback options and to identify unauthorized activities)* and reactive security management *(post-incident identification of potential root causes)*.

Any changes to your environment must be subject to your change management process. This needs to include clear parameters being defined as to what contributes to a minor or significant change and how retrospective risk assessments and recording of emergency changes are to be actioned and recorded.

All changes must be subject to change reviews in order to enable discussion, risk assessment, business justification, and formal approval.

Reality Bites

I have heard plenty of horror stories of poor people management practices and have had firsthand experience of the benefits of effectively managing your people assets and creating yourself an intelligence network, for example:

- Having established a network of Security Champions, following my first operational tour on counter intelligence field team (CIFT) duties, I soon received reports of a third-party national working acting abnormally. The individual was reported as attempting suicide on multiple occasions:

  - Attempted suicide by hanging in their living accommodation

    - *Roof beam that they had tied off their hanging noose collapsed before they had managed to hang themselves.*

  - Attempted suicide by running through an active minefield

    - *The individual missed every live mine.*

- Attempted suicide by drowning in an open water filtration facility (a.k.a. "Poo Pond")

  - *Their natural survival instincts kicked in and they scrambled themselves to the safety before ingesting sufficient sewage water.*

Being in a privileged role and suspecting that they may be undergoing external pressures to carry out actions that they were uncomfortable with, we launched initial investigations to try and ascertain the root cause for these disturbing activities. It turns out that the individual was severely depressed and that the external pressures were originating from their conflict between wanting to provide for their family and being apart from their loved ones for long periods of time.

- An old school Information Security Manager who only extended their reach to members of the IT department and who managed their ISO/IEC 27001 documentation by retaining it in a restricted file, briefing and prepping the relevant personnel on good practices, just once a year, in readiness for the annual audit. Consequently, no one knew what acceptable practices for the creation of strong passwords were and the desktop support team was just allowing members of the Board to continually reuse the same password when the password period came to expire.

- During a PCI DSS gap assessment, discovering a rogue wireless access point provides a direct insecure point of access and egress into the cardholder data environment. The compliance manager strongly objected to this having been placed there by a member of their team, despite it having been annotated an associated name. It turns out that this had been temporarily installed by their IT Manager in support of a business legitimate reason. However, the demands of the job meant that they had neglected to disconnect the connection once it was no longer required *(this had been an informal change and was not subject to any risk assessments, approval, or tracking).*

- While providing some independent oversight for a PCI DSS compliance program, I questioned why an organization still had an open connection to their penetration testing providers? This was 6 months after their annual penetration test had been carried out. The penetration testers were seen as "trusted partners," and it had been assumed that the security vendor connection would be safe/secure. However, this presumption increased the risk to their PCI DSS environment, in the event that the "trusted partner" was compromised and enabling an attacker the ability to move laterally from one environment to theirs.

- Following a spike in the number of corporate laptops being stolen from hired motor vehicles, when parked up in public car parks. The follow-up investigations revealed that the mobile device policy statement needed to be enhanced to mitigate this risk.

  - The employees were following the corporate policy, which stated that when travelling, all personnel must securely store corporate laptops (out of site) in the locked boot/trunk of their vehicle.

    - *The employees were arriving at the public parking area, with their corporate laptop in the main body of their motor vehicle. Remembering the policy, they would take the company laptop out of the main body of the car and be observed locking it into the boot/trunk of their vehicle and leaving the vehicle.*

    - *On their return to the vehicle, they were surprised to discover that the laptops had been stolen by opportunist thieves.*

Key Takeaways

Effective Data Privacy and Security programs need enterprise-wide team contributions and "Top-Level" Management support.

Do not expect a sole Information Security Manager or Data Privacy Officer (DPO) to be responsible for maintaining your compliance obligations, reducing risk, minimizing bad practices, and, thus, reducing the potential opportunities for a data breach.

Investment in the development and maintenance of your specialists is essential in helping to mature your Data Privacy and Security program.

Consider the potential benefits of having an enhanced security awareness program, delivered periodically across the entire organization and with more specialized and targeted training be provided to your payment card processing and support teams.

Security is the responsibility of EVERYONE!

- *Does your security awareness program extend beyond the PCI DSS scope?*
- *Does your Senior Executives support effective People Management?*
- *Is your security awareness training a once-a-year "tick box" approach?*
- *Do you have training development plans?*
- *Do you use a myriad of security awareness delivery mediums?*
- *Does your Data Privacy and Security program accommodate the human reactions to change?*
- *Does your change process recognize the interdependencies of your defensive/mitigation controls?*

Risks

The "Human Firewall" is an extremely effective risk mitigation countermeasure, providing you with an additional layer of monitoring and alerting.

Consequently, it is essential that this defensive layer receives sufficient investment to ensure that this is suitable and remains effective in the defense of your business.

It is important to recognize and remember that security is not a barrier to doing business but is a complementary resource that helps an organization operate securely and safely.

Ask yourself:

- *Do my personnel/employees work together in helping identify* ***ABNORMAL*** *or unsafe practices?*
- *Do all my specialists receive bespoke and tailored training to enhance their capabilities?*

- *Do I have a security committee to discuss and cascade good practices?*

- *Do I have a risk committee or change board to risk assess and approve/disapprove changes to my environment?*

- *Do I retain a record of all changes for audit purposes?*

- *Are changes considered against the potential planning and implication on other control requirements?*

- *Do I have a resilient "Human Firewall" or do I have risks associated to single points of failure?*

- *What is the potential impact of a single point of failure not being available?*

CHAPTER 15

The Ripple Effect

In this book I have been a strong advocate of the PCI DSS integrated data security controls framework, its strong heritage built from other industry security controls and its effectiveness to defend your business against your ever-present threats. I am still amazed to hear of those payment card security businesses who

- Bury their heads in the sand (ignoring their obligations to safeguard payment card data processing operations)

- Merely regard PCI DSS as a tick box approach

- Do not see any business benefits (return on investment (ROI))

- Don't perceive themselves to be of interest to the opportunist attackers

- Don't believe that they have any valuable data assets or business impacting IT systems

Imagine the potential costs of a critical system outage due to poorly maintained IT systems!

© Jim Seaman 2020
J. Seaman, *PCI DSS*, https://doi.org/10.1007/978-1-4842-5808-8_15

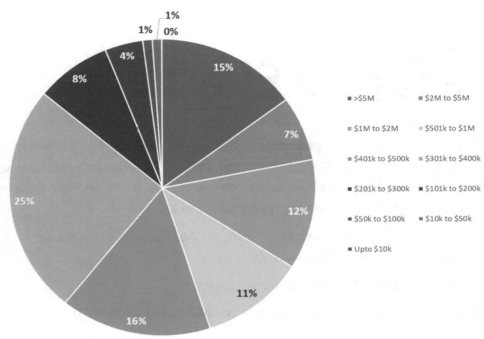

Figure 15-1. *Downtime Costs[1]*

With **25%** of businesses suffering downtime costs of between **£301k to $400k per hour**, have you calculated the cost of maintaining and protecting your operational, business critical systems vs. the potential revenue losses from having systems downtime[2]?

Can you afford not to have done so?

---

[1]www.statista.com/statistics/753938/
 worldwide-enterprise-server-hourly-downtime-cost/

[2]www.ntirety.com/calculating-the-real-cost-of-downtime-for-your-business/

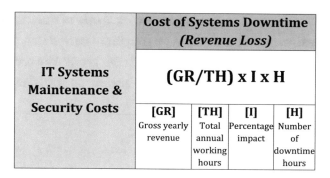

IT Systems Maintenance & Security Costs	Cost of Systems Downtime (Revenue Loss)			
	(GR/TH) x I x H			
	[GR] Gross yearly revenue	[TH] Total annual working hours	[I] Percentage impact	[H] Number of downtime hours

Figure 15-2. *Calculating Business ROI*

For example:

($10 million (GR) / 8760 (TH) × 10 (I) × 24 (H) = **$2,739.72 per day**

In this chapter, I will discuss some of the unseen benefits and advantages that occur in a business that embraces the implementation and maintenance of an effective PCI DSS program.

Throughout my career, I have observed businesses doing the bare minimum practices to secure their sensitive company and customer/employee personal data, often with the Board/Senior Management wanting to be secure but not understanding the actual costs associated with maintaining a protected data processing operations and systems, or with the responsibility being left with the IT teams who purchase ad hoc solutions, as the result of an effective sales pitch.

This frequently leads to a plethora of security tools being procured that do not integrate together to create a holistic defensive model. PCI DSS changes all of this, as this integrated controls framework has a layered architecture that culminates in requirements 10 and 11 for the effective monitoring and testing of your environment.

Consequently, an effective implementation of the requirements can significantly enhance your defensive posture and even with the smallest of scope can help create a "Ripple Effect" on your corporation's security culture.

Think of it like the ripples on a body of water.

If you think of your business as a calm body of water and the PCI DSS scope being the perfectly formed globule of water being dropped into the heart of your business, the ripples that are created will be seen to have much wider influences on other areas of your business.

Additionally, as the PCI DSS controls framework is one of the most detailed and specific for the protection of a single data type (payment card data), you can use this as a template for the protection of your other sensitive data types. However, without the need to be as prescriptive in the application of the appropriate controls needed to ring-fence your most valued data/systems.

Introduction

I recall the furious rantings of a business Director, who was trying to understand the first-line[3] Information Security team's[4] cyber security strategy and was unable to see how this was delivering a cohesive approach to effectively defend against their known threats. Consequently, they had two consistent responses:

- *"Are we 'Boiling the Ocean'?"*

  - Are we investing in the highest priority areas or are we trying to fix EVERYTHING?

- *"So what?"*

  - What does this mean? Should I be worried? What is the potential impact on the business?

Until this point, I had never appreciated the frustration of Senior Management, as I had been engrained into the belief that developing and maintaining secure environments just makes common sense. However, in business, a data privacy and security program needs to make business sense, for example:

When considering the purchase of a 24/7 network detection solution, which monitors the potential use of malicious software, this might appear to be an essential investment. However, what if this "standalone" security service has an annual cost of around $500k and does not include the centralized monitoring of the systems logs?

---

[3]www.iia.org.uk/resources/audit-committees/governance-of-risk-three-lines-of-defence/
[4]*First-line operational management has ownership, responsibility, and accountability for directly assessing, controlling, and mitigating risks.*

- Could this potentially be an extremely expensive service that only notifies me once the attackers have initiated the final step (Actions On Objectives) of their Cyber Kill Chain[5] without any detection of steps 1 to 6?

- Would this be too late to stop a mass exfiltration of data?

- Does this complement the other security tools and services?

This is where the integrated PCI DSS controls framework differs from the majority of the other Cyber/InfoSec controls frameworks, as each control is compartmentalized against a specific scope (payment card data systems and impacting/connecting IT systems). The Payment Card Industry Security Standards Council have identified the mitigation security controls that are needed to safeguard against the commonly known risks.

Applying these controls supports the creation of secure payment card data processing environments and can help create a team of security-aware personnel *(both in the engine room (IT systems support) and crew (data processing teams))*, who develop a greater understanding of what good practice looks like and who will be able to identify and report instances of ABNORMAL activities.

Even a small PCI DSS scope will provide interactions with other business areas. All of a sudden, you have an embedded security team that are interacting with other areas of the business. As a result, they will be encouraging good practice to other business departments.

Imagine that you are a software development business, which, in addition to providing PCI DSS compliant e-commerce solutions,[6] provides creative branding, marketing and strategy, interactive, software development services.

As a result of your PCI DSS scope, all your web development services have security considerations embedded into them, something that both your PCI DSS clients and non-PCI DSS clients will appreciate. However, only your in-scope PCI DSS environment is subject to an annual PCI DSS onsite assessment. Additionally, you have more security-aware employees influencing other business departments that may be handling other types of sensitive data (personal, financial, intellectual property, coding, etc.), which may need to be processed, stored, and transmitted in a secure manner.

---

[5]www.lockheedmartin.com/en-us/capabilities/cyber/cyber-kill-chain.html
[6]www.gamcreative.com/

For example, customers' personal data is increasingly being subject to legal requirements for secure processing:

- **European Union General Data Protection Regulation (EU GDPR: Article 32**[7]

  "Implement appropriate technical and organizational measures to ensure a level of security appropriate to the risk."

- **Canada's Personal Information Protection and Electronic Documents Act (PIPEDA): Principle 7**[8]

  "Personal information shall be protected by security safeguards appropriate to the sensitivity of the information."

- **Singapore's Personal Data Protection Act (PDPA): Data Protection by Design**[9]

  "An organization shall protect personal data in its possession or under its control by making reasonable security arrangements to prevent unauthorized access, collection, use, disclosure, copying, modification, disposal or similar risks."[10]

- **California Consumer Privacy Act of 2018 (CCPA)**[11]

  "Implement and maintain reasonable security procedures and practices appropriate to the nature of the information to protect the personal information."

---

[7] www.privacy-regulation.eu/en/article-32-security-of-processing-GDPR.htm

[8] www.priv.gc.ca/en/privacy-topics/privacy-laws-in-canada/the-personal-information-protection-and-electronic-documents-act-pipeda/pipeda-compliance-help/pipeda-compliance-and-training-tools/pipeda_sa_tool_200807/#principle7

[9] www.pdpc.gov.sg/-/media/Files/PDPC/PDF-Files/Other-Guides/Guide-to-Data-Protection-by-Design-for-ICT-Systems-(310519).pdf

[10] https://sso.agc.gov.sg/Act/PDPA2012#P1VI-

[11] www.isipp.com/resources/full-text-of-the-california-consumer-privacy-act-of-2018-ccpa/

- **Australian Privacy Principles (APP): APP 11 – Security of personal information**[12]

  "An APP entity must take reasonable steps to protect personal information it holds from misuse, interference and loss, as well as unauthorized access, modification or disclosure."

Consequently, with minimal effort, PCI DSS compliance is known to be extremely influential in enhancing other business areas, which may be subject to legal data protection requirements.

PCI DSS: Appropriate Technical and Organizational Measures

Okay, so we should now know that compliance with PCI DSS is extremely prescriptive, whereas compliance with your personal data laws and regulations is far less prescriptive and the responsibility is down to your organization to apply defensive measures that are commensurate with the risk.

However, how do you ensure that these are suitable and commensurate to the risk?

Are there further lessons that can be taken from your PCI DSS compliance program?

Well, payment card data is both financial data and personal data that is a high-value data asset for criminals and needs to be safeguarded as you might protect high volumes of cash, for instance, layering your physical security measures, keeping the cash under lock and key (when stored or in transit), minimizing retention periods, restricting access, and ensuring that supporting systems are well maintained to minimize the risk of failure/compromise.

We know that today's criminals are scavengers, seeking to exploit opportunities to harvest together pieces of the "Identity jigsaw" puzzles in order to monetize personal data (Identity Theft). Consequently, all pieces of the "Identity Jigsaw" have an intrinsic value, and the greater the number of pieces they are able to harvest, the greater their aggregated value.

---

[12]www.oaic.gov.au/privacy/australian-privacy-principles-guidelines/
  chapter-11-app-11-security-of-personal-information/

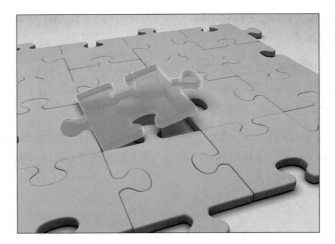

Figure 15-3. *Piecing Together the "Identity Jigsaw"*

In a recent report by the University of Texas (2019 International Identity Theft Assessment and Prediction Report[13]), digital vulnerabilities were perceived to represent almost **75%** of the cases of Identity theft.

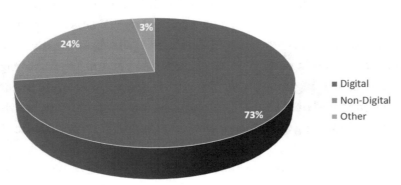

Figure 15-4. *Digital vs. Non-digital*

In addition, according to UK Finance,[14] unauthorized financial fraud losses across payment cards, remote banking, and checks totaled **£844.8 million** in 2018, an **increase of 16%** *(compared with 2017)* – both of which need a combination of personal data and

---

[13]https://identity.utexas.edu/assets/uploads/publications/CID_ITAP_Report_2019.pdf
[14]www.ukfinance.org.uk/system/files/Fraud%20The%20Facts%202019%20-%20FINAL%20
ONLINE.pdf

payment card data to enable the criminals to monetarize their activities and make it a profitable business.

Each year the Federal Trade Commission's (FTC's) Consumer Sentinel Network Data Books[15] continue to confirm that identify theft remains a consistent and ever-present threat to today's businesses and consumers:

- 2018 – **3 Million** reported incidents

Top Three Categories

1. Imposter scams

2. Debt collection

3. Identity theft

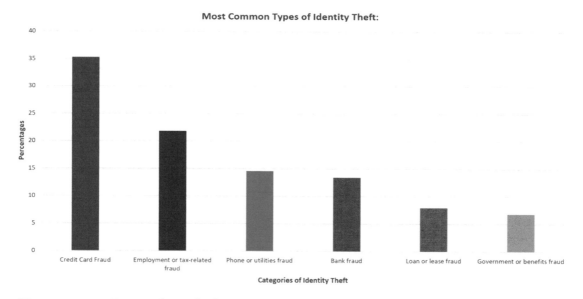

Figure 15-5. *Types of ID Theft*

At the heart of all these cases is the misuse of personal data, so with this being the case, do businesses need to do more for the protection of their consumers and employees?

If so, can we apply lessons learned from the PCI DSS requirements?

---

[15]www.ftc.gov/reports/consumer-sentinel-network-data-book-2018

Requirement 1: Install and Maintain a Firewall Configuration to Protect Sensitive Data

Increasingly we are seeing reported instances of cyber criminals gaining a persistent presence within corporate network environments. Often, once the criminals have managed to compromise a poorly managed perimeter asset or third-party-connected asset, they will then seek to identify opportunities to move laterally across the compromised networks.

During this period of Command and Conquer, the criminals are known to carrying out reconnaissance of the internal systems and connections. Having identified all the systems, the criminals then seek to map their potential attack pathways to intercept data in transit or at rest. They are seeking to identify points of potential ingress and egress, where they are more likely to identify the weaker areas of a network and the location of the corporation's "Crown Jewels." It is worrying that the criminals will not be deterred by encrypted data and, in the impact of not being able to profit from their actions, are reported to resort to impacting the business operations through the disabling of business critical systems[16] – essentially the criminals are making a statement:

If we can't make use of your data/IT systems, neither can you!

Considerable components of requirement 1 are similar to the content of the United Kingdom's National Cyber Security Centre's (NCSC's) Network Security section of their recommended ten steps to Cyber Security[17]:

- **Manage the network perimeter.**

   "Manage access to ports, protocols and applications by filtering and inspecting all traffic at the network perimeter to ensure that only traffic which is required to support the business is being exchanged. Control and manage all inbound and outbound network connections."

---

[16]www.europol.europa.eu/newsroom/news/cybercrime-becoming-bolder-data-centre-of-crime-scene

[17]www.ncsc.gov.uk/collection/10-steps-to-cyber-security?curPage=/collection/10-steps-to-cyber-security/the-10-steps/network-security

- **Protect the internal network.**

  "Ensure that there is no direct routing between internal and external networks (especially the Internet), which limits the exposure of internal systems to network attack from the Internet."

- ***Segregate networks as sets.***

  "Identify, group and isolate critical business systems and apply appropriate network security controls to them."

- ***Secure wireless access.***

  "All wireless access points should be appropriately secured, only allowing known devices to connect to corporate Wi-Fi services. Security scanning tools may be useful to detect and locate unauthorized or spoof wireless access points."

Clearly the criminals see a value in identifying and documenting your corporate network, so it is essential that your business does the same.

Do you maintain periodic scans of your perimeter and internal systems and connecting systems so that you understand?

- Data flows

- Critical business systems

- Personal data processing systems

- Personal data storage systems

- Interconnecting systems

- Internal gateways

- Delineations between trusted and untrusted environments

- Any potential exploitation opportunities

Requirement 2: Do Not Use Vendor-supplied Defaults for System Passwords and Other Security Parameters

Step 2 of the NCSC's ten steps to Cyber Security[18] shows a strong affiliation to PCI DSS requirement 2 and clearly demonstrates the integrated nature of the PCI DSS controls framework:

- ***Create and maintain hardware and software inventories.***

  "Create inventories of all authorized hardware and software used across the organization. Ideally the inventory should capture the physical location, business owner and purpose of hardware together with the version and patch status of all software. Tools can be used to help identify unauthorized hardware or software."

- ***Manage your operating systems and software.***

  "Implement a secure baseline build for all systems and components, including hardware and software. Any functionality or application that does not support a user or business need should be removed or disabled. The secure build profile should be managed by a configuration control process and any deviation from the standard build should be documented and approved."

Requirements 1 and 2 combine to make the unauthorized infiltration and extraction increasingly more difficult for opportunist attackers. The network architecture should be visualized in network and data flow diagrams, with the identified systems being correlated against the asset inventory and with all changes being subjected to documented approval. Anything not confirming to these records would require immediate investigation, and any systems approaching their end-of-life (EOL) or end-of-support (EOS) were subject to risk assessment practices.

---

[18]www.ncsc.gov.uk/collection/10-steps-to-cyber-security/the-10-steps/secure-configuration

Requirement 3: Protect Stored Sensitive Data

If you need to store sensitive data, ensure that unnecessary retention is avoided and that all aggregated/high-value sensitive data is kept in a vault under, strictly controlled, lock and key, so that if your corporate network is compromised, the sensitive data remains protected.

Periodic checks should be carried out to ensure that unnecessary or ad hoc data storage (outside your vaults) is avoided and to ensure that all personal data stores are identified to ensure that the retention remains within your business's risk tolerances. How well do you understand?

- The nature, scope, context, and purposes of the processing

- The necessity, proportionality, and compliance measures

- The risks to individuals

- Any additional measures to mitigate those risks

It is important to ensure that you have identified all potential areas where payment card data may have been deliberately, or accidentally, retained. This can be achieved through the use of automated sensitive data discovery scanning solutions, such as

- Memoryze[19]

- Groundlabs[20]

- DataSecurity Plus[21]

- Spirion[22]

---

[19]www.fireeye.com/services/freeware/memoryze.html

[20]www.groundlabs.com/

[21]www.manageengine.com/data-security/index.html?topMenu

[22]www.spirion.com/sensitive-data-discovery/

Requirement 4: Encrypt Transmission of Sensitive Data Across Open, Public Networks

In order to make use of sensitive data, your business will need to ensure that this data remains under lock and key while in transit. Modern criminals have become increasingly proficient at intercepting sensitive data while in transit. Consequently, in the event that these transmissions are intercepted, the sensitive data should remain under lock and key to ensure that it cannot be used by criminals. Public-facing technologies (e.g., Web, virtual private networks (VPNs), email, etc.) are easy targets for opportunist criminals.

Therefore, you should periodically identify the public-facing points of egress/ingress, where sensitive data assets will be moved from one corporate environment to another.

This can be easily achieved and included into your data privacy and security program using tools such as

- ExtraHop[23]
- Glassware[24]
- Wireshark[25]
- Qualys SSL Labs[26]
- SSL Checker[27]
- GeekFlare[28]
- Wormly[29]
- DigiCert[30]

---

[23]www.extrahop.com/products/security/
[24]www.glasswire.com/
[25]www.wireshark.org/
[26]www.ssllabs.com/ssltest/
[27]www.thesslstore.com/ssltools/ssl-checker.php
[28]https://gf.dev/tls-test
[29]www.wormly.com/test_ssl
[30]www.digicert.com/help/

Requirement 5: Protect All Systems Against Malware and Regularly Update Anti-virus Software or Programs

This is another of the UK NCSC's top 10 steps for cyber security:

- **Malware Prevention**

  "Malicious software, or malware is an umbrella term to cover any code or content that could have a malicious, undesirable impact on systems. Any exchange of information carries with it a degree of risk that malware might be exchanged, which could seriously impact your systems and services. The risk may be reduced by implementing appropriate security controls as part of an overall 'defense in depth' approach."

  - Malware threats remained an ever-present threat[31] during 2019.[32]

  - Botnets, Ransomware, and Cryptomining/Jacking were reported as the top 3 malware threats of 2019.[33]

Requirement 6: Develop and Maintain Secure Systems and Applications

A common avenue of attack is through poorly managed IT systems and software applications. Consequently, it is essential that any sensitive data processing systems are not exposed to being exploited. Frequently, out-of-date software and hardware provide criminals the opportunity to infiltrate your corporate environment, either via a public-facing system or web-coding error that allows the criminal unauthorized access to the supporting system layers.

It is important to ensure that any newly identified vulnerabilities are risk assessed and prioritized for timely remediation, based upon their criticality, and that the web developers use SecDevOps[34] best practices to ensure that they do not inadvertently

---

[31]www.cybok.org/media/downloads/Malware__Attack_Technology_issue_1.0.pdf

[32]https://threatpost.com/biggest-malware-threats-of-2019/151423/

[33]www.eweek.com/security/webroots-listing-of-the-nastiest-malware-of-2019

[34]www.pcisecuritystandards.org/documents/PCI-Secure-Software-Standard-v1_0.pdf?agreement=true&time=1547813202710

introduce any new exploitable vulnerabilities to the external facing, high-risk interfaces. Remember, the web-based customer interfaces have significantly changed, and they are now increasingly used as customer interfaces and not just information "read-only" interfaces.

Of course, as with anything related to systems or software integrity, any changes need to be strictly controlled, risk assessed, and monitored.

Requirement 7: Restrict Access to Sensitive Data by Business Need to Know

The Need to Know/Need to Access principles should be based upon least privilege, so as to minimize the potential impact and risk. As a consequence, this is another of the UK NCSC's top 10 steps to cyber security:[35]

- **Limit user privileges.**

  "Users should be provided with the reasonable minimum rights and permissions to systems, services and information that they need to fulfill their business role."

Requirement 8: Identify and Authenticate Access to System Components

Why wouldn't you limit and control access management to your estate? Very few would have unrestricted access to the keys to your house or motor vehicle, so why would we do this with access to our corporate network and sensitive data processing systems? All personnel should be strictly limited and educated as to the importance of creating and managing robust access credentials.

This is an increasingly difficult element to maintain, given the volume of passwords (both business and personal) are expected to commit to memory, ensuring that they are not duplicating credentials or sharing credentials. Additional measures can be applied through the use of multi-factor authentication (MFA) for higher-risk accounts/access (e.g., Privileged users, Remote users, etc.).

---

[35]www.ncsc.gov.uk/collection/10-steps-to-cyber-security/the-10-steps/
  managing-user-privileges

Remember, if it is more convenient for the authorized user, it can become even more convenient for the attacker wishing to gain unauthorized access to your corporate network, information systems, and sensitive data.

To assist your employees, you may wish to consider the benefits of the following resources:

- Password Management Systems (e.g., 1password,[36] Dashlane,[37] Lastpass,[38] etc.)

- Have I Been Pwned[39]?

  - Pwned Passwords[40]

- Password strength checker[41]

Requirement 9: Restrict Physical Access to Sensitive Data

If your attackers are unable to gain a foothold within your virtual environment, they will look for opportunities to gain unauthorized access to your physical environment where the supporting networks, information systems, or removable media may reside. Probably one of the easiest type of attacks, the perpetrator only needs a limited toolset and a combination of guile and imagination to gain unauthorized access to your physical assets.

It is important to note that testing for the non-digital-style attack (social engineering) is not a requirement in the current version of the PCI DSS integrated controls framework. However, this is a well-known tactics for cyber criminals and organized criminal gangs:

- KVM Switch Attack[42]

- Keylogger Attack[43]

---

[36]https://1password.com/

[37]www.dashlane.com/

[38]www.lastpass.com/

[39]https://haveibeenpwned.com/

[40]https://haveibeenpwned.com/Passwords

[41]https://howsecureismypassword.net/

[42]www.theregister.co.uk/2014/04/25/kvm_crooks_jailed/

[43]https://securelist.com/keyloggers-how-they-work-and-how-to-detect-them-part-1/36138/

Requirement 10: Track and Monitor All Access to Network Resources and Sensitive Data

This is another of the UK NCSC's recommended top 10 steps to Cyber Security:[44]

- ***Monitoring***

    "System monitoring provides a capability that aims to detect actual or attempted attacks on systems and business services. Good monitoring is essential in order to effectively respond to attacks. In addition, monitoring allows you to ensure that systems are being used appropriately in accordance with organizational policies. Monitoring is often a key capability needed to comply with legal or regulatory requirements."

Criminals having a median dwell time of **78 days**[45] demonstrates that businesses are recognizing the importance of being able to identify and respond to ABNORMAL activities *(reduced from **416 days** in 2011)*.

Requirement 11: Regularly Test Security Systems and Processes

Independent security testing enables you to be reassured that everything continues to operate securely while enabling you to rapidly identify and remediate any vulnerabilities before an attacker has the opportunity to exploit and profit from any poorly maintained network, systems, and practices. Periodic testing should be regarded as an integral and supportive component of your data privacy and security program, ensuring that any identified deviations or issues are investigated to ensure that these are not originated from poor practices.

It is essential that any testing is carried out by independent and suitable skilled personnel to ensure that appropriate testing is established. All periodic testing of critical systems and sensitive data processing systems should be documented, along with the tracking of any remediation activities, ensuring that any lessons learned opportunities can be applied.

---

[44]www.ncsc.gov.uk/collection/10-steps-to-cyber-security/the-10-steps/monitoring
[45]https://content.fireeye.com/m-trends

Requirement 12: Maintain a Policy that Addresses Information Security for All Personnel

You cannot expect your personnel to know what is expected of them and to understand what "good" looks like unless you provide them with the corporate rules and procedures for the specific roles and responsibilities. This is essential for ensuring that they can adhere to these rules and to operate in a safe and secure manner.

However, setting the rules that articulate the "Tone at the top" is only a small part of the job and your personnel should be periodically tested as to the intent and content of your rules and procedures.

Think of it as being licensed to drive a motor vehicle. The extent of the rules and procedures are commensurate with the potential damage/impact that is presented by the vehicle type. Personnel should be policed and periodically re-educated to refresh their understanding of these documented rules and procedures. Failure to adhere to the rules should result in disciplinary or re-education or, in some cases, the removal of their "licenses to drive."

Conclusion

The PCI DSS heritage has a clear alignment with other cyber security controls frameworks, and the implementation into your business environment should be regarded as being complementary to the success of your brand, ensuring that good practices are introduced for application of security by default/security by design concepts.

This, in turn, will be influential in helping develop more secure data processing practices for other sensitive data processing business operations.

Modern businesses have an increasingly heavy reliance on digital processing of sensitive data. Consequently, the enhancement of these "out-of-scope" environments using lessons learned from the PCI DSS integrated controls framework can provide additional defense of your environment.

This will further enhance the protection of your company's Brand/Reputation and reduce your risks of a breach of sensitive data assets or sensitive data processing systems.

Key Takeaways

There are valuable lessons that can be learned from the PCI DSS integrated security controls framework. These principles can be applied to enhance other sensitive data processing environments.

The PCI DSS integrated security controls framework has a strong heritage, with many similarities apparent between other industry security controls frameworks.

The application of consistent controls, using the PCI DSS security controls practices, across both the in-scope and out-of-scope environments can help enhance your business and reduce the opportunities for attackers to compromise your supporting corporate networks/systems and sensitive data processing environments should be regarded as a business enhancement.

Calculating the cost of a breach, or system downtimes, against the costs of maintaining the Confidentiality, Integrity, and Availability of these supporting systems will help your business leaders appreciate the potential ROI of your data privacy and security program.

PCI DSS compliance should be treated as an integral part of business operations and as being essential to the protection of your business's reputation!

Customers expect you to provide secure and resilient business systems to ensure that sensitive data is protected and systems availability is maintained.

- *Does your business see PCI DSS compliance as a business enhancement or as a hindrance?*

Risks

Payment card data is only one of the items listed on the shopping lists of today's cyber criminals. They will seek to exploit any unprotected network/systems and to steal any data assets that they are able to use or monetarize for their profit.

Consequently, it is essential that businesses consider the potential for applying the defensive benefits of the PCI DSS integrated controls framework beyond the confines of your "In-scope" environments.

You can significantly reduce your associated risks by treating PCI DSS compliance with a reduced scope *(periodically validated (e.g., Report on compliance (RoC), self-assessment questionnaire (SAQ))* and applying the intent of these security controls across wider areas of your business *(periodically validated by your internal audit process)*.

Ask yourself:

- *Do I have sensitive data processing operations that extend wider than payment card data?*

- *Is this data a target of the modern cyber criminals?*

- *Do I have an effective data privacy and security program that helps mitigate the risks associated with my sensitive data processing operations?*

- *Could my business apply lessons learned from the PCI DSS compliance program?*

- *Would the application of consistent controls, beyond the PCI DSS scope, help protect other data types?*

CHAPTER 16

Cometh the Year, Month, Day, Hour

Given the importance of PCI DSS compliance to level 1 Merchant/Service Provider businesses, a great deal of nervousness is felt by organizations. As a result, they may end up feeling pressured into staying with the same qualified security assessment company (QSAC) to validate their compliance. These companies often become disenfranchised with the whole process. Either they feel that they start to receive less of a level of service that they received at the start of their engagement, they do not receive a consistent level of quality service from the QSAC, they receive promises that never come to bear, or they do not receive consistent QSA approaches. However, because of the inconsistencies between QSACs, they feel that they would be disadvantaged if they were to shop around.

This is far from being close to the truth!

As a consumer of QSA professional services, the Payment Card Industry Security Standards Council (PCI SSC) stipulate that all QSACs must meet a minimum standard and all QSAs must adhere to their principles outlined within the PCI SSC Code of Professional Responsibility.[1]

Additionally, at the outset the company applying to become a registered QSAC must ensure that they and all their QSAs meet and maintain the qualification requirements for qualified security assessors (QSA).[2]

---

[1]www.pcisecuritystandards.org/documents/PCI_SSC_Code_of_Professional_
Responsibility.pdf

[2]www.pcisecuritystandards.org/documents/QSA_Qualification_Requirements_v3_0.pdf?agr
eement=true&time=1516980594990

© Jim Seaman 2020
J. Seaman, *PCI DSS*, https://doi.org/10.1007/978-1-4842-5808-8_16

These provisions include

- **QSAC**

  - Business Legitimacy

  - Independence

  - Business Insurance Coverage

  - Payment of PCI SSC Processing Fees

  - Maintain PCI SSC Agreement

  - Capabilities – Services and Experience

    - Maintain a dedicated information security practice that includes staff with specific job functions that support the information security practice

  - Maintain an internal Quality Assurance program

  - Inform each client of the QSA Feedback Form[3] upon commencement of each PCI SSC Assessment

- **QSA**

  - Pass background checks

  - Possess enough information security knowledge and experience to conduct technically complex security assessments

  - Possess a minimum of one-year experience in each of the following information security disciplines

    - Application security

    - Information systems security

    - Network security

---

[3]www.pcisecuritystandards.org/assessors_and_solutions/
qualified_security_assessors_feedback

- Possess a minimum of 1-year experience in each of the following audit/ assessment disciplines

  - IT security auditing

  - Information security risk assessment or risk management

- Possess a current Information Security (e.g., CISM, CISSP, etc.) and Audit (e.g., CISA, ISO/IEC 27001 Internal Auditor, etc.) qualification

- Maintain knowledge about the PCI DSS and all applicable documents on the PCI SSC web site

- Attend annual QSA Employee training provided by PCI SSC, and legitimately pass, of their own accord without any unauthorized assistance, all examinations conducted as part of training

  - *If a QSA Employee fails to pass any exam in connection with such training, the QSA Employee must no longer lead or manage any PCI SSC Assessment until successfully passing the exam.*

- Adhere to the PCI SSC Code of Professional Responsibility

Consequently, as the consumer, businesses should expect to receive a minimum standard and consistent level of professional management consultancy services.

In order to ensure that the QSA professional management consultancy services remain consistent and meet an organization's expectations for the paid-for services, it is essential that QSACs provide specific, measurable, achievable, realistic, and timebound (SMART) objectives as part of their commitment to complying with the PCI SSC principles.

As a level 1 business, the QSA and supporting professional security testing fees (Web Application testing, approved scanning vendor (ASV), penetration testing, segmentation testing, etc.) can prove to be an extremely high ongoing expense.

It is essential that such organizations are supported by their QSAC, so that they are well prepared for their annual onsite assessment. Additionally, these businesses should be encouraged to shop around each year, so that they evaluate their existing QSAC against the offerings of a sample of rival competing QSACs. This is essential for ensuring that the best value for money service is being received *(This should not be based purely on the unit cost of the services provided but also based on what is included in their proposals).*

Remember that QSACs need to remain completely independent which means that you are not disadvantaged by using a variety of different security testing vendors, in addition to the QSAC.

Additionally, periodic rotation of QSAC providers can be extremely beneficial with differing approaches, helping you gain differing perspectives on your compliance efforts.

The purpose of this chapter is to outline what should be expected from a professional management consultancy service provider (PMCSP) offering.

Introduction

Okay, so you're a business that has successfully negotiated your way through the complexities of PCI DSS and are now looking to engage the services of a PMCSP to achieve the required sign off that your efforts are aligned with the PCI DSS controls framework.

An effective offering needs to provide a better understanding and transparency between the client and the PMCSP. Additionally, the PMCSP needs to align to a consistent standard to provide better value and to reduce in the PCI DSS level 1 assessments. The objective of the standard is to enhance the quality, professionalism, and interoperability of the provided management services.

The PMCSP needs to ensure that the adherence to their standard is supported by Senior Management and that all their personnel adhere to and endorse the standard. Such a standard will be formalized and applied against every engagement. Think of it as being like the investigative interviewing training (a.k.a. PEACE Model[4]) received and followed by the police service.

In essence, your annual PCI DSS compliance is much more than an onsite audit and is more aligned to a security investigation, where the QSA needs to investigate your adherence to the PCI DSS rules, observe the supporting standard operating procedures (SOPs), review systems configurations, and interview the supporting personnel (interacting with cardholder data (CHD) and systems support staff) to ensure that you

---

[4]www.app.college.police.uk/app-content/investigations/investigative-interviewing/

are suitably applying the appropriate controls and are effectively mitigating the risks associated with your high-risk operations.

As per a formal police investigation, a formal report needs to be written (and subject to an independent quality assurance review) and all supporting evidence collated. For every control, a QSA statement is required with supporting evidence for each and every statement collated.

Both the formal report (report on compliance (RoC)) and the supporting evidence are to be securely retained for a period of 3 years and made available to the PCI SSC/Card Brands upon request in support of a post-incident investigation.

For lower-risk card payment operations, these businesses are permitted to complete a self-assessment questionnaire (SAQ) as their validation of compliance. These can be completed without the need for a QSA; however, this should be completed by someone who is familiar with the PCI DSS controls framework and who has experience of auditing/assessing IT systems and processes. It is advisable to imitate the procedures involved in a formal level 1 RoC assessment, ensuring that the person completing the review is independent to the card payment operations and making sure that the completed SAQs, and supporting evidence, are securely retained for the same 3-year period.

Background

Having been an RAF Policeman for 22 years and having spent the last 10 years of service as an InfoSec and CompSec specialist investigator, the transition to becoming a QSA in early 2013 came naturally to me. However, it is worth knowing the process for becoming a QSA to appreciate why there may be potential differences in the delivery of PCI DSS onsite assessments.

An individual selected to become a QSA, initially, needs to have 1-year experience of **EACH** of the following five security disciplines:

- Application security
- Information systems security
- Network security
- IT security auditing
- Information security risk assessment/management

Additionally, they need to have a certification from both List A[5] (Information Security) and List B[6] (auditing) *(Remember, passing an exam can be achieved through intensive "Boot Camps"! (these can be as short as a weekend to 5 days)).*

This enables them to be selected to attain the **2-day** intensive residential QSA training course. Having completed this course, they are deemed to be the qualified to deliver PCI DSS onsite assessments *(Instant Expert, Just Add Water!)*. The reality is that their certifications and experience may not have been as explicit as may be required to be considered a good PCI DSS generalist, who has had sufficient exposure to incidents within the aforementioned five security disciplines.

For most information security professionals entering the QSA environment, post qualification is a very steep learning curve as they try to apply their knowledge, skills, and experience with a PCI DSS lens. It is not reasonable to expect a newly qualified QSA to know all the "ins and outs" of the PCI DSS controls framework. However, this does often happen as the QSACs look to redeem some return on their investments.

Don't get me wrong; there are some outstanding QSAs out there and that younger QSAs need to be given the opportunity to "cut their teeth!" and it is the responsibility of the PMCSP (QSAC) to be transparent with you at the start of any engagement.

Note

- If dealing with a "Sales"-focused customer relationship, ensure that you get the guarantees written into your contracts. If you're being sold a "Gold" service at "Gold" prices, it is fair that it is what you should expect to receive.

- Remember, do your due diligence to ensure you know what service you are likely to get!

Be wary, ensure that you are getting value for money when hiring the services you're desiring!

---

[5](ISC)2 Certified Information System Security Professional (CISSP), ISACA Certified Information Security Manager (CISM), or Certified ISO 27001 Lead Implementer.

[6]ISACA Certified Information Systems Auditor (CISA), GIAC Systems and Network Auditor (GSNA), Certified ISO 27001 Lead Auditor/Internal Auditor, IRCA ISMS Auditor or higher (e.g., Auditor/Lead Auditor, Principal Auditor), or IIA Certified Internal Auditor (CIA).

Formal Assessment Expectations

Principles

A professional QSAC should "Do as They Preach!" and, as they expect of you, have a policy framework and a consistent defined approach, employing a suite of formal principles.

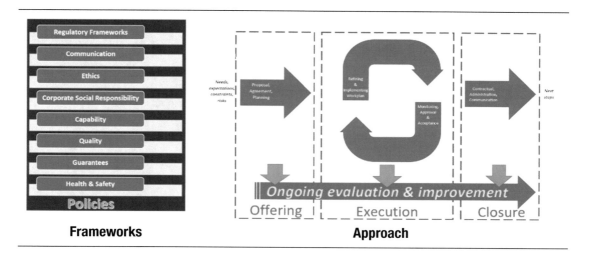

Frameworks   **Approach**

Policies

The PMCSP (QSAC) should maintain a suite of policies to outline the expected behaviors of their personnel.

Regulatory Framework

PMCSP (QSAC) maintain an appropriate level of awareness of the relevant laws, policies, rules, regulations, and standards that govern their offered services.

Communication

Maintaining a clear understanding between the client and the PMCSP (QSAC) is critical to the success of the assessment. Effective communication maximizes understanding, creating confidence, and minimizing risks.

Ethics

- **Code of conduct**

  Professional codes of conduct and business ethics should be engrained into every client engagement to help guide the conduct of the PMCSP (QSAC) personnel.

- **Values**

  A statement of values helps guide the professional conduct of the PMCSP (QSAC) personnel, for example:

  - Efficiency

  - Quality

  - Stability

  - Confidentiality

  - Honesty

  - Transparency

  - Responsibility

  - Flexibility

  - Commitment to continual improvement

  - Respect

  - Mutual benefit

  - Commitment to excellence

  - Common understanding

Corporate Social Responsibility

A statement of corporate social responsibility helps guide the professional conduct of the PMCSP (QSAC) personnel.

Capability

The PMCSP (QSAC) should only accept those assessments in which they are able to fulfill in a professional manner and in accordance with the PCI SSC's principles.

In the event that the PMCSP (QSAC) personnel has reason to believe that the agreed outcomes of the assessment cannot be met within the terms of the agreement, the PMCSP (QSAC) should immediately inform the client of the findings and renegotiate the agreement. For example, this might be that the PMCSP (QSAC) is not licensed to deliver the assessment in all of the client's card payment processing locations. Consequently, these additional regional assessments may need to be outsourced to another PMCSP (QSAC), resulting in onsite collaborative assessments.

Quality

The PMCSP (QSAC) should prepare a quality plan to anticipate, manage, and quantify any risks and issues *(e.g., aligned with the ISO/IEC 9000 series[7])*.

Guarantees

The PMCSP (QSAC) should negotiate and agree on the conditions of any guarantees to the services being provided. This should be guarantees from both the PMCSP (QSAC) and the clients.

Health and Safety

The PMCSP (QSAC) should maintain a statement of Health and Safety to help guide the professional conduct of their personnel.

Ongoing Evaluation and Improvement

The PMCSP (QSAC) should ensure that all assessments are subject to independent peer reviews. This needs to be a formalized and structured process for the proactive evaluation and with all reviews and changes being subject to documented change and controls tracking. The reviews should include

---

[7]`www.iso.org/iso-9001-quality-management.html`

- Diagnosis of the effectiveness of the assessment

- Recommendations for corrective actions

- Implementation of new/enhanced processes and methods

An effective evaluation strategy and policy should exist for the duration of the relationship between the client and the PMCSP (QSAC).

The evaluation strategy should be subject to period reviews to confirm the effectiveness of the process.

Offering

There are several activities that can be expected before the execution of an assessment, for example:

- Identification of pre-sale and client requirements, to be performed between the PMCSP (QSAC) and the client

- Supplier selection, to be performed by the client, considering the technical/economic proposals submitted by the PMCSP (QSAC)

  - *3 x PMCSP (QSAC) proposals are recommended for review/ comparison.*

- Specifications' definition, to be performed by the client/ PMCSP (QSAC) – or by both, as a combined effort

  - *Includes analysis and conceptualization of the problem to be solved, approach to service to be asked for, and the budget for these activities*

The purpose of the offering is to reach an agreement between the PMCSP (QSAC) and the client on the services to be provided. The offering should detail the PMCSP (QSAC)'s understanding of the client needs, the expectations, and the client's objectives, as well as any constraints or risks associated with the assessment, and any significant changes that are beyond the scope of the change control process. Additionally, the offering must include the outcome of the assessment, which is the legally binding agreement between the PMCSP (QSAC) and the client *(e.g., Specifications of the services and deliverables to be provided and the rights and obligations for each of the parties).*

Execution

A detailed and bespoke work plan should be provided, detailing how the assessment will be executed, for example:

- Information gathering

- Analysis

- Scenarios and/or Recommendations

- Decisions taken

- Implementation of decisions

- Preparation for acceptance and closure

    - This is an extremely important part of the assessment, whereby both the client and PMCSP (QSAC) agree and close the findings.

    - *Consider the implications of a conflict of findings between previous QSA reviews.*

Essential to the success is the management and monitoring of the assessment, ensuring that planning and continuous coordination between the client and PMCSP (QSAC) is enabled. This includes

- Project governance

- A project management approach (e.g., PIE FARM)

- Effective resources management *(both from the PMCSP (QSAC) and the client to ensure that the right people and systems are made available at the right time).*

- Monitoring the progress and change control

- Risk management

- Quality

- Communication and reporting

Closure

Having successfully completed the assessment and delivered the report on compliance (RoC) and support attestation on compliance (AoC) does not mean that the engagement is closed.

Final closure should include

- Legal and contractual matters

- Final evaluation and improvement

  - Continual learning and development opportunity for both PMCSP (QSAC) and the client

  - *What went well?*

  - *What areas could be improved?*

- Administrative matters

- Communication

- Any outstanding minor issues

Too often, PMCSPs (QSACs) fail to fully close out the assessment and treat the delivery of the final documentation as the end of the engagement. However, this is the point where the client is provided the opportunity to ask any final questions and to agree that the engagement has met *(and hopefully exceeded)* their original expectations.

Annual PCI DSS Assessment

Now that you understand what "Good" looks like, you are better placed to work in conjunction with your PMCSPs (QSACs). Whether you are a level 1 Merchant or Service Provider, you need to ensure that you are able to maintain your PCI DSS compliance. To achieve this, you need to be well prepared, which involves early planning and engagement and obtaining agreed guarantees from your chosen PMCSP (QSAC).

Planning and Preparation

Having successfully achieved your annual PCI DSS compliance after a short period of recovery, it is important to review the findings/observations identified during the assessment and to take the opportunity to implement opportunities for improvement.

Next, as a team effort, start planning your schedule for the following year's PCI DSS activities by identifying and scheduling the mandatory control actions (e.g., CTRL F of the latest version of PCI DSS).

See the following data for example.

Quarterly Activities

Data Discovery	• Identify person responsible for activity.
	    • Schedule dates for activity.
	• Identify and agree methodology to be used.
	• Identify person responsible for review *(Governance)*.
	    • Schedule dates for review.
	• Identify location for secure storage of supporting evidence *(ASV reports, review comments, re-scans, etc.)*.

Rogue Wireless Checks	• Identify person responsible for activity.
	    • Schedule dates for activity.
	• Identify and agree methodology to be used.
	• Identify person responsible for review *(Governance)*.
	    • Schedule dates for review.

Internal Vulnerability Scans	• Identify person responsible for activity.
	    • Is the individual still independent, suitably trained, and skilled?
	        • Schedule dates for activity.
	• Identify person responsible for review *(Governance)*.
	    • Schedule dates for review.
	• Identify personnel responsible for remediation activities.
	    • Schedule potential deadlines for remediation activities.
	        • Schedule potential dates for confirmatory re-scans.
	• Identify location for secure storage of supporting evidence *(ASV reports, review comments, re-scans, etc.)*.

(continued)

External Vulnerability (ASV) Scans	• Identify Approved Scanning Vendor (ASV) responsible for activity.
	• Identify Approved Scanning Vendor.
	    • *Consider 3 x potential vendors for the delivery of 4 x ASV scans over the year.*
	• Ensure that the vendors are on the approved list.[8]
	• Review contracts.
	• Procure services of preferred ASV.
	    • Agree and schedule dates for activity.
	• Identify person responsible for review *(Governance)*.
	    • Schedule dates for review.
	• Identify personnel responsible for remediation activities.
	    • Schedule potential deadlines for remediation activities.
	        • Schedule potential dates for confirmatory re-scans.
	• Identify location for secure storage of supporting evidence *(ASV reports, review comments, re-scans, etc.)*.

Periodic Supplier Security Management	• Identify third-party suppliers.
	    • Review outsourced controls.
	    • Identify Supplier Relationship Managers.
	• Engage with third-Party Suppliers Relationship Managers.
	• Request evidence of the effectiveness of the management of their control responsibilities.

Internal Audits	• Identify person responsible for activity.
	    • Schedule dates for activity.
	• Identify and agree methodology to be used.
	• Identify person responsible for review *(Governance)*.
	    • Schedule dates for review.
	• Identify location for secure storage of supporting evidence *(Reports, review comments, re-scans, etc.)*.

Security and Risk Steering Committee meetings	• Review and discuss the results of the quarterly activities. • Document meeting minutes.

(continued)

---

[8]www.pcisecuritystandards.org/assessors_and_solutions/approved_scanning_vendors

½ Yearly Activities

Firewall ruleset reviews	• Identify person responsible for activity.
	   • Schedule dates for activity.
	• Identify and agree methodology to be used.
	• Identify person responsible for review *(Governance)*.
	   • Schedule dates for review.
	• Identify location for secure storage of supporting evidence *(Reports, review comments, re-scans, etc.)*.

Terminated User Accounts	• Confirmation of six-month retention records of terminated user accounts.
	   • Identify person responsible for activity.
	      • Schedule dates for activity.
	   • Identify and agree methodology to be used.
	   • Identify person responsible for review *(Governance)*.
	      • Schedule dates for review.
	   • Identify location for secure storage of supporting evidence *(Reports, review comments, re-scans, etc.)*.

Network Segmentation Testing	• Identify person/vendor responsible for activity.
	   • Schedule dates for activity.
	• Identify and agree methodology to be used.
	• Identify person responsible for review *(Governance)*.
	   • Schedule dates for review.
	• Identify location for secure storage of supporting evidence *(Reports, review comments, re-scans, etc.)*.

PMCSP (QSA) Preparations	• Identify 3 X PMCSP (QSAs) from the PCI SSC approved list:[9]
	   • Ensure that they are listed for your payment card processing environments.
	      • Issue request for tenders.
	      • Review tenders and select best option.

(continued)

---

[9]www.pcisecuritystandards.org/assessors_and_solutions/qualified_security_assessors

Penetration/Web Application Testing Preparations	• Identify 3 X Testing Services from the PCI SSC approved list:[10]
	• Review their proposed methodology to test your environment.
	   • Issue request for tenders.
	   • Review tenders and select best option.

Incident Scenario workshop	• Team development of plausible incident scenarios, for your company, based upon the latest threat intelligence feeds. • Record and document scenarios into your playbook.

3/4 Yearly Activities

PMCSP (QSAC) Annual Assessment Preparations	• Engage with PMCSP (QSAC) to agree and schedule the dates for the next annual assessment.
	   • Ensure that the PMCSP (QSAC) confirms the dates (commencement, onsite, report writing, report QA, report delivery, etc.) and identifies the QSA/QSAs that will be scheduled to complete the assessment.
	   • Proposal for their methodology.
	      • *This will enhance the efficiency of the service deliverables and ensure the expectations are agreed.*
	• Identify internal resources required.
	   • Schedule their timings.
	• Schedule the commencement date to ensure that the assessment and delivery of the report can be concluded to align with the annual compliance date.

Annual Activities

Policy reviews	• Carry out reviews of all supporting policies, SOPs, and supporting documents. • Record review details. • Ensure in-scope personnel have read and signed as having acknowledged and understood their applicable policies.
Risk reviews	• Carry out review of identified risks, recorded in the Risk Register. • Identify and document any new risk assessments.

(continued)

---

[10]www.pcisecuritystandards.org/assessors_and_solutions/qualified_security_assessors

Annual Security Refresher training	• Review records of training/nominal roles to ensure that all in-scope personnel have received PCI DSS refresher training.
Supplier Management Review	• Identify all in-scope third-party suppliers. • Engage with third-party suppliers. • Review contracts. • Review quarterly due diligence evidence. • Review third-party AoCs. • Confirm understanding of outsourced PCI DSS services. • Third-party suppliers acknowledge their PCI DSS controls responsibilities.
Annual Security Muster	• Review quarterly internal audit reports.
Annual Security Incident Response exercise	• Test the effectiveness of the incident response plan. • Document the testing and the post-incident review.

Asset Inventory review	• Review hardware and software asset life-cycle dates.
	  • Upcoming End-of-Life (Eol)/End-of-Support (EoS) assets should be risk assessed and added to the risk register.
	  • Plan to align changes to quieter period of operations and, where possible, scheduled with the annual penetration/web application testing.
	    • *Minimize additional cost and impact.*

Validate the effectiveness of the PCI DSS program	• Review output of Business-As-Usual (BAU) activities and the internal audits, ensuring that the SOPs remain effective.

Assessment Process

Having engrained the PCI DSS checks into your routine business operations, you will have all the evidence needed for your QSA to arrive onsite to validate that you are aligned with the PCI DSS controls framework.

For me, I would always align my approach to conducting a formal onsite PCI DSS assessment in the same manner that I would complete an RAF Police security investigation. This involved the application of a six-step methodical approach:

1. **Briefing**

    Before engaging in the commencement of the PCI DSS assessment, I would request a meeting with all the in-scope members of the "In-scope" personnel. This would enable me to brief all considered on what they would I would be expecting from them and allow them the opportunity to ask any questions.

    -   Confirm agenda, timings, locations, etc.

        -   *Typically, starting at requirement 12 and working backward toward requirement 1*

    -   Inform client of the QSA feedback process.

2. **Documenting reviews**

    Next, I would do a "deep dive" analysis of the client's policies, SOPs, and supporting documents and (if necessary) ask any confirmatory questions on the content.

    -   The results providing the content needed for the creation of my interview plans

3. **Interviews**

    Employing some of the principles from the PEACE investigative interviewing model, each person with responsibilities would be interviewed so that they could provide independent accounts of their duties.

    -   The notes from these interviews would then be securely retained as supporting evidence.

4. **Processing observations**

    Having reviewed the documentation and interviewed the in-scope personnel, each member of the team is then asked to demonstrate the practical application of their policies and SOPs.

    -   Supporting evidence is collated during these observations.

5. **Reporting write-up and Quality Assurance review**

   Having collected all the supporting evidence and comprehensive notes from the onsite assessment, I was then able to work remotely to write up the draft RoC, following which the RoC would be subject to an independent peer review and returned for finalization of the draft version.

6. **Client Sign Off**

   Finally, a review session is completed with the client to ensure that they understand the observations made and to help them identify opportunities for further improvement. Having completed the review session and made any updates, following the review session, the RoC is finalized and provided to the client.

Reality Bites

During a gap assessment for a client, I was asked whether I would be willing to carry out some work for the client's sister company based in the United States. They had suffered a breach, involving just 13 payment card details, and their bank had requested that their improvement works be validated by a QSA.

Further discussions with their Acquiring confirmed that they would be content with a QSA-validated SAQ, as they had adjusted the card payment process to a fully outsourced operation, using a PCI DSS compliant payment service provider.

I advised them that I could assist them (being a QSA, at the time) but that it would probably be more cost-effective to hire a US-based QSAC.

Several weeks later, I received notice that I had been chosen to deliver this tasking and would be flying out to carry out the assessment at their US locations.

It turns out that if they had heeded my advice and approached three local QSACs, all of which had quoted for full RoC assessment, despite the task being to complete the objectives set by their Acquiring bank.

Consequently, not only was my approach a more cost-effective option but by being completely transparent with them and having spent time analyzing the requirements of the task, I became their preferred option.

Recommendations

Having gleaned an understanding of what is involved in the assessment process will enable you to be better prepared for such an annual commitment and to appreciate what might be required from your team members. It is worth noting that each QSAC may have differing approaches. Therefore, it is recommended that you request details of their approach, with an explanation on why they deliver it in this way, what the benefits are for you, and what is expected from you.

When looking at opportunities to mature your BAU activities, consider the potential benefits of automating (e.g., using scrypts) and scheduling the activities and consolidating your PCI DSS program into a suitable risk platform.

For example, in 2013, during my role as a Baseline Security Controls Manager, I was responsible for the development and implementation of a myriad of security controls (e.g., ISO27k, PCI DSS, COBIT 4.1) applied to the departmental level. In order to successfully achieve this, the use of hundreds of departmental control spreadsheets would have been impossible to manage. However, I identified that an existing risk platform (Acuity STREAM[11]) could be a very good tool to support this objective.

---

[11]https://acuityrm.com/use-benefits/control-assurance

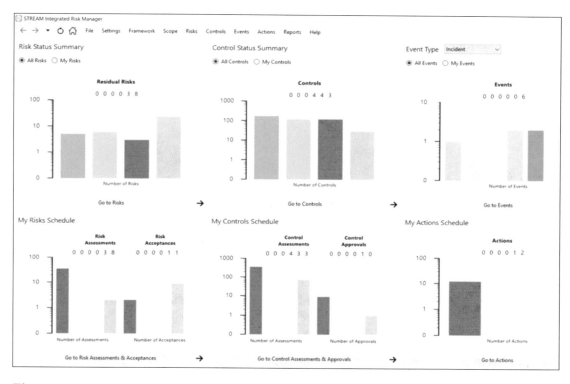

Figure 16-1. *Acuity STREAM Dashboard*

Conclusion

You should not fear the annual PCI DSS assessment and do not be afraid to "shop around" each year to review how the PCI QSA consultancy and security testing markets may have changed.

Remember that the annual process is a two-way process to evaluate the effectiveness of your business processes for the maintenance of the confidentiality and integrity of your payment card operations.

The QSACs must ensure that they deliver a service that meets the PCI SSC's principles and, as such, need to remain fair and neutral in their PCI DSS-related activities.

Each QSAC is likely to have a differing approach *(but all must adhere to the PCI SSC's principles)*, which may be more suitable and cost-effective for your type of business operations and more relevant to your specific objectives. However, if you have developed an integrated and comprehensive compliance program, where you have collated and reviewed the output of your mandatory and additional internal audit checks to cover the full year, it should not matter which QSAC you choose to employ.

Knowing that you are willing to "shop around" and weighing up your best options will make the PCI DSS annual assessment a far less restrictive process, helping you to feel reassured that you need not be locked into the same QSAC and security testing providers, year in and year out.

Key Takeaways

Having to maintain PCI DSS compliance, year in and year out, can seem like a very laborious, time-consuming, and nerve-racking process. However, with sufficient planning, scheduling, and reviews, this does not have to be the case.

The most important part of any engagement with a PCI QSAC is gaining an in-depth understanding of the way they operate and establishing the ground rules at the very outset of the engagement.

You should not feel that achieving a successful annual PCI DSS should "Pigeon hole" you into staying forever and a day, with the same PCI QSAC, ASV, and security testing providers. The market is full of multiple different providers and each with differing approaches but all having to adhere to the same principles provided by the PCI SSC.

The maintenance of PCI DSS is a yearlong process and with the annual assessment merely being the "Icing On The Cake!"

- *Do you have yearlong scheduled compliance activities?*

- *Do you have established automated processes in place?*

- *Have you identified suitable tools to help manage your compliance efforts?*

- *Have you collected sufficient evidence throughout the year?*

- *Have your Subject Matter Experts identified the means to provide the required evidence?*

- *Is this evidence securely retained?*

- *Do you periodically canvas your market options?*

Risks

Criminals seek to exploit missed controls management, enabling them the opportunity to infiltrate your corporate environment.

Consequently, it is essential that at a minimum the environment is protected against the PCI DSS controls framework.

In addition, it is essential that you implement a yearlong program of works to validate the alignment and effectiveness of the PCI DSS controls.

Failure to achieve this minimum standard increases your risk of a missed control countermeasure being actioned. This can leave you vulnerable to exploitation and being unable to achieve/maintain your PCI DSS obligations.

Ask yourself:

- *Do I have comprehensive PCI DSS audit program?*

- *Do the personnel understand their responsibilities?*

- *How they are to fulfill these obligations?*

- *Does the program monitor the effectiveness of the controls to mitigate the risks of data/system compromise?*

- *Do I have a mutual relationship with my QSAC, ASV, and security testing providers?*

- *Do I consider changing providers, or am I too uncomfortable to risk moving to new suppliers?*

- *Do I understand the different approaches of my suppliers' competitors?*

- *Do I know the principles that the PCI QSACs must adhere to?*

CHAPTER 17

Quick Fire Round – Five Commonly Asked Questions

I hope that you have found the previous chapters informative and interesting and that you have gleaned the additional knowledge you were seeking to help your businesses fortify their defenses against malicious or accidental actions that could lead to a potential compromise on your corporate networks or a breach of your sensitive data assets.

The application of the Payment Card Industry Data Security Standard (PCI DSS) should be regarded as an enhancement to your business, ensuring that everyone involved supports "Safe Driving" practices:

- *"Well-maintained vehicles"*

- *"Skilled and safe driving"*

- *"Risk-aware drivers"*

However, I appreciate that getting your heads around the concept can feel extremely daunting and you might still be looking for further answers to your questions, without the need to engage in the procurement of a qualified security assessor (QSA).

Think of your PCI DSS projects as like learning to drive. You can still learn to drive through the coaching/mentoring of a seasoned and experienced driver. However, you may well feel that it is better to pay for the services of a qualified driving instructor.

Validating your PCI DSS compliance has specific requirements for the higher risk (e.g., Level 1 Merchants, Level 1 Service Providers, Breached Entities), who are mandated to undergo a QSA onsite assessment.

© Jim Seaman 2020
J. Seaman, *PCI DSS*, https://doi.org/10.1007/978-1-4842-5808-8_17

Bearing in mind that the PCI DSS integrated is ever evolving in accordance with new technologies and threats, you need to ensure that your compliance programs remain current.

In support of this, the Payment Card Industry Security Standards Council are constantly using their special interest groups (SIGs) to develop additional guidance and provide a wide range of helpful resources on their web site.[1]

Assessor and Solutions[2]

Assessors	Products and Solutions	Additional Resources
• 3DS Assessors	• 3DS Software Development Kits	• PCI Forensic Investigators
• Approved Scanning Vendors	• Approved PTS Devices	• PCI Professionals
• Card Production Security Assessors	• Payment Applications	• Qualified Integrators and Resellers
• Internal Security Assessors	• Point-to-Point Encryption Solutions	• PCI Recognized Laboratories
• Payment Application Assessors		
• Point-to-Point Encryption Assessors	• Software-based PIN Entry on COTS (SPoC) Solutions	• Give Feedback
• Qualified PIN Assessors		
• Qualified Security Assessors		

Document Library[3]

Training and Qualification[4]

• Overview	• PCI Professional	• PROGRAM FEES
• 3DS Assessor	• P2PE Assessors	• BECOME QUALIFIED
• Approved Scanning Vendor	• Qualified Integrator and Reseller	• CORPORATE GROUP TRAINING
• Associate QSA		
• Informational Training	• Qualified PIN Assessors	
• Internal Security Assessor	• Qualified Security Assessor	
• Payment Application QSA	• Secure SLC Assessor	
• PCI Acquirer Training	• Secure Software Assessor	
• PCI Awareness Training	• Webinars	
• PCI Forensic Investigator	• Meet Our Trainers	
	• Training FAQ	

(*continued*)

[1]www.pcisecuritystandards.org/

[2]www.pcisecuritystandards.org/assessors_and_solutions/

[3]www.pcisecuritystandards.org/document_library

[4]www.pcisecuritystandards.org/program_training_and_qualification/

About Us[5]

- *Overview*
- *Leadership*
- *Jobs at PCI*
- *Contact Us*

- *Antitrust Policy*
- *Privacy Policy*
- *IPR Policy*

Get Involved[6]

- *Overview*
- *Affiliate Members*
- *Board of Advisors*
- *Global Executive Assessor Roundtable*
- *Participating Organizations*
- *Regional Engagement Board*
- *Special Interest Groups*
- *Strategic Members*
- *Strategic Regional Members*

- *COMMUNITY MEMBERS*
- *PAST COMMUNITY MEETINGS*
- *Event Photo Gallery*

- *REQUEST FOR COMMENTS*

FAQs[7]

Additionally, I thought I would conclude this book with a quick fire round of my responses to five commonly asked questions, which you might find useful.

---

[5]www.pcisecuritystandards.org/about_us/
[6]www.pcisecuritystandards.org/get_involved/
[7]www.pcisecuritystandards.org/faqs

Five Commonly Asked Questions

Where can I enhance my or my team's knowledge on securing the business's payment card security?

Your first point of call that I would recommend is to familiarize yourself with the PCI SSC's guidance documents (available in their document library):

a) *Visit PCI SSC web site.*[8]

b) *Select Document Library.*[9]

c) *Select "GUIDANCE DOCUMENTS" in the "Filter by" drop-down list.*

d) *Choose "CATEGORY."*

Additionally, checking out the PCI SSC's FAQ interface *(extract at Table 17-1)* will more than likely have the answer to one of your burning question that you may have.

What are the biggest inhibitors to a successful PCI DSS strategy for the protection of my customer cardholder data?

There are many factors that can impede the effectiveness of your PCI DSS strategy, but my top 5 would be

1. *A lack of governance*

2. *Poor planning and preparation*

3. *Apathy from within the business*

4. *No security steering committee support*

5. *Poor resource management*

---

[8]www.pcisecuritystandards.org/

[9]www.pcisecuritystandards.org/document_library

I have outsourced all payment card operations to a third-party supplier, so as neither my business systems nor personnel interact with *any* cardholder data, surely, I do not need to validate my compliance?

Unfortunately, if you are a business that provides goods or services in exchange for payment through a payment card, you are still accountable for ensuring that your third-party suppliers are carrying out these support services in accordance with PCI DSS.

The most difficult part of transferring your risk and responsibilities to a third-party supplier (a.k.a. Service Provider[10]/Merchant Agent[11]) is ensuring that the services you are paying for cover the full extent of your PCI DSS obligations.

It is extremely likely that your chosen supplier will be in the business of providing PCI DSS support services to numerous clienteles and the services offered could be wide-ranging. Consequently, you need to ensure that you fully understand the services being supplied by all your third parties and that your contracts legally oblige the supplier to fulfill their security requirements.

This concept is very similar to that seen in Article 29[12] of the European Union's General Data Protection Regulation (EU GDPR). In the event of a breach, both the Processor (Third Party) and the Controller can be subject to an administrative fine (Article 83[13]).

Consequently, as part of your PCI DSS validation, you need to

- *Identify all your suppliers.*

- *Review your contracts to ensure that they are still appropriate.*

- *Ask for evidence against a sample of the controls that they are responsible for.*

---

[10]https://globalrisk.mastercard.com/wp-content/uploads/2018/06/Service-Provider-Categories-and-PCI.pdf

[11]www.visa.co.uk/dam/VCOM/regional/ve/unitedkingdom/PDF/risk/ve-merchant-agent-list-june-2019.pdf

[12]www.privacy-regulation.eu/en/article-29-processing-under-the-authority-of-the-controller-or-processor-GDPR.htm

[13]www.privacy-regulation.eu/en/article-83-general-conditions-for-imposing-administrative-fines-GDPR.htm#4

- *Review their compliance status by requesting a copy of their latest attestation on compliance (AoC).*

- *Collate all the outsourced PCI DSS controls into a responsible, accountable, consulted, and informed (RACI) matrix – this will help you identify and confirm that all the PCI DSS controls are being managed by your suppliers.*

I am not a Merchant or a Service Provider, so does PCI DSS apply to me and how am I meant to validate my annual compliance?

If you are asking this question, I can safely presume that in some way your business has a reliance on the processing, transmission, or storage of cardholder data (or have the potential to impact the payment card operations (e.g., Data Center housing the infrastructure (requirement 9)).

*PCI DSS is a catalogue of baseline security controls that have been developed by the PCI SSC (on behalf of the Card Brands (Mastercard, Visa, American Express, JCB, and Discover) for the protection of their cardholder data. Therefore, if you are interacting, or able to impact the Confidentiality or Integrity, with any cardholder data aligned to any of the Card Brands, then you **MUST** ensure that you are applying the appropriate protection afforded by the adherence to the PCI DSS integrated suite of controls.*

As PCI DSS provides you with all the protective controls needed to safeguard your cardholder data operations, you should ensure that you maintain an oversight of your PCI DSS compliance status and annually self-validate your compliance. This will ensure that you can confirm your PCI DSS compliance to both the Regulators (in the event of a data breach) and the Card Brands (on request).

In addition, organizations that need to adhere to the Mastercard Rules[14] now need to ensure that they maintain a comprehensive security program, as per para 2.2.7.

---

[14]www.mastercard.us/content/dam/mccom/global/documents/mastercard-rules.pdf

> **2.2.7 Information Security Program**
> A Customer must maintain a comprehensive written information security program that includes technical, physical, administrative, and organizational safeguards designed to:
>
> 1. Ensure the security and confidentiality of Personal Data;
> 2. Protect against any anticipated threats or hazards to the security, confidentiality, and integrity of Personal Data;
> 3. Protect against any actual or suspected unauthorized processing, loss, or unauthorized acquisition of any Personal Data; and
> 4. Ensure the proper and secure disposal of Personal Data.
>
> *A Customer's information security program must regularly test or monitor the effectiveness of the safeguards stated in this Rule.*

Figure 17-1. *Mastercard Rules Extract*

I have undergone multiple onsite assessments and there appears to be a wide range of inconsistencies in the way that different QSAs interpret the PCI DSS controls.

Why is this?

It is important to remember that every QSA company needs to ensure that all their QSAs meet the minimum qualification requirements,[15] their QSAs adhere to the PCI SSC's Code of Professional Responsibility,[16] and all QSA work is subject to quality control.

However, despite these minimum requirements, it is inevitable that different QSAs will have differing strengths, qualities, and experiences. Consequently, it is increasingly likely that these factors will result in differing interpretations of the intent of specific controls and how these controls should be implemented.

---

[15]www.pcisecuritystandards.org/documents/QSA_Qualification_Requirements_v3_0.pdf
[16]www.pcisecuritystandards.org/documents/PCI_SSC_Code_of_Professional_Responsibility.pdf?agreement=true&time=1515177926566

Your QSA should be able to explain the reason for their specific interpretation and understanding of these controls and how they believe that their approach will still ensure that your organization is still ensuring that the risks are being effectively mitigated.

Some of the most commonly misinterpreted controls are as follows:

- ***Marking wireless controls as N/A because no wireless environment is used***

  - ***1.2.3:*** *Configuring firewalls to prohibit unauthorized wireless traffic flows*

  - ***11.1.:*** *Quarterly testing to test for the presence of wireless access points*

Consider

How does marking these controls as being N/A reduce the risk associated with rogue wireless devices?

- ### AT&T Security Incident

"In return, the employees engaged in various illegal activities, including unlocking expensive iPhones meant exclusively for AT&T's network, installing two pieces of malware on AT&T's network at the Bothell call center, as well as installing rogue wireless access points at the same location."

Source: *www.itproportal.com/news/atandt-employees-took-bribes-to-put-malware-on-network/*

- ***Not including the testing of REST application programmable interfaces (APIs) for common vulnerabilities***

    - ***6.5.1–6.5.6*** – *Applicable to all applications (internal or external)*

Consider

How does this help mitigate the risks associated with your REST APIs having a commonly known vulnerability?

- ***Authentication***
- ***Cross-Site Script***
- ***Cross-Forge Request Forgery***
- ***Injection***

Source: *https://dzone.com/articles/rest-api-security-vulnerabilities*

Treat your procurement of QSA services the same as you might regard the hiring of a driving instructor. This is a service you are paying for, and if this service is failing to meet your expectations, do not be afraid to challenge the QSA and engage with their QSA to provide you with a satisfactory resolution.

Furthermore, do not be afraid to change your suppliers as this will help you avoid becoming complacent and if you periodically bring in "new pairs of eyes" can actually enhance your PCI DSS compliance strategy.

Table 17-1. *PCI SSC Index of FAQs*

Ref #	Frequently Asked Question (FAQ)
#1003	Where is the PCI Security Standards Council Located?
#1004	Does the PCI Security Standards Council enforce compliance?
#1009	In case of a suspected breach, should the PCI Security Standards Council be contacted directly?
#1014	Do QSAs and ASVs need to send reports of compliance (ROCs) or scanning results to the PCI Security Standards Council directly?
#1015	What are the consequences to my business if I do not comply with the PCI DSS?
#1016	I want to add input into this process. How do I become a member of the Council?
#1017	How can my organization find assistance in completing the Self-Assessment Questionnaire?
#1018	Will the PCI Security Standards Council list compliant service providers and/or merchants on its web site?
#1019	If my business was deemed compliant but my system was still breached and payment account data compromised after the fact, what liability would my business incur?
#1020	How does PA-DSS support a merchant's PCI DSS compliance?
#1021	How much will it cost for a vendor to have their products validated to PA-DSS by a PA-QSA?
#1022	Do small merchants with limited transaction volumes need to comply with PCI DSS?
#1023	What are the requirements that have to be satisfied to be in compliance with the PCI Data Security Standard?
#1024	Is PCI DSS a global standard?
#1032	Can you provide clarification of PCI DSS requirement 10.3.6?
#1033	Can you provide clarification for logging/audit trail per PCI DSS requirements 10.2.5 and 10.2.6?
#1034	What are system-level objects, as identified in PCI DSS Requirement 10.2.7?
#1035	What is the definition of "remote access"?
#1036	How can I provide feedback (negative or positive) about my QSA/ASV?

(continued)

Table 17-1. (*continued*)

Ref #	Frequently Asked Question (FAQ)
#1037	Do hosting providers have responsibility for liabilities/fines?
#1038	Does PCI DSS apply to "hot cards," expired, cancelled, or invalid card account numbers?
#1039	Does PCI DSS apply to debit cards, debit payments, and debit systems?
#1040	Is it required that all of a company's sites, even those located in other countries, must be included in the company's PCI DSS review?
#1041	What is the scope of a PCI DSS assessment for a network that is not segmented?
#1042	Should cardholder data be encrypted while in memory?
#1043	Is frame relay considered a private network and are there any encryption requirements?
#1044	Do ISPs that provide only Internet connection need to comply with the PCI DSS?
#1045	Is MPLS considered a private or public network when transmitting cardholder data?
#1046	Will the PCI Security Standards Council "approve" my organization's implementation of compensating controls in my effort to comply with the PCI DSS?
#1050	I make ATMs, what do I need to do for PTS?
#1051	Can application whitelisting be used to meet PCI DSS Requirement 5?
#1052	Can a payment application that implements the same cryptographic keys across multiple installations be PA-DSS compliant?
#1053	Can a payment application that uses cryptographic keys hard-coded by the vendor be PA-DSS compliant if they cannot be changed by the customer?
#1054	Does the PCI Security Standards Council provide information on security breaches, status of investigations, or PCI DSS compliance status?
#1055	Should I complete the Prioritized Approach milestones in sequential order?
#1060	How would an identified Denial of Service (DoS) vulnerability affect a company's ability to pass a PCI DSS vulnerability scan from an Approved Scanning Vendor (ASV)?
#1061	How frequently will the PCI Security Standards Council update the PCI DSS and PA-DSS?
#1062	What is meant by a "payment application" in Part 2d of the Attestation of Compliance?
#1063	Does SAQ C-VT replace SAQ C?

(continued)

Table 17-1. (*continued*)

Ref #	Frequently Asked Question (FAQ)
#1064	What is a VT or Virtual Terminal?
#1065	Should service providers demonstrate PCI DSS compliance as part of their client's assessment or in their own separate assessment?
#1066	What is an "inactive user account" as used in PCI DSS Requirement 8.1.4?
#1067	What is meant by "non-consumer users" in PCI DSS Requirement 8?
#1068	Are digital leased lines considered public or private?
#1069	Does PCI DSS apply to paper with cardholder data (e.g., receipts, reports, etc.)?
#1070	Are digital images containing cardholder data and/or sensitive authentication data included in the scope of the PCI DSS?
#1071	Can the full credit card number be displayed within a browser window?
#1072	What is the purpose of requiring account lockout, per PCI DSS Requirements 8.1.6 and 8.1.7?
#1073	What are the PCI DSS requirements regarding transmission of cardholder data via Bluetooth technology?
#1074	Is intrusion detection required if centralized log correlation is in place?
#1075	Is it permissible to use self-decrypting files for encryption to send cardholder data?
#1076	Is it permissible to use FTP if proper security measures are implemented?
#1077	How extensive must background checks be for employees who have access to cardholder data?
#1078	In what circumstances is multi-factor authentication required?
#1079	What is the definition of "merchant"?
#1080	Are administrators allowed to share passwords?
#1081	Do PCI DSS Requirements 10.2 and 10.3 mean that both database and application logging are required?
#1082	If a merchant has multiple processing environments, should the merchant complete multiple SAQs to validate their PCI DSS compliance?

(*continued*)

Table 17-1. (*continued*)

Ref #	Frequently Asked Question (FAQ)
#1083	What is the mission of the PCI Security Standards Council?
#1084	What is the intent of PCI DSS Requirement 3.4.1?
#1085	Can unencrypted PANs be sent over email, instant messaging, SMS, or chat?
#1086	How does encrypted cardholder data impact PCI DSS scope?
#1087	For vulnerability scans, what is meant by quarterly?
#1088	What is meant by "adequate network segmentation" in the PCI DSS?
#1089	Are hashed Primary Account Numbers (PAN) considered cardholder data that must be protected in accordance with PCI DSS?
#1091	What are acceptable formats for truncation of primary account numbers?
#1092	Does PCI DSS apply to merchants who outsource all payment processing operations and never store, process, or transmit cardholder data?
#1093	Does Requirement 3.4 apply to mainframes?
#1094	Will the PCI Security Standards Council be involved in performing forensic investigations as a result of an account data compromise event?
#1095	What will be the role of the PCI Security Standards Council in expanding the global coverage of both QSAs and ASVs?
#1096	When a QSA or ASV is newly approved, who is the contact at the PCI Security Standards Council to request a press release?
#1115	How does PCI DSS apply to individual PCs or workstations?
#1117	Are truncated Primary Account Numbers (PAN) required to be protected in accordance with PCI DSS?
#1122	What is the scope of the PCI Security Standards Council's activities?
#1123	In what way does the PCI Security Standards Council make payment card data more secure?
#1124	PCI DSS provides a common data security standard across all payment brands. Are there any plans to provide a common structure of penalties and/or fines for non-compliance to this standard?

(*continued*)

Table 17-1. (*continued*)

Ref #	Frequently Asked Question (FAQ)
#1125	Are there any plans for PCI SSC to be a single point of contact for a merchant, financial institute, or processor to send a PCI DSS compliance report to?
#1126	How do I determine whether my business would be required to conduct an independent assessment or a self-assessment?
#1127	Is there opportunity to provide feedback on the PCI Council's standards?
#1128	What happens if I'm using a PA-DSS-validated payment application that is breached?
#1129	Does media containing cardholder data (e.g., backup tapes or disks) need to be physically labeled as confidential for PCI DSS Requirement 9.6.1?
#1130	Are operating systems that are no longer supported by the vendor non-compliant with the PCI DSS?
#1131	Does the council have a mapping between PCI DSS and ISO 27002 (formerly ISO 17799) or other standards?
#1132	What is an Attestation of Compliance?
#1133	Why are there multiple PCI DSS Self-assessment Questionnaires (SAQs)?
#1134	What are the steps needed to perform a self-assessment to validate compliance with PCI DSS?
#1135	Can VLANS be used for network segmentation?
#1136	Can the full payment card number be printed on the consumer's copy of the receipt?
#1137	How can I validate if a number is a legitimate credit card number?
#1138	Does PCI SSC provide a list of PCI DSS-compliant service providers?
#1139	Can I fax payment card numbers and still be PCI DSS Compliant?
#1140	Which Self-assessment Questionnaire (SAQ) should I complete?
#1141	What are the fines and penalties assessed to companies for non-compliance with the PCI DSS?
#1142	How do I contact the payment card brands?
#1146	What is the difference between masking and truncation?

(continued)

Table 17-1. (*continued*)

Ref #	Frequently Asked Question (FAQ)
#1147	What is the purpose of requiring consoles/PCs to become "locked" after 15 minutes of idle time, per PCI DSS Requirement 8.1.8?
#1152	Can an entity be PCI DSS compliant if they have performed quarterly scans, but do not have four "passing" scans?
#1153	How does PCI DSS apply to VoIP?
#1154	Is pre-authorization account data in-scope for PCI DSS?
#1155	Which service provider category should I use for Part 2 of the PCI DSS Attestation of Compliance (AOC) for Service Providers?
#1156	Are call center environments considered "sensitive areas" for PCI DSS Requirement 9.1.1?
#1157	What should a merchant do if cardholder data is accidentally received via an unintended channel?
#1158	What effect does the use of a PCI-listed P2PE solution have on a merchant's PCI DSS validation?
#1162	Can merchants use encryption solutions not listed on the PCI Council's web site to reduce their PCI DSS validation effort?
#1163	Is a "P2PE Assessor" required for a merchant's PCI DSS assessment if the merchant uses a Council-listed P2PE solution?
#1164	Is the PCI P2PE Standard applicable for merchants that have developed/implemented their own encryption solution?
#1165	Are P2PE solution providers required to have their solutions validated and listed by the Council?
#1166	Which PCI PTS point-of-interaction (POI) devices can be used in a validated P2PE solution?
#1168	What assurances does the Council provide regarding the quality of organizations assessing my systems for compliance with the PCI standards?
#1169	What are the Council's requirements for QSA and ASV Companies to maintain a Quality Assurance (QA) manual?

(*continued*)

Table 17-1. (*continued*)

Ref #	Frequently Asked Question (FAQ)
#1170	How does the Prioritized Approach work?
#1171	Is the Prioritized Approach mandatory?
#1172	Does the Prioritized Approach replace the PCI DSS?
#1173	Who is qualified to perform PA-DSS assessments?
#1174	For the list of Validated PA-DSS Applications, what is the difference between Revalidation Date and Expiry Date?
#1175	If a merchant is using a payment application listed as "acceptable only for pre-existing deployments," is the merchant allowed to install more copies of the application?
#1176	How does an organization maintain compliance when a standard changes?
#1177	How does my company become a qualified assessor (QSA, PA-QSA, QSA (P2PE), PA-QSA (P2PE)) or Approved Scanning Vendor (ASV)?
#1178	How do I reduce the scope of a PCI DSS assessment?
#1181	How can I check whether a payment application is PA-DSS validated?
#1182	Is it acceptable to make minor changes to a PA-DSS-validated application and retain the existing version number?
#1183	The PA-DSS Program Guide says application version numbers may consist of a combination of fixed and variable alphanumeric characters. What does this mean?
#1195	What is the difference between a Validated Payment Application which is shown on the PCI SSC web site as "Acceptable for New Deployments" and one which is shown as "Acceptable only for Pre-Existing Deployments"?
#1196	If I am deemed PCI DSS compliant today by one of the payment card brands, will the other brands in the PCI Security Standards Council recognize this designation of compliance, and if so, what information must be put forth to achieve such recognition?
#1210	Are audio/voice recordings permitted to contain sensitive authentication data?
#1211	To whom should media inquiries or requests for interviews about the PCI Security Standard Council be directed?

(*continued*)

Table 17-1. (*continued*)

Ref #	Frequently Asked Question (FAQ)
#1212	What is the involvement of the PCI SSC on the compliance validation processes for PCI DSS assessments and scan reports?
#1213	Are there any plans to standardize the reporting requirements (reports) for the PCI DSS, PA-DSS, ASV, QSA, and PTS programs that are sent to each of the payment brands?
#1214	Do the PCI DSS requirements apply to card manufacturers, embossers, card personalizers, or entities that prepare data for card manufacturing?
#1216	Does the PCI DSS apply to acquirers?
#1217	Does the PCI DSS apply to issuers?
#1220	Are compliance certificates recognized for PCI DSS validation?
#1221	Do shared hosting providers need to comply with PCI DSS?
#1222	Does cardholder name, expiration date, etc. need to be rendered unreadable if stored in conjunction with the PAN (Primary Account Number)?
#1223	Does PCI DSS, PA-DSS, or PTS apply to ATMs?
#1224	What does one function per server mean?
#1225	What is the relationship between the PCI Data Security Standard and the Payment Application Data Security Standard and PTS Device Security Requirements?
#1226	What is the role of the Advisory Board?
#1227	Who are the founders of the PCI Security Standards Council?
#1228	Will the PCI Security Standards Council approve and list vendors for participation in forensic investigations?
#1229	What is SAQ C-VT?
#1233	How does encrypted cardholder data impact PCI DSS scope for third-party service providers?
#1234	I have had an external vulnerability scan completed by an ASV, does this mean I am PCI DSS compliant?

(*continued*)

Table 17-1. (*continued*)

Ref #	Frequently Asked Question (FAQ)
#1235	If a merchant or service provider has internal corporate credit cards used by employees for company purchases like travel or office supplies, are these corporate cards considered "in-scope" for PCI DSS?
#1246	Can a QSA that is not also a P2PE Assessor validate if an encryption solution meets P2PE Requirements?
#1247	Who can use SAQ P2PE?
#1248	In P2PE, how do "hybrid" decryption environments differ from "hardware" decryption environments?
#1251	What is the process to use previously deployed POI devices in a PCI P2PE solution?
#1252	Do all PCI DSS requirements apply to every system component?
#1253	Does hashing of passwords meet the intent of PCI DSS Requirement 8.2.1?
#1254	What is the intent of PCI DSS requirement 10?
#1257	Can I report on my Prioritized Approach progress instead of producing a Report on Compliance or Attestation of Compliance?
#1258	Does PCI SSC endorse specific products to meet PCI DSS requirements?
#1261	Does a P2PE-validated application also need to be validated against PA-DSS?
#1262	Will PA-DSS-validated applications continue to be Acceptable for New Deployments if they run on an unsupported operating system?
#1263	What are the Card Production Logical and Physical Security Requirements?
#1265	Can I combine sections from different versions of the PCI DSS?
#1266	I'm in the middle of a PCI DSS assessment when a new version is released, should I start again using the new version?
#1270	How do the requirements in PCI DSS version 3 that are "best practices" until June 30, 2015, impact my PCI DSS assessment?
#1271	Can I combine sections from different versions of the PA-DSS?
#1272	Can my payment application be validated using PA-DSS Version 1.2.1?
#1273	Can my payment application be validated using PA-DSS Version 3.0 or 3.1?

(*continued*)

Table 17-1. (*continued*)

Ref #	Frequently Asked Question (FAQ)
#1274	Can my payment application be validated using PA-DSS Version 2?
#1275	What are the PA-DSS Expiry Dates?
#1277	Are merchants required to meet PCI DSS Requirement 12.9?
#1278	Are PA-DSS applications considered valid if installed on an operating system that is not included in the payment application listing?
#1279	How does using a PA-DSS-validated application affect the scope of a merchant's PCI DSS assessment?
#1280	Can card verification codes/values be stored for card-on-file or recurring transactions?
#1281	Are point-of-sale devices required to be physically secured (e.g., with a cable or tether) to prevent removal or substitution in order to meet PCI DSS Requirement 9.9?
#1282	Can an entity be PCI DSS compliant if they use a service provider that is validated to a previous version of PCI DSS?
#1283	If a merchant develops an application that runs on a consumer's device (e.g., smartphone, tablet, or laptop) that is used to accept payment card data, what are the merchant's obligations regarding PCI DSS and PA-DSS for that application?
#1284	Are acquirers considered service providers for the purpose of PCI DSS Requirements 12.8 and 12.9?
#1285	Does PCI DSS apply to one-time or single-use PANs?
#1286	Does PCI DSS apply to virtual (electronic-only) PANs?
#1287	Why does PA-DSS v3 require passwords to be protected by a one-way hash (Requirement 3.3.2), whereas PANs can be stored in an encrypted form (Requirement 2.3)?
#1288	Does PA-DSS Requirement 3.3.2 apply to passwords used by the payment application to access other systems/applications (e.g., for the payment application to access a third-party database)?
#1289	Does the PA-DSS v3 requirement for hashing stored passwords meet PCI DSS Requirement 8.2.1?

(*continued*)

Table 17-1. (*continued*)

Ref #	Frequently Asked Question (FAQ)
#1290	If a merchant uses a service provider to host part or all of their CDE and the service provider has been validated as PCI DSS compliant, is the merchant's assessor required to go onsite to the third-party location and retest the PCI DSS requirements?
#1291	Why is SAQ A-EP used for Direct Post while SAQ A is used for iFrame or URL redirect?
#1292	Why is there a different approach for Direct Post implementations than for iFrame and URL redirect – what are the technical differences and how do they impact the security of e-commerce transactions?
#1293	If a merchant's e-commerce implementation meets the criteria that all elements of payment pages originate from a PCI DSS-compliant service provider, is the merchant eligible to complete SAQ A or SAQ A-EP?
#1299	Are manual imprinter machines in-scope for PCI DSS requirements?
#1300	How does PCI DSS apply to payment terminals?
#1301	How do PTS-approved payment terminals support PCI DSS compliance?
#1302	How does use of an expired PTS device affect my PCI DSS compliance?
#1304	What devices does PCI DSS Requirement 10.6.2 apply to?
#1305	Do you offer examination accommodation?
#1306	Are PCI Forensic Investigators (PFIs) permitted to enter into retainer-type agreements with merchants and service providers?
#1308	How can an entity ensure that hashed and truncated versions cannot be correlated as required in PCI DSS Requirement 3.4?
#1309	Must payment applications ensure that hashed and truncated versions cannot be correlated?
#1310	Are merchants allowed to request that cardholder data be provided over end-user messaging technologies?
#1311	Are PFI Companies which are "in remediation" permitted to perform investigations?
#1312	If an entity uses a service provider that is not PCI DSS compliant, how does this impact the entity's compliance?

(*continued*)

Table 17-1. (*continued*)

Ref #	Frequently Asked Question (FAQ)
#1313	Can SAQ B-IP be used if cardholder data is transmitted over wireless?
#1314	Is storage of encrypted cardholder data considered "cardholder data" per the SAQ eligibility criteria?
#1315	Is storage of truncated PAN considered storage of "cardholder data" per the SAQ eligibility criteria?
#1316	Are merchants required to perform the "Expected Testing" in the SAQs?
#1317	What is a "significant change" for PCI DSS Requirements 11.2 and 11.3?
#1318	What is the maximum period of time that cardholder data can be stored?
#1319	Are merchants allowed to request card verification codes/values from cardholders?
#1320	Who do I report insecure merchant behavior to?
#1321	Do parent/subsidiary companies validate as a single entity or as separate entities?
#1322	What are the expiry dates for PTS POI device approvals?
#1323	Are disaster recovery (DR) sites in-scope for PCI DSS?
#1324	What changes are PFI companies allowed to make to the PFI Reporting Templates?
#1325	Does PCI SSC provide a "PCI DSS Compliant" logo?
#1326	How does PCI DSS apply to EMVCo Payment Tokens?
#1327	Do PANs need to be masked on cardholder statements sent by issuers to customers?
#1328	What version of PCI DSS should I use?
#1329	What is the current version of PA-DSS?
#1330	For P2PE solutions, can you use PCI-approved POI devices with SRED, where the PTS listing indicates "Non-CTLS"?
#1331	Can SAQ eligibility criteria be used for determining applicability of PCI DSS requirements for onsite assessments?
#1332	Is a merchant web site still in-scope for PCI DSS if it meets all the criteria for SAQ A?
#1333	Can PCI DSS compliance be determined by testing only pre-production environments using test data?

(*continued*)

Table 17-1. (*continued*)

Ref #	Frequently Asked Question (FAQ)
#1334	Where can I find unlocked versions of the AOCs and SAQs?
#1335	Does PCI DSS apply to bank account data?
#1338	What is the difference between POI firmware and additional software that may be present on the POI device?
#1339	Are POI devices with only the PTS-approved firmware (i.e., no additional software) eligible for use in a PCI P2PE solution?
#1354	Can the AOC be redacted to protect sensitive information?
#1355	Are applications listed as Acceptable only for Pre-existing Deployments able to meet the current PA-DSS and PCI DSS?
#1356	What does "Duly Authorized Officer" mean?
#1358	Which version of the P2PE Standard should be used for a P2PE assessment?
#1367	Can PCI-listed P2PE v1.1 applications be used in PCI P2PE v2 solutions?
#1368	Can PCI-listed P2PE v2 applications be used in a PCI P2PE v1.1 listed solution?
#1369	Does PCI P2PE v2 allow for partial assessments of third parties with services that will be used in one or more P2PE solutions?
#1372	How should entities apply the new SSL/TLS migration dates to Requirements 2.2.3, 2.3, and 4.1 for PCI DSS v3.1?
#1373	How should entities complete their ROC or SAQ for PCI DSS v3.1 using the new SSL/TLS migration dates?
#1374	Is Payment Account Reference (PAR) as defined by EMVCo considered PCI Account Data?
#1375	Can an Attestation of Compliance (AOC) be provided to an assessed entity before the Report on Compliance (ROC) is finalized?
#1382	Can a partial PCI DSS assessment be documented in a Report on Compliance (ROC)?
#1383	To whom do the PCI Token Service Provider Security Requirements apply?
#1384	What is the difference between "acquiring tokens," "issuer tokens," and "Payment Tokens"?
#1385	Which types of tokens are addressed by the PCI SSC tokenization documents?

(*continued*)

Table 17-1. (*continued*)

Ref #	Frequently Asked Question (FAQ)
#1425	What is the difference between "multi-factor" authentication and "two-factor" authentication?
#1426	Is "two-step" authentication the same as "two-factor" or "multi-factor" authentication?
#1427	Are OEMs and/or hardware/software resellers subject to PCI DSS Requirements 12.8 and 12.9?
#1434	How do PCI PTS-approved POI device expiry dates affect a PCI-listed P2PE solution?
#1435	What is the Council's guidance on the use of SHA-1?
#1436	Who has to comply with the PCI standards?
#1437	Can PCI DSS be used to protect non-payment card data?
#1438	How is the payment page determined for SAQ A merchants using iFrame?
#1439	How do PCI DSS Requirements 2, 6, and 8 apply to SAQ A merchants?
#1440	How does PCI DSS Appendix A2 apply after the SSL/early TLS migration deadline?
#1441	How do the updated SSL/early TLS migration dates apply to service providers?
#1442	Can merchants using non-console administrative access be eligible for SAQ B-IP, C-VT, or C?)
#1443	What is the intent of the SAQ eligibility criteria?
#1444	Can a PFI Company perform subsequent PFI investigations for the same entity?
#1445	How should QSA assistance with completion of Self-Assessment Questionnaire (SAQs) be documented?
#1446	How did Prioritized Approach Tool calculations change for DSS v3.2?
#1447	How does PCI DSS Requirement 11.3.4.1 impact timing of penetration tests for service providers?
#1448	What is meant by "at risk" and "at-risk timeframe" referenced in the Final PFI Report?
#1449	Is two-step authentication acceptable for PCI DSS Requirement 8.3?
#1450	Where can I find more information about the Assessment Guidance for Non-listed Encryption Solutions (a.k.a. NESA)?

(*continued*)

Table 17-1. (*continued*)

Ref #	Frequently Asked Question (FAQ)
#1451	Can PFIs provide reports to their clients before sending the report to the affected payment brands?
#1452	How does Triple DEA (TDEA) impact ASV Scan results?
#1453	Can a PFI Company provide QSA services to an entity after performing a PFI investigation for that entity?
#1454	What is the intent of "administrative access" in PCI DSS?
#1455	Does a QSA need to be onsite at the client's premises for all aspects of a PCI DSS assessment?
#1456	Can PCI SSC revoke a QSA Company's eligibility to participate in the Associate QSA Program due to quality concerns in connection with that program, and not revoke qualification as a QSA Company?
#1457	Is a Software-based PIN Entry on COTS Solution eligible for a P2PE Solution approval?
#1458	What date should be used for "Date of Report" in the ROC?
#1460	Where should reports be sent when the PFI investigation has concluded there is no evidence of a breach?
#1461	What are the security considerations for TLS 1.3?
#1462	What does "Window of Payment Card Data Storage" mean in the Final PFI Report template?
#1464	Does the use of expired PTS POI devices meet eligibility criteria for SAQ B-IP?
#1467	Can organizations use alternative password management methods to meet PCI DSS Requirement 8?
#1468	Can I have the same assessor company or individual assessor perform a PCI DSS and PIN Assessment for our organization?
#1469	How do PCI PTS-approved HSM expiry dates affect a PCI-listed P2PE Solution or Component?
#1470	Are PFIs required to fill out all the fields in the Final PFI Report?
#1471	What does "Servicing Market" on the QSA listing mean?
#1472	How can I determine whether a QSA is authorized to perform PCI DSS assessments in all countries that are in-scope for my company's PCI DSS assessment?

Bibliography

Goal 1: Build and Maintain a Secure Network and Systems

- McNab, C. (2017). Network security assessment : know your network. Sebastopol, CA: O'Reilly Media, Inc.

- Hutchens, J. (2017). Kali Linux Network Scanning Cookbook.

- Gordon Fyodor Lyon (2008). Nmap network scanning : official Nmap project guide to network discovery and security scanning. Sunnyvale, CA: Insecure.Com, LLC.

- Vacca, J.R. and Safari (2014). Network and system security. Waltham, MA: Syngress Is An Imprint Of Elsevier.

- Zero trust networks. Gilman, Evan. and Barth, Doug. 2017. Sebastopol, CA: O'Reilly Media.

- Knapp, E. and Langill, J.T. (2015). Industrial Network Security. 2nd ed. Waltham: Elsevier.

- Anderson, R. (2021). SECURITY ENGINEERING : a guide to building dependable distributed systems. S.L.: John Wiley & Sons.

- Theriault, M. and Newman, A. (2001). Oracle security handbook. Berkeley, Calif.: Osborne/McGraw-Hill.

- Theriault, M. and Newman, A. (2001). Oracle security handbook. Berkeley, Calif.: Osborne/McGraw-Hill.

© Jim Seaman 2020
J. Seaman, *PCI DSS*, https://doi.org/10.1007/978-1-4842-5808-8

Goal 2: Protect Cardholder Data

- Cammilleri-Subrenat, A. and Levallois-Barth, C. (2008). Sensitive data protection in the European Union. Bruxelles: Bruylant.

- Information Systems Audit and Control Association (2017). Implementing a privacy protection program : using COBIT 5 enablers with the ISACA privacy principles. Rolling Meadows, Ill.: ISACA.

- Buchanan, W. (2017). Cryptography. Gistrup, Denmark: River Publishers.

- Chey Cobb (2004). Cryptography for dummies. Hoboken, NJ: Wiley Pub.

- Sklavos, N. and Xinmiao Zhang (2007). Wireless security and cryptography : specifications and implementations. Boca Raton, FL: CRC Press.

- Standards Australia (Organization and Standards New Zealand (2008). Information technology : security techniques : key management. Part 4, Mechanisms based on weak secrets. Sydney, NSW: Standards Australia ; Wellington, N.Z.

Goal 3: Maintain a Vulnerability Management Program

- Dehghantanha, A., Conti, M. and Tooska Dargahi (2018). Cyber threat intelligence. Cham, Switzerland: Springer.

- Integrated risk and vulnerability management assisted by decision support systems : relevance and impact on governance. (2011). Dordrecht ; London: Springer.

- Haber, M.J. and Hibbert, B. (2018). Asset attack vectors : building effective vulnerability management strategies to protect organizations. Berkeley, CA: Apress.

- Nicastro, F.M. (2005). Curing the patch management headache. Boca Raton, Fla.: Auerbach Publications.

- Qualys (2011). Vulnerability management for dummies. Chichester: John Wiley & Sons, Cop.

- Antti Salminen (2000). Implementing organizational and operational change : critical success factors of change management. Espoo Finnish Academy of Technology.

- Clark, J. (1995). Managing innovation and change : people, technology and strategy. London ; Thousand Oaks: Sage Publications.

- Clegg, S., Kornberger, M. and Pitsis, T. (2016). Managing & organizations : an introduction to theory and practice. Los Angeles: Sage.

- King, N. and Anderson, N. (2002). Managing innovation and change : a critical guide for organizations. London: Thomson.

- Grembi, J. (2008). Secure software development : a security programmer's guide. Boston, MA: Course Technology.

- Howard, M. and Lipner, S. (2006). The security development lifecycle : SDL, a process for developing demonstrably more secure software. Redmond, Wash.: Microsoft Press.

- Kleidermacher, D. and Kleidermacher, M. (2012). Embedded systems security : Practical methods for safe and secure software and systems development. Oxford: Newnes (An Imprint of Butterworth-Heinemann Ltd).

- Cross, M. (2007). Web application vulnerabilities : detect, exploit, prevent. Burlington, MA: Syngress Pub.

- Wear, N. (2015). SCFM : secure coding field manual : programmer's guide to Owasp top 10 and Cwe/Sans top 25. North Charleston, South Carolina? CreateSpace Independent Publishing Platform.

- Barnett, R.C. (2013). The web application defender's cookbook : battling hackers and protecting users. Indianapolis, IN: Wiley Publishing, Inc.

Goal 4: Implement Strong Access Control Measures

- American National Standards Institute and INCITS (2012). Role-Based Access Control. New York, NY: American National Standards Institute, Inc.

- Honey, G. (2000). Electronic access control. Oxford: Newnes.

- Desmond, B. and Richards, J. (2013). Active Directory. Beijing ; Sebastopol: O'Reilly Media.

- Getz, K., Litwin, P., Baron, A. and Microsoft Corporation (2004). Access cookbook. United States of America (1005 Gravenstein Highway North, Sebastopol): O'Reilly.

- Kelley, J., Campagna, R. and Denzil Wessels (2009). Network access control for dummies. Hoboken, N.J.: Wiley.

- T Ertem Osmanoglu (2014). Identity and access management : controlling your network. Rockland, Massachusetts: Syngress.

- Khairallah, M. (2006). Physical security systems handbook : the design and implementation of electronic security systems. Amsterdam ; Oxford: Elsevier/Butterworth-Heinemann.

- Brotherston, L. and Berlin, A. (2017). Defensive Security Handbook : best practices for securing infrastructure. Sebastopol, California: O'Reilly Media, Inc.

- Griffor, E. (2017). Handbook of system safety and security : cyber risk and risk management, cyber security, threat analysis, functional safety, software systems, and cyber physical systems. Cambridge, Ma [Und 11 Weitere] Elsevier Syngress.

- Norman, T.L. (2017). Electronic access control. San Diego: Elsevier Science.

- Anthony, N. (2016). Physical Asset Management. Springer International PU.

Goal 5: Regularly Monitor and Test Networks

- Bejtlich, R. (2013). The practice of network security monitoring : understanding incident detection and response. San Francisco: No Starch Press.

- Dah Ming Chiu and Ram Sudama (1992). Network monitoring explained : design and application. New York: Ellis Horwood.

- Wilson, E. (2000). Network monitoring and analysis : a protocol approach to troubleshooting. Upper Saddle River, N.J.: Prentice Hall PTR ; London.

- Kim, P. (2014). The hacker playbook : practical guide to penetration testing. North Charleston, South Carolina: Secure Planet, LLC.

- Kim, P. (2015). The hacker playbook 2 : practical guide to penetration testing. North Charleston, South Carolina: Secure Planet, LLC.

- Kim, P. (2018). The hacker playbook 3 : practical guide to penetration testing. North Charleston, South Carolina: Secure Planet, LLC.

- Weidman, G. (2014). Penetration testing : a hands-on introduction to hacking. San Francisco: No Starch Press.

- Hacking : the Art of Exploitation. (2007). Erscheinungsort Nicht Ermittelbar: No Starch Press, US.

- Engebretson, P. (2013). The basics of hacking and penetration testing : ethical hacking and penetration testing made easy. Amsterdam ; Boston: Syngress, An Imprint Of Elsevier.

- Dafydd Stuttard and Pinto, M. (2018). The web application hacker's handbook : discovering and exploiting security flaws. Middletown, De: Books On Demand.

- Hassan, N.A. and Rami Hijazi (2018). Open source intelligence methods and tools : a practical guide to online intelligence. Berkeley, California: Apress, New York, NY.

- Watson, G., Mason, A.G. and Ackroyd, R. (2014). Social engineering penetration testing : executing social engineering pen tests, assessments and defense. Amsterdam ; Boston: Syngress, An Imprint Of Elsevier.

Goal 6: Maintain an Information Security Policy

- Rolf Von Roessing and Information Systems Audit And Control Association (2010). The business model for information security. Meadows, Ill.: ISACA.

- W Krag Brotby (2009). Information security management metrics : a definitive guide to effective security monitoring and measurement. Boca Raton: CRC Press.

- Loginov, M. (2018). CISO Defenders of the Cyber-Realm. Dirty deeds, hackers and heroes. Great Britain: Ascot Barclay.

- Bonney, B., Hayslip, G. and Stamper, M. (2016). CISO desk reference guide : a practical guide for CISOs. San Diego, CA: CISO DRG Joint Venture Pub.

- R Ian Tricker (2019). Corporate governance : principles, policies, and practices. Oxford ; New York, NY: Oxford University Press.

- Leron Zinatullin (2016). The psychology of information security : resolving conflicts between security compliance and human behaviour. Ely, Cambridgeshire: IT Governance Pub.

- Franke, D. (2016). Cyber security basics : protect your organization by applying the fundamentals. Don Franke.

- Saïd El Aoufi (2011). Information security economics. Norwich: TSO.

- Hayden, L. (2016). People centric security transforming your enterprise security culture. New York [U.A.] McGraw-Hill.

- And, A. (2013). COBIT 5 for risk. Rolling Meadows, Ill.: ISACA.

- Risk Scenarios: Using COBIT 5 for Risk. (2014). ISACA.

- Advanced persistent threats : how to manage the risk to your business. (2013). ISACA.

- Talbot, J. (2019). Security Risk Management Aide Memoire. Sydney, NSW: SERT Pty Ltd.

- Blyth, M. (2015). Risk and security management : protecting people and sites worldwide. Hoboken, N.J.: Wiley.

- Petrigh, M. ed., (2016). Security and Risk Management: Critical Reflections and International Perspectives. On-Demand Publishing LLC.

- Broder, J.F. and Tucker, E. (2012). Risk analysis and the security survey. Amsterdam ; Waltham, MA: Butterworth-Heinemann.

- Young, C.S. (2010). Metrics and methods for security risk management. Amsterdam ; Boston: Syngress/Elsevier.

- Slovic, P., Earthscan and Routledge (2014). The perception of risk. Abingdon, Oxon.

- Information Systems Audit And Control Association (2015). CRISC review manual. Rolling Meadows, IL: ISACA.

- Clarke, G.E., Tetz, E. and Warner, T.L. (2019). CompTIA A+ certification : all-in-one. Hoboken, NJ: John Wiley & Sons Inc.

- Wm Arthur Conklin, White, G.B., Cothren, C., Davis, R.L. and Williams, D. (2015). CompTIA Security+ all-in-one exam guide (exam SY0-401). New York: McGraw-Hill Education.

- Meyers, M. and Computing Technology Industry Association (2018). CompTIA Network+ certification exam guide : (exam N10-007). New York: McGraw-Hill Education

- Gallacher, L. (2019). ITIL 4 FOUNDATION EXAM STUDY GUIDE : 2018 update. S.L.: Wiley-Sybex.

- Information Systems Audit And Control Association (2015). CISM review manual. ISACA.

- Cissp, J. (2015). Cissp study guide. Syngress Media,U.S.

- Gordon, A. and Malik, J. (2015). Official (ISC)2 guide to the CISSP CBK: Certified Information Systems Security Professional. Boca Raton: CRC Press.

- Information Systems Audit And Control Association (2019). CISA review manual. Schaumburg, IL, USA: ISACA.

- Information Systems Audit And Control Association (2014). Vendor management using COBIT 5. Rolling Meadows, Il: ISACA.

BIBLIOGRAPHY

- Waters, D. (2015). Supply chain risk management : vulnerability and resilience in logistics. London: Kogan Page.

- Conboy, N., Jan Van Bon and Stationery Office (Great Britain (2017). Service rescue! : an implementation and improvement guide for incident management. Norwich: The Stationery Office.

- Information Systems Audit And Control Association (2014). IT control objectives for Sarbanes-Oxley : using COBIT́ 5 in the design and implementation of internal controls over financial reporting. Rolling Meadows, Il: ISACA.

- American Institute Of Certified Public Accountants (2018). Guide : SOC 2 reporting on an examination of controls at a service organization relevant to security, availability, processing integrity, confidentiality, or privacy. New York, N.Y.: American Institute Of Certified Public Accountants.

- Ramos, M. (2012). The Sarbanes-Oxley Section 404 Implementation Toolkit Practice Aids for Managers and Auditors. Hoboken, NJ, USA John Wiley & Sons, Inc.

- Wright, S. (2011). PCI DSS : a practical guide to implementing and maintaining compliance. Ely: It Governance Publishing.

- ISACA (n.d.). (PCI DSS) A Practical Guide to the Payment Card Industry Data Security Standard. ISACA.

- Williams, B.R. and Chuvakin, A. (2012). PCI compliance : understand and implement effective PCI data security standard compliance. Waltham, MA, USA: Elsevier/Syngress.

Index

A

Ammunition and Explosives Detection (AED), 99

Annual PCI DSS assessment
  acuity STREAM dashboard, 487
  asset inventory review, 483
  incident response exercise, 483
  policy reviews, 482
  process, 483–485
  QSAC, 487
  quarterly activities, 479–80
  refresher training, 483
  risk reviews, 482
  supplier management review, 483
  3/4 yearly activities, 482
  ½ yearly activities, 481–482

Approved scanning vendor (ASV), 14, 96, 469, 480

Asset inventory
  detailed-level overview, 225, 227
  high-level overview, 225
  RED, 224

Attestation of Compliance (AOC), 286, 293, 379, 478

Automated Teller Machine (ATM), 286, 292

B

BLACK assets, 214, 225
BROWN assets, 215, 226

Business-As-Usual (BAU) processes, 7, 90, 330, 483

Business Model for Information Security (BMIS), 74

C

California Consumer Privacy Act (CCPA), 80, 450

Card Data Environment (CDE), 257

Cardholder data (CHD), 470, 496

Cardholder data environment (CDE), 213, 214, 266

Card Not Present (CNP)
  E-commerce, 291, 295
  payload delivery attacks, 297
  perimeter attacks, 302
  perimeter network attacks, 302–305
  perimeter web attacks, 305, 306
  psychological consequence, 296
  runaway trolley conundrum, 296
  social media intelligence gathering tools, 299–301
  Spear Phishing-style tactics, 298–299
  telephone-based, 292
  TTPs, 297

Card Present (CP) attack vectors
  ATM attacks, 308–310
  cyber criminals, 307
  European payment terminal crime report, 308

© Jim Seaman 2020
J. Seaman, *PCI DSS*, https://doi.org/10.1007/978-1-4842-5808-8

Card Present (CP) attack vectors (*cont.*)
  Face to Face, 292
  POI/PTS/POS/PDQ device
      attacks, 310, 311
      problems, 311
      research, 311, 312
Center for Internet Security Risk
      Assessment Method (CIS RAM), 139
Certified Information Security
      Management (CISM), 237
Certified in risk and information systems
      control (CRISC), 122
Chief information officer (CIO), 317,
      337, 356
Closed circuit television (CCTV), 52, 311
CM-Alliance TI Pyramid, 294
Cognitive attack loop approach, 218
Compliance
  breach vectors, 329
  cash *vs.* payment card, 330, 331
  cohesive team-based approach
      (*see* Team tactics)
  Cyber/InfoSec cognizance, 346
  data breach trends, 328
  data privacy and security
      program, 331
  data types, 329
  events, 325–327
  military lesson (*see* Military)
  risk mitigation, 358
  risks, 324
  security awareness, 357
  skills gaps, 346
  team player development, 335, 337
  team sport, 331
  team structure, 332, 333
Confidentiality, integrity, and availability
      (CIA), 254

Confidentiality, integrity, availability, and
      authenticity (CIAA), 109
Counter Intelligence (CI), 234, 351
Counter intelligence field team (CIFT),
      323, 407, 439
Cyber/InfoSec strategy
  BMIS, 74
  CIAA, 109
  components
      BMIS triangle, 77
      data security, 78
      integrated data security, 79
  external or internal attackers, 75–77
  problem, 74
Cybernetics, 83
Cyber security
  CIAA triad, 84
  definition, 84
  external facing attack surfaces
      opportunist attacker, 86–89
      PCI DSS application
        controls, 91–98
      tactics, techniques, and
        protocols, 85
      technologies, 90

D

Data Encryption Standard (DES), 205
Data life support system
  blood cycle management, 68
  circulatory system
      organs, 62
      quality data, 61, 62
  human body system, 69
  human *vs.* data security, 70
  incident response process, 67
  integral monitoring system, 65

layered defenses, 63, 64

physical security, 66

SIEM security tool, 65

skeletal system, 66

Data privacy

CCPA, 80

definition, 79, 80

ISACA privacy principles, 81–83

PIPEDA, 80

Data privacy and security

behaviors, 19–22

business types, 13, 14

consent or legitimate use, 25

documentation, 420

hierarchy tree, 421

leadership, 24, 25

payment card

breach, 414, 416, 417

policies development, 422

program, 16, 17

standardized approach, 418, 419

validation requirements, 14, 16

De-militarized zone (DMZ), 40, 99, 249

De-scoping

compliance efforts, 228

DNS Dumpster, 222

Landry's data breach, 220

network, 215

POS, 220

potential opportunities, 229, 230

risk reduction, 229

safety deposit box, 219

security controls, 218

VirusTotal, 223

Dual-tone multi-frequency (DTMF)

technologies, 252, 375

E

Electronic automated access control

system (EAACS), 51, 398

Enterprise risk management (ERM)

array of interfaces, 178–183

associated action requirements, 178

audit tracking, 184

data privacy tracking, 186

incident tracking, 185

PCI DSS control framework, 188

PCI DSS control reporting, 189

PCI DSS control types, 187

EU Data Privacy laws, 7, 9, 10, 12

European Union's General Data Protection

Regulation (EU GDPR), 495

Explosive formed projectiles (EFPs), 141

F

Flat Network, 216, 246

G, H

General Data Protection Regulation

(GDPR), 73

I, J, K

Improvised explosive device (IED), 100,

141, 256

Incident management

designing scenario, 405, 406

elements, 403, 404

Information security

definition, 98

requirements, 99–102, 104

Infrastructure as a service (IAAS), 216
Integrated project management
    PCI DSS requirements, 360–363
    PEACE framework, 366
    SCRUM framework, 366
    waterfall methodology, 364, 365
Internal detection system (IDS), 64
Internal security assessor (ISA), 379, 492
ISACA's Open PCI Scoping Toolkit, 224
Issuer Identification No (IIN), 201

L

Luhn algorithm, 202

M

Magecart-style attacks, 115, 221
Major Identifier No. (MII), 200
Malicious software or malware, 459
Manifoil combination locks (MCL), 250
Man-In-The Middle (MITM)
    attack, 216, 398
Mersey-style locking mechanisms, 250
Military
    Blues course, 347
    career path, 350
    counter intelligence subjects, 351
    CSy1 subjects, 352
    CSy2 subjects, 353
    data breach, 354, 355
    Greens course, 347
    operations supply chain, 347
    RAF Provost Marshal's UK Dog
        Trails, 349
    weapons, 348
Multi-factor authentication (MFA), 85,
    277, 396, 460

N

National Cyber security and
    Communications Integration
    Center (NCCIC) cyber security
    evaluation tool, 392
National Institute of Standards and
    Technology (NIST), 287–289
Network attacks, 310

O

Open System Interconnection (OSI), 247
Open Web Application Security Project
    (OWASP), 47, 94, 396

P

Password spraying, 355, 402
Payment card industry data security
    standard (PCI DSS)
    annual independent inspection, 196
    AT&T security incident, 498
    business operations, 159, 161
    business requirement
        data security controls framework,
            156–158
        ICO, 155
        information security standards, 154
    cardholder data, 195
    careless operations, 197
    criminal gang hierarchy, 208
    FAQs, 500–514
    framework, 323
    guidance documents, 494
    information security performance
        metrics, 159
    insecure operations, 197
    maintenance checks, 196

mastercard rules extract, 497

PAN entry, 207

precious cargo categories (*see* Precious cargo)

pyramid, 324

REST APIs, 499

risk, 199, 210

SAD, 209

strategy, 494

structure, 199

tick box audit, 195

validation, 495

Payment Card Industry Qualified Security Assessor (PCI QSA), 234

Payment Card Industry Security Standards Council (PCI SSC), 114, 231, 286, 324, 449

Payment card industry's (PCI's), 238

Payment channel

risks, 321

technological advancements, 285

threat intelligence, 320

tick box solution, 319

Payment Service Provider(PSP), 382

PCI DSS compliance, 488

obligations, 489

QSAC, 467

PCI DSS controls framework

AMEX payment card, 31

application, 232, 233

card brands, 34

CI, 234, 236

CISM, 237

customer goods and services, 29, 30

e-commerce, 33

gate keeping

CDE, 257

reality bites, 258

goals, 242

information security policy, 57

JSP 440, 235, 237

layered defense, 37

malware software, 46–48

mobile payments, 32

monitor and test networks, 54–56

non-compliance data breach, 35

payment card processing, 36

PCI QSA, 234

PCI SSC, 231

people, polices and processes

compliance goal, 243

documentation, 243, 244

reality bites, 244

POS payment methods, 32

primary (core ring), 37

protect cardholder data, 45

quaternary ring, 38

quinary ring, 38

reality bites, 58, 250, 251

requirements, 241

assurance testing, 280–282

design/default, secure, 270, 271

entry search, 275

layering network, 266, 267, 269

logical access restrictions, 277

monitor and detect, 279

physical entry control, 278

Ps (people, polices, and processes), 265, 266

role-based restrictions, 276

secure in motion, 273, 274

security vulnerabilities, 276

vault, 271–273

routine assurance

CDE testing, 259

reality bites, 260, 262

PCI DSS controls framework (*cont.*)
    secondary ring, 38
    secure architecture
        IT assets, identify and
            manage, 247
        layered defense, 246
        reality bits, 249
        traffic control, 248
    secure by design/secure by default, 249
    secure data
        CHD, 253
        payment service provider, 252
        reality bites, 253
    secure maintenance
        reality bites, 255, 256
        vulnerabilities, 254
    security network, build and maintain,
        40–42, 44, 45
    senary (outer) ring, 38–40
    storage access control
        measures, 49–54
    structure, 240, 263, 264
    tertiary ring, 38
    tick box approach, 238, 239
PCI DSS integrated data security controls
    framework
    measures (*see* Technical and
        organizational measures)
Perimeter intruder detection system
    (PIDS), 64
Personal identification
    number (PIN), 51, 311
Personal Information Protection and
    Electronic Documents Act
    (PIPEDA), 80
Physical security, 217
    definition, 105
    PTS devices, 105–107

PIE FARM methodology
    FARMing
        assess, 375–377
        fix gaps, 375
        maintain, 380, 381
        report, 378, 379
    making PIE
        CMMI maturity
            levels, 373, 374
        identify and isolate, 370
        PCI DSS controls RACI matrix,
            371–373
        plan and prepare, 368, 369
Pin transaction security (PTS), 53, 278,
    306
Point-Of-Interaction (POI), 306
Point-of-Sale (PoS) payment
    methods, 32, 220, 306
Point-of-Sale (PoS)/PTS devices, 105
Policies
    development
        policy statements, 425
        senior management, 424
        SOPs, 426–429
        supporting documents, 429–432
        terminologies, 422, 423
Precious cargo
    CHD storage, 206
    front of payment card
        breakdown, 200–203
    PIN/PIN blocks, 205
    rear of payment card
        breakdown, 203, 205
Pretty Damn Quick (PDQ), 95, 306
Primary Account Number (PAN), 37, 199
Prioritized conceptual approach, 410
Privacy and Electronic Communications
    Regulations (PECR), 8

Privileged access management (PAM), 399, 400

Proactive defense
  asset management, 386
    categorization, 393
    counter intelligence operations, 387
    industry security controls
      frameworks, 387–390
    intangible assets, 387
    IT Asset Management process, 387
  compliance levels, 409, 410
  layered approach, 411
  prioritized conceptual approach, 410
  reality bites, 406–408

Public-facing technologies, 458

Q

Qualified security assessment company
  (QSAC), 467, 468
  capability, 475
  closure, 478
  communication, 473
  corporate social responsibility, 474
  ethics, 474
  guarantees, 475
  health and safety, 475
  offering, 476, 477
  ongoing evaluation and
    improvement, 475
  policy framework, 473
  quality plan, 475
  regulatory framework, 473
  values, 474

Qualified security assessor (QSA), 293,
  367, 467–469
  security disciplines, 471

  training course, 472

Qualitative risk assessment, 161

Quantitative risk assessment, 162

R

RED assets, 214

Report on compliance (RoC), 293, 471

Responsible, accountable, consulted, and
  informed (RACI), 496

Return on investment (ROI), 356

Revolution or evolution
  EU data privacy laws, 7
    NIS, 8
    PECR, 8
  financial services, 11, 12
  GDPR, 7
  legal and regulatory enhancements, 5, 6
  polished payment card operations, 2, 3
  secure data processing, 7
  technological advances, 1

Risk assessment
  CISM, 122
  CRISC, 122
  PCI DSS threat and risk, 123
  processes, 120, 140
  SANS, 121
  scenario assessment, 135
  scenario development
    advantages, 143, 144
    attacker, 124–127
    e-Commerce retailer, 129–134,
      136–138
    ISACAs, 127
    NASA process, 139
    structure, 128
  treatment, 122

Risk management
assessment cycle, 118
mitigation principles, 116, 117
NIST principles, 114–116
PCI DSS controls, 118–120
PCI SSC, 114
reality bites, 141–143
scenario development, 138
vs. compliance based
approach, 151, 154
reality bits, 189, 191
risk management, 148, 149
Rugby League, 334, 335

S

Sales-focused customer relationship, 472
SAQ D-Service Providers (SAQ D-SP), 292
Secure Software Life Cycle (Secure SLC), 395
Security
awareness training
investment, 433, 434
knowledge/skillsets,
maintaining, 436
methods of delivery, 435
payment card processing, 442
building security culture, 437, 438
management process, 438
reality bites, 439–441
Security information and event
management security (SIEM)
security tool, 65, 400–402
Security policy, 57
Self-assessment questionnaire (SAQ), 239,
379, 471
Senior Aircraftman (SAC), 255

Sensitive Authentication Data (SAD), 37,
199, 271, 311
Spear Phishing Attachment, 298
Special interest groups (SIGs), 492
Specific, measurable, achievable, realistic,
and timebound (SMART), 469
Standard operating procedures (SOPs),
38, 426, 470

T

Tactics, techniques, and protocols (TTPs),
125, 320
Team tactics
1LOD, 341
2LOD, 342
3LOD model, 341–345
requirement, 340
Technical and organizational measures
encrypt transmission, sensitive data, 458
firewall configuration, protect sensitive
data, 454, 455
information security, personnel, 463
malware, protect systems, 459
MFA, 460
payment card data, 451
restrict physical access, sensitive
data, 461
secure system and application, 459
security testing, 462
sensitive data, restrict access, 460
store sensitive data, 457
track and monitor network access, 462
vendor supplied defaults, 456
Telephone-based Payments risk balance
case

    components, 164

    example, 165–177

Third-party attack vectors

    supply chain compromise, 313

    trusted relationships, 314

Threat intelligence, 293

Three lines of defense (3LOD) model, 341

U

Unit security officers (USyOs), 354

V, W, X, Y, Z

Voice Over Internet Protocol (VOIP), 210

Vulnerability and Patch management

    application, 399

    human firewall, 396

    infrastructure, 398

    network, 399

    OWASP, 396

    risk assess, 395

    TechTarget, 394

Vulnerability management, 394

Printed in the United States
By Bookmasters